Film Theory

Film Theory

An Introduction

Robert Stam

Department of Cinema Studies, New York University

Blackwell
Publishing

BLACKWELL PUBLISHING
350 Main Street, Malden, MA 02148-5020, USA
9600 Garsington Road, Oxford OX4 2DQ, UK
550 Swanston Street, Carlton, Victoria 3053, Australia

First published 2000

17   2010

Library of Congress Cataloging-in-Publication Data has been applied for.

ISBN 978-0-6312-0653-8 (hardback)
ISBN 978-0-6312-0654-5 (paperback)

A catalogue record for this title is available from the British Library.

Set in 11 on 14 pt Galliard
by Ace Filmsetting Ltd, Frome, Somerset
Printed and bound in Malaysia
by Vivar Printing Sdn Bhd

The publisher's policy is to use permanent paper from mills that operate a sustainable
forestry policy, and which has been manufactured from pulp processed using acid-
free and elementary chlorine-free practices. Furthermore, the publisher ensures that
the text paper and cover board used have met acceptable environmental accreditation
standards.

For further information on
Blackwell Publishing, visit our website:
www.blackwellpublishing.com

Contents

Contents

[handwritten annotations in margin: "look at in relation to new media"; "semiotics"]

Contents

Preface

Film Theory: An Introduction was conceived as part of a trilogy of Blackwell books dedicated to Contemporary Film Theory, a trilogy which also includes two collections (both co-edited with Toby Miller): *Film and Theory*, an anthology of theoretical essays from the 1970s up to the present, and *A Companion to Film Theory*, in which leading figures in the field chart out their own areas of expertise while prognosticating about future developments.

While the literature of film theory is vast, and while there are numerous anthologies of film theory and criticism (Nichols, 1985; Rosen, 1986), there are relatively few historical overviews of film theory as an international enterprise. Guido Aristarco's *Storia della Teoriche del Filme* (History of Film Theory) was published in 1951, almost a half-century ago. Dudley Andrew's *The Major Film Theories* and Andrew Tudor's *Theories of Film*, despite their many good qualities, were both written in the mid-1970s and therefore do not cover recent developments as I have attempted to do here. (It was only when *Film Theory: An Introduction* was already in press that I became aware of the French translation of Francesco Casetti's excellent *Teorie del Cinema 1945–1990* (Film Theories since 1945), published in Italian in 1993 and in French in 1999.

I do not consider myself a theorist as such; rather, I am a user and a critical reader of theory, an *interlocutor* with theory. I have generally deployed theory not for its own sake, but in order to analyse specific texts (e.g. *Rear Window, Zelig*) or specific issues (e.g. the role of language in film, the role of cultural narcissism in spectatorship).

My dialogue with theory began in the mid 1960s when I was living and teaching in Tunisia, North Africa. There I began to read in French the film theory associated with the beginnings of film semiology, and I also participated in Tunis's vibrant film culture of ciné-clubs and cinématèques. I went to Paris in 1968 to study at the Sorbonne, where I combined the study of French literature and theory with daily (often thrice daily) trips to the cinématèque, and visits to classes on film, including those taught by Eric Rohmer, Henri Langlois, and Jean Mitry. When I returned to the USA in 1969 as a graduate student in the Comparative Literature Department at the University of California, Berkeley, I kept in touch with theory through Berkeley's many courses on film, dispersed through various departments, and especially through the inspirational work of Professor Bertrand Augst, who always kept us abreast of the latest Parisian developments. In Berkeley I was also part of a film discussion group, which included Margaret Morse, Sandy Flitterman-Lewis, Janet Bergstron, Leger Grindon, Rick Prelinger, and Constance Penley, where we read theoretical texts with avid attention. In 1973 I followed Bertrand Augst, then my dissertation advisor, to the Centre Americain d'Études Cinématographiques in Paris, where I attended seminars with Christian Metz, Raymond Bellour, Michel Marie, Jacques Aumont, and Marie-Claire Ropars Weulleumier. A seminar on Glauber Rocha with Marie-Claire Ropars resulted in a jointly written essay, published in Portuguese, on Rocha's *Land in Anguish*. My studies in Paris also led to a long correspondence with Christian Metz, an extraordinarily generous figure who commented regularly on my work as well as on his own.

Since then I have maintained a dialogue with theory by teaching such courses as "Theories of Spectatorship," "Film and Language," "Semiology of Film and Television," and "Bakhtin and the Media," and by writing books thoroughly laced with film theory: *Reflexivity in Film and Literature*, *New Vocabularies in Film Semiotics* (with Sandy Flitterman-Lewis and Bob Burgoyne), *Subversive Pleasures:*

Bakhtin, Cultural Criticism, and Film, and *Unthinking Eurocentrism: Multiculturalism and the Media* (with Ella Shohat). On occasion, some of the material here recasts and reconfigures some of the work that appeared in those books. The section on "reflexivity" reworks material from *Reflexivity in Film and Literature*; the section on "alternative aesthetics" reworks material from *Subversive Pleasures*; the section on "intertextuality" and the question of film language recasts material from *New Vocabularies in Film Semiotics*; and the section on "Multiculturalism, Race, and Representation" recapitulates some materials from *Unthinking Eurocentrism.*

I should like to thank a number of people for their help. Andrew McNeillie of Blackwell Publishers showed unwavering support and enthusiasm. He is one of those rare editors who actually develops a human and intellectual dialogue with writers. Alison Dunnett and Jack Messenger of Blackwell Publishers have been delightful editors and e-mail correspondents. I should also like to thank the NYU research assistants – Elizabeth Botha, Michelle Brown, and Jeff de Oca – who did the indispensable backup work not only for this book but also for the other two in the series (*Film and Theory* and *A Companion to Film Theory*). I also want to thank the four people who blessed me with a close and meticulous reading of the manuscript: Richard Allen, James Naremore, Ella Shohat, and Ismail Xavier. One could not ask for better interlocutors. Finally, my thanks to the Rockefeller Foundation for offering me a residency at the Bellagio Center in Italy, where I corrected the proofs of this book. It is hard to imagine a more serene setting in which to do such work.

Introduction

My hope in this book is to provide a reasonably comprehensive over-view of film theory during "the century of the cinema," for both those already familiar with the subject and those with little previous knowledge. What follows, then, is a kind of "user's guide" to film theory. It is a very personal guide, since it is inevitably colored by my own interests and concerns. At the same time, however, I am not personally committed to theories of my own construction, so I hope I have maintained some "ecumenical distance" from all the theories I discuss. I do not pretend to be neutral, of course (clearly, I find some theories more congenial than others), but neither am I con-cerned to defend my own position or to malign my ideological op-ponents. Throughout this book I am shamelessly eclectic, synthetic, anthropophagic even. To paraphrase Godard, one should put what-ever one likes in a book of film theory. If I am a partisan of anything it is of "theoretical cubism": the deployment of multiple perspec-tives and grids. Each grid has its blind spots and insights; each needs the "excess seeing" of the other grids. As a synaesthetic, multi-track medium which has generated an enormously variegated body of texts, the cinema virtually *requires* multiple frameworks of understanding.

Although I make frequent reference to Bakhtin, I am not a Bakhtinian (if such a thing exists). Rather, I use Bakhtin's theoreti-cal categories to illuminate the limitations and potentialities of other grids. I have learned from many theoretical schools, but none of them has a monopoly on the truth. I refuse to believe that I am the

1

only person in the field who can read both Gilles Deleuze and Noël Carroll with pleasure, or more accurately, who reads both with mingled pleasure and displeasure. I refuse the Hobson's Choice between approaches which often strike me as complementary rather than contradictory.

There are many possible ways to describe the history of film theory. It can be a triumphant parade of "great men and women": Munsterberg, Eisenstein, Arnheim, Dulac, Bazin, Mulvey. It can be a history of orienting metaphors: "cine-eye," "cine-drug," "film-magic," "window on the world," "camera-pen," "film language," "film mirror," "film dream." It can be a story of the impact of philosophy on theory: Kant and Munsterberg, Mounier and Bazin, Bergson and Deleuze. It can be a history of cinema's *rapprochement* with (or rejection of) other arts: film as painting, film as music, film as theater (or anti-theater). It can be a sequence of paradigmatic shifts in theoretical/interpretative grids and discursive styles – formalism, semiology, psychoanalysis, feminism, cognitivism, queer theory, postcolonial theory – each with its talismanic keywords, tacit assumptions, and characteristic jargon.

Film Theory: An Introduction combines elements of all these approaches. It assumes, first of all, that the evolution of film theory cannot be narrated as a linear progression of movements and phases. The contours of theory vary from country to country and from moment to moment, and movements and ideas can be concurrent rather than successive or mutually exclusive. A book of this type must deal with a dizzying array of chronologies and concerns. It has to confront the same logistical problem that confronted early film-makers like Porter and Edison: the problem of the "meanwhile," i.e. the problem of relaying simultaneous events taking place in widely separated locales. This book has to convey a sense of "meanwhile, back in France," or "meanwhile, over in genre theory," or "meanwhile, in the Third World." While more-or-less chronological, the book's approach is not *strictly* so, otherwise we might lose the drift and potential of a given movement, preventing us, for example, from tracing the lines that lead out from Munsterberg to Metz.

A strict chronology can also be deceptive. The mere fact of

sequencing risks implying a false causality: *post hoc ergo propter hoc* (after this therefore because of this). The ideas of theorists working in one historical period might bear fruit only much later. Who would have guessed that the philosophical ideas of Henri Bergson would reemerge a century later in the work of Gilles Deleuze? The work of the Bakhtin Circle, similarly, was published in the 1920s, yet Bakhtinian ideas "entered" theory only in the 1960s and 1970s, at which point a retrospective reassessment defined him as a "proto-poststructuralist." Often the sequencing of influence depends on the hazards of translation: the bulk of the writings of Dziga Vertov in the 1920s, for example, was translated into French only in the 1960s and 1970s. In any case, I do not generally subscribe to the "great person" approach to film theory. The section rubrics in this book designate theoretical schools and research projects rather than individuals, although individuals obviously play a role in schools.

This book also has to cope with the difficulties inherent in all such surveys. Chronology deceives and patterns falsify. Generalizations about theoretical "schools" elide the manifest exceptions and anomalies. Synthetic accounts of given theorists (for example, Eisenstein) fail to register changes in their theories over time. The slicing up of a theoretical continuum into neatly separated movements and schools, moreover, is always somewhat arbitrary. "Feminism," "psychoanalysis," "deconstruction," "postcoloniality," and "textual analysis" are here discussed separately and in succession, for example, yet nothing prevents a psychoanalytic postcolonial feminist from using deconstruction as part of textual analysis. Many of the theoretical "moments," furthermore – feminism, psychoanalysis, poststructuralism, postcolonial theory – are maddeningly intertwined and concurrent; ordering them in a linear fashion implies a temporal succession that doesn't exist. (Hypertext and hypermedia might have handled this challenge more effectively.)

While this book tries to survey the field impartially, it is – as I have already indicated – a very personal account of film theory. I am therefore confronted by the question of voice, of how to interweave my own voice with the voices of others. On one level, the book is a form of "reported speech," an enunciatory modality where the social evaluations and intonations of the "reporter" inevitably color and shade the report. To put it differently, the book is written in what literary theorists call "free, indirect discourse," a style which slides between the direct reporting of speech – quoting Eisenstein, for example – and a more ventriloqual speech – my version of Eisenstein's thinking – all interlaced with more personal ruminations. To make a literary analogy, it is as if I were mingling the authorial interventionism of a Balzac with the filtrations of a Flaubert or a Henry James. At times I will present the ideas of others; at times I will extrapolate or expand on the ideas of others; and at times I will present my own ideas as they have evolved over the years. When a passage is not marked as summarizing the work of others, the reader can assume that I am speaking in my own voice, especially in relation to issues that have always concerned me: the historicity of theory, intertextuality theory, Eurocentrism and multiculturalism, alternative aesthetics.

My goal is not to discuss any single theory or theorist in exhaustive detail, but rather to show overall shifts and movements in terms of the questions asked, the concerns expressed, the problematics explored. In a sense, my hope is to "deprovincialize" theory in both space and time. In temporal terms, theoretical issues trace their antecedents far back into pre-cinematic history. Issues of genre, for example, have been present at least since Aristotle's *Poetics*. In spatial terms, I see theory as implicated in a global, international space. Nor do film-theoretical concerns follow the same sequence in every locale. While feminism has been a strong presence in Anglo-American film theory since the 1970s, feminism (including French feminism) has had relatively little impact in French film critical discourse. While film theorists in countries like Brazil or Argentina have long been concerned with issues of "national cinema," such issues have been more marginal and recent in Europe and America.

Film theory is an international and multicultural enterprise, yet too often it remains monolingual, provincial, and chauvinistic. French theorists have only recently begun to reference work in English, while Anglo-American theory tends to cite only that work in French which has been translated into English. Work in Russian, Spanish, Portuguese, Italian, Polish, Hungarian, and German, not to mention Japanese, Korean, Chinese, and Arabic, often goes untranslated and is therefore slighted, as is work in English from countries like India and Nigeria. A good deal of important work, for example Glauber Rocha's voluminous writings on film – analogous in some ways to Pasolini's written oeuvre, combining theory and criticism with poems, novels, and screenplays – has never been translated into English. While Bordwell and Carroll are right to mock the servile Francophilia of that post-1960s strain of film theory that genuflects to Parisian gurus long after their aura has faded in France itself, its corrective is not Anglophilia or "United Statesian" jingoism, but rather a true internationalism. I therefore hope to multiply the perspectives and locations from which film theory is spoken, although I have hardly succeeded to the degree I might have hoped, since the focus here still remains more or less constricted to theoretical work undertaken in the United States, France, Great Britain, Russia, Germany, Australia, Argentina, Brazil, and Italy, with all-too occasional "visits" to "Third World" and "postcolonial" theory.

The fiction feature film *à la* Hollywood is often regarded as the "real" cinema, much in the same way as an American tourist abroad might ask: "How much is this in *real* money?" I assume that "real" cinema comes in many forms: fiction and non-fiction, realist and non-realist, mainstream and avant-garde. All are worthy of our interest.

Film theory is rarely "pure"; it is usually laced with an admixture of literary criticism, social commentary, and philosophical speculation. The status of those who practice film theory, moreover, varies widely, from film theorists *strictu sensu* (Balazs, Metz), through filmmakers reflecting on their own practice (Eisenstein, Pudovkin, Deren, Solanas, Kluge, Tarkovsky), to freelance intellectuals who also write about the cinema (James Agee, Parker Tyler), through practicing film critics whose collective oeuvre "hides," as it were, an embryonic theory to be teased out by the reader (the case of Manny Farber or Serge Daney). Recent decades have witnessed the "academicization" of film theory, in a situation where most theorists have a university base.

The semiotic film theory of the 1970s and 1980s presumed a kind of quasi-religious initiation into the sacred texts of the then-reigning *maîtres à penser*. Much of film theory came to consist of ritualistic invocations (and crude summaries) of Lacan and other poststructuralist thinkers. In the 1970s "theory" became "Theory"; the Religion of Art transmuted into the Religion of Theory. For Lindsay Waters, theory was the crack cocaine which got people high and then let them down. Current theory, thankfully, is more epistemologically modest and less authoritarian. Grand Theory has abandoned its totalizing ambitions, while many theorists have called for more modest approaches to theory, in tandem with philosophers like Richard Rorty who redefine philosophy not as system-building *à la* Hegel but rather as a civil "conversation" without any claims to ultimate truth. Theorists such as Noël Carroll and David Bordwell, similarly, have called for "middle-level theorizing" which would "countenance as film theory any line of inquiry dedicated to producing generalizations pertaining to, or general explanations of, filmic phenomena, or devoted to isolating, tracking, and/or accounting for any mechanisms, devices, patterns, and regularities in the field of cinema." Film theory, then, refers to any generalized reflexion on the patterns and regularities (or significant irregularities) to be found in relation to film as a medium, to film language, to the cinematic apparatus or to the nature of the cinematic text, or to cinematic reception. Instead of Grand Theory, then, only theories and the "activity of theorizing," and the workmanlike production of general concepts, taxonomies, and explanations.

To slightly modify the formulation, film theory is an evolving body of concepts designed to account for the cinema in all its dimensions (aesthetic, social, psychological) for an interpretive community of scholars, critics, and interested spectators.

While I endorse the "modesty" of the Bordwell–Carroll perspective, this modesty should not become an alibi for censuring larger philosophical or political questions about the cinema. There is a danger that "middle-range" theory, like "consensus history" or "end-of-ideology" discourse, will assume that all the big questions are unanswerable as posed, leaving us only with small-scale inquiries susceptible to direct empirical verification. That some questions, such as the role of the cinematic apparatus in engendering ideological alienation, were answered ineptly or dogmatically does not mean that such questions were not worth asking. Indeed, even unanswerable questions might be worth asking, if only to see where they take us and what we discover along the way. Film theory, to put it paradoxically, can generate productive failures and calamitous successes. Modesty, furthermore, can lead in many directions not necessarily anticipated by the cognitivists. The patterns and regularities noted in the field of cinema, for example, might have to do not only with predictable stylistic or narratological procedures but also with patterns of gendered, racialized, sexualized, and culturally inflected representation and reception. Why are materials on "race," for example, or on "third cinema," not seen as "theoretical?" While on one level this exclusion might have to do with the artificial boundaries constructed around areas of theoretical inquiry, one wonders if it might not also have to do with the colonialist hierarchy which associates Europe with reflecting "mind" and non-Europe with unreflecting body? In a sense, this book broadens film theory to include the larger field of theorized film-related writing: cultural studies, film analysis, and so forth. I have therefore tried to include such diverse schools as multicultural media theory, postcolonial theory, and queer theory, in short the entire gamut of all the complex, subtle, and theoretically sophisticated film-related work performed under a wide variety of banners.

Although film theory has often involved debates, argument is only one, rather narrow, dimension of film theorizing. Theorists are often at their worst, moreover, precisely when they are hell-bent on annihilating an opponent; the stupidity the polemicist projects onto the straw-man antagonist ends up, through a kind of boomerang, by implicating the polemicist. Indeed, there is something disturbingly masculinist and testosterone-driven in the view of theory as cockfight or shouting match *à la Crossfire*. A real dialogue depends on the ability of each side to articulate the adversary's project fairly before critiquing it.

Introduction

The analytical method of distilling a theoretical text into its separate premises, as deployed by a Richard Allen or a Gregory Currie or a Noël Carroll, has clearly demonstrated its usefulness in clearing up logical ambiguities, conceptual confusions, and misfired deductions. But not everything is reducible to the dessicated skeleton of an abstract "argument." The complex, historically situated, densely intertextual theories of a Bertolt Brecht, for example, cannot be reduced to a "truth claim" to be rebutted. The analytic method sometimes commits what literary critics used to call the "heresy of paraphrase"; it fails to recognize that the playful, oxymoronic, paradoxical writing of a Walter Benjamin or a Roland Barthes cannot always be broken down without loss into an arid sequence of "propositions," a syllogistic armature from which all the vital juices have been drained. Sometimes tension and ambiguity *are* the point. Nor is film theory a kind of conceptual chess leading to an indisputable checkmate. Theories of art are not right or wrong in the same way as scientific theories. (Indeed, some would argue that even scientific theories are merely a sequence of metaphorical approximations.) One cannot discredit Bazin's theorized defence of Italian neo-realist films in the same way as one can discredit the defence of outmoded "sciences" like phrenology and craniology.

Rather than being simply right or wrong – although on occasion they are one or the other – these diverse grids are relatively rich or impoverished, culturally dense or shallow, methodologically open or closed, fastidiously anal or cannibalistically oral, historically informed or ahistorical, one-dimensional or multidimensional, monocultural or multicultural. In theory, we find brilliant exponents of impoverished paradigms, and mediocre exponents of rich paradigms. Some film theories try to amplify meaning, while others try to discipline it, close it down. Robert Ray contrasts the impersonal, positivist approach to theory with what he calls the baroque, surrealist, essayistic approach. Indeed the history of film theory exhibits a kind of dialogue between two necessary moments, that of imaginative creation and that of analytical critique, a productive oscillation between ecstatic enthusiasms (those of an Eisenstein, for example) and the dry analytical rigor of those who tidy up the enchanting mess the creative enthusiasts have made. (Which is not to say that critique cannot display its own enthusiasm and creativity.)

At the same time, theoretical research programs, or metaphors like "film language" and "film dream," can obey a law of diminishing returns, exhausting their capacity to generate new knowledge. Theoretical movements can begin as exciting and then become boring and predictable, or they can begin as boring and then suddenly become interesting as they "mate" with other theories. Theories can be safely correct in positivist terms or ambitiously interesting but wrong-headed. Profoundly mistaken theorists can make brilliant points "along the way." Theory can be methodical and rigorous or it can consist of the anarchic play of a sensibility over a text or an issue. Theory can liberate the energies of its users or inhibit them. Theories are also task-specific. "Ideology critique" is well-suited for exposing pro-capitalist manipulations in Hollywood films, but it is rather ill-equipped for delineating the kinesthetic pleasures of a camera movement in Murnau's *Sunrise*. Analytic or post-analytic film theory, like analytic philosophy, is good at taking things apart; it is less adept at discerning correspondences and relationalities.

Theories do not supersede one another in a linear progression. Indeed, there are Darwinian survivalist overtones in the view that theories can be "retired," that they can be "eliminated" in competition. It would be silly to adopt a scorched earth policy that suggests that one movement or other got everything wrong. Theories do not usually fall into disuse like old automobiles relegated to a conceptual junkyard. They do not die; they transform themselves, leaving traces and reminiscences. There are shifts in emphasis, of course, but many of the major themes – mimesis, authorship, spectatorship – have been reiterated and reenvisioned from the beginning. At times, theorists broach the same questions, but answer them in light of different goals and in a different theoretical language.

Finally, I offer this book as a kind of antechamber to film theory, an invitation into its mansion. Needless to say, I hope readers will visit the various rooms in the mansion by reading, if they have not done so already, the theorists themselves.

The Antecedents of Film Theory

Film theory, like all writing, is palimpsestic; it bears the traces of earlier theories and the impact of neighboring discourses. Saturated with the memory of longer histories of reflection, theory embeds many antecedent debates. Film theory must be seen as part of a long-standing tradition of theoretical reflection on the arts in general. Film theorists from the turn of the twentieth century through André Bazin and Jean-Louis Baudry and Luce Iragaray have been struck, for example, by the uncanny resemblance between Plato's allegorical cave and the cinematic apparatus. Both Plato's cave and the cinema feature an artificial light, cast from behind the prisoners/spectators. In Plato's cave the light plays over effigies of people and animals, leading the deluded captives to confuse flimsy simulations with ontological reality. Contemporary theorists hostile to the cinema often replay, consciously or not, Plato's rejection of the fictive arts as nurturing illusion and fomenting the lower passions.

Some of the antecedent debates inherited by film theory concern aesthetics, medium specificity, genre, and realism, themes which will become leitmotifs throughout this book. The discussion of film aesthetics, for example, draws on the long history of aesthetics in general. Aesthetics (from the Greek word *aisthesis* meaning perception, sensation) emerged as a separate discipline in the eighteenth century as the study of artistic beauty and related issues of the sublime, the grotesque, the humorous, and the pleasurable. In philosophy, aesthetics, ethics, and logic made up the triad of "normative" sciences devoted to devising rules concerning the Beautiful, the Good, and the True, respectively. Aesthetics (and Anti-Aesthetics) tries to answer such questions as: What is beauty in a work of art? Is beauty "real" and objectively verifiable, or subjective, a matter of taste? Are aesthetics medium-specific? Should a film exploit the distinctive traits of the medium? Is "art" an honorific to be attributed only to a few films, or are all films works of art simply because of their institutionally defined social status? Do films have a natural "vocation" for

10

realism, or for artifice and stylization? Should technique call attention to itself or be self-effacing? Is there an ideal style? Is there a
correct way of telling a story? Are notions of the beautiful eternally
true or are they shaped by ambient social values? To what extent are
aesthetics linked to larger ethical and social issues? Can beauty be
separated from social use and function, as a certain Kantian tradition
suggests? What is the relation between film technique and social
responsibility? Is a tracking shot, as Godard put it, a question of
morality? Are there aesthetic correlatives to specific ideologies such
as fascism discernible in the films of Leni Riefenstahl and Busby
Berkeley, as Susan Sontag has suggested? Can fascist or racist films
like *Triumph of the Will* or *Birth of a Nation* be "masterpieces" in
artistic terms and still be repugnant in ethical/political terms? Are
aesthetics and ethics so easily separable? Has all art been irrevocably
changed by Auschwitz, as Adorno suggested? Do we even need aesthetics, or is it hopelessly compromised, as Clyde Taylor (1998) argues, by its origins in eighteenth-century racist discourses? Or can
one distinguish between capital-A "Aesthetics," rooted in Germanic
racist thought, and small-a "aesthetics" as a concern, common to all
cultures, with the formal shaping of representations of the sensate
world?

"Medium specificity" arguments, similarly, also trace their line-
age to a long tradition of reflection. The medium specificity approach goes at least as far back as Aristotle's *Poetics*, and then to the
distinction made by the German philosopher Lessing (in *Laocoön*,
1766) between spatial and temporal arts, and his insistence on establishing what is essential to each medium, that to which it should
be "true" (film theorists from Eisenstein to Carroll explicitly reference the *Laocoön* essay). Questions of media specificity also lurk in
the background when critics (or ordinary spectators) call films "too
theatrical" or "too static" or "too literary." When spectators confi-
dently announce, as if they were themselves inventing the idea rather
than receiving it spoon-fed from the industry, that they "believe
that film is entertainment," they too are proffering a medium
specificity argument, albeit a peculiarly unreflective one.

A medium specificity approach to the cinema assumes that each

11

art form has uniquely particular norms and capabilities of expression. As Noël Carroll points out in *Theorizing the Moving Image*, the approach has two components, one internal (the posited relation between the medium and the art form that emerges from it) and one external (its differential relation to other art forms and media). An essentialist approach assumes (1) that film is good at doing certain things (e.g. depicting animated movement) and not others (staring at a static object), and (2) that film should follow its own logic and not be derivative of other arts, i.e. that it should do what it does best and not what other media do best.

The issue of medium specificity brings with it issues of comparative prestige. Literature especially has often been seen as a more venerable, more distinguished, essentially more "noble" medium than film. The results of millennia of literary production are compared with the average productions of a century of film, and literature is pronounced superior. The written word, which brings with it the aura of scripture, is said to be intrinsically a more subtle and precise medium for the delineation of thoughts and feelings. Yet it could just as easily be argued that cinema, precisely because of its heterogenous matter of expression, is capable of *greater* complexity and subtlety than literature. Cinema's audiovisual nature and its five tracks authorize an infinitely richer *combinatoire* of syntactic and semantic possibilities. The cinema has extremely varied resources, even if some of those resources are rarely used (just as some of the resources of literature are rarely used). Film forms an ideal site for the orchestration of multiple genres, narrational systems, and forms of writing. Most striking is the high density of information available to the cinema. If the cliché phrase suggests that an "image is worth a thousand words" how much more worthy are the typical film's hundreds of shots (each formed by hundreds if not thousands of images) as they interact simultaneously with phonetic sound, noises, written materials, and music? Interestingly, literature itself sometimes expresses a kind of "envy" of cinema, as when novelist Robbe-Grillet aspires to cinema's perpetual present tense, or when Nabokov's Humbert Humbert laments in *Lolita* that he, unlike a film director, has to "put the impact of an instantaneous vision into a sequence of words" in such a way that "their physical accumulation on the page impairs the actual flash, the sharp unity of impression."

The question of cinematic specificity can be approached (a) *technologically*, in terms of the apparatus necessary to its production; (b) *linguistically*, in terms of film's "materials of expression"; (c) *historically*, in terms of its origins (e.g. in daguerreotypes, dioramas, kinetoscopes); (d) *institutionally*, in terms of its processes of production (collaborative rather than individual, industrial rather than artisanal); and (e) in terms of its *processes of reception* (individual reader versus gregarious reception in movie theater). Whereas poets and novelists (usually) work alone, filmmakers (usually) collaborate with cinematographers, art directors, actors, technicians, etc. While novels have characters, films have characters and performers, a quite different thing. Thus Pierre Louÿs's 1898 novel *The Woman and the Puppet* features one entity (the character Conchita) while the Buñuel adaptation of the novel *That Obscure Object of Desire* features three (or more) entities: the character, the two actresses who play the role, and the dubber who dubs both actresses.

Film theory also inherits the history of reflection on literary genre. Etymologically drawn from the Latin *genus* ("kind"), "genre" criticism began, at least in what came to be known as the "West," as the classification of the diverse kinds of literary texts and the evolution of literary forms.[1] In the *Poetics* Aristotle proposed to treat "poetry in its various kinds, noting the essential quality of each." Aristotle's famous definition of tragedy touched on diverse aspects of genre: the kinds of events portrayed (an action of a certain magnitude); the social rank of the characters (nobles, better than ourselves); the ethical qualities of the characters (their "tragic flaws"); narrative structure (dramatic reversals); and audience effects (the purging of pity and fear through "catharsis"). In the third book of Plato's *Republic*, Socrates proposed a tripartite division of literary forms, based on their manner of presentation: (1) pure imitation of dialogue (tragedy, comedy); (2) direct recital (dithyramb); and (3) the mixture of the two (as in epic). Refining on Plato, Aristotle distinguished between the medium of representation, the objects represented and the mode of representation. The "mode of representation" produced

13

the familiar triad of epic, drama, and lyric, while the "objects" of imitation generated class-based distinctions between tragedy (the actions of nobles) and comedy (the actions of the nobles' presumed inferiors). The film world, as we shall see shortly, inherited this habit of arranging artworks into types, some drawn from literature (comedy, tragedy, melodrama) and others more specifically cinematic: views, actualities, tableaux, travelogues, animated cartoons.

A number of perennial doubts plague genre theory. Are genres really "out there" in the world, or are they merely the constructions of analysts? Is there a finite taxonomy of genres or are they in principle infinite? Are genres timeless Platonic essences or ephemeral, time-bound entities? Are genres culture-bound or transcultural? Does the term "melodrama" have the same meaning in Britain, France, Egypt, and Mexico? Should genre analysis be descriptive or proscriptive? Genre taxonomies in film have been notoriously imprecise and heterotopic, having some of the qualities of Foucault's Chinese encyclopedia. While some genres are based on story content (the war film), others are borrowed from literature (comedy, melodrama) or from other media (the musical). Some are performer-based (the Astaire–Rogers films) or budget-based (blockbusters), while others are based on artistic status (the art film), racial identity (Black cinema), locate (the Western) or sexual orientation (Queer cinema). Some, like documentary and satire, might better be seen as "transgenres." Subject matter is the weakest criterion for generic grouping because it fails to take into account *how* the subject is treated. The subject of nuclear war, for example, can be generically rendered as satire (*Dr Strangelove*), docu-fiction (*War Game*), porn (*Café Flesh*), melodrama (*Testament, The Day After*), and satiric compilation documentary (*Atomic Café*). The Hollywood-on-Hollywood film can be a melodrama (*A Star is Born*), a comedy (*Show People*), a musical (*Singin' in the Rain*), a vérité documentary (*Lion's Love*), a parody (*Silent Movie*), and so on.

Filmic genre, like literary genre before it, is also permeable to historical and social tensions. The entire course of western literature, Erich Auerbach (1953) argues in *Mimesis*, has worked to erode the elitist "separation of styles" inherent in the Greek tragic model, through a democratizing impulse (rooted in the Judaic notion of "all souls equal before God") by which the dignity of a noble style was gradually accorded to ever "lower" classes of people. Genres come equipped, then, with class connotations. In literature, the novel, rooted in the common-sense world of bourgeois facticity, challenges the romance, linked to aristocratic notions of courtliness and chivalry. Art revitalizes itself by drawing on the strategies of previously marginalized forms and genres, in conformity with what Viktor Shklovsky calls the "law of the canonization of the junior branch." Some films explicitly connect class and genre. King Vidor's *Show People*, for example, pits vaudevillian slapstick against Frenchified costume drama, portraying slapstick as the genre of the unpretentious people, and costume drama as the genre of the royalty-identified elite.

Film theory also inherits antecedent questions concerning artistic "realism." An uncommonly contested and elastic term, "realism" comes to film theory heavily laden with millennial encrustations from antecedent debates in philosophy and literature. Classical philosophy distinguished between Platonic realism – the assertion of the absolute and objective existence of universals, i.e. the belief that forms, essences, abstractions such as "beauty" and "truth" exist independent of human perception – and Aristotelian realism – the view that universals only exist within objects in the external world (rather than in an extra-material realm of essences). The term "realism" is confusing because these early philosophical usages often seem diametrically opposed to "common-sense" realism – the belief in the objective existence of facts and the attempt to see these facts without idealization.

The concept of realism, while ultimately rooted in the classical Greek conception of *mimesis* (imitation), gained programmatic significance only in the nineteenth century, when it came to denote a movement in the figurative and narrative arts dedicated to the observation and accurate representation of the contemporary world. A neologism coined by French critics, realism was originally linked to an oppositional attitude toward romantic and neo-classical models in fiction and painting. The realist novels of writers like Balzac,

15

Stendhal, Flaubert, George Eliot, and Eça de Queiròs brought intensely individualized, seriously conceived characters into typical contemporary social situations. Underlying the realist impulse was an implicit teleology of social democratization favoring the artistic emergence of "more extensive and socially inferior human groups to the position of subject matter for problematic–existential representation" (Auerbach, 1953, p. 491). Literary critics distinguished between this deep, democratizing realism, and a shallow, reductionistic, and obsessively veristic "naturalism" – realized most famously in the novels of Emile Zola – which modeled its human representations on the biological sciences.

The beginnings of cinema coincided with a kind of crisis within the veristic project as expressed in the realist novel, in the naturalist play (with real meat hanging in staged butcher shops), and in obsessively mimetic exhibitions. An ongoing aesthetic debate within film theory has to do with arguments about whether cinema should be narrative or anti-narrative, realist or anti-realist; in short, with film's relation to modernism. Artistic modernism, i.e. those movements in the arts (both in Europe and outside of Europe) which emerged in the late nineteenth century, flourished in the early decades of the twentieth century, and became institutionalized as "high modernism" after World War II, was interested in a non-representational art characterized by abstraction, fragmentation, and aggression. Despite its superficial modernity and technological razzle-dazzle, dominant cinema inherited the mimetic aspirations that Impressionism had relinquished in painting, that Alfred Jarry as well as the symbolists had attacked in the theater, and that James Joyce and Virginia Woolf had undermined in the novel. Yet in the cinema this realist/modernist dichotomy can easily be overdrawn. When Hitchcock collaborates with Salvador Dali on the dream sequence in *Spellbound* is he still pre-modernist? Was Hitchcock *ever* pre-modernist? When Buñuel makes genre films within the Mexican industry, does he remain an avant-gardist?[2]

The issue of realism also had to do with intercultural dialogue. In the case of European modernism, as Bakhtin and Medvedev (1985) suggest in *The Formal Method in Literary Scholarship*, non-European cultures became the catalysts for the supercession, within

16

Europe, of a retrograde culture-bound verism. Africa, Asia, and the Americas provided a reservoir of alternative trans-realist forms and attitudes. In film theory, Sergei Eisenstein invoked extra-European traditions (Hindi *rasa*, Japanese kabuki) as part of his attempt to construct a film aesthetic which went beyond mere mimesis. A realist or, better, illusionist style was revealed by the modernist movement to be just one of many possible strategies, and one marked, furthermore, by a certain provinciality. Vast regions of the world, and long periods of artistic history, had shown little allegiance to or even interest in realism. Kapila Malik Vatsayan speaks of a very different aesthetic that held sway in much of the world:

A common aesthetic theory governed all the arts, both performing and plastic, in South and South East Asia. Roughly speaking, the common trends may be identified as the negation of the principle of realistic imitation in art, the establishment of a hierarchy of realities where the principle of suggestion through abstraction is followed and the manifestation in the arts of the belief that time is cyclic rather than linear. . . . This tradition of the arts appears to have been persuasive from Afghanistan and India to Japan and Indonesia over two thousand years of history. (Quoted in Armes, 1974, p. 135)

In India, a two-thousand year tradition of theater, which has impacted Indian cinema, circles back to the classical Sanskrit drama, which tells the myths of Hindu culture through an aesthetic based less on coherent character and linear plot than on the subtle modulations of mood and feeling (*rasa*). Chinese painting, in the same vein, has often ignored both perspective and realism. The African art which revitalized modernist painting, similarly, cultivated what Robert Farris Thompson calls "mid-point mimesis," i.e. a style that avoided both illusionistic realism and hyperabstraction.

Non-realist traditions also exist within the West, of course, and in any case there is nothing intrinsically "bad" about occidental realism. But as the product of a specific culture and historical moment, it is just one of many possible aesthetics. Indeed, realism as a norm can be seen as provincial even within Europe. In *Rabelais and His World* Bakhtin speaks of the "carnivalesque" as a counter-hegemonic tradition with a history that runs from Greek Dionysian festivals and the Roman Saturnalia, through the grotesque realism of the medieval "carnivalesque," on through Shakespeare and Cervantes, and finally to Jarry and Surrealism. As theorized by Bakhtin, carnival embraces an anti-classical aesthetic that rejects formal harmony and unity in favor of the asymmetrical, the heterogenous, the oxymoronic, the miscegenated. Carnival's "grotesque realism" turns conventional aesthetics on its head in order to locate a new kind of popular, convulsive, rebellious beauty, one that dares to reveal the grotesquerie of the powerful and the latent beauty of the "vulgar." Within carnival, all hierarchical distinctions, all barriers, all norms and prohibitions, are temporarily suspended, while a qualitatively different kind of communication, based on "free and familiar contact," is established. Within carnival's cosmic gaiety, laughter has deep philosophical meaning; it constitutes a special perspective on experience, one no less profound than seriousness and tears.

In *Problems of Dostoevsky's Poetics* Bakhtin speaks of the "Menippea," a perennial artistic genre linked to a carnivalesque vision of the world and marked by oxymoronic characters, multiple styles, violation of the norms of etiquette, and the comic confrontation of philosophical points of view. Although not originally conceived as an instrument for cinematic analysis, the category of the Menippea has the capacity to deprovincialize film-critical discourse, which is too often tied to nineteenth-century conventions of verisimilitude. Filmmakers like Buñuel, Godard, Ruiz, and Rocha, in this perspective, are not the mere negation of the dominant tradition but rather heirs of this *other* tradition, renovators of a perennial mode characterized by protean vitality.

Film and Film Theory: The Beginnings

Film theory is what Bakhtin would call a "historically situated utterance." And just as one cannot separate the history of film theory from the history of the arts and of artistic discourse, so one cannot separate it from history *tout court*, defined by Fredric Jameson as "that which hurts" but also as that which inspires. In the long view, the history of film, and therefore of film theory, must be seen in the light of the growth of nationalism, within which cinema became a strategic instrument for "projecting" national imaginaries. It must also be seen in relation to colonialism, the process by which the European powers reached positions of economic, military, political, and cultural hegemony in much of Asia, Africa, and the Americas. (While nations had often annexed adjacent territories, what was new in European colonialism was its planetary reach, its attempted submission of the world to a single "universal" regime of truth and power.) This process reached its apogee at the turn of the twentieth century, when the earth surface controlled by European powers rose from 67 percent (1884) to 84.4 percent (1914), a situation that began to be reversed only with the disintegration of the European colonial empires after World War II.[1]

The beginnings of cinema, then, coincided precisely with the very height of imperialism. (Of all the celebrated "coincidences" – of the beginnings of cinema with the beginnings of psychoanalysis, with the rise of nationalism, with the emergence of consumerism – it is this coincidence with imperialism that has been least studied.) The first film screenings by Lumière and Edison in the 1890s occurred shortly after the "scramble for Africa" that erupted in the late 1870s, the British occupation of Egypt in 1882, the massacre of the Sioux at Wounded Knee in 1890, and countless other imperial misadventures. The most prolific film-producing countries of the silent period – Britain, France, the USA, Germany – also "happened" to be among the leading imperialist countries, in whose clear interest it was to laud the colonial enterprise. The cinema combined narrative and spectacle to tell the story of colonialism from the colonizer's perspective. Thus dominant cinema has spoken for the "winners" of history, in films which idealized the colonial enterprise as a philanthropic civilizing mission motivated by a desire to push back the frontiers of ignorance, disease, and tyranny. Programmatically negative portrayals helped rationalize the human costs of the imperial enterprise.

The dominant European/American form of cinema not only inherited and disseminated a hegemonic colonial discourse, but also created a powerful hegemony of its own through monopolistic control of film distribution and exhibition in much of Asia, Africa, and the Americas. Eurocolonial cinema thus mapped history not only for domestic audiences but also for the world, in a manner which has profound implications for theories of film spectatorship. African spectators were prodded to identify with Rhodes, Stanley, and Livingstone against Africans themselves, thus engendering a battle of national imaginaries within the fissured colonial spectator. For the European spectator, then, the cinematic experience mobilized a rewarding sense of national and imperial belonging, but for the colonized, the cinema produced a sense of deep ambivalence, mingling the identification provoked by cinematic narrative with intense resentment.

The medium of cinema, as Ella Shohat has pointed out, formed part of the same discursive continuum that included such disciplines as geography, history, anthropology, archeology, and philosophy. The cinema could "chart a map of the world, like the cartographer; it could tell stories and chronicle events, like the historiographer; it could 'dig' into the past of distant civilizations, like the archeologist; and it could narrate the customs and habits of exotic peoples, like the ethnographer."[2] The audiovisual media, in sum, were available as instruments for the intellectual dispossession of non-European cultures. That the implications of this dispossession were noted, overall, only by the victims of these processes suggests the extent to which Eurocentric habits of mind have been taken as axiomatic by most film scholars and theorists. It took hard work, as Toni Morrison might say, *not* to notice such things.

The common assumption that the cinema is an exclusively western technology is incorrect. Science and technology are often thought of as western, but historically Europe has largely borrowed them from others: the alphabet, algebra, astronomy, printing, gunpowder, the magnetic compass, mechanical clockwork, irrigation, vulcanization, and quantitative cartography all came from outside Europe. While the cutting-edge of technological development over

20

recent centuries has undoubtedly centered on Western Europe and North America, this development has been very much a "joint venture" (in which Europe owned most of the shares) facilitated in the past by colonial exploitation and now by neo-colonial "brain draining" of the "Third World." The wealth of Europe, as Fanon put it in *The Wretched of the Earth*, "is literally the creation of the Third World." If the industrial revolutions of Europe were made possible by the control of the resources of colonized lands and the exploitation of slave labor – Britain's industrial revolution, for example, was partially financed by infusions of wealth generated by Latin American mines and plantations – then in what sense is it meaningful to speak only of *Western* technology, industry, and science?

The object of film theory – films themselves – is profoundly international in nature. Although the cinema *began* in such countries as the United States, France, and Britain, it quickly spread throughout the world, with capitalist-based film production appearing roughly simultaneously in many places, including in what are now called Third World countries. Brazil's cinematic *bela epoca*, for example, occurred between 1908 and 1911, before the country was infiltrated by American distribution companies in the wake of World War I. In the 1920s India was producing more films than Great Britain, and countries like the Philippines were producing over 50 films a year by the 1930s. What we now call Third World cinema, taken in a broad sense, far from being a marginal appendage to First World cinema, has actually produced *most* of the world's feature films. If one excludes made-for-TV films, India is the leading producer of fiction films in the world, producing between 700 and 1,000 feature films a year. Asian countries, taken together, produce over half of the yearly world production. Burma, Pakistan, South Korea, Thailand, the Philippines, Indonesia, and even Bangladesh produce over 50 feature films a year. Despite its hegemonic position, then, Hollywood has contributed only a fraction of the annual worldwide production of feature films. "Standard" film histories, and standard film theory, unfortunately, rarely engage with the implications of this filmic cornucopia. The Hollywoodcentric formulation reduces India's giant film industry, which produces more films than Hollywood, and whose

21

hybrid aesthetics mingle Hollywood continuity codes and production values with the anti-illusionist values of Hindu mythology, to a mere mimicry of Hollywood. Even the branch of cinema studies that is critical of Hollywood often recenters Hollywood as a kind of *langue* in relation to which all other forms are but dialectal variants; thus the avant-garde becomes little more than the shadowy alter ego of Hollywood, a festival of negations of dominant cinema.

Early Silent Film Theory

Reflexion on film as a medium began virtually with the medium itself. Indeed, the etymological meanings of the original names given to the cinema already point to diverse ways of "envisioning" the cinema and even foreshadow later theories. "Biograph" and "animatographe" emphasize the recording of life itself (a strong current, later, in the writings of Bazin and Kracauer). "Vitascope" and "Bioscope" emphasize the *looking* at life, and thus shift emphasis from recording life to the spectator and scopophilia (the desire to look), a concern of 1970s psychoanalytic theorists. "Chronophotographe" stresses the writing of time (and light) and thus anticipates Deleuze's (Bergsonian) emphasis on the "time image," while "Kinetoscope," again anticipating Deleuze, stresses the visual observation of movement. "Scenarograph" emphasizes the recording of stories or scenes, calling attention both to decor and to the stories that take place within that decor, and thus implicitly privileges a narrative cinema. "Cinematographe," and later "cinema," call attention to the transcription of movement.

One might even expand the discussion to examine the proto-theoretical implications of the etymologies of the words for *pre*-cinematic devices: "camera obscura" (dark room) evokes the processes of photography, Marx's comparison of ideology to a camera obscura, and the name of a feminist film journal. "Magic lantern" evokes the perennial theme of "movie magic" along with Romanticism's creative "lamp" and the Enlightenment's "lantern." "Phantasmagoria" and

22

"phasmotrope" (spectacle-turn) evoke fantasy and the marvelous, while "cosmorama" evokes the global world-making ambitions of the cinema. Marey's "fusil cinématographique" (cinematic rifle) evokes the "shooting" process of film while calling attention to the aggressive potential of the camera as a weapon, a metaphor resurrected in the "guerrilla cinema" of the revolutionary filmmakers of the 1960s. "Mutoscope" suggests a viewer of change, while "phenakistiscope" evokes "cheating views," a foreshadowing of Baudrillard's simulacrum. Many of the names for the cinema include some variant on "graph" (Greek "writing" or "transcription") and thus anticipate later tropes of filmic authorship and *écriture*. The German *lichtspiel* (play of light) is one of the few names to reference light. Not surprisingly, given the "silent" beginnings of the medium, the appelations given the cinema rarely reference sound, although Edison saw the cinema as an extension of the phonograph and gave his pre-cinematic devices such names as "optical phonograph" and "kinetophonograph" (the writing of movement and sound). The initial attempts to synchronize sound and image generated such coinages as "cameraphone" and "cinephone." In Arabic the cinema was called *sura mutaharika* (moving image or form), while in Hebrew the word for cinema evolved from *reinoa* (watching movement) to *kolnoa* (sound movement). Otherwise, the names themselves imply that film is "essentially" visual, a view often buttressed by the "historical" argument that cinema existed first as image and then as sound; in fact, of course, cinema was usually accompanied both by language (intertitles, visible mouthings of speech) and by music (pianos, orchestras).

In the earliest writings on the cinema, theory is often only an implicit embryonic presence. We find in some journalistic critics, for example, a discourse of wonderment, a kind of religious awe at the sheer magic of mimesis, at seeing a convincing simulacral representation of an arriving train or of the "wind blowing through the leaves." Responding to an 1896 screening of the Lumière films in Bombay, a *Times of India* (July 22, 1896) reporter remarked on the "life-like manner in which the various views were portrayed on the screen . . . [with] something like seven or eight hundred photographs being thrown on the screen within the space of a minute."[1] A 1989 article in the Chinese paper *Yo-shi-Bao* (The Amusement Journal) speaks of one reporter's initial experience of cinema:

Last night . . . my friends took me to the Chi Gardens to see a show. After the audience gathered, the lights were put out and the performance began. On the screen before us we saw a picture – two occidental girls dancing, with puffed-up yellow hair, looking rather silly. Then another scene, two occidentals boxing. . . . The spectators feel as though they are actually present, and this is exhilarating. Suddenly the lights come on again and all the images vanish. It was indeed a miraculous spectacle. (Quoted in Leyda, 1972, p. 2)

Responding to a Lumière screening in Mexico City in December 1895, Luis G. Urbina noted not only the deficiencies of the "new contraption" which "entertains us by reproducing life" but which "lacks color,"[2] but also the cultural "lacks" of the popular audience:

The popular masses, uncouth and infantile, experience while sitting in front of the screen the enchantment of the child to whom the grandmother has recounted a fairy tale; but I fail to understand how, night after night, a group of people who have the obligation of being civilized can idiotize themselves [in movie theaters] with the incessant repetition of scenes in which the abberations, anachronisms, inverisimilitudes, are made ad hoc for a public of the lowest mental level, ignorant of the most elementary educational notions. (Mora, 1988, p. 6)

Much of the early writing on cinema was produced by literary figures. Here is the Russian novelist Maxim Gorky responding to an 1896 screening of a film:

Last night I was in the Kingdom of Shadows. If you only knew how strange it is to be there. It is a world without sound, without colour. Everything there – the earth, the trees, the people, the water and the air – is dipped in monotonous grey. . . . It is no life but its shadow. . . . And all this in a strange silence where no rumble of wheels is heard, no sound of footsteps or of speech. Not a single note of the intricate symphony that always accompanies the movements of people. (Quoted in Leyda, 1972, pp. 407–9)

24

Many early commentators, like Gorky, were ambivalent about the cinema. From the beginning, there were simultaneous tendencies to either over-endow the cinema with utopian possibilities, or to demonize it as a progenitor of evil. Thus while some promised that the cinema would reconcile hostile nations and bring peace to the world, others gave expression to "moral panics," the fear that film might contaminate or degrade the lower-class public, prodding it toward vice or crime. In such reactions, we sense the convergence of the long shadow of three discursive traditions: (1) Platonic hostility to the mimetic arts; (2) the puritanical rejection of artistic fictions; and (3) the historical scorn of bourgeois elites for the unwashed masses.

A common leitmotif in early film writing was the cinema's potential for democratization, a perennial theme which emerges with every new technology up through the computer and the Internet. A writer for *Moving Picture World* argued in 1910 that "The motion picture brings its note of sympathy alike to the cultured and the uncultured, to the children of opportunity and the sons of toil. It is literature for the illiterate. . . . It knows no boundary lines of race or nation." In tones that point back to Walt Whitman and forward to cyber-discourse, the writer continues:

[The spectator] goes to see, to feel, to sympathize. He is taken for the time out of the limitations of his environment; he walks the streets of Paris; he rises with the cowboy of the West; he delves in the depths of the earth with swarthy miners, or tosses on the ocean with sailor or with fishermen. He feels, too, the thrill of human sympathy with some child of poverty or sorrow. . . . The motion picture artist may play on every pipe in the great organ of humanity.[3]

A cognate theme was the celebration of film as a new "universal language," a theme which resonated, as Miriam Hansen points out, with sources as diverse as the French Enlightenment, the metaphysics of Progress, and Protestant Millennialism (Hansen, 1991, p. 76). The cinema could thus "repair the ruins of Babel" and transcend barriers of nation, culture, and class. As a contributor writes in *American Magazine* (July 1913), there is in the cinema *no bar of language for the alien or the ignorant . . . for a mere nickel, the wasted man . . . sees alien people and begins to understand how like they are to him; he sees courage and aspiration and agony, and begins to understand himself. He begins to feel himself a brother in a race that is led by many dreams. (Quoted in Hansen, 1991, p. 78)*

Despite this theoretical claim of universality, some community groups protested against the actual representations of their communities in Hollywood movies. The August 3, 1911, issue of *Moving Picture World* reports on a Native American delegation to President Taft protesting against erroneous representations and even asking for a Congressional Investigation.[4] In the same vein, African American newspapers like the Los Angeles-based *California Eagle* protested against the racism of films like Griffith's *Birth of a Nation*. It was only in the late 1920s, as we shall see, that we find an in-depth discussion of cinematic racism in the avant-garde journal *Close Up*.

In the silent period we sometimes find a colonized mentality in the film journalism of countries like Brazil. The film magazine *Cinearte* (founded in 1926), for example, was a tropical version of Hollywood's *Photoplay*. Largely financed through advertisements for Hollywood films, the magazine proclaimed its cinematic and social ideals in an editorial:

A cinema which teaches the weak not to respect the strong, the servant to respect his boss, which shows dirty, bearded, unhygienic faces, sordid events and extreme realism is not cinema. Imagine a young couple who go to see a typical North American film. They will see a clean-faced, well-shaven hero with well-combed hair, agile, a gentleman. And the girl will be pretty, with a nice body and cute face, modern hair-style, photogenic . . . the couple which sees such a film will comment that they had already seen such images twenty times before. But over their dreaming hearts, there will not fall the shadow of any shocking brutality, any dirty face which might take away the poetry and enchantment. Young people today cannot accept revolt, lack of hygiene, the struggle and eternal fight against those who have the right to exercise power.[5]

Here the notion of *photogenie,* later developed by French filmmaker-theorists like Jean Epstein to advance the specific potentialities of

26

the "seventh art," becomes a normative epidermic notion of beauty, associated with youth, luxury, stars, and, at least implicitly, whiteness. Although the passage does not mention race, its call for "clean" and "hygienic" as opposed to "dirty" faces, and its generally servile stance toward the lily-white Hollywood model, suggest a coded reference to the subject.[6] At times, the racial reference becomes more explicit. One editorialist calls for Brazilian cinema to be an "act of purification of our reality," emphasizing "progress," "modern engineering," and "our beautiful white people." The same author warns against documentaries as more likely to include "undesirable elements:"

We should avoid documentaries, for they do not allow for total control over what is shown and therefore might allow for the infiltration of undesirable elements: we need a studio cinema, like that of Hollywood, with well-decorated interiors inhabited by nice people.[7]

Thus racial hierarchies impact even on issues of genre and production method.

The film theory of the silent period was concerned, albeit in an intuitive manner, with what turned out to be perennial questions about the cinema: Is cinema an art or merely a mechanical recorder of visual phenomena? If it is an art, what are its salient characteristics? How does it differ from other arts such as painting, music, and theater? Other questions had to do with film's relation to the three-dimensional world. What distinguishes reality in the world, as it were, from reality as presented in the cinema? Still other questions bear on spectatorial processes. What are film's psychological determinants? What mental processes are involved in spectatorship? Is film a language, or a dream? Is cinema art, or commerce, or both? What is the social function of the cinema? Is it to stimulate the perceptive intelligence of the spectator, to be beautifully useless, or to promote the cause of justice in the world? Although these questions have been transformed and reformulated by contemporary film theory, they have never been completely discarded. On the other hand, there has been a clear evolution in preoccupations. While the early theorists

27

were very much concerned with *proving* cinema's artistic potentialities, for example, later theorists, less defensive and less elitist, take film's status as art for granted, as not in need of proof.

Much of the early film criticism/theory had to do with defining the film medium and its relation to other arts. Drawing on Lessing, Wagner, and the futurists, Ricciotto Canudo, in his 1911 manifesto "The Birth of a Sixth Art," envisioned the cinema as absorbing the three spatial arts (architecture, sculpture, and painting) and the three temporal arts (poetry, music, and dance), transforming them into a synthetic form of theater called "Plastic Art in Motion" (Abel, 1988, Vol. I, pp. 58–66). Anticipating Bakhtin's notion of the "chronotope" – the necessary relationality of time and space in artistic representation – Canudo saw the cinema as the redemptive *telos* of the antecedent spatial and temporal arts, that toward which they had been tending all along. Rather than Bazin's later "myth of total cinema," Canudo promoted the "myth of the total art form."

In the first few decades of the cinema much of the theorizing about film was unformed and impressionistic. A good example of this kind of ad hoc, unsystematic theorizing is found in the work of American poet–critic Vachel Lindsay. In *The Art of the Moving Picture* (1915, revised 1922), Lindsay ruminates over a number of issues, mingling personal anecdotes with speculations about literature and film. Writing against an assumed backdrop of high literary scorn for film as a medium, Lindsay defends popular film to his specified target audience: the directors of art museums, the members of English departments, and "the critical and literary world generally" (ibid., p. 45). Film, for Lindsay, is a democratic art, a new American hieroglyphic in the Whitmanesque tradition. Some of Lindsay's speculations have to do with genre, defined, rather imprecisely, on the basis not of structure but of content and tone. Lindsay cites three "genres": action, intimacy, and splendor. Lindsay appeals to the example of other arts to define the cinema, seeing it as at once "sculpture in motion," "painting in motion," and "architecture in motion," with "motion" forming the common substratum of definition (Lindsay's visual orientation is not surprising given his painterly training at the Art Institute of Chicago). Lindsay thus adopted a differential approach to film specificity, defining the cinema in opposition to other media. In one chapter, for example, he inventories the differences between photoplays (i.e. films) and theatrical performances: while the stage has its exits and entrances at the side and back, "the standard photoplays have their exits and entrances across the imaginary footlight line"; and while the stage is dependent on actors, movies depend on "the genius of the producer" (ibid., pp. 187–8). A decade later, Gilbert Seldes (1924) showed himself to be a partial heir of Lindsay in his enthusiastic defense of cinema as a popular art in *The Seven Lively Arts*.

However quirky in his argumentation, Lindsay did anticipate a number of later currents. His fascination with the analogy between film and hieroglyphics foreshadows both Eisenstein and Metz, and his vision of Thomas Edison as a "new Gutenberg" anticipates McLuhan's claims about new media and the "global village." His suggestion that spectators should talk during films, meanwhile, anticipates Brecht's notion of a "smokers' theater" and a "theater of interruptions." Lindsay also pays a kind of ethnographic attention to audience reaction. Action pictures, for example, "gratify the incipient or rampant speed-mania in every American" (Lindsay, 1915, p. 41). "People love Mary Pickford," he argues, "because of a certain aspect of her face in her highest mood" (ibid., p. 55). Anticipating Vertov's later comparison of film to narcotic drugs ("cine-nicotine," "cine-vodka"), but without Vertov's censorious tone, Lindsay compares the gregarious pleasures of the movie theater to those of the saloon. Since many of Lindsay's somewhat scattershot ruminations are highly speculative, even frivolous – at one point he posits Rimbaud-style correspondences between filmic genres and specific colors – it makes more sense to read him largely in terms of issues raised and possibilities opened up.

Systematic film theory *per se* traces its origins to the first comprehensive study of the film medium: *The Photoplay: A Psychological Study* by Harvard psychologist and philosopher Hugo Munsterberg (1916). Drawing both on the categories of neo-Kantian philosophy and on research in perceptual psychology, as well as on his knowledge of what was then a relatively small corpus of films – the author was ashamed to be seen at the movies – Munsterberg's book argued for film as an "art of subjectivity" which mimics the ways that consciousness shapes the phenomenal world: "The photoplay tells us a human story by overcoming the forms of the outer world, namely space, time and causality, and by adjusting the events to the forms of the inner world, namely attention, memory, imagination and emotion."[8]

In his introduction, Munsterberg distinguishes between "inner" and "outer" developments of the cinema, with the former referring to aesthetic principles and the latter referring to the evolution from pre-cinematic devices such as the kinetoscope to the first "real" films. (In this sense, he anticipates an intense area of interest for contemporary historians of silent cinema.) On the technological origins and future potential of cinema, Munsterberg takes a refreshingly non-teleological position:

It is arbitrary to say where the development of the moving pictures began and it is impossible to foresee where it will lead. . . . If we think of the moving pictures as a source of entertainment and aesthetic enjoyment, we may see the germ in that camera obscura which allowed one glass lid to pass before another . . . on the other hand if the essential feature of the moving pictures is the combination of various views into one connected impression, we must look back to the days of the phenakistoscope which had scientific interest only. (Munsterberg, 1970, p. 1)

But what really interests Munsterberg is the cinema's "inner forms," i.e. the advances in film language which transform "trite episodes" into "a new and promising art" (ibid., pp. 8–9). The filmmaker's selection of what is significant and consequential, for Munsterberg, turns the "chaos" of sense impressions into the "cosmos" of film.

Munsterberg is thus concerned with both aesthetics and psychology. The filmic deployment of space and time, for Munsterberg, transcends theatrical dramaturgy through such devices as the close-up, special effects, and quick changes of scene through editing. For Munsterberg, it is precisely film's *distance* from physical reality which brings it into the mental sphere. Working out of the tradition of philosophical idealism, where thought shapes reality, Munsterberg argues that film reconfigures three-dimensional reality according to the "laws of thought." Unlike the theater, the cinema creates pleasure by triumphing over the material principle, freeing the palpable world from the heaviness of space, time, and causality, decking it out instead in the forms of our own consciousness. Yet there is an aesthetic tension within Munsterberg. On the one hand he calls for the "perfect unity of plot and pictorial appearance" and "complete isolation from the practical world," phases evocative of Hollywood illusionism; but on the other hand he calls for a more open-ended and unpredictable "free play of mental experiences," evocative of art film subjectivism.

Munsterberg can be seen as the spiritual father of a number of currents within film theory. Munsterberg's emphasis on the active spectator, who compensates for cinema's lacunae through intellectual and emotional investments and thus participates in the "game" of cinema, anticipates later theories of spectatorship. In Munsterberg's notion that the spectator accepts the impression of the depth offered by the filmic image, despite his or her knowledge of its factitiousness, for example, we find the germ of the later psychoanalytic notion of "split belief," the "je sais mais quand meme" of 1970s film theory. Munsterberg's notion that films generate mental events, that the film exists, ultimately, not on celluloid but in the mind that actualizes the film, similarly, anticipates the "reception theory" of the 1980s. Munsterberg's work on the "phi-phenomenon," the process by which the mind makes kinetic sense out of static images, finally, makes him the granddaddy of the cognitivists, for whom mimetic processes do not reflect a link between film and "reality" but rather between filmic processes and those of the mind itself. And as a trained philosopher turning his attention to the cinema, Munsterberg anticipates such later figures as Maurice Merleau-Ponty and Gilles Deleuze.

While Munsterberg emphasized the psychological dimensions of film, other theorists saw film as a kind of language, with its own grammar, syntax, and vocabulary. For Vachel Lindsay (1915), film constituted a new language of picture-words and hieroglyphs, a kind of Esperanto. We also encounter the notion of film language in the 1920s writings of Riccioto Canudo and Louis Delluc in France, both of whom saw the language-like character of the cinema as linked, paradoxically, to its non-verbal status and its capacity for transcending the barriers of national language.[9] Hungarian film theorist Bela Bálázs, meanwhile, repeatedly stressed the language-like nature of film in his work from the 1920s through the late 1940s. Film spectators, Bálázs argued, have to learn the "grammar" of the new art, its conjugations and declensions of close-ups and editing.[10] (The trope of film language, as we shall see, was also developed by the Russian Formalists and, much more rigorously, by the film semiologists of the 1960s.)

Another strand of theory can be teased out of the commentaries on their craft by filmmakers themselves. Griffith's claim that he borrowed his chiaroscuro lighting techniques from Rembrandt, for example, implied a quasi-theoretical stance on the relation between film and painting. Louis Feuillade's description of his films as "slices of life" representing "people and things as they are rather than as they would like to be" surely implies a stance on artistic realism.[11] Brazilian filmmaker Humberto Mauro's aphorism that "the cinema is waterfalls," similarly, suggests that the cinema should privilege natural beauty, in this case Brazilian natural beauty. Non-filmmakers also offered embryonic "theories" of the cinema. Woodrow Wilson's praise for *Birth of a Nation* as "history written with lightning" could be seen as making a theoretical claim about the cinema's potential for historiographical *écriture*, albeit one with disturbingly racist implications. Lenin's proclamation that "film was for us the most important of all the arts," in the same way, could be seen as making an implicitly theoretical claim about the political–ideological uses of film.

Many incipient "theories" built on pre-existing traditions concerning other arts. The idea of the filmmaker as "author," for example, was inherited from millennia of literary tradition. Although auteurism came into vogue only in the 1950s, the root idea itself emerged in the silent period, a function of cinema's search for artistic legitimation. Already in 1915, Vachel Lindsay anticipated auteurism by predicting in *The Art of the Moving Picture* that "we will some day distinguish the different photoplay masters as we now delight in the separate tang of O. Henry and Mark Twain" (Lindsay, 1915, p. 211). In 1921 the filmmaker Jean Epstein, in "Le Cinéma et les lettres modernes," applied the term "author" to the filmmaker, while Louis Delluc analyzed the films of Griffith, Chaplin, and Ince in what Stephen Crofts has called a "proto-auteurist" manner (Crofts, in Hill and Gibson, 1998, p. 312). The characterization of the cinema as the seventh art, similarly, implicitly gave film artists the same status as writers and painters.

The Essence of Cinema

Since the beginning of film as a medium, analysts have sought its "essence," its unique and distinguishing features. Some early film theorists argued for a cinema untainted by the other arts, as in Jean Epstein's notion of "pure cinema." Other theorists and filmmakers proudly asserted cinema's links to the other arts. Griffith claimed to have borrowed narrative cross-cutting from Dickens while Eisenstein found prestigious literary antecedents for cinematic devices: the changes of focal length in *Paradise Lost*; the alternating montage of the agricultural fair chapter in *Madame Bovary*. The often-cited definitions of cinema in terms of other arts – "sculpture in motion" (Vachel Lindsay); "music of light" (Abel Gance); "painting in movement" (Leopold Survage); "architecture in movement" (Elie Faure) – simultaneously established links with previous arts while positing crucial differences: cinema was painting, but this time in movement, or it was music, but this time of light rather than notes. The common point of agreement was that cinema was an art. Indeed, Rudolf Arnheim in 1933 expressed astonishment that the cinema had not been received with open arms by art lovers. The cinema, he wrote, is "the art *par excellence*. With unrestrained exclusivity it served to entertain and distract; it won out over all the older arts in the beauty pageant; and its muse was as scantily clad as could possibly be desired" (Arnheim, 1997, p. 75). The insistence on both the differences and the similarities between cinema and the other arts provided a way of legitimizing a fledgling medium, a way of saying not only that the cinema was as good as the other arts, but also that it should be judged in its own terms, in relation to its own potentials and aesthetics.

With its many specialized film journals and important figures (Jean Epstein, Abel Gance, Louis Delluc, Germaine Dulac, and Riccioto Canudo), France became a privileged site of reflection on both commercial and avant-garde cinema. A constellation of institutions (a "cultural field" in Bourdieu's terminology) facilitated the exhibition and discussion of films. Many of the theorists of this period, despite their manifold differences, were preoccupied with the status and essential nature of the cinema as an art. Already in 1916 a futurist manifesto ("The Futurist Cinema") called for recognition of cinema as "an autonomous art" which must never "copy the stage" (quoted by Hein, in Drummond et al., 1979, p. 19). Within "pure cinema," the goal, as Fernand Leger put it, was to "break away from the elements which are not purely cinematographic" (ibid., p. 41). Still another expression of this concern was the theme of *photogenie*, which Delluc called the "law of cinema," and which Epstein, in *Le Cinématographe vu de l'Etna*, called the "purest expression of cinema": "With the notion of *photogenie* was born the idea of cinema art. For how better to define the indefinable *photogenie* than by saying that it is to cinema as color is to painting and volume to sculpture, the specific element of this art" (Drummond et al., 1979, p. 38). Elsewhere, Epstein defined *photogenie* as "any aspect of things, beings, or souls whose moral character is enhanced by filmic reproduction."[1] *Photogenie* was thus that ineffable quintessence that differentiated the magic of cinema from the other arts. In another sense, the emphasis on the generation of new knowledge linked the cinema to artistic modernism as a project of challenging conventional perception and understanding.

The impressionists were also concerned with the cinema's relation to other arts. In his *L'Usine aux images* (The Image Factory, 1926), Canudo suggested that cinema, as a "sixth art," would be like a "painting and a sculpture developing in time, as in music and poetry, which realize themselves by transforming air into rhythm for the duration of their execution."[2] In Canudo's gregarious concep-

34

tion, this "plastic art in motion" fulfilled the rich utopian promise of the Festival – a notion akin to Bakhtin's "carnival" – redolent of ancient theater and contemporary fairgrounds. Louis Delluc in his *Cinema et cia* (1919) spoke of the cinema as the only truly modern art because it used technology to stylize real life. Germaine Dulac invoked the musical analogy of a "visual symphony:"

Should not cinema, which is an art of vision, as music is an art of hearing . . . lead us toward the visual idea composed of movement and life, toward the conception of an art of the eye, made of a perceptual inspiration evolving in its continuity and reaching, just as music does, our thought and feelings. (Quoted in Sitney, 1978, p. 41)

Movement and rhythm, for Dulac, formed "the unique and intimate essence of cinematic expression" (Drummond et al., 1979, p. 129).

Many of the early theorists displayed what Annette Michelson calls a "euphoric epistemology" (Michelson, 1990, pp. 16–39). Filmmaker Abel Gance proclaimed in *L'Art cinématographique* (1927) that "the time of the image has arrived!" The cinema, for Gance, would endow human beings with a new synaesthetic awareness: spectators "will hear with their eyes."[3] Anticipating Bazin's epiphanic view of the cinema, Delluc saw the cinema, and especially the close-up, as providing us with "impressions of evanescent eternal beauty . . . something beyond art, that is, life itself."[4] Within a kind of transcendental iconophilia, the cinema was envisioned as delivering up life itself in its felt presence and immediacy. Jean Epstein spoke in *Bonjour cinéma* (1921) of the cinema as "profane revelation," a means of mobilizing the spectator's sensibility through direct contact with the human organism (hands, faces, feet). For Epstein, the cinema is "essentially supernatural. Everything is transformed" (quoted in Abel, 1988, p. 246). The cinematic experience, for Epstein, was embodied, visceral. Thanks to the cinema

we experience hills, trees, faces in space as a new sensation. Given motion or its appearance, the body as a whole experiences depth. . . . The cine-camera, more than the car or the airplane, makes possible particular, personal trajectories that reverberate through the entire physique. (Quoted in Williams, 1980, pp. 193–4)

35

Anticipating Bazin, but on a different register and in a distinct, more mystical vocabulary, Epstein took what he imagined as the automatic, non-mediated nature of the cinema to be a guarantee of its ineffable "sincerity." For Epstein, the close-up was the "soul of the cinema:" "I will never find the way to say how I love American close-ups. Point blank. A head suddenly appears on screen and drama, now face to face, seems to address me personally and swells with an extraordinary intensity. I am hypnotized."[5] At the same time, Epstein was not opposed to manipulation of the image. In a 1928 text, he argues that

Slow motion actually brings a new range to dramaturgy. Its power of laying bare the emotions of the dramatic enlargements, its infallibility in the designation of the sincere movements of the soul, are such that it outclasses all tragic modes at this time. I am certain and so are all those who have seen part of La Chute de la maison Usher, *that if a high-speed film of an accused person under interrogation were to be made, then from beyond his words, the truth would appear, writ plain, unique, evident; that there would be no further need of indictment, of lawyers' speeches, nor of any proof other than that provided from the depths of the images.*[6]

In his survey of impressionist usages of the term *photogenie,* David Bordwell speaks of the "bewildering compendium of variants" of idealism in which "Baudelairian theosophy mingles with Platonic idealism with Bergsonian movementism" in an "assemblage of various assumptions never raised to theoretical self-consciousness" (quoted in Willemen, 1994, p. 125). The concept of *photogenie* enabled the impressionist critics to speak of the ways the cinema can not only highlight the poetic movement of things in the world but also render the transmuted perceptions generated by contemporary urban life, namely speed, simultaneity, multiple information. At the same time, Epstein believed the cinema could explore "the non-linguistic, non-rational operations of the 'unconscious' in human existence" (Liebman, 1980, p. 119).

Many of the silent-period theorists warned against the temptation of verism. In his essay "A New Realism: The Object" (Jacobs, 1960, p. 98), experimental filmmaker Fernand Leger complained that most films waste their energy in constructing a recognizable world, while neglecting the spectacular power of the fragment. Another experimentalist, Hans Richter, argued that the "main aesthetic problem for the movies, which were invented for reproduction is, paradoxically, the overcoming of reproduction" (ibid., p. 282). Germaine Dulac foresaw a cinema freed of the responsibility of telling stories or realistically reproducing "real life." "Pure" cinema could be inspired by dreams, as with Epstein, or by music, as with Abel Gance and Germaine Dulac in France, and Mario Peixoto in Brazil, all of whom spoke of film as essentially rhythm, or better, a "visual symphony made up of rhythmic images."[7] Purity thus implied a rejection of plots. Anticipating the existential skepticism of Sartre's *La Nausée*, Jean Epstein called cinematic stories "lies:" "There are no stories. There have never been stories. There are only situations without tail or head; without beginning, middle or end."[8] Germaine Dulac accused those who promote narrative of a "criminal error."[9] As something promiscuously shared with many other arts, narrative was thought to form a very fragile basis for establishing film's special qualities. Usually associated with written texts, narrative could not provide the basis for the construction of a purely visual art form.

The Soviet Montage-Theorists

What might be called the *bricolage* style of the film theory of the early silent period gave way in the 1920s to the more thoroughgoing reflexions of the Soviet montage-theorists/filmmakers. These theorists worked against the backdrop of the remarkable flowering of diverse avant-garde tendencies in theater, painting, literature, and cinema (much of it state-financed) in the Soviet Union. As practitioner–intellectuals linked to the State Film School founded in 1920, these filmmaker–theorists were concerned not only with grand ideas but also with the practical questions of constructing a socialist film industry which reconciled authorial creativity, political efficacy, and mass popularity. They asked such questions as: what kind of cinema should we promote? Fiction or documentary? Mainstream or avant garde? What is revolutionary cinema? They also had in common a view of themselves as "cultural workers" forming part of a broad social spectrum engaged in revolutionizing and modernizing Russia. Trained in practical fields like engineering and architecture, their emphasis was on technique, on construction, on experiment.

Despite the diversity of their film styles – ranging from the pragmatic clarity of Pudovkin to the epic–operatic density of Eisenstein – these theorists all emphasized montage as the basis of cine-poetics. Montage, as Eisenstein, Pudovkin, and Alexandrov put it in their 1928 manifesto on sound, "has become the indisputable axiom on which the worldwide culture of the cinema has been built" (Eisenstein, 1957, p. 257). "Montage" is the ordinary word for editing, not only in Russian but also in the romance languages. As Geoffrey Nowell-Smith points out, the word has strong practical and even industrial overtones (for example *chaine de montage* for "assembly line" in French). The alchemy of montage, for the Soviet theorists, brought life and luster to the inert base materials of the single shot. The montage-theorists were also, in a sense, structuralists *avant la lettre*, in that they saw the filmic shot as being without intrinsic meaning prior to its placement within a montage structure. The shot gained meaning, in other words, only relationally, as part of a larger system. In film as in language, to paraphrase Saussure, "there were only differences."

For the practically minded Kuleshov, founder of the world's first film school, the art of cinema consisted in strategically managing the spectator's cognitive and visual processes through the analytic segmentation of partial views. What distinguishes the cinema from other arts, for Kuleshov, is montage's capacity to organize disjointed fragments into meaningful, rhythmical sequence. In the early 1920s Kuleshov devised a series of experiments to show that editing could engender emotions and associations that went far beyond the content of individual shots. One experiment, later dubbed the "Kuleshov effect," juxtaposed the same shot of the actor Mosjoukine with diverse visual materials (a bowl of soup, a baby in a coffin, and so forth) to convey very different emotional effects (hunger, grief, etc.).

It was film technique, rather than "reality," then, that generated spectatorial emotion. Kuleshov suggested that film actors should become "models" or "mannequins," or even "monsters" who could train the body to "achieve complete mastery of its material construction." As for Hitchcock later, meaning was generated less through the expressive performance of actors as "cattle" than through the manipulation of performance through editing. (Mark Rappaport performs a brilliant filmic excursus on the Kuleshov effect in his film *From the Journals of Jean Seberg.*) The success of American films, for Kuleshov, derived from their clear, rapid storytelling, their invisible cutting, and the efficient matching of montage techniques with lively action sequences: fights, cavalcades, chases.

While Vertov's work was aesthetically ambiguous, pointing both to the experimentalism of Eisenstein and to the efficacy of the mainstream, the work of Kuleshov's student Pudovkin was more conventional. In books like *Film Technique* and *Film Acting* Pudovkin elucidated the basic principles of narrative and spatiotemporal continuity, largely from the point of view of the practicing filmmaker. (Pudovkin's books were translated and used in film schools and even studios throughout the world.) For Pudovkin, the key to the cinema lay in its protocols for organizing the look and managing the perceptions and feelings of the spectator through editing and staging and through such rhetorical devices as contrast, parallelism, and symbolism (Pudovkin, 1960). Editing, for Pudovkin, both resembled and engendered the shifts in focus and attention typical of ordinary, everyday perception. Pudovkin's account of these mechanisms anticipates, in some respects, later cognitive accounts of what came to be called "classical cinema."

The most influential of the Soviet montage-theorists was Sergei Eisenstein; here the prestige of the films and the prestige of the theory went hand in hand. A prodigious thinker of encyclopedic interests, Eisenstein's theoretical discourse was a high-flying amalgam: part philosophical speculation, part literary essay, part political manifesto, and part filmmaking manual. Indeed, Eisenstein's writing often gives the impression of a constellation of remarkable insights in search of an overarching theory. Within Eisenstein's inspired eclecticism, a technicist, reductive approach – filmmaker as engineer, or as Pavlovian lab technician – coexisted with a quasi-mystical approach emphasizing "pathos" and "ecstasy," an oceanic feeling of oneness with others and the world. Although Eisenstein's theories evolved over two decades of theoretical production – Jacques Aumont in *Montage Eisenstein* (1987) suggests that there are "several Eisensteins" — he always favored a highly stylized and intellectually ambitious cinema. Within Eisenstein's millennial approach, the cinema not only inherited but also transformed the achievements of the history of all the arts and of "the entire experience of mankind through the ages" (Eisenstein, quoted in Bordwell, 1993, pp. 492–3). Rather than "purify" the cinema, Eisenstein preferred to enrich it through synesthetic cross-fertilization with the other arts, whence his citations of artists as diverse as da Vinci, Milton, Diderot, Flaubert, Dickens, Daumier, and Wagner. Eisenstein's thinking was also what would nowadays be called "multiculturalist," in that he showed a more than exotic interest in African sculpture, Japanese kabuki, Chinese shadow plays, Hindu *rasa* aesthetics, and American indigenous forms, all seen, in a relatively non-primitivist manner, as germane to the forging of a "modern" cinema. (He also wanted to make a film called *Black Majesty*, based on the Haitian revolution.)

In an early stage, Eisenstein, fresh from his experience with the politicized avant-garde theater, stressed the "montage of attractions" – the image was drawn from the circus and the amusement park – and the reflexological shock effects of what he called the "kino-fist" as opposed to Vertov's "kino-eye." Eisenstein's "montage of attractions" proposed a carnival-like aesthetic favoring small sketch-like blocks, sensational turns, and aggressive moments such as drum rolls, acrobatic stunts, sudden bursts of light, organized around specific themes and designed to administer a salutary shock to the spectator. Eisenstein opted for an anti-naturalistic cinema based on the powers of pictorial composition and stylized acting. He also stressed the value of *typage*, a casting technique designed to evoke social stratifications through the choice of performers based on the connotations of their physiognomies as easily recognizable social types. Where Kuleshov spoke of "linkage," Eisenstein spoke, in "A Dialectic Approach to Film Form,"

40

of "conflict:" "In the realm of art this dialectical principle of dynamics is embodied in conflict as the fundamental principle for the existence of every art-work and every art-form."

Eisenstein was less interested in linear cause–effect plot construction than in a disrupted, disjunctive, fractured diegesis, interrupted by digressions and extra-diegetic materials like the shots of the mechanical peacock in *October* that metaphorize the vanity of Prime Minister Kerensky. Eisenstein saw the cinema as potentially stimulating thought and ideological interrogation through constructivist techniques. Rather than *tell* stories through images, Eisensteinian cinema *thinks* through images, using the clash of shots to set off ideational sparks in the mind of the spectator, product of a dialectic of precept and concept, idea and emotion.[1]

Later commentators found Eisenstein's approach totalitarian and suffocating. Andrei Tarkovsky, for example, complains in *Sculpting in Time* that "Eisenstein makes thought into a despot; it leaves no 'air,' nothing of that unspoken elusiveness which is perhaps the most captivating quality of all art." Arlindo Machado (1997, p. 196) suggests that Eisenstein's dream of an audiovisual spectacle made up of concepts and sensations is more appropriate to contemporary video than to the cinema. When shorn of its dialectical basis, moreover, Eisensteinian "associationist" montage could easily be transformed into the commodified ideograms of advertising, where the whole is more than the sum of its parts: Catherine Deneuve plus Chanel No. 5 signifies charm, glamour, and erotic appeal.

The essays gathered in *Film Sense* (1942) and *Film Form* (1949) show an extraordinary range of interests. In "The Cinematographic Principle and the Ideogram," Eisenstein modeled his alternative filmmaking on ideogrammatic (mistakenly called "hieroglyphic") writing, i.e. stylized vestiges of an ancient pictorial language. The appeal both to "attractions" and to ideographic writing facilitated a theoretical end-run around conventional dramatic realism. For Eisenstein, a shot signified largely through its relationships to other shots within a montage sequence. Montage was therefore the key to both aesthetic and ideological mastery. For Eisenstein, the cinema was above all transformative, ideally triggering social practice rather

41

than aesthetic contemplation, shocking the spectator into consciousness of contemporary problems. Appealing to the analogy of contemporary technology, Eisenstein compared film to a tractor, which "plows" – the word has sexual as well as agricultural connotations – the spectatorial psyche. While dismissive of avant-garde "trickery," Eisenstein favored a popular, experimental avant-garde cinema, one intelligible to the masses of people.

Eisenstein was also the theorist of the contrapuntal use of sound, an idea developed in a 1928 manifesto signed by himself, Pudovkin, and Alexandrov, where the three directors warned against the temptation of synchronous phonetic sound, arguing instead for a counterpoint of sound and image. Indeed, notions of counterpoint, tension, and conflict are central to the Eisensteinian aesthetic. For Eisenstein, influenced both by Hegel and Marx, a dialectical struggle of contraries animates not only social life but also artistic texts. Eisenstein aestheticizes Hegelian/Marxist dialectics, while temporalizing, as it were, the essentially spatial juxtapositions of Cubist collage. His ideal in montage is that of a dissonant sound–image concatenation, where tensions remain unresolved. If any single trope characterizes Eisenstein's way of thinking, it is the oxymoron, the yoking of opposites, a trope in evidence in many of his most famous expressions, such as "sensuous thinking" or "dynamic of opposites." Indeed, it is hard to write about Eisenstein without reaching for oxymoronic formulations – "Pavlovian mysticism," "Marxist aestheticism," "Hegelian formalism," "disruptive organicism," "transcendant materialism" – in order to capture the contradictory impulses contained in his thought.

In "Methods of Montage" Eisenstein developed a full-scale montage typology consisting of progressively more complex forms: metric (based solely on length); rhythmic (based on length and content); tonal (based on dominant mood generated by manipulation of light or graphic form); overtonal (based on more subtle expressive resonances); and intellectual (a complex overlay of all the strategies). Each of these types, for Eisenstein, generated specific spectatorial effects. The schema is less interesting as a descriptive paradigm for the cinema than as a suggestive cornucopia of formal possibilities. In "The Filmic Fourth Dimension" Eisenstein suggested that filmmakers work with "overtones" as well as with the "dominant" to create a filmic "impressionism" reminiscent of that of Debussy in music. Eisenstein, as David Bordwell (1997) points out, often makes implicit appeal to musical analogies, whence the frequent recourse to musical concepts such as meter, overtones, dominant, rhythm, polyphony, and counterpoint. (Eisenstein shared this musical orientation with many of his contemporaries: Bakhtin, who was also working out ideas of artistic "polyphony" and "tact" in his late 1920s work on Dostoevsky; writer Henri-Pierre Roché, who spoke of "polyphonic novels"; and Brazilian artist Mario de Andrade, who spoke of "polyphonic poetry.")

Drawing on his vast knowledge of languages, cultures, arts, and disciplines, and working always in a synergistic dialectic of theory and practice, Eisenstein privileged artistic discontinuity, seeing each fragment of film as part of a powerful semantic construction based on principles of juxtaposition and conflict rather than organic seamlessness. In Eisenstein, phenomenal appearances of volume, shape, light, and velocity became the energetic raw material for a subtle form of alchemical, ideogrammatic writing which could shape thought, affect the senses, and even convey abstract or recondite forms of reasoning, consciousness, and conceptual analysis (Eisenstein famously contemplated adapting both Marx's *Capital* and Joyce's *Ulysses*). Eisenstein left a rich intellectual legacy. We find echoes of Eisensteinian principles in Metz's "Grande Syntagmatique," in Burch's *Praxis du cinéma*, in Roland Barthes's "third meaning," and in countless other later reflections on the cinema. Marie-Claire Ropars made Eisenstein a key figure in her notion of a filmic *écriture* based on montage, and in the 1980s Cuban filmmaker Tomás Gutiérrez Alea, in his *Dialectica del Espectador*, attempted to synthesize Eisensteinian *pathos* with Brechtian *verfremdung* (estrangement).

Dziga Vertov, meanwhile, was in many ways even more radical than Eisenstein. (By calling his late 1960s collective with Jean-Pierre Gorin the "Dziga Vertov group," Jean-Luc Godard opted for the more politically and formally radical Vertov over the putatively "re-

43

visionist" Eisenstein.) In a series of incendiary essays and manifestos, Vertov pronounced a "death sentence" on a "profiteering" commercial cinema. Here is Vertov's "We: Variant of a Manifesto:"

We declare the old films, based on the romance, theatrical films and the like, to be leprous.

> *– Keep away from them!*
> *Keep your eyes off them!*
> *They're mortally dangerous!*
> *Contagious!*
> *(Vertov, 1984, p. 7)*

Inviting readers/spectators to "flee the sweet embraces of the romance / the poison of the psychological novel / the clutches of the theater of adultery" (ibid.), Vertov called instead for the "sensory exploration of the world through the kino-eye." With Whitmanesque projective glee, Vertov anthropomorphized the camera:

I am kino-eye. I am a mechanical eye. I, a machine, show you the world as only I can see it.

Now and forever, I free myself from human immobility. I am in constant motion. I draw near, then away, from objects. I crawl under, I climb onto them. I move apace with the muzzle of a galloping horse. I plunge full speed into a crowd. (Ibid., p. 17)

In his "Provisional Instructions to Kino-Eye Groups" Vertov points out that the human eye is inferior to the camera:

Our eye sees very poorly and very little – and so men conceived of the microscope in order to see invisible phenomena; and they discovered the telescope in order to see and explore distant, unknown worlds. The movie camera was invented in order to penetrate deeper into the visible world, to explore and record visual phenomena. (Vertov, 1984, p. 67)

Editing, for Vertov, could assemble a man "more perfect than Adam." The dominant social structures, unfortunately, prevented the cinema from realizing its potential:

But the camera experienced a misfortune. It was invented at a time when there was no single country in which capital was not in power. The bourgeoisie's hellish idea consisted of using the new toy to entertain the masses or rather to divert the workers' attention from their aim: the struggle against their masters. (Ibid., p. 67)

Vertov's basic, programmatic objective, as he put it in "The Essence of Kino-Eye," was to "aid each oppressed individual and the proletariat as a whole in their effort to understand the phenomena of life around them" (Vertov, 1984, p. 49).

Vertov also called for "kino pravda," literally "cinema truth" but also an allusion to the communist newspaper *Pravda*. There is a tension, in Vertov's writing, between his emphasis on film as a medium of truth and fact and his emphasis on film as a form of "writing," a tension captured in his designation of his own films as "poetic documentaries." On a practical level, Vertov advocated documentary filming in the streets, far from studios, in order to show people without masks or make-up and to reveal what lurks beneath the surfaces of social phenomena. Influenced by the Italian futurists, but wary of that movement's fascist politics, Vertov lauded the "poetry of machines" and the perfectible "cine-eye" (*kino glas*) as a means of celebrating the brave new world of speed and machines – "epics of electric power plants" – to be placed in the service of socialism.

For Vertov, montage permeates the entire process of film production, taking place during observation, after observation, during filming, after filming, during editing (the search for montage fragments) and during the definitive montage. Vertov spoke of musical-style montage "intervals," i.e. the movement and proportional relation between frames. In "We: Variant of a Manifesto" (1922), Vertov spoke of "Kinokism" and of the "kinogram," the filmic counterpart to the musical scale which maps out the figural combinatory of filmic construction:

Kinochestvo [Kinokism] is the art of organizing the necessary movements of objects in space as a rhythmical artistic whole, in harmony with the properties of the material and the internal rhythm of each object.

45

The Intervals (the transitions from one movement to another) are the material, the elements of the art of movement, and by no means the movements themselves. It is they (the intervals) which draw the movement to a kinetic conclusion. (Vertov, 1984, p. 8)

The obligation of the filmmaker, for Vertov, was to decipher mysteries and expose mystifications, whether found on the screen or in three-dimensional life, as part of the "communist deciphering of the world" (ibid., p. 79). Vertov defined his kind of cinema diacritically, in opposition to the mystifications of the "artistic drama," a cinematic form designed to intoxicate the spectator and insinuate certain reactionary notions into the unconscious. Echoing simultaneously the Bolshevik fight against Tsarism and the Kino-Glas struggle against the Hollywood star system, Vertov called for the overthrow of the "immortal kings and queens of the screen" and the reinstatement of "the ordinary mortal, filmed in life at his daily tasks" (ibid., p. 71).

Apart from tropes of royalty, Vertov's denunciations of illusionistic cinema drew on three other families of tropes: (1) magic ("the cinema of enchantment"); (2) drugs ("cine-nicotine," "electric opium"); and (3) religion (the "high priests of cinema"). (The revolutionary Trotsky had written an essay entitled "Vodka, the Church, and the Cinema.") Against a Kantian valorization of "disinterested" art, Vertov argued for films as "useful as shoes." Film, for Vertov, did not transcend productive life: rather, it existed on a continuum of social production. Vertov's film *The Man with a Movie Camera*, as Annette Michelson points out, treats cinema as a branch of industrial production, systematically juxtaposing virtually every aspect of cinematic activity with labor as it is conventionally conceived.[2] Despite his emphasis on montage at every stage of film production, Vertov's condemnation of "fairy tale scripts" as merely a form of bourgeois representation makes him, ultimately, a realist (although not an illusionist). Vertov's theories had international impact. He was admired in the United States by such leftist groups as the Workers Film and Photo League, and in 1962 the New York journal *Film Culture* published a selection of his writings, prior to entire translated volumes in French in the 1970s and in English in the 1980s.

All the supposed differences between the diverse montage-theorists meant little in the eyes of the official Stalinist regime, since virtually all of them got into political trouble after 1935, when "socialist realism" was adopted as the official aesthetic of the Soviet Communist Party, at which point they came under attack for their "idealism," "formalism," and "elitism."

Russian Formalism and the Bakhtin School

The work of the Soviet filmmakers in theorizing their own practice coincided with, and was concretely influenced by, another important source-movement for film theory – the Russian Formalists – who, like them, were also subsequently denounced as "idealists." Eisenstein had personal contact with key Formalists like Shklovsky and Eikhenbaum as well as with the Futurist poets who were their mutual friends, and he shared with the Formalists a fascination with film/language, montage as construction, ¹ inner speech. The Formalist movement, which flourished roughly from 1915 through 1930, revolved around two groups: the Linguistic Circle of Moscow and the Society for the Study of Poetic Language. The Formalists, some of whom were involved in the cinema as scriptwriters and consultants, hoped to construct a sound foundation or "poetics" for film theory, comparable to their poetics for literature. (The title of their most ambitious collection – *Poetika Kino* [The Poetics of Cinema, 1927] – echoed not only Aristotle's *Poetics* but also *Poetika*, an earlier Formalist volume on literary theory.) In *Poetika Kino* and in other important essays on the cinema, most notably Shklovsky's "Literature and Cinema" (1924) and Tynyanov's essay "Cinema–Word–Music" (also 1924), the Formalists explored a wide range of issues, laying the groundwork for much of subsequent theory. The cinema, then in the process of establishing itself as a legitimate art,

47

provided the Formalists with an intriguing arena to extend the "scientific" ideas that they had already developed in their work on literature, in a field they variously called "cinematology" (Kazanski), "cinepoetics" (Piotrovsky), or "cine-stylistics" (Eikhenbaum). The cinema offered an ideal terrain for testing the intersemiotic translation of Formalist concepts such as story, fable, dominant, materials, and automatization.

The Formalists shared with Eisenstein a kind of "techicism," a preoccupation with the *techne*, the materials and devices, of the artist/artisan's "craft." Rejecting the bellettristic traditions which had dominated previous literary study, the Formalists favored a "scientific" approach concerned with literature's "immanent" properties, structures, and systems, those not dependent on other orders of culture. In this sense, the Formalists sought a scientific basis for what would seem to be a highly subjective field: aesthetics. The subject of this science was not literature as a whole or even individual literary texts but rather "literariness" (*literaturnost*), i.e. that which makes a given text a work of literature. "Literariness," for the Formalists, inhered in a text's characteristic ways of deploying style and convention, and especially in its capacity to meditate on its own formal qualities.

Downplaying the representational and expressive dimensions of texts, the Formalists focused on their self-expressive, autonomous dimensions. Shklovsky coined the terms *ostrenanie* ("defamiliarization" or "making strange") and *zatrudnenie* ("making difficult") to denote the way that art heightens perception and short-circuits automatized responses. The essential function of poetic art, for Shklovsky, was to explode the encrustations of customary, routinized perception by making forms difficult. Defamiliarization was to be achieved through unmotivated formal devices based on deviations from established norms, the way Tolstoy, for example, could probe the institution of property through the surprising perspective of a horse. Literary evolution was shaped by the perennial attempt to disrupt regnant artistic conventions and generate new ones. The contemporaneous "Bakhtin School" mocked this kind of literary Oedipalism, with its perpetual adolescent rebellion against whatever happened to be the dominant, preferring to take a much longer and more tolerant view of artistic history.

The early Formalists were, as their name implies, rigorously aestheticist; for them, aesthetic perception was autotelic, an end in itself. Art was largely a means for experiencing what Shklovsky called the "artfulness of the object," for feeling the "stoniness of the stone." Their consistent emphasis upon the *construction* of artworks led the Formalists (particularly Jakobson and Tynyanov) to an understanding of art as a system of signs and conventions rather than the registration of natural phenomena. Formalists believed in what Eikhenbaum called the "inescapable conventionality of art" (Eagle, 1981, p. 57). Indeed, the role of art was to call attention to the conventionality of all art, including realist art. Naturalism in the cinema, Eikhenbaum argued, "is no less conventional than literary or theatrical naturalism" (Eikhenbaum, 1982, p. 18). Shklovsky extended the notion of literariness to the cinema by analyzing the structure of Charlie Chaplin films, seeing the tramp figure as constructed by a series of devices (pratfalls, chases, fights), only some of which were motivated by plot. In a neo-Kantian language, Tynyanov argued that art "strives toward the abstractions of its means" (Eagle, 1981, p. 81).

The Formalists were the first to explore, with a modicum of rigor, the analogy between language and film. Following the cues offered by the Swiss linguist de Saussure, the Formalists sought to systematize the apparently chaotic world of filmic phenomena. "The visible world," wrote Tynyanov, "is presented in cinema not as such, but in its semantic correlativity . . . as semantic sign." In *Poetica Kino*, with contributions by Eikhenbaum, Shklovsky, Tynyanov, and others, the Formalists stressed a "poetic" use of film analogous to the "literary" use of language they posited for verbal texts. For Tynyanov, montage was comparable to prosody in literature. Just as plot is subordinate to rhythm in poetry, so plot is subordinate to style in cinema. The cinema deployed cinematic procedures like lighting and montage in order to render the visible world in the form of semantic signs. While Eikhenbaum compared the syntax of film to that of narrative prose, Tynyanov saw poetry as a more appropriate model.

49

(Pasolini picked up this theme in his "Cinema of Poetry" essay four decades later.) In "Problems in Film Stylistics," Eikhenbaum, meanwhile, saw film in relation to "inner speech" and "image translations of linguistic tropes." Inner speech, for Eikhenbaum, completed and articulated what was only latent in the on-screen images and thus facilitated spectatorial comprehension. Verbal language was thus implicated in the "readability" of the filmic image. Inner speech also mediated between what Lev Vygotsky called "egocentric speech," on the one hand, and "socialized" discourse on the other, as well as between the written and the oral, thus opening the way for another kind of expression – elliptical, fragmentary, dislocated – linked to the "rhetoric of the Unconscious." At the same time, the Formalists were not insensitive to what might be called the phenomenology of spectatorship, as in Eikhenbaum's remarks in "Problems of Cine-Stylistics" on the necessary solitude of spectatorship:

The spectator's condition is close to solitary, intimate contemplation – he observes, as it were, somebody's dream. The slightest outside noise unconnected with the film annoys him much more than it would if he were in the theater. Talking by spectators next to him (e.g. reading the titles aloud) prevents him from concentrating on the movement of the film; his ideal is not to sense the presence of the other spectators, but to be alone with the film, to become deaf and dumb. (Eikhenbaum, 1982, p. 10)

Here Eikhenbaum anticipates a number of later theoretical currents – Metz's metapsychology of spectatorship, comparative media study, the metaphor of film as dream, and cognitive theory.

Eikhenbaum saw montage as a stylistic system quite independent of plot. The cinema, for Eikhenbaum, was a "particular system of figurative language," the stylistics of which would treat filmic "syntax," the linkage of shots into "phrases" and "sentences." The "cine-phrase" grouped a string of shots around a key image such as a close-up, while a "cine-period" developed a more complex spatio-temporal configuration. Analysts could use shot-by-shot analysis to identify a typology of such phrases – a project taken up some four decades later by Christian Metz in his "Grande Syntagmatique of the Image Track." While Eikhenbaum did not develop a full-blown typology, some of his principles of syntagmatic construction – such as contrast, comparison, and coincidence – resemble in embryo the conceptions later developed by Metz. But the Formalist focus, unlike that of Metz, was in the end less linguistic than stylistic and poetic. "Anti-grammatical" and anti-normative, the Formalist aesthetic valorized not the correct rules for selecting and combining elements but rather deviations from aesthetic and technical norms of the kind proffered by avant-garde movements like Futurism.

During the later period of Russian Formalism, the so-called "Bakhtin Circle" or "Bakhtin School" developed a provocative critique of the Formalist method, a critique rich in implications for film theory. In *The Formal Method in Literary Scholarship* (1928), Bakhtin and Medvedev dissected the underlying premises of first-phase Formalism. On the one hand, Bakhtin and Medvedev's "sociological poetics" shared certain features with Formalist poetics: the refusal of a romantic, expressive view of art; the rejection of the reduction of art to questions of class and economics; an insistence on art's self-purposeful specificity. Both saw "literariness" as inhering in a differential relation between texts, which the Formalists called "defamiliarization" and which Bakhtin and Medvedev refer to under the more comprehensive rubric of "dialogism." Both schools rejected naively realist views of art. An artistic structure does not reflect reality, Bakhtin and Medvedev argued, but rather the "reflections and refractions of other ideological spheres." Bakhtin and Medvedev praised the "productive role" of Formalism in formulating the central problems of literary scholarship, and doing so "with such sharpness that they can no longer be avoided or ignored." But they engaged critically with Formalism on the question of artistic "specification." Recognizing this issue as a legitimate one, they proposed a translinguistic and materialist approach. In most cases, Bakhtin and Medvedev argued, the Formalists simply reverse preexisting dyads – practical/poetic language; material/device; story/plot – turning them inside out in an undialectical manner, enthroning intrinsic form, for example, where extrinsic content had once been supreme. But for Bakhtin and Medvedev every artistic phenomenon is simultaneously determined from within and without; the barrier between "inside" and "outside" is an artificial one, for in fact there is great permeability between the two.

Formalism, for Bakhtin and Medvedev, fails to discern the social nature of literature even in its specificity. By dissolving history into an "eternal contemporaneity," Formalists created a model which was inadequate even to the immanent evolution of literature, not to mention its relation with the other "series" – ideological, economic, political. The Formalist fetishization of the artwork as the "sum of its devices" left readers with nothing more than their own empty sensation, the hedonistic pleasure of "defamiliarization" experienced by the individual consumer of the artistic text. The purpose of art, the Formalists argued tautologically, is "about" being aesthetic, about renewing perception, about making the reader/spectator feel the "stoniness of the stone."

The critique of Formalism as mechanistic, ahistorical, and hermetically sealed-off life began to be addressed by the Formalists themselves in Tynyanov's notion of "dynamic structure" and later in the Prague School work of Jakobson, who spoke of "dynamic synchrony," and others who tried to correlate the literary and the historical "series." Indeed, many of the fundamental positions of Russian Formalism were adopted and elaborated by Prague structuralism in the late 1920s and early 1930s, with Roman Jakobson as a key figure linking the two movements. The Prague School was especially concerned with "aesthetic functions," an idea that formed the basis for import-ant essays on the cinema by Roman Jakobson and Jan Mukarovsky. In his essay "Art as a Semiotic Fact" (1934) and in his book *Aesthetic Function* (1936), Mukarovsky outlined a semiotic theory of aesthetic autonomy, whereby two different functions, communicative and aesthetic (roughly comparable to the Formalists' "practical" and "poetic" language), coexist within a text, but where the aesthetic function serves to isolate and "foreground" and "focus attention" on the object. Writing in the wake of the advent of sound, Jakobson, in an essay entitled "Is the Cinema in Decline?," argued that (1) the presence of sound does not alter the fact that the cinema still transforms "reality" into sign, and (2) the use of sound has historically evolved into a highly conventional system with only a remote connection to real sound (see Eagle, 1981, p. 37).

Russian Formalism and its cognate movements have left a vast legacy within film theory. Later film theory extrapolated Formalist formulations concerning literary specificity into cinema theory, especially when Christian Metz expanded and synthesized the insights of Saussurean linguistics and Formalist poetics in his *Langage et cinéma* (1971). David Bordwell and Kristin Thompson, meanwhile, drew on some aspects of the defamiliarization theory of the Formalists and the "norms" and "schemata" theory of the Prague structuralists to construct their version of "Neo-Formalism" as a basis for "historical poetics" – the word "poetics" goes back not only to Aristotle but also to the Formalists' *Poetica Kino* as well as Bakhtin's "chronotope" essay – notably in Bordwell's *Narration in the Fiction Film* (1985), Thompson's *Ivan the Terrible: A Neo-Formalist Analysis* (1980) and *Breaking the Glass Armour* (1988), and their jointly written (and widely used) *Film Art* (1996). But even if the Formalists had not written about the cinema *per se*, their conceptualizations would have been influential. Bertolt Brecht subsequently politicized the Formalist concept of "defamiliarization," reconceiving it as his *verfremdungseffekt* (variously translated as "alienation effect" or "distanciation"), whereby the work of art would simultaneously reveal its own processes of production along with those of society. The structuralist project of "denaturalization," i.e. revealing the socially coded aspect of what was taken to be "natural," was anticipated by the Formalist project of *ostrenanie* or "making strange," even if the Formalists themselves saw such devices in a purely formal way.

The distinction between "story" (*fabula*) – the putative sequence of events in their "factual" order and narration – and "plot" or "discourse" (*sjuzet*) – the story as narrated within an artistic structure – also came to influence film theory and analysis indirectly via such literary theorists as Gerard Genette, and directly in the work of David Bordwell and Kristin Thompson in their (generally non-semiotic) work. The issue of "inner speech," meanwhile, lay dormant until the 1970s, when it was "rediscovered" by theorists like Paul Willemen, Ronald Levaco, and David Bordwell. Willemen, for example, argued that inner speech was not just relevant to silent cinema as Shklovsky had suggested, but rather ultimately formed a kind of Unconscious substratum of the filmic system in general.

Also crucial to subsequent film semiotics was the Formalist view of the text as a battleground between rival elements, as dynamic systems structured in relation to a "dominant." Although first conceptualized by Tynyanov, the concept was further developed by Jakobson, who argued in his landmark 1927 essay ("The Dominant") that artistic works are constituted by a constellation of interacting codes governed by the "dominant," i.e. the process by which one element, for example rhythm or plot or character, comes to regulate the artistic text or system. As "the focusing component of a work of art," the dominant manages to rule, determine, and transform the remaining components.[1] As Jakobson elaborates it, the notion applies not only to the individual poetic work, but also to the poetic canon and even to the art of a given epoch when seen as a totality. In the 1980s Fredric Jameson adopted the term when he called postmodernism the "cultural dominant" of the era of transnational capitalism.

Yet another current within Formalism was formed by Vladimir Propp's work on narrative in his *Morphology of the Folktale* (1968). Propp examined 115 Russian folk tales in order to discern common structures based on minimal units of action, called "functions," such as "leaving home." Propp discerned a relatively small number of 31 such functions, as opposed to a much larger number of persons, objects, and events (corresponding to the traditional "motif"). Propp's legacy for film theory is evident, for example, in Peter Wollen's analysis of *North by Northwest* and in Randal Johnson's analysis of *Macunaima*. Finally, Formalist ideas on film were also developed in the 1970s by the "semiotics of culture" groups in Moscow and Tartu. In *Semiotics of Cinema* (1976), Juri Lotman, the most active member of the school, discusses cinema as both language and "secondary modeling system," while trying to integrate the analysis of cinema into a broader cultural theory in ways that clearly echo but also reinvoice Formalist formulations.

The Historical Avant-Gardes

The 1910s and 1920s were the period of "historical avant-gardes," the zenith of experimentalism in the arts: Impressionism in France, Constructivism in the Soviet Union, Expressionism in Germany, Futurism in Italy, Surrealism in Spain and France, Muralism in Mexico, and Modernismo in Brazil. Modernism, according to Perry Anderson, emerged as a cultural force-field with three coordinates: "(1) the official art of regimes still linked to the old aristocracies; (2) the impact of the new technologies of the second industrial revolution; and (3) the hope of social revolution" (Anderson, 1984). The film theory of these movements was expressed not only in manifestos and in occasional essays in journals like *Close-Up* and *Experimental Cinema*, but also in later filmic manifestos like *L'Age d'Or* (1930) and *Zéro de Conduite* (1933). The films of the avant-garde were defined not only by their distinct aesthetics, but also by their mode of production, usually artisanal, independently financed, without links to studios or the industry. Yet the avant-garde was hardly a monolith. Ian Christie usefully distinguishes between three distinct movements: (1) the Impressionists (Abel Gance, Louis Delluc, Jean Epstein, and early Germaine Dulac), who are closer to a kind of national "art cinema;" (2) the partisans of "pure cinema" (Fernand Leger, later Dulac); and (3) the Surrealists (Christie, in Drummond et al., 1979). In political terms one can distinguish between a high-modernist avant-garde preoccupied with autotelic form, and a "low," carnivalized, anti-institutional, and anti-grammatical avant-garde which attacked the art-system (see Burger, 1984; Stam, 1989). Although modernism grows out of "high art," as Patrick Brantlinger and James Naremore (1991) point out, it is also deconstructive of certain high art values. Indeed, Michael Newman posits two artistic modernisms, one derived from Kant and stressing the absolute

55

autonomy of art, the other deriving from Hegel and stressing the dissolution of art into life and praxis.[1] It is also possible to see the more irreverent avatars of modernism as renewing a carnivalesque tradition going at least as far back as the medieval period.

The Surrealists, for their part, stressed what they saw as the deep affinities between moving images and the metaphorical processes of *écriture automatique,* in a movement defined by André Breton as "psychic automatism in its pure state, by which one proposes to express . . . the actual functioning of thought." This link to automatic writing prompted Philippe Soupault, for example, to write "cinematographic poems." Despite the erudite origins of some of their concepts, the Surrealists were also passionate fans of popular films. Even the worst films, Ado Kyrou suggested, could be "sublime." The Surrealists discerned subversive undercurrents in the films of such artists as Mack Sennett, Buster Keaton, and Charlie Chaplin. Antonin Artaud, meanwhile, lauded the anarchic energies of the Marx Brothers. Robert Desnos spoke of the "madness" presiding over Sennett's scripts, while Louis Aragon developed a "synthetic criticism" designed to extract intense, libidinal meanings from ordinary sequences. Even American crime films, for Aragon, "speak of daily life and manage to raise to a dramatic level a banknote on which our attention is riveted, a table with a revolver on it, a bottle that on occasion becomes a weapon, a handkerchief that reveals a crime" (quoted in Hammond, 1978, p. 29).

For the Surrealists, the cinema had the transcendent capacity to liberate what was conventionally repressed, to mingle the known and the unknown, the mundane and the oneiric, the quotidian and the marvelous. Luis Buñuel and Robert Desnos took positions opposed both to Hollywood narrative cinema and to the Impressionist avant-garde of filmmakers like L'Herbier and Epstein. While they were enthusiastic about the cinema, they expressed disappointment with both of these modes for not exploiting its subversive potential and opting instead for bourgeois love dramas and what Buñuel called "the sentimental infection." By opting for narrative logic and bourgeois decorum, Buñuel argued, conventional cinema had squandered its potential for creating an insurrectionary, convulsive, anti-canonical art which would visualize the "automatic writing of the world."[2] The Surrealists used specific techniques to distance themselves from the spell of narrative cinema, whether through Man Ray's device of watching the screen through outstretched fingers or through the Surrealist habit of interruptive spectatorship, whereby the artists would visit a series of films in twenty-minute stretches, picnicking as they watched. Cinematic techniques such as superimposition, the dissolve, and slow motion were ideally suited not only for representing dream but also for mimicking its procedures of figuration. Surrealism's cheerfully creative, utopian misreading of Freud, meanwhile, proposed a cinema which would unleash, rather than tame, the anarchic, liberating energies of the Unconscious.

It is well known that the "pope" of Surrealism, André Breton, was partially inspired by Freud's *Interpretation of Dreams*, even though Breton's various attempts to form an alliance between Surrealism and Freudianism led nowhere. Buñuel was one of many Surrealists concerned with the relation between film and other states of consciousness. For Robert Desnos, cinema was the anticipatory site of "poetic liberation" and "intoxication," a magical time–space where the distinction between reality and dream could be abolished. It was the desire to dream that generated the "thirst for and love of the cinema."[3] Speaking of the "marvel of cinema," Breton wrote that "From the instant he takes his seat to the moment he slips into a fiction evolving before his eyes [the spectator] passes through a critical point as captivating and imperceptible as that uniting waking and sleeping" (quoted in Hammond, 1978, p. 11). Further elaborating the comparison, Jacques Brunius wrote:

The arrangement of screen images in time is absolutely analogous with the arrangement thought or the dream can devise. Neither chronological order nor relative values of duration are real. Contrary to the theater, film, like the dream, chooses some gestures, defers or enlarges them, eliminates others, travels many hours, centuries, kilometers in a few seconds, speeds up, slows down, stops, goes backwards. (Ibid.)

Antonin Artaud, in a 1927 text, was even more categorical. "If the cinema is not made to translate dreams or all that which, in conscious life, resembles dreams," he argued, "then the cinema does not exist."[4] These analogies to what would later be called the "dream state" were subsequently taken up by theorists such as Hugo Mauerhofer, Suzanne Langer, and Christian Metz. The Surrealist-inflected work of Jacques Lacan later continued the tradition of "subversive Freud," a tradition which was to have a strong impact on film theory. Later avant-gardist artists such as Maya Deren, Alain Resnais, Stan Brakhage, and Alejandro Jodorovsky would also continue the intertextual dialogue with Surrealism, as would the latter-day theorists of the avant-garde such as Annette Michelson, P. Adams Sitney, and Peter Wollen.

The Debate after Sound

The advent of sound cinema generated considerable debate about the relative merits of sound versus silent cinema. In the United States Gilbert Seldes denounced sound cinema as a regression to theatrical modes (Seldes, 1928, p. 706). In France Germaine Dulac, even before the advent of sound, saw cinema as a necessarily silent art.[1] Marcel L'Herbier and Leon Poirier were also hostile to sound, while others, such as Abel Gance, Jacques Feyder, and Marcel Pagnol, cautiously embraced it. "The talking film," Pagnol argued "is the art of recording, preserving, and diffusing theater" (Pagnol, 1933, p. 8). For Epstein the *phonogénie* of sound could potentially complement the *photogénie* of the image. But Artaud, in "The Premature Old Age of the Cinema" (1933), warned that sound might prod the cinema to adopt outmoded conventions, while René Clair proclaimed that "the cinema must remain visual at all costs."[2] In Russia Eisenstein, Alexandrov, and Pudovkin in their 1928 manifesto called for the non-synchronous use of sound, warning that the inclusion of dialogue might reestablish the hegemony of outworn methods and trigger a flood of "photographed performances of a theatrical sort" (Eisenstein, 1957, pp. 257–9). Synchronous sound, they feared, would destroy the culture of montage and thus the very basis of the autonomy of cinema as an art form. In Germany Rudolf Arnheim, in the name of the plastic specificity of the cinema, enshrined silent cinema as the definitive, paradigmatic form of the seventh art. In what now seems like a counter-intuitive move, Arnheim argued that sound detracts from visual beauty. "When real sounds are emitted by the filmed virtuoso's violin," Arnheim lamented, "the visual picture suddenly becomes three-dimensional and tangible" (Arnheim, 1997, p. 30). The introduction of the sound film, for Arnheim, aborted the progress of film art by tempting filmmakers to submit to "the inartistic" demand for a superficial "naturalness" (ibid., p. 154). Ultimately, the sound/silent debate had to do with notions of the putative "essence" of cinema and the aesthetic and narrative implications of "realizing" that essence. (It took 1960s semiotic theory to suggest that "essence" and "specificity" were not coterminous, that the cinema could have some dimensions that were "specifically cinematic" without those traits dictating any single style or aesthetic.)

In 1933 Arnheim published in German his book *Film* (a revised version of which appeared in English as *Film as Art* in 1957). Arnheim had in common with Munsterberg a fondness for Kant and an interest in psychology, although the psychology that interested him was of the Gestalt variety. The Gestaltists under whom Arnheim studied experimented in the areas of "visual field" and "perception of movement." Influenced by neo-Kantian thought, they stressed the active role of the mind in shaping dumb matter into meaningful experience, a perceptual process hyperbolized and foregrounded by art. Arnheim's work on film thus forms part of a larger project in which the visual arts provide a kind of proving ground for the study of visual perception (Arnheim's own 1928 dissertation was on perception).

Gestalt theory, like aesthetic modernism, as Gertrud Koch points out, is constructivist; it sees the relation between art and the perceptual world as one not of imitation, but of shared *structural* principles.[3] Arnheim's *materialtheorie* emphasizes what he sees as the essential traits of the film medium and the means by which those traits might be deployed for artistic ends. According to Arnheim, misjudgments about film arise "when theatrical, painterly, or literary standards are applied" (Arnheim, 1997, p. 14). Arnheim begins by outlining all the attributes of the medium which differentiate it from everyday perception and from reality: the reduction of depth, the projection of solid objects upon a single-plane surface, the absence of color, the lack of a space–time continuum, the exclusion of all senses other than the visual. By foregrounding film's constitutive lacks, Arnheim set out to "refute the assertion that film is nothing but the feeble mechanical reproduction of real life" (ibid., p. 37). Within Arnheim's less-is-more algebraic principles, apparent deficiencies engender aesthetic strength; the lack of depth, for example, brought a welcome element of unreality into film.

For Arnheim, vision in general, and film viewing in particular, is primarily a mental phenomenon. Arnheim shared with latter-day realist theorists like Kracauer the premise that film as a reproductive art "represents reality itself," yet he moved from that premise toward the aesthetic injunction that film should go *beyond* realistic representation. Within Arnheim's *via negativa*, it was precisely film's mimetic "defects" and its facility for manipulation through lighting effects, superimposition, accelerated or slowed motion, and editing that made it more than a mechanical recording and thus capable of artistic expressiveness. By bypassing the mimetic portrayal made possible by the mechanical apparatus, film establishes itself as an autonomous art.

The Hungarian film theorist Bela Bálázs, meanwhile, began writing on cinema in the early 1920s with books like *Der Sichtbare Mensch* (The Visible Man, 1924), continued with *Der Geist des Films* (The Spirit of Film, 1930), and work subsequently gathered in English and revised in *Theory of the Film* (Bálázs, 1972). Bálázs defended popular cinema against high-art prejudice. The motion picture, he argued "is *the* popular art of our century" (ibid., p. 17). Like Arnheim, Bálázs was concerned with the specific nature of film as art: "When and how did cinematography turn into a specific independent art employing methods sharply differing from those of the theater and using a totally different form-language?" (Bálázs, 1933, p. 30). In *Theory of the Film* Bálázs answered his question by suggesting that it was montage, i.e. cinema's capacity to vary distance and angle with respect to the staged action, that differentiated film from theater. Film discarded the basic formal principles of the stage – integrity of space, fixed spectatorial position, and fixed angle of vision – in favor of varying distance between spectator and scene, the division of the scene into shots, and changing angle, perspective, and focus within the same scene. Unlike Arnheim, who defined filmic specificity in terms of the inherent constraints of the medium, Bálázs stressed the artistic intervention of montage as a synthesis of fragments creating an organic whole. Like Arnheim, Bálázs wanted film to undermine the superficial naturalism of the filmic image, but unlike Munsterberg he did not see film as a "mental phenomenon," but rather as an instrument for generating a new understanding of the real world. The cinema could democratize the act of looking. Like the "euphoric" theorists, Bálázs glorified the cinema as capable of estranging our perceptions of the world: "Only by means of unaccustomed and unexpected methods produced by striking set-ups can old, familiar and therefore never-seen things hit our eyes with new impressions" (Bálázs, 1972, p. 93).

Bálázs was the poet-laureate of the filmic close-up, not as naturalistic detail but as radiating "a tender human attitude in the contemplation of hidden things, a delicate solicitude, a gentle bending over the intimacies of life-in-the-miniature, a warm sensibility" (ibid., p. 56). The close-up "shows you your shadow on the wall with which you have lived all your life and which you scarcely knew" (ibid., p. 55). The close-up revealed the "polyphonic play of features," the impact of changing emotions on the face:

We cannot use glycerine tears in a close-up. What makes a deep impression is not a fat, oily tear rolling down a face – what moves is to see the glance growing misty, and moisture gathering in the corner of the eye – moisture that as yet is scarcely a tear. This is moving, because this cannot be faked. (Bálázs, 1972, p. 77)

The "microphysiognomy" of the close-up offered a window on the soul; the apparatus of the cinema mirrored the psychic apparatus.[4]

Bálázs also anticipated later theory by speaking of "identification" as the key to film's "absolute artistic novelty:"

61

We look up to Juliet's balcony with Romeo's eyes and look down on Romeo with Juliet's. Our eye and with it our consciousness is identified with the characters in the film, we look at the world out of their eyes and have no angle of vision of our own. (Bálázs, 1972, p. 48)

Anticipating later "gaze" and apparatus theory, as well as later theories of identification and engagement, Bálázs argued that this kind of identification was unique to film. He also spoke of the role of "physiognomy" as revelation. After centuries of word-based culture, he argued, the cinema prepared the way for a new culture of "visible man." It could even prepare the way for a more tolerant, international kind of human being, thus contributing to the lessening of "differences between the various races and nations, thus becoming one of the most useful pioneers in the development of a universal, international, humanity" (quoted in Xavier, 1983, p. 83).

As a practicing filmmaker, Bálázs was sensitive to the concrete procedures of film, whence chapter headings like "changing set-up," "optical tricks, composites, cartoons," and "the script." Although he complained initially that the sound film had undermined the expressiveness of film acting, he later became an astute analyst of sound in the cinema, with suggestive comments on the dramaturgy of sound, the dramatic possibilities of silence, and the "intimacy of sound" which makes us perceive sounds which are usually drowned out by the accustomed din of everyday life (Bálázs, 1972, p. 210). He also points out that the anti-sound critics never objected to sound *per se* in the cinema – for example, Chaplin's sound gags – but only to dialogue as the real enemy (ibid., p. 221).

Siegfried Kracauer also began writing in this period. As a columnist for the *Frankfurter Zeitung* he wrote on such topics as the "Cult of Distraction" and "The Little Shopgirls Go To the Movies." Kracauer was concerned with the potential for both alienation and liberation of the mass media. For him the task of the cinema was to look unblinkingly at social malaise, to promote a kind of activist pessimism, to show that we do not live in the best of all possible worlds, and thus to provoke doubts about the Panglossian ideology of the reigning system. "Were [the cinema] to depict things as they really are today,"

Kracauer wrote in 1931, "moviegoers would get uneasy and begin to have doubts about the legitimacy of our current social structure" (Kracauer, 1995, p. 24). As early as the 1920s Kracauer exalted the cinema's capacity to capture the mechanized surfaces of modern life. What interested him was what might be called the profundity of the superficial, the micro-calamities and everyday epiphanies that make up human experience. The cinema, in this sense, could help spectators "read" the phenomenal surfaces of contemporary life. Films also gave expression to the "daydreams of society," revealing its secret mechanisms and repressed desires. In his 1928 essay "The Little Shopgirls Go to the Movies" Kracauer spoke of the ideological function of films – here projected onto women spectators exclusively – in ways that anticipated Adorno and Horkheimer, but unlike them he saw the "distraction" of popular spectacles as in some ways a positive force, a subjunctive escape from Taylorization and uniformity. (We will return to Kracauer subsequently.)

Finally, it is important to mention the work of the film journal *Close Up*, which from 1927 to 1933 discussed a wide range of film-theoretical issues. It was here, as Anne Friedberg points out, that the female literary modernists – H. D., Dorothy Richardson, Gertrude Stein, Marianne Moore – began to write on the cinema (see Donald et al., 1998, p. 7). Just as important, the journal began a serious discussion of the question of race and racism, culminating in a special issue on "The Negro and Cinema" in August 1929, featuring contributions by black and white critics and a letter from Walter White, assistant secretary of the NAACP. Anticipating much later critiques of the "positive image," Kenneth Macpherson warned that the "white man is always going to portray the negro as he likes to see him, no matter how benevolently. Benevolence, indeed, is the danger" (Donald et al., 1998, p. 33). As if to illustrate his own warnings about white projections, Macpherson himself speaks in primitivist tones of the "jungle, lissom lankness" of Stepin Fetchit. At the same time, Macpherson called for "confederated negro socialist cinema," while Robert Herring called for films "by and about" blacks. Harry Potamkin, in "The Aframerican Cinema," surveys black roles in film (Bert Williams, Farina) within the context of a comparative study of black representation in the graphic arts, the theater, and the cinema. An essay by Geraldyn Dismond, identified as a "well-known American Negro writer," finally, stresses the co-implication of white and black representation, in that "no true picture of American life can be drawn without the negro" (ibid., p. 73). Although blacks entered the cinema through the "servant's entrance," Dismond points out, "the negro [has turned out] some of the best acting on the American screen and stage" (ibid., p. 74). Wide-ranging, the essay addresses issues of "primitivism," the stereotypical casting of blacks as comic menials, and self-representation, in ways that at times anticipate the multicultural film studies of the 1980s and 1990s.

The Frankfurt School

If the Surrealists had expressed both hope for and disappointment in the cinema, others from both left and right lauded and critiqued the cinema for different reasons. The critique often coincided with an intense and anti-democratic form of anti-Americanism. Herbert Jhering warned in 1926 that the American film was more dangerous than Prussian militarism: millions of people were being "co-opted by American taste; they are made equal, made uniform."[1] One prominent leitmotif was the idea that the cinema rendered its audience bovine and passive. For the conservative Frenchman Georges Duhamel, the cinema was the slaughterhouse of culture, and movie theaters were "Gargantuan maws" where hypnotized pilgrims, corraled into long lines, went "like lambs to the slaughter." Reacting to what he saw as the desecration of literature in the form of filmic adaptations, Duhamel wrote:

And no one cried murder! . . . All those works which from our youth we have stammered with our hearts rather than with our lips, all those sublime songs which at the age of passionate enthusiasms were our daily bread, our study, and our glory . . . were dismembered, hacked to pieces, and mutilated. (Duhamel, 1931, p. 30)

64

The apologists of mass culture were responsible for "having allowed the cinema to become the most powerful instrument of moral, aesthetic and political conformism" (ibid., p. 64). While film theorists like Arnheim were trying to decide exactly what kind of art the cinema was, Duhamel denied that the cinema was an art at all: "The cinema has sometimes diverted me and sometimes moved me; it has never required me to rise superior to myself. It is not an art. It is not art" (ibid., p. 37). From a self-consciously elitist perspective, Duhamel ridiculed cinema as "a pastime for slaves, an amusement for the illiterate, for poor creatures stupefied by work and anxiety . . . a spectacle that demands no effort, that does not imply any sequence of ideas . . . that excites no hope, if not the ridiculous one of someday being a 'star' at Los Angeles" (ibid., p. 34).

Cultural critic Walter Benjamin took a contrary view. At the end of his essay "The Work of Art in the Age of Mechanical Reproduction" (first published in France in 1936) Benjamin argued, against Duhamel, that the new medium had a progressive epistemological impact. For Benjamin, capitalism planted the seeds of its own destruction by creating conditions which would make it possible to abolish capitalism itself. Mass-media forms like photography and the cinema created new artistic paradigms reflective of new historical forces; they could not be judged by the old standards. Anticipating Andy Warhol's "15 minutes of fame," Benjamin argued that in the age of mechanical reproduction every human being had an inalienable right to be filmed. More important, the cinema enriched the field of human perception and deepened critical consciousness of reality. For Benjamin, film's uniqueness derived, paradoxically, from its non-uniqueness, the fact that its productions were multiply available across barriers of time and space, in a situation where easy access made it the most social and collective of the arts. Film's mechanical reproduction triggered a world-historical aesthetic rupture: it destroyed the "aura," the luminous cult-value or presence, of the putatively unique, remote, and inaccessible art object. The modernity of the cinema reveals the artistic aura as the product either of illusory nostalgia or of exploitative domination. Thus critical attention shifts from the venerated object of art to the dialogue between work and spectator. Just as Dada had turned respectable art into an object of scandal and thus perturbed the passive contemplation of artistic beauty, the cinema had shocked the audience out of its complacency, forcing it to participate actively and critically.

Benjamin turned the much maligned "distraction" of film viewing into a cognitive advantage. Distraction did not entail passivity; rather, it was a liberating expression of collective consciousness, a sign that the spectator was not "spellbound in darkness." Through montage, film administered shock-effects which effectuated a break with the contemplative conditions of bourgeois art consumption. Thanks to mechanical reproduction, film acting, too, lost the literal presence of the performer which characterized the theater, thus diminishing the aura of the individual. (Metz would later argue that the very lack of real presence of the actor would paradoxically induce spectators to invest the "imaginary signifier" with their own projections and thus render the image even more charismatic.) For Benjamin, film exemplified and itself shaped a kind of mutated perception appropriate to a new era of social and technological evolution. Duhamel's critique of film was for Benjamin merely the "same ancient lament that the masses seek distraction whereas art demands concentration of the spectator" (Benjamin, 1968, p. 241). As opposed to the solitary absorption provoked by the reading of a novel, film spectatorship was necessarily gregarious and potentially interactive and critical.[2] The cinema could therefore transform and energize the masses for purposes of revolutionary change. The politicized aesthetics of socially conscious and formally experimental films provided one poss-ible response to fascism as the "aestheticization of politics."

On one level Benjamin's thinking reflected a perennial tendency, evidenced later in McLuhan's utopian claims about the "global village," as well as in the more giddy proclamations of contemporary cyber-theorists, to over-invest in the political and aesthetic possibilities of new media and technologies. And indeed the publication of "The Work of Art in the Age of Mechanical Reproduction" triggered a lively polemic about the social role of film and the mass media. In a series of epistolary responses to Benjamin's essays, Frankfurt School critical theorist Theodor Adorno attacked Benjamin for a technological utopianism which fetishized technique while ignoring the alienating social functioning of that technique in reality. Adorno expressed skepticism about Benjamin's claims for the emancipatory possibilities of new media and cultural forms. Benjamin's celebration of film as a vehicle for revolutionary consciousness, for Adorno, naively idealized the working class and its supposedly revolutionary aspirations. Adorno worried over the effects of what Frankfurt theorists called the "culture industry," discerning vast potential for alienation and commodification. Ironically, although a man of the left, Adorno expressed the same scorn for the passive popular audience as was shown by an extreme right-winger like Duhamel, but this time reformulated in a Marxist idiom. In *Minima Moralia* Adorno almost seems to echo Duhamel when he says that "every visit to the cinema leaves me, against all my vigilance, stupider or worse" (Adorno, 1978, p. 75). Representing the more pessimistic wing of the Frankfurt School, Adorno placed his faith not in what he regarded as circus-like popular distractions but in what would later be called the difficult "high modernist" art of an Arnold Schoenberg or a James Joyce, art which staged the dissonances of modern life. At the same time, Adorno knew that even the high art of erudite modernists was caught up in capitalist processes, although at the "higher," more sublimated level of patronage, museum exhibition, state subsidy, and independent wealth. High art could be "difficult" precisely because it did not have to sell itself directly on the open market. Nevertheless, high art did have the capacity to dramatize through form the social reality of alienation. What Adorno missed was the fact that popular art, for example jazz, might also be difficult, discontinuous, complex, challenging.

Artistic modernism reached its zenith in the 1920s. But if the 1920s constituted an orgy of theoretical experimentalism, the 1930s were the hangover after the party, as Nazism, fascism, and Stalinism (and in a very different way the Hollywood Studio system) began to close down the various insurrectionary aesthetics and art movements. Thus the 1930s became a period of intense anxiety about the social effects of mass media. Both Benjamin and Adorno were affiliated with the Frankfurt Institute of Social Research, which was established in 1923, moved to New York in the 1930s after Hitler came to power, and was reestablished in Germany in the early 1950s. The Frankfurt School, which also included Max Horkheimer, Leo Lowenthal, Erich Fromm, Herbert Marcuse, and (on its outskirts) Siegfried Kracauer, became a key center of institutional reflection, inaugurating critical studies on mass communication. The Frankfurt School was shaped by vast historical events such as the defeat of left-wing working-class movements in Western Europe after World War I, the degeneration of the Russian revolution into Stalinism, and the rise of Nazism. One of the School's main concerns was to explain why the revolution envisaged by Marx had not occurred. Departing from Benjamin's *via positiva*, they counterposed their own *via negativa*, a faith in the power of critical negation. The Frankfurt School studied the cinema synecdochically, as a part-for-whole emblem of capitalist mass culture, deploying a multifaceted and dialectical approach that paid simultaneous attention to issues of political economy, aesthetics, and reception. Deploying such Marxist concepts as commodification, reification, and alienation they coined the term "culture industry" to evoke the industrial apparatus which produced and mediated popular culture, as well as the market imperatives underlying it. They chose the term "industry" rather than "mass culture" to avoid the impression that culture arises spontaneously from the masses (see Kellner in Miller and Stam, 1999).

In "Culture Industry: Enlightenment as Mass Deception," published in 1944 as part of *The Dialectic of Enlightenment*, Adorno and Horkheimer outlined their critique of mass culture. That critique formed part of a larger critique of the Enlightenment, whose egalitarian promises of liberation had never been fulfilled. If scientific rationality had on the one hand freed the world from traditional forms of authority, it had also facilitated new, oppressive forms of domination of the kind exemplified by the high-tech Holocaust engineered by the Nazis. But Adorno and Horkheimer were equally critical of liberal capitalist societies, whose cinemas produced spectators as consumers. As opposed to those who saw the mass media as "giving the public what it wanted," Adorno and Horkheimer saw mass consumption as a consequence of the industry which dictated and channelled public desire. The cinema, as the "*mésalliance* of the novel and photography," created a fictive homogeneity reminiscent of the Wagnerian *Gesamtkunstwerk*. Commercial films were simply mass-produced commodities engineered by assembly-line techniques, products which themselves stamped out their own passive, automatized audience. Adorno's and Horkheimer's overwhelming concern was with the question of ideological legitimation: how does the system integrate individuals into its program and values and what is the role of the media in this process? As they put it, "the deceived masses are today captivated by the myth of success even more than the successful are. Immovably, they insist on the very ideology that enslaves them." The culture industry, caught up as it is in the world of commodification and exchange-value, stupefies, narcotizes, zombifies, and objectifies what is symptomatically called its "target" audience. A difficult, modernist art, in contrast, fosters, for Adorno especially, the development in its audience of the critical capacities necessary for a truly democratic society. Interestingly, Adorno and Horkheimer share with Brecht the critique of "stupefying" art, but unlike Brecht they did not applaud popular forms like boxing, vaudeville, the circus, and slapstick, although they did make an exception for Chaplin. At the same time, their condemnation was not unnuanced. Adorno and Horkheimer did show some sympathy for the undisciplined, anarchic, pre-Taylorized silent cinema, before it became "streamlined." (Adorno's major direct contribution to film theory *per se* was the book – co-written with Hanns Eisler in 1947 – *Composing for the Films* – which discerns progressive possibilities in such techniques as sound–image disjunction, which go against the *Gesamtkunstwerk* tradition.)

For Adorno and Horkheimer, the emergence of the cultural industry signified the death of art as the site of corrosive negativity. The Adorno–Horkheimer denunciations of the culture industry, and indirectly of its audience, were subsequently criticized as simplistic, positing the audience as "cultural dopes" and "couch potatoes." The modernist "difficult" art they praise, meanwhile, has been criticized as elitist. Noël Carroll argues that the idea of "disinterested art" traces its origins to a misreading of Kant, a hand-me-down aesthetic of "purposeful purposelessness" based on a misunderstanding of "The Analytic of the Beautiful" in Kant's *Critique of Judgement* (Carroll, 1998, pp. 89–109). Film theory and cultural theory are still very much under the influence of these debates. The Adorno–Benjamin debates, and the attendant oscillation between melancholic and euphoric attitudes toward the social role of the mass media, returned in force in the late 1960s, 1970s, and 1980s. The Adorno–Horkheimer claim that "real life" has become "indistinguishable from the movies" clearly anticipates Debord's "Society of the Spectacle," Borstin's notion of "pseudo-events," and Baudrillard's proclamations about the "simulacrum." It could also be argued that 1970s proposals for "counter-cinema" and for a cinema of production rather than consumption are indebted to Adorno's call for "difficult" art. Another influential aspect of "Critical Theory," broadly defined, was the attempt by figures such as Wilhelm Reich, Erich Fromm, and Herbert Marcuse to forge a synthesis of Marxism and psychoanalysis. Germany before Hitler, after all, was the country where psychoanalysis was strongest, and Frankfurt was also the home of the Frankfurter Psychoanalytisches Institut. Both Freudianism and Marxism were seen there as two revolutionary forms of liberatory thinking; one aimed at transforming the subject, the other at transforming society through collective struggle. This project would be approached differently, and in a Saussurean–Lacanian vocabulary, by Althusserians and theoretical feminists in the 1960s and 1970s and by Slavoj Žižek in the 1990s.

Later theory also took up again the 1930 debates about "realism" which opposed Bertolt Brecht (and Walter Benjamin) to Marxist theorist Georg Lukács. For Lukács, realist literature portrays the social totality through the use of "typical" characters. While Lukács took the novels of Balzac and Stendhal as his model for a dialectical realism, Brecht favored a theater realist in its intentions – aimed at exposing society's "causal network" – but modernist–reflexive in its forms. To cling to the ossified forms of the nineteenth-century realist novel constituted for Brecht a formalistic nostalgia which failed to take altered historical circumstances into account. That particular artistic formula, for Brecht, had lost its political potency; changing times called for changing modes of representation. Haunted by the Nazis' fondness for overwhelming spectacle which exploited blinkered, visceral emotion, Brecht called for a fragmented, distantiated "theater of interruptions" which fostered critical distance through the systematic demystification of dominant social relations. Walter Benjamin (1968) took Brecht's epic theater as a model of how the forms and instruments of artistic production could be transformed in a socialist direction. Epic theater, he argued, "derives a lively and productive consciousness from the fact that it is theater" (Benjamin, 1973, p. 4). Through interruptions, quotations, and tableau effects, epic theater supersedes the old illusionistic, antitechnical, auratic art. Benjamin compared epic theater, somewhat speciously, to film:

Epic theater proceeds by fits and starts, in a manner comparable to the images on a film strip. Its basic form is that of the forceful impact on one another of separate sharply distinct situations of the play. The songs, the captions, the gestural conventions, differentiate the scenes. As a result intervals tend to occur which destroy illusion. These intervals paralyze the audience's capacity for empathy. (Ibid., p. 21)

While one might question Benjamin's analogy (since the images on a film strip, unlike the sketches of epic theater, proceed in *apparent* continuity), and while one might wonder if empathy *per se* is *necessarily* reactionary, such ideas were to have immense impact on the practice and theory of film over subsequent decades.

The Frankfurt School had a major impact on subsequent theories of the culture industry, on theories of reception, and on theories of high modernism and the avant-garde. Walter Benjamin was influential not only through "the age of mechanical reproduction" essay, but also through his ideas on the "author as producer" and on the necessity of artistic as well as social subversion, the idea that revolutionary art must first of all be revolutionary in formal terms, *as art*. His readiness to embrace new forms of mass-mediated art provided a foundational insight for what came to be known as "cultural studies."

His rejection of classical ideals of beauty in favor of an aesthetic of fragments and ruins prepared the way for the postmodern "anti-aesthetic." Benjamin's ideas on allegory and the *trauerspiel*, meanwhile, had an impact on theorists of national allegory like Fredric Jameson and Ismail Xavier. The Frankfurt School, more generally, had a long-distance impact – via such thinkers as Hans Magnus Enzensberger, Alexander Kluge, John Berger, Miriam Hansen, Douglas Kellner, Rosewitta Muehler, Roberto Schwarz, Fredric Jameson, Anton Kaes, Gertrud Koch, Thomas Levin, Patrice Petro, Thomas Elsaesser, and many others – who later reworked its theories.

The Phenomenology of Realism

Apart from debates within Marxism (such as that between Brecht and Lukács about "realism" and between Benjamin and Adorno about the progressive potential of the mass media), the decades following the advent of sound were dominated by arguments about the "essence of cinema," and more specifically by the tensions between the "formative" theorists who thought the artistic specificity of cinema consisted in its radical differences from reality, and the "realists" who thought film's artistic specificity (and its social *raison d'être*) was to relay truthful representations of everyday life. As already discussed, one current of film theory was dominated by "formative" theorists like Rudolf Arnheim (*Film as Art*) and Bela Bálázs (*Theory of the Film*), who insisted on film's differences not only from "reality" but also *vis-à-vis* other arts such as theater and the novel. If some theorists, like Arnheim and Bálázs, favored an interventionist cinema which flaunted its differences from the "real," other, later theorists, partially under the impact of Italian neo-realism, favored a mimetic, revelatory, and realist cinema. The realist aesthetic predated the cinema, of course, and could trace its roots to the ethical stories of the Bible, to the Greek fascination with surface detail, to Hamlet's "mirror up to nature," on through the realist novel and Stendhal's "un miroir que se promene lelong la rue."

But in the 1940s, realism takes on a new urgency. In a sense, postwar film realism emerged from the smoke and ruins of European cities; the immediate trigger for the mimetic revival was the calamity of World War II. Surveys of film theory too often forget the essential contribution of Italian theorists, including filmmaker–theorists, to the debates about film realism. In the postwar period, Italy became a major scene not only of filmmaking but also of film-theoretical production, through film journals such as *Bianco e Nero*, *Cinema*, *La Revista del Cinema Italiano*, *Cinema Nouvo*, and *Filmcritica*, and through prestigious publication series like "Biblioteca Cinematografica." In his film *Histoires du Cinema*, Godard suggests that there was a historical logic behind this filmic Renaissance. As a country which was formally part of the Axis powers, but which had also suffered under the Axis, Italy had lost its national identity and therefore had to reconstruct it through the cinema. With *Rome Open City*, Italy regained the right to look at itself in the mirror, hence the extraordinary harvest of Italian film. The war and the liberation, filmmaker–theorist Cesare Zavattini argued, had taught filmmakers to discover the value of the real. Against those like the Formalists, who saw art as inescapably conventional and inherently different from life, Zavattini called for annihilating the distance between art and life. The point was not to invent stories which resembled reality, but rather turn reality into a story. The goal was a cinema without apparent mediation, where facts dictated form, and events seemed to recount themselves. (Metz, basing himself on Benveniste's categories, would later call this form of telling "histoire" [story] as opposed to "discours" [discourse].) Zavattini also called for a democratization of the cinema, both in terms of its human subjects and in terms of what kinds of events were *worth* talking about. For Zavattini, no subject was too banal for the cinema. Indeed, the cinema made it possible for ordinary people to know about each other's lives, not in the name of voyeurism but in the name of solidarity.

Guido Aristarco, meanwhile, in his critical essays as well as in his *Storia delle Teoriche del Film*, argued against Zavattini that realism, in the sense of registering daily life, was never simple or unproblematic. Inspired both by the work of Hungarian Marxist

73

theorist Georg Lukács and by Italian Marxist Antonio Gramsci, Aristarco called for a "critical realism" which would reveal the dynamic causes of social change through exemplary situations and figures. (For an excellent overview of neo-realist theory, see Casetti, 1999.) Partly inspired by the anti-fascist achievements of Italian neo-realism, theorists such as André Bazin and Siegfried Kracauer made the camera's putatively intrinsic realism the cornerstone of a democratic and egalitarian aesthetic. The mechanical means of photographic reproduction, for these theorists, assured the essential objectivity of film. Here we find a converse ju-jitsu from Arnheim's. For Arnheim the cinema's defects (for example, the lack of a third dimension) were a trampoline for artistic excellence. But what Arnheim saw as something to be transcended – film's mechanical reproduction of phenomenal appearances – was for Bazin and Kracauer the very key to its strength. As Bazin put it in "The Ontology of the Photographic Image" (1945), "the objective nature of photography confers on it a quality of credibility absent from all other picture making" (Bazin, 1967, pp. 13–14). For the first time, as Bazin put it, "an image of the world is framed automatically, without the creative intervention of man" (ibid., p. 13). For Bazin, the fact that the photographer, unlike the painter or poet, could work in the absence of a model guaranteed an ontological bond between the cinematographic representation and what it represents. Since photochemical processes entail a concrete link between the photographic analogon and its referent, the charismatic indexicality of photography was presumed to make possible unimpeachable witness to "things as they are." It is this same "impersonality" that makes film comparable, for Bazin, to the process of embalming and "mummification." The cinema instantiates a deeply rooted desire to replace the world by its double. The cinema combines static photographic mimesis with the reproduction of Time: "the image of things is likewise the image of their duration, changed, mummified as it were" (ibid., p. 15). In an overly veristic formulation subsequently critiqued by film semiologists, Bazin went so far as to claim that "the photographic image is the object itself, the object freed from the conditions of time and space that govern it" (ibid., p. 14).

The formative/realist dichotomy – Lumière vs. Méliès, mimesis vs. discourse – has often been overdrawn, obscuring what the two currents have in common.[1] Both relied on an essentialist notion of the cinema – as being intrinsically good at certain things and not others – and both were normative and exclusivist: they thought that the cinema should follow a certain path. Both formalist and realist currents featured their own brand of "progressive" teleology of technique. For Arnheim, the advent of sound derailed what would have been the normal train-like progress toward a consciously artificial cinema, while for Bazin the "Old Testament" of silence, in a telling formula which reveals the religious–providential substratum to his thinking, prepared the way for its fulfillment in the "New Testament" of sound. Although Bazin did praise what he calls the "narrational dialectic" of opposing styles in *Citizen Kane*, stylistic counterpoint, or what Bakhtin called the "mutual relativization" of styles, was not generally seen as a viable option.

For Bazin, the valorization of realism had an ontological, apparitical, historical, and aesthetic dimension. In apparitical terms, realism was the mediumistic realization of what Bazin (1967) called the "myth of total cinema." This myth animated the inventors of the medium: "In their imaginations they saw the cinema as a total and complete representation of reality; they saw in a trice the reconstruction of a perfect illusion of the outside world in sound, color, and relief" (ibid., p. 20). Thus silent, black-and-white cinema gave way to cinema in sound and color, part of an inexorable technological progression toward an ever-more persuasive realism. (One discerns an interesting tension in Bazin between the mimetic megalomania of the desire for a total simulacrum of life, and the quiet, self-effacing modesty of his stylistic preferences.) In 1963 Charles Barr extended Bazin's myth to include the development of widescreen cinema, and the phrase "total cinema" obviously resonates with later innovations such as 3-D, IMAX, Dolby Sound, and Virtual Reality. (In a reverse chronology, Jean-Louis Baudry's 1970s linking of the cinema to Plato's allegory of the cave certainly has Bazin's "myth of total cinema" as its dialogizing backdrop.)

Bazin also generated novel accounts of film history and aesthetics.

In his essay "The Evolution of Film Language" he postulated a kind of triumphal progress of realism in the cinema not unlike a telescoped version of Auerbach's account in *Mimesis* of an ever-more verisimilar western literature. Bazin distinguished between those filmmakers who placed their faith in the "image" and those who placed their faith in "reality." The "image" filmmakers, especially the German Expressionists and the Soviet montage filmmakers, dissected the integrity of the time–space continuum of the world, cutting it up into fragments. The "reality" directors, in contrast, deployed the duration of the long take in conjunction with staging in depth to create a multi-plane sense of reality in relief. Bazin's annointed realist tradition began with Lumière, continued with Flaherty and Murnau, was strengthened by Welles and Wyler, and reached quasi-teleological fulfillment with Italian neo-realism. Bazin particularly valued the down-to-earth, relatively eventless plots, the unstable character motivations, and the relatively slow and viscous quotidian rhythms characteristic of early neo-realist films. He distinguished between a shallow Zola-like naturalism, which seeks superficial verisimilitude, and a profound realism which plumbs the depths of the real. For Bazin, realism had less to do with literal mimetic adequation between filmic representation and the "world out there" than with the testimonial honesty of mise-en-scène. Deleuze takes on certain aspects of Bazin's historical teleology in his 1980s work, especially in terms of neo-realism as a crucial break.

According to Bazin, new approaches to editing and mise-en-scène, especially long-take cinematography and depth of field, allowed the filmmaker to respect the spatiotemporal integrity of the pro-filmic world. These advances facilitated a more thoroughgoing mimetic representation, one linked, in Bazin's thinking, to a spiritual notion of "revelation," a theory with theological overtones of the presence of the divine in all things. Indeed, Bazin's critical language – real presence, revelation, faith in the image – often reverberates with religiosity. Cinema becomes a sacrament; an altar where a kind of transsubstantiation takes place. At the same time, this in-depth conception was linked for Bazin to a political notion of the democratization of filmic perception, in that the spectator enjoyed the freedom to scan the multi-planar field of the image for its meaning. Although Bazin did speak in favor of "impure cinema," i.e. a mixture of theater and film, in general Bazinian stylistics left little room for the self-conscious mixing of styles, and indeed Bazin played down the mixing of long takes and montage, of Expressionism and realism, that characterized the work even of some of his favorite directors, such as Orson Welles. Bazin's favored techniques like the single-shot sequence, as Peter Wollen points out, could also be used for ends diametrically opposed to those endorsed by Bazin; for example, *de*-realization and reflexivity.[2] At the same time, Bazin was never the "naive realist" that he is often caricatured as being; he was well aware of the artifice required to construct a realist image. The automatization of the cinematic apparatus is a necessary but not sufficient condition for realism. Indeed, Bazin is on some levels a formalist, in that he is less concerned with any specific "content" than with a style of mise-en-scène. Nor can Bazin be reduced to a theorist only of realism; his ideas about genre, authorship, and "classical cinema" also had immense impact.

Like Bazin, Siegfried Kracauer was also concerned with issues of realism, and like him he cannot be reduced to being a "naive realist." As Thomas Levin points out, Kracauer is often made out to be a kind of anti-Benjamin, when in fact he had much in common with Benjamin. Indeed, it is ironic that 1970s film theoreticians, in their anti-veristic rage, often used Kracauer as a kind of whipping boy, when in many ways his views were aligned with theirs. Kracauer's *The Mass Ornament*, dedicated as it was to topical analyses of ephemera such as street maps, hotel lobbies, and boredom, clearly anticipated Barthes's *Mythologies*. Some of the confusion arises from the fact that Kracauer's works in the 1920s and 1930s – especially the essays later collected in *The Mass Ornament* – only became available decades after they were written (1977 in Germany, 1995 in English).

In the background of Kracauer's analysis was a concern with the democratic and anti-democratic potentialities of the mass media. In *From Caligari to Hitler* (1947), a study of German cinema from 1919 to 1933, Kracauer showed how a highly artificial Weimar cinema "really" reflected "profound psychological tendencies" and the institutionalized madness of German life. Films could reflect the national psyche because (1) they are not individual but collective productions and (2) they address and mobilize a mass audience, not through explicit themes or discourses but through the implicit, the unconscious, the hidden, the unsaid desires. Within Kracauer's figural approach Weimar cinema foreshadowed the Caligaresque insanity of Nazism. Kracauer discerned a kind of morbid teleology in Expressionist masterpieces such as *The Cabinet of Dr Caligari* (1921) and *M* (1931), a movement toward Nazism evidenced in the authoritarian tendencies of the films themselves. In this sense, Kracauer explores another kind of social mimesis, to wit the historicity of form itself as figuring social situations. In aesthetic terms this cinema represented the "complete triumph of the ornamental over the human. Absolute authority asserts itself by arranging people under its domination in pleasing designs" (Kracauer, 1947, p. 93; Kracauer's analysis indirectly enabled Susan Sontag in "Fascinating Fascism" to align the aesthetics of Riefenstahl's *Triumph of the Will* with those of Busby Berkeley musicals). While not completely persuasive, and vitiated by a sense of *post hoc ergo propter hoc*, Kracauer's overall argument interestingly displaces the question of realism onto another level, whereby films are seen as representing, in an allegorical manner, not literal history but rather the deep, roiling, unconscious obsessions of national desire and paranoia.

Much of the view of Kracauer as the ayatollah of realism is based on his magnum opus *Theory of Film: The Redemption of Physical Reality* (1960), which laid the foundations for what he called a "materialist aesthetics." Kracauer spoke of the film medium's "declared preference for nature in the raw" and its "natural vocation for realism." For Kracauer, film was uniquely equipped to register what he variously called "material reality," "visible reality," "physical nature," or simply "nature." At times, Kracauer seems to posit a quasi-Platonic hierarchy of realities, running from the "sort of real" to the "really real," with "natural reality" at the apex. Although everything which exists is hypothetically filmable, some subjects are *inherently* cinematic. Within a kind of romantic ecologism, Kracauer seems to want to keep nature "virginal" and "intact." But a skeptic might ask why a film of a staged performance, or a shot of a computer screen, is less "real" than a shot of a forest. As usual, the implicit ontological claims of the word "real" lead into dead ends and aporias. Writing in the wake of World War II and the Holocaust, Kracauer was perfectly aware of the dystopian, Hitlerian potential of the mass media. Nevertheless, he maintained his faith in film as the artistic expression of a democratizing modernity, besieged but not yet overcome by barbarism and catastrophe. Central to Kracauer's valorization of the cinema was its capacity to register the quotidian, the contingent, and the random, the world in its endless becoming. As Miriam Hansen puts it:

Kracauer's investment in the photographic basis of film does not rest on the iconicity of the photographic sign, at least not in the narrow sense of a literal resemblance or analogy with a self-identical object. Nor, for that matter, does he conceive of the indexical, the photochemical bond that links image and referent, in any positivist way as merely anchoring the analogical "truth" of the representation. Rather, the same indexicality that allows photographic film to record and figure the world also inscribes the image with moments of temporality and contingency.[3]

Although Kracauer at times seems to confuse aesthetics with ontology, he was not ultimately the partisan of a single style such as neorealism. The anarchistic slapstick of a Mack Sennett, for Kracauer, could critically foreground the well-ordered abuses of instrumental reason. (Here Kracauer anticipates the later French radical deconstructionist embrace of the films of Jerry Lewis.)

Film for Kracauer stages a rendezvous with contingency, with the unpredictable and open-ended flux of everyday experience. It is no accident that Kracauer cites that other great theorist of democratic realism, Erich Auerbach, who speaks of the modern novel's registering of "the random moment which is comparatively independent of the controversial and unstable orders over which men fight and despair; it passes unaffected by them, as daily life."[4] Perhaps in visceral recoil from the authoritarian certitudes and monumentalist hierarchies of fascist aesthetics, Kracauer, like Auerbach, stresses the "ordinary business of living." The vocation of the filmmaker, in this conception, was to initiate the spectator into the passionate knowledge and critical love of everyday existence. Speaking overall, Kracauer's work anticipates Metz's later emphasis on the analogy between film and daydream, Jameson's work on national allegory and the "political unconscious," and the cultural studies notion of culture as a "discursive continuum."

Theorists of this period were also concerned with the perennial issue of cinematic specificity, and whether this specificity was of a technical, stylistic, or thematic nature, or some combination of the three. Bazin asked the question in his title *What is Cinema?* and answered it by grounding cinema's essence in the charismatic indexicality of photography, with its existential link to the pro-filmic referent. Kracauer, similarly, saw cinema as rooted in photography and its registry of the indeterminate, random flow of everyday life. Film theory in the 1950s and 1960s also revisited the perennial question of cinema's relation to the other arts. Theorists quarreled, more specifically, about precisely *which* arts or media should be seen as allies or antecedents. Should cinema flee from theater or embrace it, see itself as analogous to painting or deny any relationship? Film theory is particularly haunted by its prestigious forebear, literature. A famous essay by Bazin was entitled "For an Impure Cinema: In Defense of Adaptation." Others were less interested in adaptation than in the fact that filmmakers should proceed *like* novelists, an idea implicit in Alexandre Astruc's metaphor of the "camera pen." Maurice Scherer (the future Eric Rohmer) once wrote: "Cinema should recognize the narrow dependence which links it, not to painting or to music, but to the very arts from which it had always tried to distance itself," literature and the theater (Clerc, 1993, p. 48). Cinema, in sum, need not give up its right to draw on or be inspired by other arts.

In postwar France film theory marched hand-in-hand with developments in philosophical phenomenology, the dominant movement of the period. Following up on Husserl, philosophers returned to "things themselves" and their relation to embodied, intentional consciousness. The leading phenomenologist, Merleau-Ponty, discerned a kind of "match" not only between the film medium and the postwar generation but also between film and philosophy. "The movies," he argued, "are peculiarly suited to make manifest the union of mind and body, mind and the world, and the expression of one in the other. . . . The philosopher and the moviemaker share a certain way of being, a certain view of the world which belongs to a generation."[5] Anticipating Deleuze, Merleau-Ponty saw film and philosophy as cognate forms of intellectual labor. In "The Film and the New Psychology," based on a 1945 lecture, Merleau-Ponty discussed the phenomenological parameters of the cinema as a "temporal gestalt" whose palpable realism was even more exact than that of the real world itself. A film is not thought, Merleau-Ponty pointed out, "it is perceived." Applying an amalgam of Gestalt psychology and existential phenomenology to the cinema, Merleau-Ponty suggested, would provide a psychological basis for the basic structures of the cinematic experience as a mediated experience of being-in-the-world. A number of later theorists came to build on Merleau-Ponty-style phenomenology, for example Henri Agel in *Le Cinéma et le Sacré* (1961), Amadee Ayfre in *Conversion aux images* (1964), Albert Laffay in *Logique du cinéma* (1964), Jean-Pierre Meunier in his *Les Structures de l'experience filmique* (1969), Jean Mitry in his two-volume *Esthetique et psychologie du cinéma* (1963–5), and much later, Dudley Andrew in "The Neglected Tradition of Phenomenology in Film" (1978) and *Major Film Theories* (1976), and Alan Casebier in *Film and Psychology* (1991). In *The Address of the Eye: A Phenomenology of Film Experience* (1992) Vivian Sobchack used Merleau-Ponty's method of phenomenological interpretation to suggest that "The film experience not only *represents* and reflects upon the prior direct perceptual experience of the filmmaker *by means of* the modes and structures of direct and reflective perceptual experience, but also *presents* the direct and reflective experience of a perceptual and expressive existence *as* the film" (Sobchack, 1992, p. 9).

Concurrent with Merleau-Ponty's work, an academically based French movement called Filmology gave rise to a research institute (Association pour la Recherche Filmologique), an international jour-

81

nal (*La Revue internationale de filmologie*), and a collective text (*L'Univers filmique*). The movement's inaugural tome was Gilbert Cohen-Seat's *Essai sur les principes d'une philosophie du cinéma* (Essay on the Principles of a Philosophy of the Cinema, 1946). Partly inspired by phenomenology, the "filmologists" sought to organize various academic disciplines – sociology, psychology, aesthetics, linguistics, psychophysiology – around the project of a comprehensive and scientific theory of film. At their First International Congress, the filmologists defined five categories of interest: (1) Psychological and Experimental Research; (2) Research in the Development of Cinematic Empiricism; (3) Aesthetic, Sociological and General Philosophical Research; (4) Comparative Research on Film as a Means of Expression; and (5) Normative Research – application of studies of the filmic fact to problems of teaching, of medical psychology, etc. (Lowry, 1985, p. 50). In subsequent years Henri Agel wrote on "Cinematic Equivalences of Literary Composition and Language," Anne Souriau wrote on "Filmic Functions of Costumes and Decor," and Edgar Morin and Georges Friedman wrote on "Sociology of the Cinema." In his paper "Filmologie et esthetique comparée," Souriau argues, somewhat problematically, that four structural properties of the novel – time, tempo, space, and angle of approach – render it difficult to "translate" into film.

The filmology group undertook a systematic study of all aspects of the cinema, from the "cinematic situation" (theater, screen, and spectator) to the social rituals surrounding the cinema, to the phenomenology and even the physiology of spectatorship. The filmologists elaborated a number of concepts – "cinematic situation" (Cohen-Seat), "diegesis" (Etienne Souriau), "cognitive mechanisms" (Rene and Bianka Zazzo) – which were subsequently deployed (and reworked) by both Metzian semiotics and, much later, cognitive theory. In Souriau's proposal (in *La Correspondance des arts*, 1947) for a comparative study of the specificities of the various arts, for example, we see the partial source of Metz's attempts to classify and differentiate media in terms of their "specificity," just as Romano's work on the "character of reality" provoked by film anticipates Metz's work on "the impression of reality." Filmology's investigation of such issues as the perception of movement, the impression of depth, the role of immediate and deferred memory, motor reactions, empathic projections and the physiology of spectatorship, by the same token, prefigured many of the concerns of cognitive theory in the 1980s.

The Cult of the Auteur

In the late 1950s and early 1960s a movement called auteurism came to dominate film criticism and theory. Auteurism was in some ways the expression of an existentialist humanism inflected by phenomenology. Echoing Sartre's pithy summary of existentialism – "existence precedes essence" – Bazin claimed that the *cinema's* "existence precedes its essence." Bazin's vocabulary, moreover, as James Naremore points out, was a Sartrean one, fond of words like "freedom," "fate," and "authenticity" (Naremore, 1998, p. 25). Bazin's essays "Ontology of the Photographic Image" and "Myth of Total Cinema" were roughly concurrent with Sartre's essay entitled "Existentialism and Humanism." Sartre and Bazin share a fundamental tenet: "the centrality of the activity of the philosophical subject, the premise of all phenomenologies" (Rosen, 1990, p. 8). Auteurism was also the product of a cultural formation which included film magazines, ciné-clubs, the French cinématèque, and film festivals, and it was fueled by the screening of newly available American films during the Liberation period.

Novelist and filmmaker Alexandre Astruc prepared the way for auteurism with his 1948 essay "Birth of a New Avant-Garde: The Camera-Pen," in which he argued that the cinema was becoming a new means of expression analogous to painting or the novel. The filmmaker, Astruc claimed, should be able to say "I" like the novelist or poet.[1] The "camera-pen" formula valorized the *act* of filmmaking; the director was no longer merely the servant of a pre-existing text (novel, screenplay) but a creative artist in his/her own right. François Truffaut also played an important role with his strategic aggressions against the established French cinema. In his famous manifesto-essay, "A Certain Tendency of the French Cinema," published in 1954 in *Cahiers du cinéma*, Truffaut excoriated the "tradition of quality" which turned the classics of French literature into predictably well-furnished, well-spoken, and stylistically formulaic films. Truffaut dubbed this archaic cinema, in a rather oedipal manner, the "cinéma de papa" (the proponents of New German Cinema, at Oberhausen in 1962, also spoke of "Daddy's Cinema"). Truffaut derided the tradition of quality as a stuffy, academic, screenwriters' cinema, while lauding the more vital American popular maverick cinema of Nicholas Ray, Robert Aldrich, and Orson Welles. The tradition of quality, for Truffaut, reduced filmmaking to the mere translation of a pre-existing screenplay, when it should be seen as an open-ended adventure in creative mise-en-scene. Although French cinema prided itself on being "anti-bourgeois," Truffaut taunted, it was ultimately made "by the bourgeois for the bourgeois," the work of *littérateurs* who despised and underestimated the cinema. It is difficult to overstate the provocative nature of Truffaut's intervention, and especially his support for American cinema in the era of Sartrean "engagement" and the left's domination of French culture, when the US, for French intellectuals, evoked McCarthyism and the cold war, and when "Hollywood" evoked the powerful dream factory that had destroyed grand talents like von Stroheim and Murnau.

For Truffaut, the new film would resemble the person who made it, not so much through autobiographical content but rather through the style, which impregnates the film with the personality of its director. Intrinsically strong directors, auteur theory argued, will exhibit over the years a recognizable stylistic and thematic personality, even when they work in Hollywood studios. In short, real talent will "out" no matter what the circumstances. *Cahiers* defended the American films of Lang against the prejudice that his work declined in Hollywood. In the case of Hitchcock, *Cahiers* not only supported his American films, but two of its members, Eric Rohmer and Claude Chabrol, argued in a book-length study that Hitchcock was both a technical genius and a profound metaphysician whose work revolved around the implicitly Catholic theme of a Christ-like "transfer of guilt." "Once the principle of directorial continuity is accepted even in Hollywood," Andrew Sarris wrote, "films can never look the same again" (Sarris, 1973, p. 37).

With its first issue in 1951 *Cahiers du cinéma* became a key organ for the propagation of auteurism. The *Cahiers* critics saw the director as the person responsible, in the last instance, for a film's aesthetics and mise-en-scène. *Cahiers* initiated a new policy of interviewing admired directors; between 1954 and 1957 Renoir, Buñuel, Rossellini, Hitchcock, Hawks, Ophuls, Minnelli, Welles, (Nicholas) Ray, and Visconti all passed through the *Cahiers* interview machine. In a 1957 article, "La Politique des auteurs," Bazin summarized auteurism as "choosing in the artistic creation the personal factor as a criterion of reference, and then postulating its permanence and even its progress from one work to the next." The auteur critics distinguished between metteurs-en-scène, i.e. those who adhered to the dominant conventions and to the scripts given them, and auteurs who used mise-en-scène as part of self expression.

Although auteurism came into vogue in the 1950s, the idea itself was in many ways a traditional one. The perennial characterization of the cinema as the "seventh art" implicitly granted film artists the same status as writers and painters. In 1921 the filmmaker Jean Epstein, in "Le Cinéma et les lettres modernes," used the term "auteur" to apply to filmmakers, and directors like Griffith and Eisenstein had compared their own cinematic techniques to the literary devices of writers like Flaubert and Dickens. In the 1930s Rudolf Arnheim was already lamenting the "exaltation" of the director (Arnheim, 1997, p. 65). In postwar France, however, the auteurist metaphor became a key structuring concept in film criticism and theory. In Sartrean terms, the film author strives for "authenticity" in the face of the castrating "regard" of the studio system.

On the other side of the Atlantic, meanwhile, American film journals of the late 1940s had anticipated the auteurist discussion by debating the relative importance of the diverse collaborators on the filmmaking team. Lester Cole defended the scriptwriter, Joseph Mankiewicz the scriptwriter–director, while Stanley Shofield compared the collaborative art of filmmaking to the collective construction of a cathedral. All these arguments were attempts to claim artistic origins and were animated by a desire to show that film could transcend its artisanal, industrial form of production and incorporate a singular, signed vision. One can also detect a romantic auteurist impulse in the writings of American avant-gardists like Maya Deren and Stan Brakhage. The former speaks in a 1960 essay of the cinema's "extraordinary range of expression," its affinities not only with dance, theater, and music, but also with poetry in that "it can juxtapose images" and with literature generally in that "it can encompass in its soundtrack the abstractions available only to language." Brakhage, in a 1963 essay, projects the artist not so much as auteur but rather as visionary, the creator of a wordless world "shimmering with an endless variety of movement and innumerable gradations of color." Cinema for Brakhage is an adventure in perception, where the director can deploy transgressive techniques – overexposure, improvised natural filters, spitting on the lens – to provoke a trans-perspectival vision of the world.

In the postwar period, film discourse, like literary discourse, became oriented around a constellation of concepts such as *écriture*, writing, and textuality. This graphological trope dominated the period, from Astruc's "camera–stylo"(camera–pen) to Metz's later discussion of "cinema and *écriture*" in *Language and Cinema* (1971). The French New Wave directors were especially fond of the scriptural metaphor – scarcely surprising, given that many of them began as film journalists who regarded articles and films as simply two forms of expression. "We are always alone," Godard (1958) wrote somewhat melodramatically, "whether in the studio or before the blank page." Agnes Varda, when she was about to make *La Pointe Courte*, announced that she would "make a film exactly as one writes a book" (quoted in Philippe, 1983, p. 17). The films by the New Wave directors "embodied" this writerly theory. It is no accident, for example, that Truffaut's first film, *Les Quatre Cents Coups*, abounds with references to writing: the opening shot of pupils writing; Antoine's mimicry of his mother's penmanship; his theft of a typewriter; his pastiche of Balzac which elicits accusations of plagiarism

86

– all point to the undergirding trope which subtends his vision of filmmaking. At the same time the New Wave was profoundly ambivalent about literature, which was both a model to be emulated, and, in the form of literary scripts and conventional adaptations, the enemy to be abjured.

A product of the conjunction of cinephilia (celluphagie) and a romantic strain of existentialism, auteurism must be seen partially as a response to (a) the elitist putdowns of the cinema by some literary intellectuals; (b) the iconophobic prejudice against cinema as a "visual medium;" (c) the mass-culture debate which projected the cinema as the agent of political alienation; and (d) the traditional anti-Americanism of the French literary elite. Auteurism was in this sense a palimpsest of influences, combining romantic expressive notions of the artist, modernist–formalist notions of stylistic discontinuity and fragmentation, and a "proto-postmodern" fondness for "lower" arts and genres. The real scandal of the auteur theory lay not so much in glorifying the director as the equivalent in prestige to the literary author, but rather in exactly *who* was granted this prestige. Filmmakers like Eisenstein, Renoir, and Welles had always been regarded as auteurs because they were known to have enjoyed artistic control over their own productions. The novelty of auteur theory was to suggest that studio directors like Hawks and Minnelli were also auteurs. American cinema, which had classically been the diacritical "other" of French film theory, that against which it had defined itself, just as the putative "vulgarity" of American culture had long provided the diacritical counterpoint for French national identity, now became, surprisingly, the model for a new French cinema.

Born in an atmosphere of violent polemics, "la Politique des Auteurs" translates literally as the "auteur policy" rather than "theory." In France auteurism formed part of a strategy for facilitating a new kind of filmmaking. Auteurism was thus both inspiration and strategic instrument for the filmmakers of the New Wave, who used it to dynamite a place for themselves within a conservative, hierarchical French film scene where aspiring directors had to wait a lifetime to direct films. Critic–directors like Truffaut and Godard were attacking the established system, with its rigid production hierarchies, its preference for studio shooting, and its conventional narrative procedures. They were also defending the rights of the director *vis-à-vis* the producer. Godard's *Contempt*, which pits the humane, cultivated, and polyglot auteur Fritz Lang against the vulgar, barely literate Hollywood producer Prokosch, filmically encapsulates this "director's lib" side of auteurism. Paradoxically, a theory that had its ideological roots in pre-modernist romantic Expressionism helped undergird a cinema, exemplified by epoch-making films like *Hiroshima Mon Amour* and *Breathless*, which was resolutely modernist in aspiration and aesthetics.

In its more extreme incarnations auteurism can be seen as an anthropomorphic form of "love" for the cinema. The same love that fans had formerly lavished on stars, or that formalists lavished on artistic devices, the auteurists now lavished on the men – and they largely *were* men – who incarnated the auteurists' idea of cinema. Film was resurrected as secular religion; the "aura" was back in force thanks to the cult of the auteur. At the same time Bazin distanced himself from the splenetic excesses of the young Turks. With his usual prescience he warned in 1957 against any aesthetic "cult of personality" which would erect favored directors into infallible masters. Bazin also pointed out the necessity of complementing auteurism with other approaches – technological, historical, sociological. Great films, he argued, arise from the fortuitous intersection of talent and historical moment. Occasionally a mediocre director – Bazin cites Curtiz and *Casablanca* – might vividly capture a historical moment, without qualifying as an authentic auteur. The quality control guaranteed by the well-oiled Hollywood industrial machine, furthermore, virtually assured a certain competence and even elegance. Bazin pointed out the paradox that auteurists admired the American cinema, "where the restrictions on production are heavier than anywhere else," while they failed to admire what was ultimately most admirable about it, "the genius of the system, the richness of its ever-vigorous tradition, and its fertility when it comes into contact with new elements" (Hillier, 1985, pp. 257–8).

The Americanization of Auteur Theory

Auteurism took a different turn when it was introduced to the United States by Andrew Sarris in his "Notes on the Auteur Theory in 1962." Like Paris, New York had a strong tradition of ciné-clubs, repertory theaters, and film journals such as *Film Culture*. Sarris picked up on the French critics' emphasis on style as creative expression: "The way a film looks and moves should have some relationship to the way a director thinks and feels." A meaningful style, Sarris argued, unites the "what" and the "how" into a "personal statement" where the director takes risks and struggles against standardization (ibid., p. 66). The critic must therefore be alert to the tensions between the directorial personality and the materials with which the director works. In Sarris's hands the auteur theory also became a surreptitiously nationalist instrument for asserting the superiority of American cinema. Sarris declared himself ready to "stake his critical reputation" on the notion that American cinema has been "consistently superior" to what Sarris dismissively and ethnocentrically called the "rest of the world." Sarris struggled against the Europhile prejudice that saw "art" in stuffy adaptations of European literary classics, but saw only "entertainment" in the films of a Hitchcock or a John Ford. At its best, Sarris's work turned film buffery and connoisseurship into an art form, deploying his broad knowledge of cinema to convey the genuine achievements of Hollywood cinema.

Sarris proposed three criteria for recognizing an auteur: (1) technical competence; (2) distinguishable personality; and (3) interior meaning arising from tension between personality and material. In *The American Cinema* Sarris constructed a nine-part schema which invited privileged directors into a "pantheon" while it relegated the lower ranks into circles reminiscent of Dante's hell.

Pauline Kael debunked Sarris's three criteria in her response article "Circles and Squares" (1963). Technical competence, she argued, was hardly a valid criterion, since some directors, such as Antonioni, went *beyond* mere technical competence. "Distinguishable personality" was meaningless since it favors repetitive direc-

89

tors whose styles are recognizable precisely because they never try anything new. The distinctive smell of skunks, she analogized, does not make their smell pleasant or superior to that of roses. Kael dismisses "interior meaning," finally, as impossibly vague and favoring "hacks who shove style into the crevices of plots." (Kael's attempt to deprive Orson Welles of legitimate authorship of *Citizen Kane*, atttributing it instead to Herman Mankiewicz, was also aimed at Sarris and auteurism.) But the heat of the Sarris–Kael debate masked the fact that they did share a key premise: the idea that film theory/ criticism should be *evaluative*, concerned with the comparative ranking of films and directors. At its most crass, this approach led to sterile quarrels about relative merit, a kind of reckless gambling on critical reputations, as arbitrary tastes were elevated into supposedly rigid hierarchies. In Sarris, metaphors of war and gambling and staking claims were in this sense symptomatic, redolent of the rough-and-tumble frontier atmosphere of competitive journalism.

Auteurism was also criticized on more practical grounds. Critics pointed out that it underestimated the impact of production conditions on authorship. The filmmaker is not an untrammeled artist; he or she is immersed in material contingencies, surrounded by the Babel-like buzz of technicians, cameras, and lights of the "happening" which is the ordinary film shoot. While the poet can write poems on a napkin in prison, the filmmaker requires money, camera, film. Auteurism, it was argued, downplayed the collaborative nature of filmmaking. Even a low-budget feature can involve more than a score of people working over an extended period. A genre like the musical requires the strong creative participation of composers, musicians, choreographers, and set designers. No single writer cam claim, Salman Rushdie writes, to be the true author of the film *The Wizard of Oz*:

No single writer can claim that honour, not even the author of the original book. Mervyn LeRoy and Arthur Freed, the producers, both have their champions. At least four directors worked on the picture, most notably Victor Fleming. . . . The truth is that this great movie, in which the quarrels, sackings and near-bungles of all concerned produced what seems like pure, effortless, and

90

somehow inevitable felicity, is as near as dammit to that will-o'-the-wisp of
modern critical theory: the authorless text. (Rushdie, 1992)

Given this kind of collaboration, some argued that producers like Selznick, performers like Brando, or writers like Raymond Chandler could be seen as auteurs. Any coherent theory of authorship must take into account these diverse intrications in terms of material circumstances and personnel within filmic authorships. Authorship also borders on complex legal issues of ownership concerning copyright, "fair use," "substantial similarity." When Art Buchwald sues Eddie Murphy over the plot of *Coming to America*, when French producers of *The Three Musketeers* refuse to acknowledge Alexander Dumas's "moral rights" as "inalienable author," we are far from the realm of unsullied inspiration and unencumbered genius evoked by romantic notions of authorship.

Auteurism also required modification to apply to television. In television, some argued, the real auteurs were producers like Norman Lear and Stephen Bochco. What happens to a person's status as authors when TV commercial directors (Ridley Scott, Alan Parker) move into feature films, or when consecrated directors (David Lynch, Spike Lee, Jean-Luc Godard) move into commercials, or when Michelangelo Antonioni choreographs a psychedelic spot for Renault? Are they always and in every circumstance auteurs, or does their auteur status depend on medium, context, format? Industry-oriented critics like Thomas Schatz, meanwhile, spoke not of the genius of authors but rather of what Bazin had called the "genius of the system," i.e. the capacity of a well-financed and talent-filled industrial machine to turn out high-quality films. While auteurists emphasized *personal* style and mise-en-scène, Bordwell, Staiger, and Thompson in their work on "classical Hollywood cinema" emphasized the *impersonal* and standardized "group style" of a homogenous corpus whose main features were narrative unity, realism, and invisible narration.

Auteurism ultimately was less a theory than a methodological focus. In any case, it clearly represented an improvement over antecedent critical methodologies, notably Impressionism (a kind of neuro-glandular response to films based solely on the critic's sensibilities and tastes) and sociologism (an evaluative approach based on a reductive view of the perceived progressive or reactionary political thrust of the characters or story line). Auteurism also performed an invaluable rescue operation for neglected films and genres. It discerned authorial personalities in surprising places – especially in the American makers of B-films like Samuel Fuller and Nicholas Ray. It rescued entire genres – the thriller, the western, the horror film – from literary high-art prejudice. By forcing attention to the films themselves and to mise-en-scène as the stylistic signature of the director, auteurism clearly made a substantial contribution to film theory and methodology. Auteurism shifted attention from the "what" (story, theme) to the "how" (style, technique), showing that style itself had personal, ideological and even metaphysical reverberations. It facilitated film's entry into literature departments and played a major role in the academic legitimation of cinema studies. But with the subsequent emergence of semiotics, as we shall see, auteurism came under attack for its romantic, apolitical valorization of authorial genius, gradually transmuting into a hybrid called "auteur-structuralism." We will address auteur-structuralism in a subsequent section.

Third World Film and Theory

Simultaneous with the development of auteurism and film phenomenology in Europe are the first stirrings of what later came to be known as "third cinema" theory, and here too both auteurism and realism were relevant to the discussion. While there had always been diverse forms of film-related writing in Latin America, Africa, and Asia – books, film magazines, and film columns in newspapers – it was in the 1950s that such writing cohered into a theory inspired by nationalist concerns. Originally coined by French journalist Alfred Sauvy in the 1950s by way of analogy to the revolutionary "third estate" of France, i.e. the commoners in contrast with the first estate (the nobility) and the second estate (the clergy), the term "Third World" posited three geopolitical spheres: the capitalist First World (nobility) of Europe, the US, Australia, and Japan; the Second World (clergy) of the socialist bloc; and the Third World proper (the commoners). "Third World" refers to the colonized, neo-colonized or decolonized nations and "minorities" of the world whose economic and political structures have been shaped and deformed within the colonial process. The term itself challenged the colonizing vocabulary which posited these nations as "backward" and "underdeveloped," mired in a presumably static "tradition." As a political coalition, the Third World broadly coalesced around the enthusiasm generated by anti-colonial struggles in Vietnam and Algeria, and specifically emerged from the 1955 Bandung Conference of non-aligned African and Asian nations. The fundamental definition of the Third World had more to do with structural economic domination than it had with crude humanistic categories ("the poor"), developmental categories (the "non-industrialized"), (binary) racial categories ("the non-white"), cultural categories ("the backward"), or geographical categories ("the East"). Such notions of the Third World were seen as imprecise because the Third World is not necessarily poor in resources (Mexico, Venezuela, Nigeria, Indonesia, and Iraq are rich in petroleum), nor culturally backward (as witnessed by the brilliance of Third World cinema, literature, and music), nor non-industrialized (Brazil and Singapore are highly industrialized), nor non-white (Ireland, perhaps the first British colony, is predominantly white, as is Argentina).

The way for filmic third-worldism was prepared, in Latin America at least, by the popularity of Italian neo-realism, partially facilitated by Italian immigrant populations but also by certain analogies between the Italian social situation and that of Latin America. The social geography of Italy, divided into rich North and poor South, uncannily homologized the world at large. Indeed, there was a good deal of cross-fertilization between Italian neo-realism and film theory and practice in Latin America (and elsewhere, for example the case of Satyajit Ray in India and Youssef Chahine in Egypt). Not only did a number of the neo-realist filmmakers visit Latin America –

Cesare Zavattini went to Cuba and Mexico in 1953 to talk about the possibilities of Latin American versions of neo-realism – but also many Latin American filmmakers themselves (Fernando Birri, Julio Garcia Espinosa, Tringuerinho Neto, Tomás Gutiérrez Alea) studied at the Centro Sperimentale in Rome. (While there, Espinosa lectured on "Neo-Realism and Cuban Cinema.") The Italian influence was also disseminated by film journals like *Tiempo de Cine* in Argentina and *A Revista de Cinema* in Brazil, and by the Latin American edition of the Italian journal *Cinema Nuovo*, published in Buenos Aires in the mid 1960s.

The Italian neo-realist films provoked optimism about new filmmaking possibilities. In 1947 Brazilian film critic Benedito Duarte wrote in the *Estado de São Paulo* of his admiration for the ways that Italian filmmakers had created an "aesthetic of poverty" by using documentary techniques and lightweight equipment to create a technically poor but imaginatively rich cinema. Writing in the Cuban journal *Cine-Guia* in 1955, Walfredo Pinera asked: "Why should we want gigantic studios when the most famous films in the world are being made in the street?" Influenced both by Gramsci and by Italian neo-realism, Brazilian critic–filmmakers like Alex Viany and Nelson Pereira dos Santos published articles in the early 1950s defending a "national" and a "popular" cinema. Often theory and practice were closely allied. Fernando Birri's film *Tire Dié*, when it came out in 1958, was accompanied by a manifesto calling for a "national, realist, and critical cinema."

Third World filmmakers and theorists resented not only Hollywood's domination of distribution circuits but also its caricatural representations of their culture and history. "No Cuban," wrote the Cuban film critic Mirta Aguirre in 1951,

will ever forget the United Artists picture Violence, *shown in Havana in 1947, in which the island's capital is presented as a brothel and an unsanitary port of bars and people in tatters. As for Mexico, it continually suffers offenses ranging from the trivial . . . to the most serious, as in Warner Brothers'* One Way Street, *in which James Mason, incarnation of a yankee tough, is the hero and benefactor, while the proud mob of Indians is humiliated beyond limit, in a one-sided picture of misery, humbug, ignorance, and banditry, designed to foment in the*

94

North American and international public the belief that [the Americas] south of Texas [are] an irredeemable and savage territory in which any fair-skinned gunman becomes a messiah. (Quoted in Chanan, 1983, p. 3)

As a response to such caricatures, Latin American critic–theorists favored a cinema made by and for Latin Americans, one which would more adequately give voice to Latin American experience and perspectives.

In the wake of the Vietnamese victory over the French in 1954, the Cuban revolution in 1959, and Algerian Independence in 1962, third-worldist film ideology was crystallized, in the late 1960s, in a wave of militant film manifesto-essays – Glauber Rocha's "Aesthetics of Hunger" (1965), Fernando Solanas and Octavio Getino's "Towards a Third Cinema" (1969), and Julio Garcia Espinosa's "For an Imperfect Cinema" (written in 1969) – and in declarations and manifestos from Third World film festivals (Cairo in 1967, Algiers in 1973) calling for a tricontinental revolution in politics and an aesthetic and narrative revolution in film form. Written during a period of intense nationalist struggles, each of the manifestos emerged from a particular cultural and cinematic context, yet there were common concerns. Just because a country was *economically* underdeveloped, Glauber Rocha suggested, it did not mean that it had to be *artistically* underdeveloped. And in this sense both Italian neo-realism and Soviet-style socialist realism were sometimes criticized as inadequate models. Playing on the Spanish word for "south," Rocha called for "neo-*sur*-realism." In Cuba director–theorists like Julio Garcia Espinosa ridiculed the "frozen forms" of socialist realism, seen as simplistic and conservative. In his incendiary 1965 essay "Aesthetics of Hunger" (alternately entitled "Aesthetics of Violence") Rocha called for a "hungry" cinema of "sad, ugly films," films which would not only treat hunger as a theme but also be "hungry" in their own impoverished means of production. In a displaced form of mimesis, the material poverty of style would signal real-world poverty. Latin America's originality, for Rocha, was its hunger, and the most noble cultural manifestation of hunger was violence. All that was needed, as the slogan went, was "a camera in the hand and an idea in the head."

In his 1963 book *Revisão Crítica do Cinema Brasileiro* Rocha called for a "free, revolutionary, and insolent cinema without stories, reflectors, or casts of thousands" (Rocha, 1963, p. 13). Rather than being an "aesthete of the absurd," on the one hand, or a "romantic nationalist" on the other, the duty of the filmmaker was simply to be "revolutionary" (Rocha, 1981, p. 36). Influenced by Brecht, Rocha proposed what might be called a "trance-Brechtianism," i.e. a Brechtianism filtered through and transformed by a complex Afromestizo culture which "exceeded" the rationalism of the Brechtian aesthetic. Cinema had to be not only dialectical but also "anthropophagic" – a reference to the cannibalist thematic of 1920s Brazilian modernism – and had to de-alienate a spectatorial taste colonized by the commercial–popular aesthetic of Hollywood, by the populist–demagogic aesthetic of the socialist bloc, and by the bourgeois–artistic aesthetic of the European art film. The new cinema, for Rocha, should be "technically imperfect, dramatically dissonant, poetically rebellious, and sociologically imprecise" (ibid.). Rocha also called for an auteurist approach which favored young directors, since if the industry was "the system," the auteur was "the revolution." But while European auteurism gave voice to the sovereign individual subject, Third World auteurism "nationalized" the author, seen as giving voice not to individual subjectivity but rather to the nation as a whole.

In their foundational and widely translated essay "Towards a Third Cinema" (1969), subtitled "Notes and Experiments toward the Development of a Cinema of Liberation in the Third World," Fernando Solanas and Octavio Getino denounced the cultural colonialism that normalized Latin American dependency. Neo-colonialist ideology, they argued, functioned even at the level of cinematic language, leading to the adoption of the ideological forms inherent in the dominant cinema aesthetic. The authors forged a tripartite schema which distinguished between "first cinema" (Hollywood and its analogues around the world); "second cinema" (the art films of a Truffaut in France, or a Torre Nilsson in Argentina); and "third cinema," a revolutionary cinema composed primarily of militant guerrilla documentaries (those of Cine-Liberacion in Argentina, but also Third World

Newsreel in the US, Chris Marker in France, and student move-ment films from around the world). Following Fanon, Solanas and Getino called for the "dissolution of the aesthetic into the life of society." They also reformulated film spectatorship as a "historical encounter," in which spectators, rather than resonating with the sensibility of an auteur, become active shapers of their own destiny, the protagonists of their own histories/stories.

The Cuban Espinosa, meanwhile, in his 1969 essay "For an Im-perfect Cinema," called in carnivalesque fashion for the erasure of the line between artist and public. At a point when Cuban cinema was just beginning to acquire the capacity of producing a well-made cinema with high production values, Espinosa warned against the temptation of perfection. Technically and artistically perfect cinema, he argued, is almost always a reactionary cinema. He therefore called for an "imperfect" cinema not beholden to European aesthetic ide-als, one energized by the "low" forms of popular culture and in creative dialogue with American cinema. If American cinema was "born to entertain," and if European cinema was "born to make art," Latin American cinema, for Espinosa, "was born for political activism." A genuine popular art will arise, he prophesied, when the masses actually create it. Rather than godlike auteur, the spectator auteur. Rather than an *a priori*, self-sufficient, contemplative cin-ema, imperfect cinema proposes art as endless critical process. Art, he concluded, will not disappear into nothingness; rather, "it will disappear into everything" (Chanan, 1983, p. 33).

The work of Frantz Fanon was a pervasive influence in these theo-ries and in the films influenced by them. Although Fanon never used the term "Orientalist discourse," his critiques of colonialist imagery provided proleptic examples of the anti-orientalist critiques of mainstream cinema which became popular in the 1980s and 1990s. In words that might have been describing any of the hundreds of orientalist films about North Africa – French films like *Pépé le Moko* and American films like *Sahara* – Fanon argued in *The Wretched of the Earth* that in Eurocentric historiography "the settler makes his-tory; his life is an epoch, an Odyssey," while against him "torpid creatures, wasted by fevers, obsessed by ancestral customs, form an almost in-organic background for the innovating dynamism of colonial mercantilism." Fanon worked at the point of convergence of anti-imperial politics and (Lacanian) psychoanalytic theory, finding a link between the two in the concept of "identification." Much in advance of 1970s film theory, Fanon deployed Lacan's notion of the "mirror stage" as part of a critique of colonial psychiatry. For Fanon, identification was at once a psychological, cultural, historical, and political issue. One of the symptoms of colonial neurosis, for example, was an incapacity on the part of the colonizer to identify with colonialism's victims. Media objectivity, Fanon pointed out, always works against the native. The issue of identification also had a cinematic dimension, one closely linked to later debates in film theory, which also came to speak of identification and projection, of narcissism and regression, of "spectatorial positioning" and "suture," and point of view, as basic mechanisms constituting the cinematic subject.

Fanon himself, interestingly, also delved into the issue of cinematic spectatorship. Long before the psychoanalytic critics of the 1970s Fanon brought Lacanian psychoanalysis into cultural theory, including film theory. Fanon saw racist films, for example, as a "release for collective aggressions." In *Black Skin, White Masks* (1952) Fanon used the example of Tarzan to point to a certain instability within cinematic identification:

Attend showings of a Tarzan film in the Antilles and in Europe. In the Antilles, the young negro identifies himself de facto with Tarzan against the Negroes. This is much more difficult for him in a European theater, for the rest of the audience, which is white, automatically identifies him with the savages on the screen.

Fanon's example pointed to the shifting, situational nature of colonized spectatorship: the colonial context of reception alters the processes of identification. The awareness of the possible negative projections of other spectators triggers an anxious withdrawal from the film's programmed pleasures. The conventional self-denying identification with the white hero's gaze, the vicarious acting out of a

98

European selfhood, is short-circuited through the awareness of being "screened" or "allegorized" by a colonial gaze within the movie theater itself. While feminist film theory later spoke of the "to-be-looked-at-ness" (Laura Mulvey) of female screen performance, Fanon called attention to the "to-be-looked-at-ness" of spectators themselves, who become slaves, as Fanon puts it, of their own appearance: "Look, a Negro! . . . I am being dissected under white eyes. I am fixed."

Countless 1960s films and manifestos paid homage to Fanon. Solanas and Getino's revolutionary film *La Hora de Los Hornos* (Hour of the Furnaces, 1968), a self-designated "ideological and political film-essay" divided into a prologue, chapters, and epilogue, not only quotes Fanon's adage that "Every Spectator is a Coward or a Traitor," but also orchestrates a constellation of Fanonian themes – the psychic stigmata of colonialism, the therapeutic value of anti-colonial violence, and the urgent necessity of a new culture and a new human being. One iconoclastic sequence entitled "Models" invokes Fanon's final exhortation in *The Wretched of the Earth*: "Let us not pay tribute to Europe by creating states, institutions and societies in its mould. Humanity expects more from us than this caricatural and generally obscene imitation." The third-worldist film manifestos also stressed, *à la* Fanon, anti-colonial militancy and violence, literal–political in the case of Solanas and Getino, metaphoric–aesthetic in the case of Rocha. "Only through the dialectic of violence," Rocha wrote, "will we reach lyricism."

The notion of "Third Cinema" emerged from the Cuban revolution, from Peronism and Peron's "third way" in Argentina, and from such film movements as Cinema Novo in Brazil. Aesthetically, the movement drew on currents as diverse as Soviet montage, Surrealism Italian neo-realism, Brechtian epic theater, cinema verité, and the French New Wave. We witness the dialogue between Third Cinema and the New Wave in Godard's *Wind from the East* (1969), where a pregnant woman holding a camera asks Rocha to show her the way to political cinema. He answers:

That way is the unknown cinema of aesthetic adventure and philosophical speculation. And this way is third world cinema, a dangerous, divine,

99

marvelous cinema where the questions are practical ones, for example in the case of Brazil, how to form 300 filmmakers to make 600 films per year, in order to supply one of the largest markets in the world.

In his *Dialectica del Espectador* (translated as "Dialectics of the Spectator" in *Jump Cut*), meanwhile, Cuban filmmaker/theorist Tomas Gutierrez Alea proposed a generous synthesis, brilliantly exemplified by his own films, one that would combine the critical distantiation of Brecht, the pathos of Eisenstein, and the social urgency and cultural vibrancy of Latin American art. Rather than console or distract the spectator, this transrealist cinema would prod the spectator to actively interrogate and transform the world

For Godard, as a "Swiss-bourgeois anarcho-moralist," Rocha wrote, "the cinema is finished, but for us it's just beginning" (Rocha, 1985, p. 240).

In relation to cinema, the term "Third World" was empowering in that it called attention to the collectively vast cinematic productions of Asia, Africa, and Latin America and of minoritarian cinema in the First World. While some such as Roy Armes define "Third World Cinema" broadly as the ensemble of films produced by Third World countries (including films produced before the very idea of "Third World" was current), others, such as Paul Willemen, prefer to speak of "Third Cinema," which they see as an ideological project, i.e. as a body of films adhering to a certain political and aesthetic program, whether or not they are produced by Third World peoples themselves. Solanas and Getino define Third Cinema as "the cinema that recognizes in [the anti-imperialist struggle in the Third World and its equivalents within the imperialist countries] . . . the most gigantic cultural, scientific, and artistic manifestation of our time . . . in a word, the decolonization of culture."[1]

The manifestos of the 1960s and 1970s valorized an alternative, independent, anti-imperialist cinema more concerned with militancy than with auteurist self-expression or consumer satisfaction. In third worldist film theory issues of production methods, politics, and aesthetics become inextricably intermingled. The idea was to turn strategic weakness – the lack of infrastructure, funds, equipment –

into tactical strength, turning poverty into a badge of honor, and scarcity, as Ismail Xavier put it, "into a signifier." The hope was to give expression to national themes in a national style. As with the auteurists, style "signified," but here it resonated not with individual authorial personality but with national issues such as poverty, oppression, and cultural conflict. The third worldist manifestos contrasted the new cinema not only with Hollywood but also with their own countries' commercial traditions, now viewed as "bourgeois," "alienated," and "colonized." Decades later, revisionist theories and aesthetics would rediscover new virtues in the previously despised commercial traditions (in places like Brazil, Egypt, Mexico, and India), while moderating the demand for militancy and didacticism.

The Third World film theorists, in their revolutionary enthusiasm and in their synergistic approach to theory and practice, recalled the 1920s montage-theorists from the Soviet Union. Like them, they too were filmmakers as well as theorists, and the questions they asked were at once aesthetic and political. In a 1958 essay Glauber Rocha suggested that Latin American film language could be invented on the basis of a fusion of two apparently antagonistic models proposed by Zavattini and Eisenstein. Indeed, the Third World theorists made frequent reference to the Soviet theorists, while rejecting the "socialist realist" model that emerged in the 1930s. The third worldists developed an ongoing problematic, a set of interrelated questions asked repeatedly and answered diversely, among them: How could cinema best give expression to national concerns? What areas of social experience had been neglected by the cinema? How were progressive, nationalist films to be produced and financed? What strategies were most appropriate to colonized or neo-colonized or newly independent countries? What was the role of the independent producer? What was the place of the author, and of auteurism, within Third World cinema? What was the role of the state in resisting Hollywood domination of exhibition? Was the state the disinterested protector of national cinema *vis-à-vis* powerful foreign interests or was it indirectly allied with them? How could Third World cinemas conquer their domestic market? What distribution strategies would be most effective? What cinematic language was most appropriate? What was the relation between production methods and aesthetics? Should Third World cinema emulate the Hollywood continuity codes and production values to which Third World audiences had become accustomed? Or should it make a radical break with Hollywood aesthetics in favor of a radically discontinuous and anti-populist aesthetic such as the "aesthetic of hunger" or the "aesthetic of garbage?" To what extent should cinema incorporate indigenous popular cultural forms? To what extent should films be anti-illusionistic, anti-narrative, anti-spectacular, and avant-garde? (This last question was also being asked by the First World avant-garde.) What was the relation between Third World filmmakers (largely middle-class intellectuals) and the "people" whom they purported to represent? Should they be a cultural vanguard speaking for the people by proxy? Should they be the celebratory mouthpieces of popular culture, or the unrelenting critics of its alienations?

Unfortunately, perhaps because of an assumption that Third World intellectuals could only express "local" concerns, or because their essays were so overtly political and programmatic, this body of work was rarely seen as forming part of the history of "universal" – read Eurocentric – film theory.

The Advent of Structuralism

The intellectual movement called structuralism was not without relation to these Third World stirrings. Both structuralism and third worldism had their long-term historical origins in a series of events that undermined the confidence of European modernity: the Holocaust (and in France the Vichy collaboration with the Nazis), and the postwar disintegration of the last European empires. Although the exalted term "theory" was rarely linked to Third World Cinema theorizing, third worldist thinking had an undeniable impact on First World theory. The structuralists codified, on some levels, what anti-colonial thinkers had been saying for some time. The subversive work of "denaturalization" performed by what one might call the left wing

102

of semiotics – for example, Roland Barthes's famous analysis of the colonialist implications of the *Paris Match* cover showing a black soldier saluting the French flag – had everything to do with the external critique of European master-narratives performed by Third World Francophone decolonizers like Aimé Cesaire (*Discourse on Colonialism*, 1955) and Frantz Fanon (*The Wretched of the Earth*, 1961). In the wake of the Holocaust, decolonization, and Third World revolution, Europe started to lose its privileged position as model for the world. Lévi-Strauss's crucial turn from biological to linguistic models for a new anthropology, for example, was motivated by his visceral aversion to a biological anthropology deeply tainted by anti-semitic and colonialist racism. Indeed, it was in the context of decolonization that UNESCO asked Lévi-Strauss to undertake the research which culminated in his "Race and History" (1952), where the French anthropologist rejected any essentialist hierarchy of civilizations.

Both the structuralist and the poststructuralist movements, in this sense, coincide with the moment of self-criticism, a veritable legitimation crisis, within Europe itself. Derrida's decentering of Europe as "normative culture of reference," for example, was clearly indebted to Fanon's earlier decentering of Europe in *The Wretched of the Earth*. Many of the source thinkers of structuralism and poststructuralism, furthermore, were biographically linked to what came to be called the Third World: Lévi-Strauss did anthropology in Brazil; Foucault taught in Tunisia; Althusser, Cixous, and Derrida were all born in Algeria, where Bourdieu also did his anthropological field work.

In terms of film, the adoption of the methods of the human sciences constituted a challenge to what were seen as the impressionistic, subjective methods of earlier schools of film criticism. In this period film semiotics and its prolongations, later called "screen theory" or simply "film theory," came to the center of the analytic enterprise. In a first stage, Saussurean structural linguistics provided the dominant theoretical model. Understanding the causes of this paradigmatic shift requires a brief detour into the origins of the structuralist movement. Although language had been an object of philosophical reflexion for millennia, it was only in the twentieth century that it came to constitute a fundamental paradigm, a virtual "key" to the mind, to artistic and social praxis, and indeed to human existence generally. Central to the project of a wide spectrum of twentieth-century thinkers – Peirce, Wittgenstein, Sapir, Whorf, Cassirer, Heidegger, Bakhtin, Merleau-Ponty, and Derrida – is a concern with the crucial importance of language in shaping human life and thought. As the methodological success story of the twentieth century, structural linguistics generated a rich proliferation of structuralisms premised on the principles of Saussurean linguistics. The overarching meta-discipline of semiotics, in this sense, can be seen as a local manifestation of a more widespread "linguistic turn," an attempt, in Fredric Jameson's words, to "rethink everything through again in terms of linguistics."[1]

Film semiotics must be seen as symptomatic not only of the general language-consciousness of contemporary thought but also of its penchant for methodological self-consciousness, its "metalinguistic" tendency to demand critical scrutiny of its own terms and procedures. The two source thinkers of contemporary semiotics were the American pragmatic philosopher Charles Sanders Peirce (1839–1914) and the Swiss linguist Ferdinand de Saussure (1857–1913). Roughly simultaneously, but without each other's knowledge, Saussure founded the science of "semiology" and Peirce the science of "semiotics." In *A Course in General Linguistics* (1916) Saussure called for a "science that studies the life of signs," a science that "would show what constitutes signs, what laws govern them." Peirce's philosophical investigations, meanwhile, led him in the direction of what he called "semiotics," specifically through a concern with symbols, which he regarded as the "woof and warp" of all thought and scientific research. (That there are two words for the semiotic enterprise, "semiotics" and "semiology," largely has to do with its dual origins in these two intellectual traditions).

It is Saussure, however, who constitutes the founding figure for European structuralism, and thus for much of film semiotics. Saussure's *Course in General Linguistics* ushered in a kind of "Copernican Revolution" in linguistic thought by seeing language not as a mere adjunct to our grasp of reality but rather as formative of it.

104

Saussurean linguistics forms part of a general shift away from the nineteenth-century preoccupation with the temporal and the historical – as evidenced by Hegel's *historical* dialectic, Marx's *dialectical* materialism, and Darwin's "*evolution* of the species" – to the contemporary concern with the spatial, the systematic, and the structural. Saussure argued that linguistics must move away from the historical (diachronic) orientation of traditional linguistics toward a synchronic approach which studies language as a functional totality at a given point in time. In fact, however, it is virtually impossible to separate out the synchronic from the diachronic. Indeed, many of the aporias of structuralism derive from its failure to recognize that history and language are mutually imbricated. For the structuralists themselves, however, the qualifiers "synchronic" and "diachronic," then, were seen as applying less to the phenomena themselves, therefore, than to the perspective adopted by the linguist. What matters is the shift in emphasis from a historical approach preoccupied with the origins and evolution of language, to a structural emphasis on language as a functional system.

More a method than a doctrine, structuralism was concerned with the immanent relations constituting language and all discursive systems. Common to most varieties of structuralism and semiotics was an emphasis on the underlying rules and conventions of language rather than on the surface configurations of speech exchange. In language, Saussure famously argued, "there are only differences." Rather than a static inventory of names designating things, persons, and events already given to human understanding, Saussure argued, language is nothing more than a series of phonetic differences matched with a series of conceptual differences. Concepts, therefore, are purely differential, defined not by their positive content, but rather by their diacritical relation with other terms of the system: "Their most precise characteristic is in being what the others are not." Within structuralism as a theoretical grid, then, behavior, institutions, and texts are seen as analyzable in terms of an underlying network of relationships; the elements which constitute the network gain their meaning from the relations that hold between the elements.

Although structuralism developed out of Saussure's groundbreaking work on language, it was not until the 1960s that it became widely disseminated. The process by which structuralism came to form a dominant paradigm is retrospectively clear. The scientific advance represented by Saussure's *Course* was transferred to literary study initially by the Russian Formalists and later by the Prague Linguistic Circle, which formally instituted the movement in the "Theses" presented in Prague in 1929. The Prague School phonologists, notably Troubetskoy and Jakobson, demonstrated the concrete fruitfulness of looking at language from a Saussurean perspective and thus provided the paradigm for the rise of structuralism in the social sciences and the humanities. Lévi-Strauss then used the Saussurean method with great intellectual audacity in anthropology and thereby founded structuralism as a movement. By seeing kinship relations as a "language" susceptible to the kinds of analysis formerly applied to questions of phonology, Lévi-Strauss made it possible to extend the same structural-linguistic logic to all social, mental, and artistic phenomena and structures. Lévi-Strauss extended the idea of binarism as the organizing principle of phonemic systems to human culture in general. The constituent elements of myth, like those of language, only acquire meaning in relation to other elements such as myths, social practices, and cultural codes, comprehensible only on the basis of structuring oppositions. When Lévi-Strauss delivered his inaugural lecture in 1961 at the Collège de France, he situated his structural anthropology within the broad field of semiology. By searching for constants within a multitude of variations, and by banishing all resort to a conscious speaking subject, Lévi-Strauss laid the bases for structuralism.

In terms of film, the structural approach implied a move away from any evaluative criticism preoccupied with exalting the artistic status of the medium or of particular filmmakers or films. Auteur-structuralism in the late 1960s built on Lévi-Strauss's concept of myth to speak of genre and authorship. In terms of directors, semiology was less interested in the aesthetic ranking of directors than in how films in general are understood. Just as Lévi-Strauss was uninterested in the "authors" of Amazonian myths, so structuralism was not particularly interested in the artsmanship of individual auteurs. While auteurism valorized specific directors as artists, for semiology all filmmakers are artists and all films are art, simply because film's socially constructed status is that of art.

The Question of Film Language

The shift from the classical film theory of Kracauer and Bazin to film semiology mirrored larger changes in the history of thought in general. Film semiology also reflects changes in French cultural institutions: the expansion of higher education and the opening up of new departments and new forms of research; new publishing venues willing to publish trans-disciplinary books like Barthes's *Mythologies*; new institutions such as the École Pratique des Hautes Études (where Barthes, Metz, Genette, and Greimas all taught); and new journals such as *Communications*. Indeed, issue 4 of *Communications* in 1964 presented the structural linguistic model as the program of the future, with Barthes's essay "Elements of Semiology" providing a blueprint for a broad research project. Issue 8, two years later, on "structural analysis of the *recit*" (story), framed a narratological project that would be carried out over decades.

In the wake of the work of Lévi-Strauss a wide range of apparently non-linguistic domains came under the jurisdiction of structural linguistics. Indeed, the 1960s and 1970s might be seen as the height of semiotic "imperialism," when the discipline annexed vast territories of cultural phenomena for exploration. Since the object of semiotic research could be anything that could be construed as a system of signs organized according to cultural codes or signifying processes, semiotic analysis could easily be applied to areas previously considered either obviously non-linguistic – fashion and cuisine, for example – or traditionally deemed beneath the dignity of literary or cultural studies, such as comic strips, photo-romans, James Bond novels, and the commercial entertainment film.

The core of the filmolinguistic project was to define the status of film as a language. Filmolinguistics, whose origins Metz attributed to the convergence of linguistics and cinéphilia, explored such questions as: Is cinema a language system (*langue*) or merely an artistic language (*langage*)? (Metz's 1964 article "Cinéma: *langue* or *langage*?" was the founding essay within this current of inquiry.) Is it legitimate to use linguistics to study an "iconic" medium like film? If it is, is there any equivalent in the cinema to the linguistic sign? If there is a cinematic sign, is the relation between signifier and signified "motivated" or "arbitrary," like the linguistic sign? (For Saussure the relation between signifier and signified is "arbitrary," not only in the sense that individual signs exhibit no intrinsic link between signifier and signified, but also in the sense that each language, in order to make meaning, "arbitrarily" divides the continuum of both sound and sense.) What is the cinema's "matter of expression?" Is the cinematic sign, to use Peircian terminology, iconic, symbolic, or indexical, or some combination of the three? Does the cinema offer any equivalent to *langue*'s "double articulation" (i.e. that between phonemes as the minimal units of sound and morphemes as the minimal units of sense)? What are the analogies to Saussurean oppositions such as paradigm and syntagm? Is there a normative grammar for the cinema? What are the equivalents of "shifters" and other marks of enunciation? What is the equivalent of punctuation in the cinema? How do films produce meaning? How are films understood? In the background lurked a methodological issue. Rather than an essentialist, ontological approach – what *is* the cinema? – attention shifted to questions of discipline and method. Quite apart from the question of whether film was a language (or like a language), there was the much broader question of whether filmic systems could be illuminated through the methods of structural linguistics, or any other linguistics for that matter.

Metz exemplified a new kind of film theorist, one who came to the field already "armed" with the analytic instruments of a specific discipline, who was unapologetically academic and unconnected to the world of film criticism. Eschewing the traditional evaluative language of film criticism, Metz favored a technical vocabulary drawn from linguistics and narratology (diegesis, paradigm, syntagma).

With Metz we move from what Casseti (1999) calls the "onto-logical paradigm" *à la* Bazin to the "methodological paradigm." Although Metz clearly built on the antecedent work of the Russian Formalists, along with that of Marcel Martin (1955) and François Chevassu (1963) and especially Jean Mitry (1963, 1965), he brought a new degree of disciplinary rigor to the field.

Within a few years a number of important studies were published on the language of film, notably Metz's *Essais sur la signification au cinéma* (1968; translated as *Film Language* in 1974); Metz's *Langage et cinéma* (1971; translated as *Language and Cinema* in 1974); Pasolini's *Empirismo Eretico* (translated into French as *L'Experience heretique: langue et cinéma* in 1971 and into English as *Heretical Empiricism* in 1988); Eco's *La Struttura Assente* (The Absent Structure); Emilio Garroni's *Semiotica ed Estetica* (Semiotics and Aesthetics, 1968); Gianfranco Bettetini's *Cinema: Lingua e Scrittura* (The Language and Technique of Film, 1968); and Peter Wollen's *Signs and Meaning in the Cinema* (1969), all of which addressed on some level the issues raised by Metz. (The Italian work, as Giuliana Muscio and Roberto Zemignan point out, has generally been filtered though French channels.)[1]

Of these, Metz's *Film Language* was the most influential. Metz's chief purpose, as he himself defined it, was to "get to the bottom of the linguistic metaphor" by testing it against the most advanced concepts of contemporary linguistics. In the background of Metz's discussion was Saussure's founding methodological question regarding the "object" of linguistic study. Thus Metz looked for the counterpart, in film theory, to the conceptual role played by *langue* in the Saussurean schema. And much as Saussure concluded that the purpose of linguistic investigation was to disengage from the chaotic plurality of *parole* (speech) the abstract signifying system of a language, i.e. its key units and their rules of combination at a given point in time, so Metz concluded that the object of ciné-semiology was to disengage from the heterogeneity of meanings of the cinema its basic signifying procedures, its combinatory rules, in order to see to what extent these rules resembled the doubly articulated dia-critical systems of "natural languages."

For Metz, the cinema is the cinematic institution taken in its broadest sense as a multidimensional socio-cultural fact which includes pre-filmic events (the economic infrastructure, the studio system, technology), post-filmic events (distribution, exhibition, and the social or political impact of film), and a-filmic events (the decor of the theater, the social ritual of moviegoing). "Film," meanwhile, refers to a localizable discourse, a text; not the physical object contained in a can, but rather the signifying text. At the same time, Metz points out, the cinematic institution also enters into the multidimensionality of films themselves as bounded discourses concentrating an intense charge of social, cultural, and psychological meaning. Metz thus reintroduces the distinction between film and cinema *within* the category "film," now isolated as the specific and proper "object" of film semiology. In this sense, "the cinematic" represents not the industry but rather the totality of films. As a novel is to literature, or as a statue is to sculpture, Metz argues, so is film to cinema. The former refers to the individual film text, while the latter refers to an ideal ensemble, the totality of films and their traits. Within the filmic, then, one encounters the cinematic.

Thus Metz closes in on the object of semiotics: the study of discourses, of texts, rather than of the cinema in the broad institutional sense, an entity much too multifaceted to constitute the proper object of filmolinguistic science, just as *parole* was for Saussure an object too multiform to form the proper object of linguistic science. The question which oriented Metz's early work was whether the cinema was *langue* (language system) or *langage* (language). Metz begins by discarding the imprecise notion of "film language" that had predominated up to that time. It is in this context that Metz explores the comparison, familiar from the earliest days of film theory, between shot and word, and sequence and sentence. For Metz, important differences render such an analogy problematic:

1 Shots are infinite in number, unlike words (since the lexicon is in principle finite) but like statements, an infinity of which can be constructed on the basis of a limited number of words.
2 Shots are the creations of the filmmaker, unlike words (which

110

preexist in lexicons) but again like statements.

3   The shot provides an inordinate amount of information and semiotic wealth.

4   The shot is an actualized unit, unlike the word which is a purely virtual lexical unit to be used as the speaker wishes. The word "dog" can designate any type of dog, and can be pronounced with any accent or intonation, whereas a filmic shot of a dog tells us, at the very minimum, that we are seeing a certain kind of dog of a certain size and appearance, shot from a specific angle with a specific kind of lens. While it is true that filmmakers might "virtualize" the image of a dog through backlighting, soft-focus, or decontextualization, Metz's more general point is that the cinematic shot more closely resembles an utterance or a statement ("here is the backlit silhouetted image of what appears to be a large dog") than a word.

5   Shots, unlike words, do not gain meaning by paradigmatic contrast with other shots that might have occurred in the same place on the syntagmatic chain. In the cinema, shots form part of a paradigm so open as to be meaningless. (Signs, within the Saussurean schema, enter into two kinds of relationship: paradigmatic, having to do with choices from a virtual, "vertical" set of "comparable possibilities" – e.g. a set of pronouns in a sentence – and syntagmatic, having to do with horizontal, sequential arrangement into a signifying whole. Paradigmatic operations have to do with selecting, while syntagmatic operations have to do with combining in sequence.)

To these disanalogies between shots and words, Metz adds a further disanalogy concerning the medium in general: the cinema does not constitute a language widely available as a code. All speakers of English of a certain age have mastered the code of English – they are able to produce sentences – but the ability to produce filmic utterances depends on talent, training, and access. To speak a language, in other words, is simply to use it, while to "speak" cinematic language is always to a certain extent to invent it. One might argue, of course, that this asymmetry is itself historically determined; one can hypothesize a future society where all citizens will have access to the code of filmmaking. But in society as we know it, Metz's point must stand. There is, furthermore, a fundamental difference in the diachrony of natural as opposed to cinematic language. Cinematic language can be suddenly prodded in a new direction by innovatory aesthetic procedures (those introduced by a film such as *Citizen Kane*, for example) or those made possible by a new technology such as the zoom or the steadicam. Natural language, however, shows a more powerful inertia and is less open to individual initiative and creativity. The analogy is less between cinema and natural language than between cinema and other arts like painting or literature, which can also be suddenly inflected by the revolutionary aesthetic procedures of a Picasso or a Joyce.

Metz concluded that the cinema was not a language system but that it was a language. Although film texts cannot be conceived as generated by an underlying language system – since the cinema lacks the arbitrary sign, minimal units, and double articulation – they do nevertheless manifest a language-like systematicity. Although film language has no *a priori* lexicon or syntax, it is nevertheless a language. One might call "language," Metz argues, any unity defined in terms of its "matter of expression" – a Hjelmslevian term that designates the material in which signification manifests itself – or in terms of what Barthes in *Elements of Semiology* calls its "typical sign." Literary language, for example, is the set of messages whose matter of expression is writing; cinematic language is the set of messages whose matter of expression consists of five tracks or channels: moving photographic image, recorded phonetic sound, recorded noises, recorded musical sound, and writing (credits, intertitles, written materials in the shot). Cinema is a language, in sum, not only in a broadly metaphorical sense but also as a set of messages grounded in a given matter of expression, and as an artistic language, a discourse or signifying practice characterized by specific codifications and ordering procedures.

Much of the early debate centered around the question of minimal units and their articulation in the sense of André Martinet's notion of the "double articulation" of minimal units of sound (phonemes) and minimal units of sense (morphemes). In response to Metz's argument that film lacked double articulation, Pier Paolo Pasolini argued that cinema did form a "language of reality" with its own double articulation of "cinemes" (by analogy to phonemes) and "im-signs" (by analogy to morphemes). The minimal unit of cinematic language, for Pasolini, is formed by the diverse real-world signifying objects in the shot. The language of im-signs, for Pasolini, was extremely subjective and extremely objective at the same time. He postulated minimal units of film, i.e. cinemes, the objects depicted in a filmic shot, but which unlike phonemes were infinite in number. The cinema explores and reappropriates the signs of reality. Eco argued that objects cannot be elements of a second articulation since they already constitute meaningful elements.

Both Eco and Emilio Garroni criticized Pasolini's "semiotic naiveté" for confusing cultural artifact with natural reality. But a number of recent analysts have argued that Pasolini was far from naive; in fact he was actually in advance of his contemporaries. For Teresa de Lauretis Pasolini was not naive but rather prophetic, anticipating the role of cinema in "the production of social reality" (ibid., pp. 48–9). As Patrick Rumble and Bart Testa point out, Pasolini saw structuralism as only one interlocutor, along with Bakhtin, Medvedev, and others. For Giuliana Bruno, Pasolini is not the naive reflectionist portrayed by Eco; rather, he sees both reality and its filmic representation as discursive, contradictory. The relation between film and the world is one of translation. Reality is a "discourse of things" which film translates into a discourse of images, what Pasolini called "the written language of reality." Like Bakhtin and Voloshinov, Pasolini was more interested in *parole* than in *langue* (see Bruno, in Rumble and Testa, 1994).

Pasolini was also interested in the issue of the analogies and disanalogies between cinema and literature. Just as written reworked oral discourse, the cinema reworked the common patrimony of human gestures and actions. Pasolini favored a "cinema of poetry" over a "cinema of prose." The former evoked an imaginative, oneiric, subjective cinema of experimental form where author and character blend, while the latter evoked a cinema founded on classical conventions of spatiotemporal continuity. In *Empirismo Eretico* Pasolini also discussed his notions of "free, indirect discourse" in the cinema. In literature "le style indirect libre" referred to the managing of subjectivity in a writer like Flaubert, whereby mediated representation conveyed through pronouns like "Emma thought" modulated into a direct presentation "How wonderful to be in Spain!" In the cinema it referred to the stylistic contagion whereby authorial personality would blend ambiguously with that of the character, where a character's subjectivity would become the trampoline for stylistic virtuosity and experiment.

Umberto Eco, whose work on the cinema was part of his work on languaged articulations in general, rejected a double articulation for the cinema in favor of a triple articulation: first, iconic figures; second, iconic figures combined into semes; and third, semes combined in "kinemorphes." Garroni, meanwhile, argued that Metz had asked the wrong question; the right question concerned the constitutive heterogeneity of the filmic/artistic message. Bettetini preferred a double articulation based on the cinematic "sentence" on the one hand, and technical units (the frame, the shot) on the other. He spoke of the "iconeme" as the privileged unit of film language. In *L'Indice del Realismo* (The Index of Realism) he applied Peirce's trichotomy to the cinema as deploying all three dimensions of the sign: the indexical, the iconic, and the symbolic. Bettetini argued that the minimal signifying unit of film, the "cineme" or "iconeme," is the filmic image and this corresponds not to the word but to the sentence. Peter Wollen too, in *Signs and Meaning in the Cinema* (1969) found Saussurean notions of the sign overly rigid for a medium whose "aesthetic niches" derived from a computer and unstable deployment of all these type of signs.

Film became a discourse, Metz argued, by organizing itself as narrative and thus producing a body of signifying procedures. As Warren Buckland points out, it is as if the "arbitrary" relation of Saussure's signifier/signified was transferred to another register, i.e. not the arbitrariness of the single image but rather the arbitrariness of a plot, the sequential pattern imposed on raw events. Here we find an echo of the Sartrean idea that life does not tell stories. The true analogy between film and language, for Metz, consisted in their common syntagmatic nature. By moving from one image to two, film becomes language. Both language and film produce discourse through paradigmatic and syntagmatic operations. Language selects and combines phonemes and morphemes to form sentences; film selects and combines images and sounds to form "syntagmas," i.e. units of narrative autonomy in which elements interact semantically. While no image entirely resembles another image, most narrative films resemble one another in their principal syntagmatic figures, their orderings of spatial and temporal relations.

The Grand Syntagmatique was Metz's attempt to isolate the principal syntagmatic figures or the spatiotemporal orderings of narrative cinema. It was proposed as a response to the question "How does film constitute itself as narrrative discourse?" against the backdrop of the notorious imprecision of film terminology, much of which had been based on theater rather than on the specifically cinematic signifiers of image and sound, shots and montage. Terms like "scene" and "sequence" had been used more-or-less interchangeably, and were based on the most heterogenous criteria. The classification was at times based on a posited unity of depicted action ("the farewell scene") or of place ("the courtroom sequence") with little attention to the precise articulations of the filmic discourse, and ignoring the fact that the same action (e.g. a wedding scene) might be rendered by a diversity of syntagmatic approaches.

Metz used the paradigm/syntagma distinction, along with the larger binary either–or method – "a shot is continuous or it is not" – to construct his Grande Syntagmatique. The Grande Syntagmatique constitutes a typology of the diverse ways that time and space can be ordered through editing within the segments of a narrative film. Using a binary method of commutation (commutation tests have to do with discovering whether a change on the level of the signifier entails a change on the level of the signified), Metz generated a total of six types of syntagma (in the version published in *Communications* in 1966), subsequently increased to eight (in the version included in *Essais sur la signification au cinéma* in 1968 and also in *Film Language*). The eight syntagmas are as follows:

1 The *autonomous shot* (a syntagma consisting of one shot), in turn subdivided into (a) the *single-shot sequence*, and (b) four kinds of inserts: the *non-diegetic insert* (a single shot which presents objects exterior to the fictional world of the action); the *displaced diegetic insert* ("real" diegetic images but temporally or spatially out of context); the *subjective insert* (memories, fears); and the *explanatory insert* (single shots which clarify events for the spectator).

2 The *parallel syntagma*: two alternating motifs without clear spatial or temporal relationship, such as rich and poor, town and country.

3 The *bracket syntagma*: brief scenes given as typical examples of a certain order of reality but without temporal sequence, often organized around a "concept."

4 The *descriptive syntagma*: objects shown successively suggesting spatial coexistence; used, for example, to situate the action.

5 The *alternating syntagma*: narrative cross-cutting implying temporal simultaneity, such as a chase alternating pursuer and pursued.

6 The *scene*: spatiotemporal continuity perceived as being without flaws or breaks, in which the signified (the implied diegesis) is continuous as in the theatrical scene, but where the signifier is fragmented into diverse shots.

7 The *episodic sequence*: a symbolic summary of stages in an implied chronological development, usually entailing a compression of time.

8 The *ordinary sequence*: action treated elliptically so as to eliminate unimportant detail, with jumps in time and space masked by continuity editing.

This is not the place to inventory the innumerable theoretical problems with the Grande Syntagmatique (for a sustained critique see Stam et al., 1992). Suffice it to say that while some of Metz's syntagmas are conventional and well established – the alternating syntagma, for example, refers to what was traditionally called narrative cross-cutting – others are more innovative. The bracket syntagma, for example, provides typical samples of a given order of reality without linking them chronologically. The audiovisual logos which open television sitcoms (for example, the initial montage-segment showing the typical activities of a day in the life of Mary Richards on the *Mary Tyler Moore Show*) might be seen as bracket syntagmas. Similarly, the fragmented shots of two lovers in bed that open Godard's *A Married Woman* provide a typical sample of "contemporary adultery;" indeed, the sequence's lack of teleology and climax form part of a Brechtian strategy of de-eroticization, a "bracketing" of eroticism. Many of the films featuring significant numbers of bracket syntagmas can be characterized, not coincidentally, as Brechtian, precisely because the bracket syntagma is especially well-equipped for representing the socially "typical." Godard's Brechtian fable about war, *Les Carabiniers*, mobilizes bracket syntagmas as part of the film's systematic deconstruction from within of the dominant cinema's traditional approach to dramatic conflict. The bracket syntagma's emphasis on the typical – here the behavioral typicalities of war – is eminently suited to the social and generalizing intentions of politicized directors.

As a kind of illustration of his method Metz performed a syntagmatic breakdown of the film *Adieu Phillipine* into 83 autonomous segments. But given Metz's methodological restrictions, his syntagmatic analysis did not address many of the most interesting features of the film: its portrayal of the TV milieu; the chronotopic implications of the frequent TV monitors in the shot; the working-class attitudes and accents of the characters; the war in Algeria (in which the protagonist enlists); gender roles and flirtation in 1960s France. Once the linguistic analysis is finished, almost everything else remains to be said, whence the need for a Bakhtinian translinguistic analysis of the film as historically situated utterance. But Metz offered the Grande Syntagmatique in a more modest spirit than was often granted by his detractors, as a first step toward establishing the main types of image orderings. To the objection that "everything remains to be said" it might first be answered that it is in the nature of science to choose a principle of pertinence. To speak of the Grand Canyon in terms of geological strata, or of *Hamlet* in

terms of syntactic functions, hardly exhausts the interest or signification of experiencing the Grand Canyon or reading *Hamlet*, yet that
does not mean that geology and linguistics are useless. Second, the
work of addressing all levels of signification in a film is the task of
textual analysis, not film theory.

In *Language and Cinema* Metz redefined the Grande Syntagmatique as merely a subcode of editing within a historically delim-
ited body of films, i.e. the mainstream narrative tradition from the
consolidation of the sound film in the 1930s through the crisis of
the studio aesthetic and the emergence of the diverse New Waves
in the 1960s. Metz's schema, clearly the most sophisticated developed up to that point, was subsequently applied (in myriad textual
analyses) and was later reconfigured by Michel Colin from the
Chomskian perspective of transformational grammar (see Colin, in
Buckland, 1995). Film theory could still use a more sophisticated
approach to the questions raised by the Grande Syntagmatique, one
that would synthesize Metz's work with other currents: Bakhtin's
suggestive notion of the chronotope as "the intrinsic connectedness
of temporal and spatial relationships" in artistic texts; Noël Burch's
work on spatial and temporal articulations between shots; Bordwell's
work on classical cinema; and Genette's narratology insofar as it is
transposable to film.

Metz was subsequently criticized for surreptitiously privileging the
mainstream narrative film and marginalizing such forms as documentary and the avant-garde. A Bakhtinian translinguistic formulation
might have saved ciné-semiologists in the Saussurean tradition a
good deal of trouble by rejecting from the outset the very notion of
a unitary (cinematic) language. Anticipating contemporary sociolinguistics Bakhtin argued that all languages are characterized by the
dialectical interplay between centripetal pressures toward normativ-
ization (monoglossia) and centrifugal energies favoring dialectal
diversification (heteroglossia). This approach provides a valuable framework for seeing the classical dominant cinema as a kind of standard
language backed and "underwritten" by institutional power, and thus
exercising hegemony over a number of divergent "dialects" such as
the documentary, the militant film, and the avant-garde cinema. A

translinguistic approach would be more relativistic and pluralistic about these diverse filmic languages, privileging the peripheral and the marginal as opposed to the central and the dominant.

Cinematic Specificity Revisited

In their attempts to legitimate film as art, as we have seen, theorists made conflicting claims about the "essence" of film. The 1920s Impressionists like Epstein and Delluc had earlier embarked on a quasi-mystical search for the photogenic quintessence of film. For theorists such as Arnheim, meanwhile, the artistic essence of cinema was linked to its strictly visual nature, and thus to its "lacks" (the limiting frame, the lack of a third dimension, etc.) that marked it as art. Others, such as Kracauer and Bazin, rooted film's "vocation for realism" in its origins in photography. Film semiology, too, was concerned with this perennial issue. For Metz, the question "Is film a language?" was inseparable from the question "What is specific to the cinema?" The pertinent sensorial traits of film language help us distinguish the cinema from other artistic languages; in changing one of the traits, one changes the language. For example, film has a higher coefficient of iconicity than does a natural language like French or English (although one could argue that ideographic or hieroglyphic languages are highly iconic). Films are composed of multiple images, unlike photography and painting which (usually) produce single images. Films are kinetic, unlike newspaper cartoons which are static. Metz's approach, then, involved teasing out the specific signifying procedures of film language. Some of the specific materials of expression of the cinema are shared with other arts (but always in new configurations) and some are unique to itself. The cinema has its own material means of cinematic expression (camera, film, lights, tracks, sound studios), its own audiovisual procedures. This question of "materials of expression" also brings up the issue of evolving technologies. Is an IMAX spectacle, or a CD-ROM narrative, or video art still a film?

Metz's most thoroughgoing exercise in filmolinguistics was *Langage et cinéma*, first published in French in 1971 and translated (disastrously) into English in 1974.[1] Here Metz substituted the broad concept of "code," a concept thankfully free of specifically linguistic baggage, for both *langue* and *langage*. For Metz, the cinema is necessarily a "pluri-codic" medium, one which interweaves (1) "specifically cinematic codes," i.e. codes that appear only in the cinema, and (2) "non-specific codes," i.e. codes that are shared with languages other than the cinema. Cinematic language is the totality of cinematic codes and subcodes insofar as the differences separating these various codes are provisionally set aside in order to treat the whole as a unitary system.

Metz describes the configuration of specific and non-specific codes as a set of concentric circles, with a differential approach to cinematic specificity. The codes range from the very specific (the inner circle; for example, those linked to film's definition as deploying moving, multiple images – codes of camera movement, continuity editing, etc.), through codes which are shared with other arts (e.g. generally shared narrative codes), to codes which are widely disseminated in the culture and in no way dependent on the specific modalities of the medium or even on the arts in general (for example, the codes of gender roles). Rather than an absolute specificity or non-specificity, then, it is more accurate to speak of degrees of specificity. Examples of specifically cinematic codes are camera movement (or lack of it), lighting, and montage; they are attributes of all films in the sense that all films involve cameras, all films must be lit, and all films must be edited, even if the editing is minimal. The distinction between specifically cinematic and non-cinematic codes, obviously, is often a tenuous and shifting one. While the phenomenon of color belongs to all the arts, the particularities of 1950s technicolor belong specifically to film. Even non-specific elements, moreover, can be "cinematized" via filmic simultaneity, by their neighboring and coexisting with the other elements featured on other "tracks" at the same moment in the filmic–discursive chain.

Within each particular cinematic code, cinematic subcodes represent specific usages of the general code. Expressionist lighting, for example, is a subcode of lighting, as is naturalistic lighting. Eisensteinian montage is a subcode of editing, which can be contrasted in its typical usage with a Bazinian mise-en-scène that would minimize spatial and temporal fragmentation. According to Metz codes do not compete, but subcodes do. While all films must be lit and edited, not all films need to deploy Eisensteinian montage. Metz notes, however, that certain filmmakers such as Glauber Rocha at times mingle contradictory subcodes in a "feverish anthological procedure" by which Eisensteinian montage, Bazinian mise-en-scène, and cinema verité coexist in tension within the same sequence. The diverse subcodes can also be made to play against one another, for example by using Expressionist lighting in a musical, or a jazz score in a western. For Metz, the code is a logical calculus of possible permutations; the subcode is a specific and concrete use of these possibilities, which yet remains within a conventionalized system. There is a tension in *Language and Cinema* between an additive, taxonomic approach to codes, developed in the first half of the book, and a more activist "writerly" deployment of the codes, developed at the end of the book.

A history of the cinema, for Metz, would trace the play of competition, incorporations, and exclusions of the various subcodes. In his essay "Textual Analysis etc.," David Bordwell points out some of the problems with Metz's analysis, arguing that Metz's characterization of subcodes shows covert dependency on received ideas about film history and the "evolution of film language," ideas which provide the unstated grounding for the recognition of subcodes. Bordwell therefore calls for the historicization of the study of cinematic subcodes.[2] The invaluable historicization suggested by Bordwell is limited to the institutional and the art-historical; it does not include what Bakhtin would call the "deep-generating series" of both life and art, i.e. history in a larger sense as it impacts on film.

Metz inherited the question of *langue/langage* from Saussure and the question of cinematic specificity from the Russian Formalists, with their emphasis on literary specificity or *literaturnost*. Metz, in this sense, inherits the combined blindspots of Saussurean linguistics (which "brackets the referent" and thus severs text from history) and of aesthetic formalism (which sees only the autotelic, autonomous object of art). If Metz, like the Formalists, could be said to have brought great "sharpness and principle to the problem of specification," he was somewhat less adept, given these inherited blindspots, at linking the specific and the non-specific, the social and the cinematic, the textual and the contextual. In this sense the Bakhtin School critique of Formalism is pertinent to Metz's notions of the "specifically cinematic," and, as I suggest later (p. 188), to the "neo-Formalism" of Kristin Thompson and David Bordwell.

What is perhaps more promising in Metz's work is his attempt to distinguish film from other media in terms of its means of expression. Metz distinguishes between film and theater, for example, by the physical presence of the actor in the theater versus the deferred absence of the performer in the cinema, a "missed rendezvous" that paradoxically makes film spectators *more* likely to "believe" in the image. In subsequent work Metz stressed that it is precisely the "imaginary" nature of the filmic signifier that makes it so powerful a catalyst of projections and emotions (Marshall McLuhan implied something similar in his contrast between "hot" and "cool" media). Metz also compares film to television, concluding that despite technological differences (photographic versus electronic), differences in social status (cinema by now a consecrated medium, television still deplored as a wasteland), differences in reception (domestic small screen versus theatrical large screen, distracted versus concentrated attention), the two media constitute virtually the same language. They share important linguistic procedures (scale, sound off and on, credits, sound effects, camera movement, etc.). Thus they are two closely neighboring systems; the specific codes which also belong to the other are much more numerous and important than those which do not belong to it; and, inversely, those which separate them are much less numerous and important than those which separate them, in common, from other languages (Metz, 1974). Although one might argue with Metz's conclusions here (for example, one might say that technologies and reception conditions have evolved since the 1970s), what is important is the differential, diacritical method: constructing or discerning film's specificity by exploring the analogies and disanalogies between it and other media.

Interrogating Authorship and Genre

Linguistically oriented semiotics had the effect of displacing auteurism, since filmolinguistics had little interest in film as the expression of the creative will of individual auteurs. At the same time, auteurism had introduced a kind of system – one based on the constructing of an authorial personality out of surface clues and symptoms – which made it reconcilable with a certain kind of structuralism, resulting in a marriage of convenience called auteur-structuralism. Undermining the cult of personality endemic to both the *Cahiers* and the Sarris models, auteur-structuralism saw the individual author as the orchestrator of trans-individual codes (myth, iconography, locales). As Stephen Crofts points out, auteur-structuralism emerged out of a precise cultural formation in the late 1960s, that of the structuralist-influenced left in London, and specifically of the film-cultural work of the British Film Institute's Education Department. Auteur-structuralism was exemplified by Geoffrey Nowell-Smith's study *Visconti* (1967), Peter Wollen's *Signs and Meaning in the Cinema* (1969), and Jim Kitses' *Horizons West* (1969). The auteur-structuralists highlighted the idea of an auteur as a critical construct rather than a flesh-and-blood person. They looked for hidden structuring oppositions which subtended the thematic leitmotifs and recurrent stylistic figures typical of certain directors as the key to their deeper meaning. For Peter Wollen, the apparent diversity of John Ford's oeuvre, for example, hid fundamental structural patterns and contrasts based on culture/nature binaries: garden/wilderness; settler/nomad; civilized/savage; married/single. Auteur-structuralism had little to say on the issue of cinematic specificity, since many of these motifs and binary structures were not specific to the cinema but were, rather, broadly disseminated in culture and the arts.

The hyphen in auteur-structuralism was ultimately a stressful one. It proved difficult to reconcile the romantic individualism of auteurism (John Ford's Cheyennes) with the impersonal scientism of structuralism (Lévi-Strauss's Bororos). The powerful structuralist currents claiming that "language speaks the author" and "ideology speaks the subject" made it likely that large, impersonal "structures" would overwhelm the puny, individual "author." At the same time, structuralists and poststructuralists scorned auteurism for formulating the theory in such a way as to make the cinema the last outpost of a romanticism long discarded by other arts. The romantic view of art saw art as an expressive "lamp" rather than as a reflective "mirror" (to draw on Meyer Abrams's dichotomy), and the artist as *vates*, magus, seer, clairvoyant, and "unacknowledged legislator of mankind." Romanticism attributes artistry to a mysterious "elan" or "genius," a view which is ultimately magical, quasi-religious.

Auteur-structuralism can be seen as a transitional moment in the historical lap-dissolve that takes us from structuralism to poststructuralism, both of which relativized the notion of the author as the sole originating and creative source of the text, preferring to see the author as site rather than point of origin. In "The Death of the Author" (1968) Barthes reconfigured the author as a byproduct of writing. The author now became nothing more than the instance of writing, just as linguistically the subject/shifter "I" is nothing more than the instance of saying "I." A text's unity, for Barthes, derived not from its origin but from its destination. Barthes's midwifery, in effect, murdered the author in order to make possible the birth of the reader.

In "What is an Author?" (1969) Michel Foucault also spoke of the death of the author. Foucault traced the emergence of the author to the cultural context of the eighteenth century, an age which produced the "individualization" of the history of ideas. Foucault preferred to speak of the "author function," seeing authorship as an ephemeral time-bound institution which would soon give way to a future "pervasive anonymity of discourse." The film author, as a consequence of the poststructuralist attack on the originary subject, shifted from being the generating source of the text to merely a term in the process of reading and spectating, a space where discourses intersect, a shifting configuration produced by the intersection of a group of films with historically constituted ways of reading and viewing. The author, in this anti-humanist reading, dissolved into more abstract, theoretical instances such as "enunciation," "subjectification," "*écriture*," and "intertextuality." (Skeptics were quick to point out that the same poststructuralist writers who had decreed the author's death were themselves consecrated authors, even stars, and that they never forgot to collect their royalty checks.)

In this same period it was argued that a monolithic auteur theory could not account for all the diverse practices of cinema. Partisans of the avant-garde censured auteurism for its exclusive devotion to commercial cinema, leaving little room for experimental cinema (see Pam Cook, in Caughie, 1981). Auteurism faltered when confronted with the work of a Michael Snow or a Hollis Frampton, and broke down completely with political film collectives like Third World Newsreel or Grupo Cine de la Base. Indeed, leftist film activists who preferred more collective and egalitarian models were naturally suspicious of the hierarchical and authoritarian assumptions undergirding auteurism. Marxists criticized auteurism's ahistorical assumption that talent will eventually "out" no matter what political or economic conditions prevail. Third World critics also gave auteurism a mixed reception. Glauber Rocha wrote in 1963 that "if commercial cinema is the tradition, auteur cinema is the revolution," but Fernando Solanas and Octavio Gettino mocked auteur cinema (their "second cinema") as politically anodyne and easily co-optable, favoring instead a "Third Cinema" which was collective, militant, and activist. Feminist analysts, too, expressed ambivalence, on the one hand pointing out the patriarchal and oedipal substratum of such tropes as the "camera-pen" and the reviled "cinéma de papa," and on the other calling for the recognition of such female auteurs as Germaine Dulac, Ida Lupino, Dorothy Arzner, and Agnes Varda. As early as 1973 Claire Johnston argued that auteur theory marked an important intervention: "stripped of its normative aspects the classification of films by director has proved an extremely productive way of ordering our experience of the cinema" (Johnston, 1973).

The period of auteur-structuralism also saw a renewed interest in

125

genre analysis. Wollen's version of auteur-structuralism, for example, was partially dependent on notions of genre. His analysis of the structures operative in the John Ford corpus was inevitably linked to the fact that the bulk of the Ford oeuvre is made up of westerns, a genre itself dependent on the wildnerness/garden dichotomy. In the 1970s film analysts like Ed Buscombe, Jim Kitses, Will Wright, and Steve Neale brought the new methods to bear on the traditional area of genre theory. In "The Idea of Genre in American Cinema" Buscombe called for more attention to the iconographic elements of films. The visual conventions, for Buscombe, provide a framework or setting within which the story can be told. The "outer form" of a genre consists of visual elements – in the western wide-brimmed hats, guns, prostitutes' bodices, covered wagons, and so forth – while the "inner form" is the means by which these visual elements are employed. The director deploys the resources provided by iconography by recombining them in ways that reconcile familiarity with innovation. Buscombe illustrates the tensions between "inner" and "outer" by way of Peckinpah's *Ride the High Country*, where a camel is substituted for a horse: "A horse in a western is not just an animal but a symbol of dignity, grace, and power. These qualities are mocked by having it compete with a camel: and to add insult to injury, the camel wins" (Buscombe, in Grant, 1995, p. 22).

In *Horizons West* (1970) Jim Kitses used the wilderness–civilization opposition proposed by Henry Nash Smith in *Virgin Land* to analyze the western. Kitses set out a table of oppositions (individual–community; nature–culture; law–gun; sheep–cattle) which structured the western, and he also called attention to the presence of chivalric codes, frontier history, and the history of other non-cinematic representations of the frontier. Will Wright's *Sixguns and Society* drew on Vladimir Propp's work on "plot functions" and character types in folk tales. The oppositions set up in earlier westerns, Wright argued, transmute into very different configurations in later westerns. The myths relayed by genre help us read history and the world, crystallizing our fears and desires, tensions and utopias.

The word "genre" had been traditionally used in at least two senses: (1) an inclusive sense which sees all films as participating in genre;

and (2) a more restricted sense of the Hollywood "genre film," i.e. the less prestigious and lower-budget productions or B-films. Genre in the latter sense is a corollary of the industrialized mode of production of Hollywood (and its imitators), an instrument of simultaneous standardization and differentiation. Genre here has institutional force and density; it implies a generic division of labor, whereby studios specialized in specific genres (MGM and the musical, for example), while within each studio, each genre had not only its sound stages but also its daylaborers: scriptwriters, directors, costume designers.

Thomas Schatz's *Hollywood Genres* (1981), like earlier work by Wright and Kitses, is informed by Lévi-Strauss's structuralist readings of myth as resolving structural tensions. Deploying the structuralist method of binary oppositions, Schatz divides Hollywood genres into those that work to reestablish social order (westerns, detective films) and those that work to establish social integration (the musical, comedy, melodrama). Genre functions as "cultural ritual" to integrate a conflictual community through romance or through a character who mediates between rival factions.

Against the Frankfurt School view of film genres as merely a symptom of massified assembly-line production, theorists began to see genre as the crystallization of a negotiated encounter between filmmaker and audience, a way of reconciling the stability of an industry with the excitement of an evolving popular art. Steve Neale, for his part, argued that genres were "systems of orientations, expectations and conventions that circulate between industry, text, and subject." Drawing on the language of reception theory, Neale saw each new film as altering our "horizon of generic expectations." Rick Altman (1984) called for an approach which would be both "semantic" in its concern with narrative content, and "syntactic" in its focus on the structures into which narrative elements are inserted, with the caveat that many films can innovate by mixing the syntactics of one genre and the semantics of another. Thus the musical renews itself by incorporating melodrama. Altman thus hoped to avoid the problems associated with over-inclusive semantic definitions of a genre (for example, Durgnat's wildly exfoliating "family tree" of film noir) on the one hand, and the interpretative definitions (for example,

Schatz's order–integration dichotomy) on the other, proposing instead a dual and complementary approach which acknowledges that a film can align semantically with one trend and yet syntactically with another.

While some genres represent established categories of studio production (e.g. westerns, musicals) recognized by both producers and consumers, others are *ex post facto* designations constructed by critics. No producer in the 1940s set out to make a film noir. The term itself was coined retrospectively by French film critics on the analogy of the *serie noire*. By the time of *Body Heat*, however, after the genre had been popularly consecrated, Lawrence Kasdan could consciously strive for a "noir effect" in his remake of *Double Indemnity*.

Genre analysis is plagued by a number of problems. First, there is the question of *extension*. Some generic labels, such as comedy, are too broad to be useful, whereas others, say "biopics about Sigmund Freud" or "disaster films concerning earthquakes," are too narrow. Second, there is the danger of *normativism*, of having a preconceived *a priori* idea of what a genre film *should* do, rather than seeing genre merely as a trampoline for creativity and innovation. Third, genre is sometimes imagined to be *monolithic*, as if films belonged only to one genre. The "law of genre" presumably forbids miscegenation between genres, yet even classical Hollywood films hybridized diverse generic strands, if only for commercial reasons (see Bordwell et al., 1985, pp. 16–17). The Bombay musical, similarly, characteristically mixes the strong emotion of melodrama with the song and dance of musical, along with any other sensational elements that can entertain the spectator.[1] Thomas Elsaesser notes that melodramatic situations have been historically embedded in different forms, in Britain in the novel, in France in the costume drama, and so forth (Elsaesser, 1973, p. 3).[2]

Fourth, genre criticism is often plagued by *biologism*. The etymological roots of the word "genre" in tropes of biology and birth, James Naremore suggests, promote a kind of essentialism (Naremore, 1998b, p. 6). Thomas Schatz argues that genres have a life cycle, moving from birth to maturity to parodic decline, but in fact we

128

find parody at the very beginning of art forms (for example, Richardson's *Pamela* and Fielding's *Shamela* in the novel, or Griffith's *Intolerance* and Keaton's *The Three Ages* in film). Genres, furthermore, are permanently available for reconfiguration, as in the perennial flowerings of carnivalesque irreverence going at least as far back as the Middle Ages. Much genre criticism suffers from *Hollywoodcentrism*, a provinciality which leads analysts to restrict their attention to the Hollywood musical, for example, while eliding the Brazilian *chanchada*, the (Bollywood) Bombay musical, the Mexican *cabaretera* film, the Argentinian tango film, and the Egyptian musicals with Leila Mourad.

Genres can also be *submerged*, as when a film appears on the surface to belong to one genre yet on a deeper level belongs to another, as when analysts argue that *Taxi Driver* is "really" a western, or that *Nashville* is ultimately a reflexive film about Hollywood. At times analysts make *genre mistakes*, mistakenly applying standards appropriate to one genre to another, as when some critics found *Dr Strangelove* cynical because it had no admirable characters, when in fact the lack of admirable characters is a constitutive feature of satire.[3] Genre mistakes also occur when carnivalesque films are criticized for not offering positive images when in fact "grotesque realism" is simply part of an alternative protocol of representation. There is also the danger of *acinematic* analysis, a failure to take into account the filmic signifier and specifically cinematic codes: the role of lighting in film noir, of color in musicals, camera movement in the western, and so forth.

At its best, genre criticism can be an exploratory cognitive instrument: What do we learn if we regard *Taxi Driver* as a western, or *Spartacus* as an allegory of the Civil Rights struggle? What features of these texts become visible through such a strategy? Politically repressive circumstances can lead to the submerging of genre, as when political allegories like dos Santos's *A Very Crazy Asylum* or Forman's *Fireman's Ball* hide their serious intentions behind a facade of farce. The most useful way of using genre, perhaps, is to see it as a set of discursive resources, a trampoline for creativity, by which a given director can gentrify a "low" genre, vulgarize a "noble" genre, inject new energy into an exhausted genre, pour new progressive content into a conservative genre, or parody a genre that deserves ridicule. Thus we move from static taxonomy to active, transformative operations.

1968 and the Leftist Turn

Alongside relatively apolitical currents such as auteur and genre theory, we also find more radical, even revolutionary, strains of theory. In the late 1960s the First World, like the Third World earlier, witnessed a period of cultural and political effervescence, a culmination of the revolutionary ferment that followed the defeat of Nazism in World War II and the postwar dissolution of the colonial empires. The film theory of the 1960s built on the earlier achievements of leftist theorizing (Eisenstein, Vertov, Pudovkin, Brecht, Benjamin, Kracauer, Adorno, Horkheimer) and indeed often revisited many earlier debates: the Eisenstein–Vertov debate about experimentalism in film, the Brecht–Lukács debate about realism, the Benjamin–Adorno debate about the ideological role of the mass media.

In May of 1968, the *annus mirabilis*, a student-led insurrection almost toppled the Gaullist regime in France. In the background of these conflicts was the crisis of western Marxism triggered by two events in 1956: the Soviet Communist Party's acknowledgment of Stalin's crimes and the crushing of the Hungarian uprising. In general, 1968 was the product not of the "Old Left," i.e. the Stalinist bureaucratic left of the orthodox communist parties, but of the "New Left," i.e. the anti-authoritarian, anti-"revisionist" left which found communist parties strangely passive and complicitous with the bourgeoisie. Spurred on not by poverty but by abundance, the revolt failed partly because of the refusal of the French Communist Party to support it. The year 1968 marked the beginning of the end of the cold war, in which the two superpowers (the USA and the USSR) had been locked in the fatal embrace of MAD (mutually assured destruction) so brilliantly spoofed in Kubrick's *Dr Strangelove*.

Anti-authoritarian, socialistic, egalitarian, and anti-bureaucratic, the New Left also moved away from the old emphasis on class exploitation and integrated the insights of psychoanalysis, feminism, and anti-colonialism into a broad critique of social alienation.

In 1968 the "political" was diasporized, spreading out into theory and everyday life. May 1968 was preceded by Godard's prophetic film *La Chinoise* (1967) about a Maoist cell in Paris, and by Guy Debord's prescient manifesto-book *Society of the Spectacle* (also 1967) in which the leader of the Situationist International argued in an aphoristic style that life in modern society "displays itself as an immense accumulation of spectacles." For Debord, both the state capitalism of the socialist bloc and the market capitalism of the West alienated workers through the ghastly unity of a passively consumed "spectacle." (Debord later turned the book into a compilation film which superimposed Marxist commentary over found film materials.) The Situationists also challenged the art-system itself, calling not for a "critique of revolutionary art" but rather for "a revolutionary critique of all art."[1]

The events of May 1968 had echoes in the world of the arts generally and in film specifically. The insurrection was preceded and foreshadowed by "L'affaire Langlois," the attempt by the French left (including filmmakers Truffaut, Godard, and Rivette, along with Roland Barthes) to reinstate Henri Langlois, fired by Culture Minister André Malraux, as director of the French Cinémateque, culminating in Godard and Truffaut literally "closing the curtain" on the 1968 Cannes Film Festival. In France, 1968 also brought the utopian proposals of the "États Generaux du Cinéma" (an allusion to the French Revolution and the "Estates General" of 1789, the same metaphor at the root of the Third World trope). Divided into various projects, the States General called for a radical break with the existing system. Among its proposals were the abolition of the CNC (National Center of Cinematography), the development of new screening sites (factories, farms), the abolition of censorship, publicly financed screenings of films, and universal initiation into the trade-secrets of filmmaking. The manifesto "Le Cinéma s'insurge" (The Cinema Rebels) reminds its readers that cinema belongs to the

131

people and that it should be produced and disseminated by its workers (see Harvey, 1978).

The phrase "May '68" often serves as a kind of shorthand for a much larger phenomenon extending over almost two decades of insurgent thought and practice in many different countries. The events in France, while the most spectacular, actually followed events elsewhere. Students and intellectuals in Berkeley and Berlin, Rio de Janeiro and Tokyo, Bangkok and Mexico City, all participated in a global revolt against capitalism, colonialism, and imperialism, as well as against authoritarian forms of communism. It was a global phenomenon partly because it was the first insurrection where the media served to amplify social movements. Some of the slogans of the time give a sense of the surrealist-tinged flavor of the period: "Power to the imagination"; "Be realistic: demand the impossible"; "It is forbidden to forbid"; "Chase the cop from your head"; "We are all German Jews"; "Open the doors of the prisons, the asylums, and the high schools"; "Don't trust anyone over thirty"; "Tune in, turn on, and drop out"; "Make love not war"; "Two, three, many Vietnams"; "Women hold up half the sky." There was no single, unified 1968: the movement was Marxist–Leninist in Western Europe, anti-Stalinist in Eastern Europe, Maoist in China, counter-cultural in North America, anti-imperialist in the Third World. Often the movement combined the embrace of the American lifestyle and the repudiation of American foreign policy, whence Godard's formula (in *Masculine, Feminine*) the "children of Marx and Coca-Cola."

In terms of film, the 1960s and early 1970s proliferated in movements of renovation. In the wake of neo-realism and the New Wave we find: Tercer Cine in Argentina, Cinema Novo in Brazil, Nueva Ola in Mexico, Neues Deutsches Kino in Germany, Giovane Cinema in Italy, New American Cinema in the United States, and New Indian Cinema in India. The period was also marked by the proliferation of Marxist and left-leaning film journals such as *Positif, Cinétique, Cinémaction,* and (the newly leftish) *Cahiers du cinéma* in France; *Screen* and *Framework* in England; *Cine-Tracts* and later *Cine-Action* in Canada; *Jump Cut* and *Cineaste* in the United States;

132

Ombre Rossi and *Filmcritica* in Italy; *Hablemos de Cine* in Peru; and *Cine Cubano* in Cuba. Marxist-inflected film theory asked such questions as the following: What are the social determinants of the film industry? What is the ideological role of the cinema as an institution? Is there a Marxist aesthetic? What is the role of social class in the production and reception of films? What style and narrative structures should filmmakers adopt, and what strategies should critics deploy to analyze film politically? How can films advance social struggles for justice and equality?

Common to the various currents of inquiry was the idea that the cinema formed a quasi-autonomous realm of political struggle; it did not merely "reflect" struggles elsewhere. If Walter Benjamin had spoken of the fascist "aestheticization of politics," (May 68) film culture moved in the reverse direction: the politicization of aesthetics.

A key term in these leftist film debates was "ideology," a word encrusted with meanings accumulated over centuries. Raymond Williams suggests in *Keywords* (1985, pp. 152–7) that the term can be understood in three senses: (1) a system of beliefs characteristic of a particular class or group; (2) a system of illusory beliefs – false ideas or false consciousness – which can be contrasted with true or scientific knowledge; and (3) the general process of meanings and ideas. The concept of "bourgeois ideology," for Marxists, was a way of explaining how capitalist social relations are reproduced by people in ways *not* involving force or coercion. How does the individual subject internalize social norms? As defined by Lenin, Althusser, and Gramsci, bourgeois ideology is that ideology generated by class society through which the dominant class comes to provide the general conceptual framework for a society's members, thus furthering the economic and political interests of that class. "Ideology" and "hegemony" were answers to a perplexing question: why did oppressed workers (for example in Weimar Germany, postwar France, or the contemporary United States) not join a socialist revolution transparently in their own interest? Why did they misrecognize themselves as free agents, misconstruing their subjection as "freedom?" Why did they cling to a capitalist system which so clearly abused them?

Althusser's structuralist rereading of Marxist theory challenged the humanist "Hegelian" understanding of Marx's work inspired by the rediscovery of Marx's early writings. To Lacan's "return to Freud" corresponded Althusser's "return to Marx"; each in his respective realm developed a complex response to a symbolic father and a founding text. In Althusser's formulation, ideology was "a system (possessing its own logic and rigor) of representation (images, myths, ideas or concepts as the case may be) existing and having a historical role within a given society." As Althusser expressed it in a widely quoted definition, ideology was "a representation of the imaginary relation of individuals to the real conditions of their existence." Using surprisingly "natural" and biological metaphors for an adherent of "denaturalization," ideology is for Althusser an "organic part" of the social totality, something "secreted" by human societies "as the very element and atmosphere indispensable to their historical reproduction and life" (ibid., p. 232).

Ideology operates through what Althusser calls "interpellation." Originally derived from French legislative procedure, the term "interpellation" evokes the social structures and practices which "hail" individuals, endowing them with a social identity and constituting them as subjects who unthinkingly accept their role within the system of production relations. The novelty of Althusser's approach, then, was to see ideology not as a form of false consciousness deriving from the partial and distorted perspectives generated by distinct class positions, but rather, as Richard Allen (1989) puts it, as an "objective feature of the social order which structures experience itself."

In the 1970s key Althusserian terms like "overdetermination," "structure in dominance," "problematic," "theoretical practice," "interpellation," and "structuring absences" came to circulate widely within film-theoretical discourse. Althusser's notion of "symptomatic reading" became especially influential in film theory and analysis. Symptomatic reading brought together diverse strands of the "hermeneutics of suspicion"; Marx's critical readings of bourgeois economists like Adam Smith; Freud's symptomatic readings of his patients' discourse; and the Brechtian notion of distanciation, this time applied not to the stagings of theater but to the readings of texts. In *Reading Capital*, where Althusser and Balibar read Marx reading Adam Smith, Althusser characterizes Marx's method of reading Smith as "symptomatic," in that "it divulges the undivulged event in the text it reads, and in the same movement relates it to a *different text*, present as a necessary absence in the first" (Althusser and Balibar, 1979, p. 28). Thus symptomatic reading involves reading the text not for its essence nor its depth, but rather for its breaking-points, its lapses and silences, its "structuring absences" and "constitutive lacks." (Pierre Macheray developed the notion of symptomatic reading in literature in his *A Theory of Literary Production*, 1978.)

Also influential was Althusser's theory of the Ideological State Apparatuses, affectionately dubbed "ISAs" in leftist circles. Building on Gramsci's concept of hegemony, Althusser divides the superstructure into two "instances," the political–legal (Law and the State) and ideology. The first, the repressive state apparatus, includes the government, the army, the police, the courts, and the prisons, while the ideological state apparatuses include churches, schools, the family, political parties, the cinema, television, and other cultural institutions. (This kind of analysis was especially appropriate to France, with its centralized state-dominated bureaucratic structure.) Althusser's characterization of theory as "theoretical practice" provided a rationale for theory as a form of activism, and at times an alibi for avoiding more risky and consequential forms of politics. (While Althusser was the fundamental reference for *Screen* theory, Gramsci, as we shall see subsequently, was the key reference for what came to be known as cultural studies.)

For Althusser, free natural-born "individuals" are actually culturally produced "subjects." Indeed, the "free" self is an imaginary construct, whose mood swings and *elan* hide, as it were, the dull weight of social domination. Freedom is imaginary in Lacan's sense of the mirror stage, where the child misrecognizes itself as unified subject. For Althusser, social subjects misrecognize their own free individuality when in fact they are "positioned" within dominant social relations, where rich corporations dominate workers, where men domi-

135

nate women, and so forth. Ideology naturalizes social inequalities and relations of domination, passing them off as natural and immutable.

Linking Althusser's idea that the primary function of ideology is to reproduce subjects acquiescent in the values necessary for maintaining an oppressive social order, with Lacan's ideas about subject construction, film theorists like Stephen Heath, Colin MacCabe, and Jean-Louis Comolli emphasized the ways in which the cinema positioned subjects in ways congenial to the capitalist system. Locked into a structure of misrecognition, spectators accept the identity assigned them and are thus fixed in a position where a particular mode of perception and consciousness appears natural. Both the cinematic apparatus and specific film devices (the perspectival image, point-of-view editing) serve to "subject" the spectator.

If Arnheim saw the camera's intrinsic realism as an *aesthetic* defect, the Althusserian theorists saw it as a kind of congenital *ideological* defect. And if Bazin and Kracauer exalted filmic realism as a catalyst for democratic participation, the Althusserians saw it as an authoritarian instrument of subjugation. It was precisely the camera's intrinsic conveyance of realism, they argued, that made it complicit with bourgeois ideology. Far from facilitating democratic access to the ambiguous field of the image, the apparatus (and its corollary the realist style) merely sutured the spectator into the *doxa* of bourgeois common sense.

A group of writers associated with two avant-garde journals – *Tel Quel* and *Cinétique* – and partly inspired by the work of art historian Pierre Francastel, argued that the cinematic apparatus incorporated the code of Renaissance perspective, a system of representation installed at a certain moment of history by a specific mercantile class. Bourgeois ideology, in this reading, inhered in the apparatus itself. The camera merely consecrated conventions of pictorial representation inherited from Renaissance humanism. The painters of the quattrocento, observing that the perceived size of objects in nature varies proportionally with the square of the distance from the eye, simply incorporated this law, which characterizes the retina, into their paintings. The resultant impression of depth planted the seeds of illusionism in painting, ultimately leading to impressive *trompe-l'oeil* effects. The camera merely incorporates this *perspectiva artificialis* into its reproductive apparatus and thus inscribes the "centered space" of the "transcendental subject" posited by Renaissance perspective. And while painters could violate the code of perspective, filmmakers could not, because that code is built into the very instrument with which they work. Even the distorted perspectives of fish-eye or telephoto lenses remain perspectival; they are distorted only in relation to normal perspective. Rather than simply recording reality, these theorists argued, the camera conveyed the world already filtered through a bourgeois ideology which makes the individual subject the focus and origin of meaning, thus giving the all-seeing spectator the illusion of being omniscient and omnipresent. The delusions of grandeur of the spectator mirrored those of the "free" subject of bourgeois society. The code of perspective, furthermore, produced the illusion of its own absence; it "innocently" denied its status as representation and passed off the image as if it were actually the world. In a morbid, dystopian reversal of Bazin's utopia of "total cinema," the cinema became the site of "total alienation," the latest stage in the realization of a primordial desire to recreate the scene of a politically alienated Unconscious.

Narrative editing conventions, meanwhile, collapsed diverse subjectivities into a singular subject through a process of "suture." This term originally referred to the surgical procedure of stitching a wound, but for Lacanians such as Jacques-Alain Miller it evoked the relation between the subject and his or her discourse, the illusory closing of the gap between imaginary and symbolic. "Imaginary" has to do with the privileged (dual) relation with the mother, while the "symbolic," for Lacan, has to do with the realm of language and the symbolic, associated with the father. The concept was first worked out for film by Jean-Pierre Oudart, for whom the function of suture was to hide the fragmentation inherent in montage and thus conjure away the threat of the cut (evoking castration) and bind the spectator into the filmic discourse. Oudart argues that films in the dominant style prod the spectator to mentally construct a unified, holistic space of fiction, one which masks a field of absence. He gives the shot/counter structure as an example. By adopting the subject position first of one interlocutor and then of the other, the spectator becomes both the subject and the object of the look, thus enjoying an illusory sense of wholeness. Point-of-view editing thus constantly opens up holes and stitches them together, creating a see-saw oscillation in the spectator, a movement between loss and compensatory plenitude. While Oudart's work allowed for a reflexive self-questioning of suture, Daniel Dayan emphasized the one-way ideological effectivity of this system, which rendered the workings of a film's codes invisible.[2] Suture theory was subsequently criticized as overly generalized and imprecise. William Rothman rejected the theory of suture as overly monolithic in relation to the classical film, which actually depended on a three-shot sequence: character seeing–object seen–character seeing.[3] Kaja Silverman, following on from Heath's "Narrative Space" essay, looked not at the shot–reverse shot procedure but rather at the larger suturing role of narrative as a whole in positioning the spectator. *Psycho*, for example, orchestrates point-of-view editing in such a way that the spectator is positioned ambivalently, both as victim and as sadistic voyeur.

Suture theory has been shot at from many directions and vantage points, rather like the target of a firing squad whose members do not even know each other. Analytic theory (Carroll, 1988; Allen, 1995; Smith, 1995) focuses on faulty reasoning and conceptualization within the theory. Cognitivists (Bordwell, 1985) point to the neglect of preconscious and conscious engagements with narrative. Narratologists point to other determinants of identification. Aestheticians (Bordwell, 1985) note the reductionist account of very different film styles. Lacanians complain that the theory misconstrues Lacan. And feminists (Penley, 1989) point to the patriarchal substratum of the kind of spectatorship posited by the theory.

The closed-in, suffocatingly determinist nature of the left-Althusserian view of the cinema inevitably provoked a backlash. In retrospect some of the Marxist theory of the 1960s and 1970s does seem somewhat hyperbolic, even hysterical, in its denunciations of the "ideological state apparatuses" and of "dominant cinema." Instead of the moral panics fostered by right-wing critics, the left-wing critics of the 1960s fostered a kind of ideological panic. The theory scapegoated a single medium for widespread social alienation, failing to see the cinema as part of a larger discursive continuum, within which most institutions played contradictory and politically ambivalent roles. An ahistorical, naively realist epistemology, which virtually equated perception itself with ideology, led in the work of some theorists to a totalizing condemnation of the apparatus as an all-powerful "influencing machine" against which all resistance was vain. (The despair of subverting the apparatus also paralleled a certain political pessimism in the wake of the defeat of the French left after 1968.) A monolithic conception of dominant ideology and dominant cinema viewed the apparatus undialectically, as if it were exempt from contradiction. The theory also allowed for little difference between texts. Was it reasonable to think that all films, in all circumstances, wielded exactly the same morbid determinism? Was there ultimately no difference in the effects of a misogynistic snuff film and *Thelma and Louise*, or between *Top Gun* and *Bulworth*? Structuralist Marxism, by privileging the formal aspects of ideological representations, seen as expressive of a general system or structure, lent itself to an ahistorical conception of the cinema. The historically dated code of perspective became itself a transcendental essence rendering the cinema forever permeable to metaphysics. The quasi-idealist positing of a transhistorical wish inherent in the psyche, and the monolithic model of the cinema, failed to allow for modifying the apparatus, "aberrant readings," or filmic texts which might alert the spectator to these very processes.

Apparatus theory at times imbued the cinematic machine with an abstract and malevolent intentionality, falling into a kind of neo-Platonic condemnation of emotional manipulation. But real-life spectators were never the pathetically deluded, shackled captives of a high-tech version of Plato's cave decreed by apparatus theorists.

There were, moreover, alternative explanations for the failure of the oppressed to overturn the capitalist system. The actual distribution of power in capitalist societies, the improbability of socialist revolution, the hope to be a "winner" in the capitalist lottery, the excesses of left sectarianism, might also explain the failure of anticapitalist revolution, perhaps much better than any abstruse theory about subject construction. Noël Carroll in *Mystifying Movies* argued that the concept of subject positioning was superfluous for political–ideological analysis, since the subject's subordination to the reigning social order was better explained by what Marx called the "dull compulsion of economic relations" than by any hypothesis concerning subject construction.

The Classic Realist Text

The apparatus debate also had an aesthetic–stylistic corollary. In the Althusserian view, the dominant style of dramatic realism inevitably expresses only the ideology implicit in conventional bourgeois notions of reality. Realism cannot challenge the received wisdom of the public, since spectators see nothing but their own flickering ideologies in the naturalistic images on the screen. Jean-Paul Fargier saw the impression of reality as a constitutive part of the ideology produced by the cinematic apparatus: "[The screen] opens like a window, it is transparent. This illusion is the very substance of the specific ideology secreted by the cinema" (Fargier, in *Screen Reader*, 1977). Comolli and Narboni (1969) argued from within an Althusserian framework that "what the camera registers in fact is the vague, unformulated, untheorized, unthought-out world of the dominant ideology . . . reproducing things not as they really are but as they appear when refracted through the ideology. This includes every stage in the process of production: subject, 'styles,' forms, meanings, narrative traditions; all underline the general, ideological discourse" (Comolli and Narboni in *Screen Reader*, 1977).

At the same time, some of these theorists were eager to leave a loophole for commercial, mainstream cinema and especially for beloved auteurs like John Ford. In an extremely influential 1969 *Cahiers* editorial, "Cinema/Ideology/Criticism," Jean-Louis Comolli and Jean Narboni (1969) provided a schema whereby mainstream cinema was simultaneously crisscrossed by dominant and subversive

140

currents, readable in formal gaps, cracks, and fissures which offered an escape from ideology. The schema posited an ideological spectrum of films, ranging from those completely complicitous with prevailing norms ("blindly faithful and blind to their own fidelity") to superficially political films which do not challenge formal conventions, to those which "point out the gap produced between film and ideology by showing how the films work." While some films constituted a frontal assault on the system, others performed a sly subversion. The typology's "category e" embraced films which at first sight seem to be under the sway of the dominant ideology but which also throw it off course, where filmic disjunctions expose the strains and limits of the official ideology, and where an oblique, symptomatic reading can reveal, underneath an apparent formal coherence, ideological cracks and faultlines. The Comolli–Narboni schema generated a host of somewhat derivative and predictable "gaps and fissures" analyses, but it at least had the virtue of opening up films to the notion of contradiction. (Interestingly, the cultural studies of the 1980s displaced contradiction from the text to the spectator, as in Stuart Hall's later analysis of "dominant," "negotiated," and "resistant" readings of the mass media.)

A corollary of the above debate had to do with the issue of realism, a term already covered, as suggested earlier, with complex encrustations from antecedent debates, notably that which had opposed two Marxist aestheticians: Bertolt Brecht and Georg Lukács. In relation to literature, "realism" designates a fictional world characterized by internal coherence, plausible causality, and psychological plausibility. Traditional realism, based on a unified and coherent narrative, was seen as obscuring contradictions and projecting an illusory "mythic" unity. The modernist text, in contrast, foregrounded contradiction and allowed the silenced to speak.

In relation to cinema, the issue of "realism" has always been present, whether posited as *aesthetic* ideal or as an object of opprobrium. The very names of many aesthetic movements in film ring the changes on the theme: The "*sur*realism" of Buñuel and Dali, the "poetic realism" of Carné/Prevert, the "neo-realism" of Rossellini and de Sica, the "subjective realism" of Antonioni. Several broad

141

tendencies coexist within the spectrum of definitions of cinematic realism. The most conventional definitions of realism make claims about verisimilitude, the putative adequation of a fiction to the facticity of the world. These definitions assume that realism is not only possible (and empirically verifiable) but also desirable. Other definitions stress the differential aspirations of an author or school to forge a *relatively* more truthful representation, seen as a corrective to the falsity of antecedent cinematic styles or protocols of representation. This corrective can be stylistic – as in the French New Wave assault on the preciousness of the "tradition of quality" – or social – Italian neo-realism aiming to show postwar Italy its true face – or both at once – Brazilian Cinema Novo revolutionizing both the social thematics and the cinematic protocols of antecedent Brazilian cinema.

Still other definitions acknowledge the conventionality of realism, seeing realism as having to do with a text's degree of conformity to widely disseminated cultural models of "believable stories" and "coherent characters." Plausibility also correlates with *generic* codes. The crusty conservative father who resists his show-crazed daughter's entrance into show-business can "realistically" be expected, in a backstage musical, to applaud her on-stage apotheosis at the end of the film, no matter how statistically infrequent such a denouement might be in real life. Psychoanalytically inclined definitions of realism, meanwhile, invoke a realism of subjective response, rooted less in mimetic accuracy than in spectatorial credence. A purely formalist definition of realism, finally, emphasizes the conventional nature of all fictions, positing realism simply as a constellation of stylistic conventions that, at a given moment in the history of an art, manage, through the fine-tuning of illusionistic technique, to crystallize a strong *feeling* of authenticity. Realism, it is important to add, is both culturally relative – for Salman Rushdie, the self-flaunting irreality of Bollywood (Bombay) musicals makes Hollywood musicals look like Italian neo-realism – and somewhat arbitrary. Generations of filmgoers, for example, found black-and-white more "realistic" than color film, even though reality itself came in color. It is also possible to speak not of realism but rather of mimesis (imitation) in a broader sense: the ways that texts imitate other texts, the ways that performers mimic the behavior of prototypes, the ways that spectators mimic the behavior of characters or performers, or the way a film style can analogize its subject or historical period.

The term "realism" also evokes the debates about "classical cinema" and the "classic realist text." These terms denote a set of formal parameters involving practices of editing, camerawork, and sound which promote the appearance of spatial and temporal continuity. This continuity was achieved, in the classical Hollywood film, by an etiquette for introducing new scenes (a choreographed progression from establishing shot to medium shot to close shot); conventional devices for evoking the passage of time (dissolves, iris effects); editing techniques to smooth over the transition from shot to shot (the 30 degree rule, position matches, direction matches, movement matches, inserts to cover up unavoidable discontinuities); and devices for implying subjectivity (interior monologue, subjective shots, eyeline matches, empathetic music).

The classical realist film was "transparent" in that it attempted to efface all traces of the "work of the film," making it pass for natural. The classical realist film also drew on what Roland Barthes (in *S/Z*) called "reality effects," i.e. the artistic orchestration of apparently inessential details as guarantors of authenticity. The representational accuracy of the details was less important than their role in creating an optical illusion of truth. By effacing the signs of production, dominant cinema persuaded spectators to take what were really nothing but constructed effects as transparent renderings of the real.

By combining the codes of visual perception introduced in the Renaissance – monocular perspective, vanishing points, impressions of depth, accurate scale – with the codes of narration dominant in nineteenth-century literature, the classical fiction film acquired the emotional power and diegetic prestige of the realistic novel, whose social function and aesthetic regime it prolonged. It was within this perspective that Colin MacCabe, in "Realism and the Cinema: Notes on some Brechtian Themes" (in MacCabe, 1985), starting from his study of George Eliot's *Middlemarch*, offered an immanent analysis of realism as a discursive system, a set of strategies with textual

143

effects. MacCabe's notion of the classic realist text embraced both the novel and the fiction film, definable as a text in which a clear hierarchy regulates and adjudicates between the discourses composing the text, and where this hierarchy is defined in terms of an empirical notion of truth. Dominant cinema inherited from the nineteenth-century novel a precise kind of textual structuration which positioned the reader/spectator as a "subject who is supposed to Know." The alternative is to fracture and disperse this Knowing subject. The classic text, whether literary or filmic, was reactionary not because of any mimetic "inaccuracies" but rather because of its authoritarian stance toward the spectator. Stephen Heath, in his analysis of realism as "narrative space," carried this further by examining the ways that this same hierarchical logic pervades the formulaic conventions of orthodox film technique, for example those defended by filmmaking manuals (the 180 degree rule, movement, position, eyeline matches, and so forth), all of which promote the surface appearance of seamless continuity (Heath, 1981). Yet it may be argued that such a one-size-fits-all account totalizes and oversimplifies a very variegated field. David Bordwell (1985) argued that MacCabe's analysis could benefit from the more nuanced Bakhtinian notion of the novel as the privileged site of heteroglossia (many-languagedness) or the competition of discourses. Even in the most realistic novels "the narrator's language will interact dynamically with several discourses, not all of them attributable to direct character speech" (ibid., p. 20).

Bordwell delineated with great empirical precision the procedures of the classic Hollywood cinema. Combining issues of denotative representation and dramaturgical structure, he highlighted the ways in which classical Hollywood narration constitutes a particular configuration of normalized options for representing the story and manipulating style. The classical Hollywood film presents psychologically defined individuals as its principal causal agents. These agents struggle to solve clear-cut problems or to attain specific goals, the story ending with either a resolution of the problem or a clear achievement or non-achievement of the goals. Causality revolving around character provides the prime unifying principle, while spatial configurations are motivated by realism as well as compositional necessity. Scenes are demarcated by neo-classical criteria – unity of time, space, and action. Classical narration tends to be omniscient, highly communicative, and only moderately self-conscious. If time is skipped over, a montage sequence or scrap of dialogue informs us; if a cause is missing, we are informed about its absence. Classical narration operates as an "editorial intelligence" that selects certain stretches of time for full-scale treatment, while paring down or scissoring out other "inconsequential" events. In *Classical Hollywood Cinema* Bordwell, Staiger, and Thompson (1985) further developed their analysis of what they called an "excessively obvious cinema."

The Presence of Brecht

Leftist film theory of the 1960s and 1970s in Europe and the Third World continued an aesthetic discussion begun in the 1930s by Bertolt Brecht, who developed a strong Marxist-inflected critique of the dramatic realist model operative both in traditional theater and in the Hollywood film. The performances of *Mother Courage* by Brecht's Berliner Ensemble at the Theater of Nations in Paris in 1956, attended by many French critics and artists, and the laudatory essays penned by Roland Barthes and Bernard Dort, fueled enthusiasm for Brecht. In 1960 *Cahiers du cinéma* dedicated a special issue to the German playwright, marking the first stages of a politicizing tendency which reached its apogee in the early 1970s. In his essay "Towards Brechtian Criticism of the Cinema" theater critic Bernard Dort argued that a Brechtian film criticism would place politics at the center of discussion. The Brechtian critique influenced not only film theorists (Jean-Louis Comolli, Peter Wollen, Colin MacCabe) but also countless filmmakers around the world (among them Welles, Godard, Resnais, Duras, Rocha, Straub-Huillet, Makavejev, Fassbinder, Alea, Tanner, Oshima, Sen, Ghatak, Herbert Ross, and Haskell Wexler).

There are many possible ways to approach the subject of Brecht and cinema: Brecht's own use of film in his theater work (for ex-ample, productions of *Mother Courage* featuring footage from *October*); the influence of cinema (e.g. Chaplin) on Brecht's work; Brecht's own work on film (*Kuhle Wampe, Hangmen Also Die*, his many unpublished film scripts); and filmic adaptations of Brecht's work (by Pabst, Cavalcanti, Schlöndorff, and others). What interests us here, however, is Brecht's aesthetic relevance for film. In the various essays collected in *Brecht on Theater* Brecht theorized certain general goals for the theater which are equally applicable to film. These goals can be summarized to include the following:

1   The nurturing of the active spectator (as opposed to the dreamily passive "zombies" engendered by bourgeois theater or the goose-step automatons generated by Nazi spectacle).
2   The rejection of voyeurism and the "fourth-wall convention."
3   The notion of *becoming* rather than *being* popular, i.e. transforming rather than satisfying spectatorial desire.
4   The rejection of the entertainment–education dichotomy, seen as implying that entertainment is useless while education is pleasureless.
5   The critique of the abuses of empathy and pathos.
6   The rejection of a totalizing aesthetic where all the "tracks" are enlisted in the service of a single, overwhelming feeling.
7   The critique of Fate/Fascination/Catharsis typical of Aristotelian tragedy in favor of ordinary people making their own history.
8   Art as a call to praxis, whereby the spectator is led not to contemplate the world but to change it.
9   Character as contradiction, a stage on which social contradictions are played out.
10   Immanence of meaning, whereby the spectator has to work out the meaning of the play of contradictory voices in the text.
11   Dividing the audience, according to class, for example.
12   Transforming production relations, i.e. critiquing not only the system in general but also the apparatuses that produce and distribute culture.

13 Laying bare the causal network, in spectacles that are realist not in style but in terms of social representation.

14 Alienation effects (*verfremdungseffekt*), which decondition the spectator and "make strange" the lived social world, freeing socially conditioned phenomena from the "stamp of familiarity," revealing them as other than "natural."

15 Entertainment, i.e. theater as critical yet fun, in some ways analogous to the pleasures of sport or the circus.

As well as these general goals Brecht also proposed specific techniques to achieve them, techniques transposable, up to a point, to the cinema. These include the following:

1 Fractured mythos, i. e. an anti-organic, anti-Aristotelian "theater of interruptions" based on sketch-scenes as in the music hall or vaudeville.

2 The refusal of heroes/stars, a rejection of the dramaturgy which constructs heroes through lighting, mise-en-sène, and editing (for example, the way Hitler is constructed as hero in Riefenstahl's *Triumph of the Will*).

3 De-psychologization in an art more interested in collective patterns of behavior than in the nuances of individual consciousness.

4 *Gestus*, the mimetic and gestural expression of social relationships between people in a given period.

5 Direct address: in the theater, direct address to the audience, and in film, direct address by characters, narrators, or even cameras (as in the famous opening of Godard's *Contempt* where the camera, or at least *a* camera, is trained on the spectator).

6 Tableau effects, easily transposable to the cinema in the form of freeze-frames.

7 Distantiated acting: a distantiation between actor and part, and between actor and spectator.

8 Acting as quotation: a distanced style of acting, as if the performer is speaking in the third person or the past tense.

9 Radical separation of elements, i.e. a structurating technique

147

which sets scene against scene and track (music, dialogue, lyric) against track, so that they mutually discredit rather than reinforce one another.

10   Multimedia, the mutual alienation of "sister arts" and parallel media.

11   Reflexivity, a technique whereby art reveals the principles of its own construction.

Peter Wollen was very much influenced by Brecht in his formulations of "counter-cinema." Wollen's schema mapped the contrasts between mainstream cinema and counter-cinema – best exemplified by the work of Godard – in the form of seven binary features:

1   Narrative *intransitivity* versus narrative *transitivity* (i.e. the systematic disruption of the flow of the narrative).

2   *Estrangement* versus *identification* (through Brechtian techniques of acting, sound–image disjunction, direct address, etc.).

3   *Foregrounding* versus *transparency* (systematic drawing of attention to the process of construction of meaning).

4   *Multiple* versus *single* diegesis.

5   *Aperture* versus *closure* (rather than a unifying authorial vision, an opening out into an intertextual field).

6   *Unpleasure* versus *pleasure* (the filmic experience conceived as a kind of collaborative production/consumption).

7   *Reality* versus *fiction* (the exposure of the mystifications involved in filmic fictions).

Other theorists aligned Brechtian materialism with Derridean poststructuralism, arguing for films which deconstructed and made visible the operative codes and ideologies of dominant cinema. Jean-Louis Baudry spoke of the revolutionary "text of écriture" as being characterized by (1) a negative relation to narrative; (2) a refusal of representationality; (3) a refusal of an expressive notion of artistic discourse; (4) a foregrounding of the materiality of signification; (5) a preference for non-linear, permutational, or serial structures.[1]

Many such schemas, while they were suggestive, could also be seen as simply up-ending old dyads rather than moving beyond them. Indeed, in retrospect we can see a number of dangers within Brechtianism itself:

- *Scientism*, an exaggerated faith in the progressive narrative of science.
- *Rationalism*, an exorbitant faith in reason and suspicion of identification.
- *Puritanism*, the valorization of the "working" as opposed to the "enjoying" spectator.
- *Masculinism*, a bias against "feminine" values linked stereotypically to empathy and consumerism.
- *Classocentrism*, the privileging of only one axis of social oppression to the detriment of other axes such as race, gender, sexuality, and nation.
- *Monoculturalism*, in that Brechtian theater might not necessarily "work" for non-European cultures.

Other dangers have to do with the way that Brechtians departed from some of Brecht's own axioms. While Brecht endorsed popular forms of culture such as sport and the circus, the new theories offered only a festival of negations of the dominant cinema. While Brecht revelled in stories and fables, Brechtians rejected narrative. While Brecht assumed that his theater was a form of entertainment, Brechtians rejected entertainment altogether. In this sense they echoed Adorno's call for an austere, formalist, and difficult art. Some of the theories were built on the idea of destroying spectatorial pleasure. Peter Gidal (1975) spoke of "structural materialist" films which would refuse all illusion, representing nothing beyond their own fabrication. Peter Wollen spoke positively of "unpleasure," while Laura Mulvey in "Visual Pleasure and Narrative Cinema" called for "the destruction of pleasure as a radical weapon," adding that it was her explicit intention to analyze pleasure, or beauty, in order to destroy it. But while such a move is understandable in the light of feminist anger at masculinist representations, and while it is fine to denounce the alienations provoked by dominant cinema, it is also important to recognize the desire that brings spectators to the cinema. A theory based simply on negations of the conventional pleasures of cinema – the negation of narrative, mimesis, identification – leads to a dead-end anhedonia, leaving little for the spectator to connect with. To be effective a film must offer its quantum of pleasure, something to discover or see or feel. Brechtian distantiation, after all, can only be effective if there is something – an emotion, a desire – to *be* distanced. The view that simply laments the delight that audiences take in spectacle and narrative betrays a puritanical attitude toward filmic pleasure. It is of little value for films to be "correct" if no one is interested in participating in them (see Stam, 1985; 1992).

The critique-of-ideology approach performed an enormous service by unmasking the ideology at work within cinematic forms themselves and denouncing the potential for exploitation in identification with streamlined plots, glamorous stars, and idealized characters. But as Metz points out, totally deconstructive films require a libidinal transfer whereby traditional satisfactions are replaced by the pleasures of intellectual mastery, by a "sadism of knowledge."[2] The pleasure in the toy is transmuted into the pleasure of breaking the toy, a pleasure, ultimately, no less infantile. Why should the spectator or theorist give up pleasure, rather than look for a *new kind* of pleasure? While assuming the pleasures of conventional narrative, film might also mobilize the spectator to interrogate those pleasures and make that interrogation itself pleasurable. Films can play with fictions rather than do away with them altogether; tell stories, but also question them; articulate the play of desire and the pleasure principle *and* the obstacles to their realization. In literary fiction, for example in *Don Quixote*, it was possible to love fiction and narrativity but at the same time interrogate that love. The enemy was never fiction *per se* but rather socially generated illusions; not stories but alienated dreams.

The Politics of Reflexivity

A key term in many of these debates was "reflexivity" and its satellite terms such as "self-referentiality," "metafiction," and "anti-illusionism." Borrowed from philosophy and psychology, reflexivity referred originally to the mind's capacity to take itself as object – for example, Descartes's *cogito ergo sum* – but was extended metaphorically to the capacity for self-reflexion of a medium or language. The penchant for reflexivity must be seen as symptomatic not only of the general language-consciousness of contemporary thought but also of what one might call its methodological self-consciousness, its tendency to scrutinize its own instruments. For artistic modernism – those movements in the arts (both within Europe and outside of it) which emerged in the late nineteenth century, flourished in the first decades of the twentieth century, and became institutionalized as high modernism after World War II – reflexivity evokes a non-representational art characterized by abstraction, fragmentation, and the foregrounding of the materials and processes of art. In the broadest sense, *filmic* reflexivity refers to the process by which films foreground their own production (for example, Truffaut's *La Nuit Américaine*), their authorship (Fellini's *8½*), their textual procedures (the avant-garde films of Hollis Frampton or Michael Snow), their intertextual influences (the parodic films of Mel Brooks), or their reception (*Sherlock Jr., The Purple Rose of Cairo*).[1] By calling attention to filmic mediation, reflexive films subvert the assumption that art can be a transparent medium of communication, a window on the world, a mirror promenading down a highway.

Much has been made of what might be called the political valences of realism and reflexivity. The left wing of 1970s film theory, especially that influenced by Althusser as well as Brecht, came to regard reflexivity as a *political* obligation. Some version of this idea pervades the 1970s and 1980s work of such theorists as Peter Wollen, Chuck Kleinhans, Laura Mulvey, David Rodowick, Julia Lesage, Robert Stam, Colin MacCabe, Michael Walsh, Bernard Dort, Paul Willemen, and many others. Film theory in this period thus "relived," and explicitly cited and reworked, the Brecht–Lukács debate about realism in the 1930s, and sided with the Brechtian critique of realism. The tendency at this time was simply to equate "realist" with "bourgeois" and "reflexive" with "revolutionary." "Hollywood" (a.k.a. "dominant cinema") became synonymous with all that was retrograde and passivity-inducing. The identity of "deconstructive" and "revolutionary," meanwhile, led in the pages of journals such as *Cinetique* to the rejection of virtually all cinema, past and present, as "idealist." Since the problem was the effacing of signs of production in the dominant cinema, the solution, it was thought at the time, was simply to foreground the work of production in self-reflexive texts.

But all these equations do not stand up to close scrutiny (see Stam, 1992). It is a mistake, first of all, to regard reflexivity and realism as necessarily antithetical terms. A novel such as Balzac's *Lost Illusions* and a film like Godard's *Numéro Deux* can be seen as at once reflexive and realist, in the sense that they illuminate the everyday lived realities of the social conjunctures from which they emerge, while they also remind the reader/spectator of the constructed nature of their own mimesis. Realism and reflexivity are not strictly opposed polarities but, rather, interpenetrating tendencies quite capable of coexisting within the same text. It is therefore more accurate to speak of a "coefficient" of reflexivity or realism, and to recognize that it is not a question of a *fixed* proportion. The coefficient of reflexivity varies from genre to genre (musicals like *Singin' in the Rain* are classically more reflexive than social realist dramas like *Marty*), from era to era (in the contemporary postmodernist era reflexivity is the norm rather than the exception), and from film to film by the same director (Woody Allen's *Zelig* is more reflexive than *Another Woman*). Illusionism, meanwhile, has never been monolithically dominant even in the mainstream fiction film. Even the most paradigmatically realist texts – as Barthes's reading of *Sarrasine* and *Cahiers'* reading of *Young Mr Lincoln* demonstrate – are marked by gaps and fissures in their illusionism. Few classical films perfectly fit the abstract category of transparency often taken to be the norm for mainstream cinema.

Nor can one simply assign a positive or negative value to realism or reflexivity as such. What Jakobson calls "progressive realism" has been used as an instrument of social criticism in favor of the working class (*Salt of the Earth*), women (*Julia*), and racial minorities (*Rosewood*), and by emergent Third World nations (*The Battle of Algiers*). Brechtian theory showed the compatability between reflexivity as an aesthetic strategy and realism as an aspiration. Brecht's critique of realism centered on the ossified conventions of naturalist theater, but not on the goal of truthful representation. Brecht distinguished between realism as "laying bare society's causal network" – a goal realizable within a reflexive, modernist aesthetic – and realism as a historically determinate set of conventions.

The generalized equation of the reflexive with the progressive is also problematic. Texts may foreground the work of their signifiers or obscure it; the contrast cannot always be read as a political one. Jane Feuer speaks of the "conservative reflexivity" of musicals like *Singin' in the Rain*, films which foreground cinema as an institution, which emphasize spectacle and artifice, but ultimately within an illusionistic aesthetic devoid of any subversive, demystificatory, or revolutionary thrust. The reflexivity of a certain avant-garde, similarly, is eminently co-optable within Art World formalism.

Reflexivity, in sum, does not come equipped with an *a priori* political valence; it can be grounded in art-for-art's sake aestheticism, in media-specific formalism, in commercial propagandizing, or in dialectical materialism. It can be narcissistic or intersubjective, a sign of politically motivated urgency or nihilistic lassitude.

The Search for Alternative Aesthetics

The challenge to the classical Hollywood aesthetic has come from many directions, including from within the mainstream tradition. In fact the dominant model was challenged – to put it anachronistically – even before it established itself as the dominant. The conventional view that the cinema evolved logically and inexorably toward the *telos* of an ever greater realism and verisimilitude has been questioned by scholars of silent cinema such as Noël Burch and Tom Gunning, who have argued that the so-called "primitive cinema" was not a bumbling attempt to achieve what were to become the dominant norms, but rather an alternative to those norms. Burch (1990) speaks of an international "Primitive Mode of Representation" (PMR) as the dominant practice from 1894 to 1914, the style of which was non-linear, anti-psychological, and discontinuous. Tom Gunning delineates the non-linear aesthetics of what he calls a "cinema of attractions," a strong presence prior to 1908, whose aesthetics were exhibitionistic rather than voyeuristic, closer to circus and to vaudeville than to what later became the dominant story film.

It is common knowledge that the dominant model was challenged by the historical avant-gardes – doda, expressionism, Surrealism – and by latter-day avant-gardes such as New American Cinema. Strict dramatic realism was never the only model available even within mainstream cinema. Such films as the Keaton parodies of Griffith (*The Three Ages*) and of the western (*Go West*), the more irreverent of the Chaplin films, and certain films of the Marx Brothers represented a homegrown anti-realist tradition rooted in the popular intertext of fairground, vaudeville, and burlesque. The "boiling anarchy" animating *Animal Crackers* and *Monkey Business*, according to Antonin Artaud, led to "an essential disintegration of the real by poetry."[1] The Marx Brothers' films combine an anti-authoritarian stance toward official institutions with a cinematic and linguistic *gramatica jocosa* which involves, in Patricia Mellenkamp's words, "breaking and entering the narrative as well as houses, constantly shattering any imposed cause–effect logic."[2]

In a series of innovative texts, Nöel Burch describes the moments of tension within the classical system, its interstices, its abberations, its anomalies, as well as the alternatives to that system. In "Propositions," (1974) Burch and Jorge Dana ransacked film history for exemplary films which undermined the dominant illusionist codes: *Caligari* with its perverse expressionist construction of space; *Man with a Movie Camera* with its reflexive demonstration of cinematic technique; *Citizen Kane* with its hyperbolic personalizations of the dominant style. In the wake of Comolli/Narboni, Burch/Dana too constructed an ideological spectrum ranging from films which completely relayed the dominant codes to those which subtly undermined them. In *Praxis du Cinema* (1969; English version 1973) Burch analyzed cinematic style in terms of the "dialectics" operating between specifically cinematic elements – on-screen and off-screen space, normal and accelerated movement – which typify the modernist cinema of Antonioni, Godard and Hanoun. (Burch's work looks back to Eistenstein and forward to the "conflictual écriture" analyzed by Marie-Claire Ropars.)

The 1970s ideological critique of anti-illusionism tended to favor an austere minimalism; rarely did theorists think about the possibilities of *excess* as a strategy. Many theorists assumed as their point of departure a false dichotomy between an alienated popular art on the one hand and a difficult modernist art on the other. They forgot that the art of a Shakespeare, for example, the partial model for some of Brecht's work, could be pleasurable *and* difficult. Shakespeare's plays could entertain the Globe's motley crowd because they were multidimensional, with farce and slapstick for the groundlings and subtlety and allusion for the culturally privileged. Indeed, much of the greatest art, that of Chaucer and Cervantes and Shakespeare, one might argue, was deeply rooted in a millennial substratum of popular irreverence and playfulness.

The formulations of counter-cinema, in this sense, lost touch with the long tradition of popular forms summed up by the word "carnival." The work of Mikhail Bakhtin, which began to be translated into English and French in the 1960s, provided a way to conceptualize an alternative kind of cinematic pleasure. Although Bakhtin never directly addressed the cinema, his theories were nonetheless influential on film theory, especially through Julia Kristeva's rendering of Bakhtin's idea of dialogism, in the mid 1960s, as intertextuality. Some analysts (Mercer, Willemen, Mellencamp, Stam, Rowe) extrapolated Bakhtin's notion of carnival, developed in *Rabelais and His World* and *Problems of Dostoevsky's Poetics*, for a cinema of raucous and extravagant, rather than ascetic, subversion. Within Bakhtin's carnival, all hierarchical distinctions, all barriers, all norms and prohibitions, are temporarily suspended, while a qualitatively different kind of communication, based on "free and familiar contact," is established. Carnival, for Bakhtin, generates a special kind of universal laughter, a cosmic gaiety directed at everyone, including the carnival's participants. For the carnivalesque spirit, laughter has deep philosophical meaning; it constitutes a special perspective on experience, one no less profound than seriousness and tears. As theorized by Bakhtin, carnival embraces an anti-classical aesthetic that rejects formal harmony and unity in favor of the asymmetrical, the heterogenous, the oxymoronic, the miscegenated.

Carnival's "grotesque realism" turns conventional aesthetics on its head in order to locate a new kind of popular, convulsive, rebellious beauty, one that dares to reveal the grotesquerie of the powerful and the latent beauty of the "vulgar." In the carnival aesthetic everything is pregnant with its opposite, within an alternative logic of permanent contradiction and non-exclusive opposites that transgresses the monologic true-or-false thinking typical of a certain kind of positivist rationalism. Within this perspective, the dichotomy of alienating mass art, on the one hand, and liberatory but difficult avant-garde art on the other, is a false one. It leaves no room for hybrid forms that mob-ilize mass-cultural forms in a critical way, which reconcile popular appeal with social critique.

Although Fredric Jameson implies in his essay "Third World Allegory" that Third World cinema, with rare exceptions, has always been realist and pre-modernist, Third World cinema has also been rich in avant-garde, modernist, and postmodernist movements. Quite apart from the confluence of Brechtian modernism and Marxist modernization in the "new cinemas" of Cuba (Alea), Brazil (Guerra), Egypt (Chahine), Senegal (Sembene), and India (Sen), there have been many modernist and avant-garde films in the Third World, going all the way back to films like *São Paulo: Sinfonia de una Cidade* (São Paulo: Symphony of a City, 1928) and *Limite* (1930), both from Brazil, and forward through Mambete's *Touki-Bouki* (1973) and Med Hondo's *Soleil O* (1970) and *West Indies* (1975), to the underground movements of Argentina and Brazil, through Kidlat Tahimik's anti-colonialist experiments in the Philippines. The point is not to brandish terms like "reflexive" or "postmodern" as honorifics

156

– you see, the Third World is postmodern too! – but rather to set the debates within a broader relational framework in terms of both space and time.

Alternative cinemas, often rooted in the Third World or in First World minoritarian communities, have explored a wide spectrum of alternative aesthetics, crystallized in suggestive epithets and neologisms: Rocha's "aesthetic of hunger," Rogerio Sganzerla's "aesthetic of garbage," Claire Johnston's feminist "Counter Cinema," Paul Leduc's "salamander" (as opposed to dinosaur) aesthetic, Guilhermo del Toro's "termite terrorism," Teshome Gabriel's "nomadic aesthetics," Kobena Mercer's "diaspora aesthetics," Clyde Taylor's "Aesopian aesthetics," and Espinosa's *cine imperfecto*. The films aligned with these resistant practices are neither homogenous nor static; they vary over time, and from region to region. What these aesthetic strategies have in common is that they bypass the formal conventions of dramatic realism in favor of such modes and strategies as the carnivalesque, the anthropophagic, the magical realist, the reflexive modernist, and the resistant postmodernist. They are often rooted in non-realist, often non-western or para-western cultural traditions featuring other historical rhythms, other narrative structures, other views of the body, sexuality, spirituality, and the collective life. Many incorporate para-modern traditions into clearly modernizing or postmodernizing aesthetics, and thus problematize facile dichotomies such as traditional and modern, realist and modernist, modernist and postmodernist (Shohat and Stam, 1994).

In Brazil, to take just one example, the Tropicalist movement in the 1960s, as expressed in films such as *Macunaima* and *How Tasty was My Frenchman*, reinvoiced the anthropophagy movement of the 1920s. Like Brazilian modernism (and unlike European modernism), Tropicalism fused political nationalism with aesthetic internationalism. As recycled for the 1960s, anthropophagy implied a transcendence of Cinema Novo's Manichean opposition between "authentic Brazilian Cinema" and "Hollywood alienation." As expressed in the theater, music, and cinema, Tropicalism aggressively juxtaposed the folkloric and the industrial, the native and the foreign. Its favored technique was an aggressive collage of discourses,

157

an anthropophagic devouring of varied cultural stimuli in all their heterogeneity. Tropicalist filmmakers framed a resistant strategy premised on a low-cost "aesthetic of garbage." Where Rocha's earlier metaphor of an aesthetic of hunger had evoked famished victims redeeming themselves through violence, the garbage metaphor conveyed an aggressive sense of marginality, of surviving within scarcity, of being condemned to recycle the materials of dominant culture. A garbage style was seen as appropriate to a Third World country picking through the leavings of an international system dominated by First World capitalism.

In their attempts to forge a liberatory language, alternative film traditions draw on para-modern phenomena such as popular religion and ritual magic. In some recent African films such as *Yeelen* (1987), *Jitt* (1992), and *Kasarmu Ce* (This Land is Ours, 1991), magical spirits become an aesthetic resource, a means for breaking away, often in comical ways, from the linear, cause-and-effect conventions of Aristotelian narrative poetics, a way of defying the "gravity," in both senses of that word, of chronological time and literal space. The values of African religious culture inform not only African cinema but also a good deal of Afro-diasporic cinema, for example Brazilian films like *Barravento* (1962) and *A Forca de Xango* (The Force of Xango, 1977), and African American films like Julie Dash's *Daughters of the Dust*, all of which inscribe African (usually Yoruba) religious symbolism and practice. Indeed, the preference for Yoruba symbolism is itself significant, since the arts – music, dance, costume, poetry, narrative – are at the very kernel of the Yoruba religions themselves, unlike other religions where the performing arts are grafted onto a theological/textual core. Aesthetics and culture, in this sense, are inseparable.

From Linguistics to Psychoanalysis

Within First World film theory, meanwhile, linguistically oriented semiology was giving way to a "second semiology," where psychoanalysis became the preferred conceptual grid, as attention shifted from film language and film structure to the "subject-effects" produced by the cinematic apparatus. The encounter between psychoanalysis and the cinema was in one sense the culmination of a long flirtation, since both were born around the same time (Freud first used the term "psychoanalysis" in 1896, just one year after the first screenings of the Lumière films in the Grand Café). There had also been character-oriented psychoanalytic studies of the cinema prior to the second semiology, such as *Movies: A Psychological Study* (1950), where Martha Wolfenstein and Nathan Leites argued that the cinema crystallized the common dreams, myths, and fears of the general population, and *Hollywood: The Dream Factory* (also 1950), where Hortense Powdermaker described, in quasi-ethnographic terms, the Hollywood "tribe" that manufactured these same dreams and myths.

There was also the pioneering work of sociologist, psychologist, and filmmaker Edgar Morin. In *Cinéma, ou l'homme imaginaire* (1958) Morin revisited the venerable trope of "cinema magic," but this time in order to highlight cinema's capacity to infantilize and overpower the spectator. According to Morin the spectator does not merely watch a film; he or she lives it with a neurotic intensity, as a form of socially approved regression, a theme which would be taken up by the psycho-semioticians. The cinema, for Morin, implicates spectators in their very depths. Both contemporary and archaic, the cinema as an "archive of souls" allows us to photograph our own movements, attitudes, and desires. Imbuing the cinema with their own sensibility and imagination, spectators experience powerful emotions and even a cultic devotion.

Beginning in the mid 1970s, and notably with the special 1975 issue of the French journal *Communications* devoted to "Psychoanalysis and the Cinema," semiotic discussion came to be inflected by psychoanalytic notions such as scopophilia, voyeurism, and fetishism, and by Lacan's conception of the mirror stage, the imaginary, and the symbolic. While North American "ego psychology" stressed the development of the individual, conscious self, Lacanian psychoanalysis privileged the id, the Unconscious, and the notion of

159

the "subject." Synthesizing psychoanalysis with the philosophical tradition, Lacan explored the subject in its multiple senses – psychological, philosophical, grammatical, logical – contrasting the sovereign self of "ego psychology" with the "subject of the unconscious." Lacan was also concerned with "identification," the process by which the subject constituted itself by appropriating aspects of other human interlocutors such as parents. The term "other," for Lacan, designated the symbolic place where the subject was constituted in relation to his or her "desire." Lacan conceived desire not as a biological impulse but rather as a phantasmatic movement toward an obscure "object" exercising spiritual or sexual attraction. Catalyzed by the Law, desire was by definition unsatisfiable since it was a desire not for an achievable object but rather for "the desire of the other," a struggle for amorous recognition reminiscent of the Hegelian dialectic between master and slave. As Lacan summed it up in a La Rochefoucauld-like aphorism: "Love is giving what one does not have to someone who doesn't want it." (One is reminded of Denis de Rougemont's melancholy anatomy of passion in his *Love in the Western World*, where desire is indelibly marked with pathos and impossibility.) The differences between "French Freud" and American ego psychology also reflect large-scale cultural/political contrasts between the optimistic country of pragmatic success and the pursuit of happiness, and the more pessimistic "old world" country emerging from two world wars and a Holocaust on its own soil. While ego psychology was concerned with therapy and cure, Lacanian psychoanalysis was more concerned with developing a powerful intellectual system which synthesized the anthropology of Lévi-Strauss, the philosophy of Heidegger, and the linguistics of Saussure. By cinematic analogy, Lacanianism favored the tense ambiguities of European psychoanalysis (the art film) over the (Hollywoodean) "happy end" of ego psychology.

In film theory, at any rate, it was the French Freud that predominated. The focus of interest, in the psychoanalytic phase of semiotics, shifted from the relation between filmic image and reality to the cinematic apparatus itself, not only in the sense of the instrumental base of camera, projector, and screen, but also in the sense of the spectator as the desiring subject on which the cinematic institution depends as its object and accomplice. The psychoanalytic approach highlighted the meta-psychological dimension of the cinema, its ways of both activating and regulating spectatorial desire. The practitioners of this approach were not interested at all in what other "psychological" approaches had classically been interested in: the psychoanalysis of authors, plots, or characters. Rather, the interest shifts, in this phase, from questions such as "What is the nature of the cinematic sign and the laws of their combination?" and "What is a textual system?" to other questions, such as "What do we want from the text?" and "What are our spectatorial investments in it?" Many of the psychoanalytic questions were interarticulated with Marxist issues of ideology. How is the spectator/addressee "interpellated" as subject? What is the nature of our identification with the cinematic apparatus and with the stories and characters offered by the cinema? What kind of subject–spectator is fashioned by the cinematic apparatus? Why does the cinema provoke passionate reactions? What explains its fascination? Why does so much seem to be at stake? How do films resemble dreams or daydreams? What are the analogies between the condensations and displacements typical of the "dreamwork" and the textual "work" of film? Can the cinema serve as the "poor man's couch," as Félix Guattari suggested? How do film narratives replay the Oedipus story, the conflict of law and desire?

Although much has been made of the faddish nature of the shift from linguistic semiotics to psychoanalysis, in fact this change forms part of a coherent trajectory toward the "semio-psychoanalysis" of the cinema. Linguistics and psychoanalysis were not chosen for arbitrary voguish reasons but because they were seen as two sciences that dealt directly with signification as such. The shift was facilitated by the fact that Jacques Lacan, the major influence in psychoanalytic film theory, had placed language at the very center of psychoanalysis. If classically the Unconscious was seen as a prelinguistic, instinctual reserve, for Lacan the Unconscious was an effect of the subject's entry into the linguistic (symbolic) order. Language was the very condition of the Unconscious. Rather than read the Oedipus Complex biologistically, Lacan read it linguistically. The reference to linguistics, Lacan promised, "will introduce us to the method which, by distinguishing synchronic and diachronic structurings in language, will enable us to understand better the different value that our language assumes in the interpretation of the resistances and the transference" (Lacan, 1997, p. 76). Lacan's nostrum that the "Unconscious is structured like a language" provided a further bridge between the two fields of language and the psyche. (Voloshinov and Bakhtin, from a different angle, had performed a linguistic reading of Freud in their 1927 book *Freudianism: A Marxist Critique*.)

Psychoanalytic theorists were especially interested in the psychic dimension of the film medium's overpowering "impression of reality." They were concerned, that is, with explaining the extraordinary *power* of the cinema over human feelings. The persuasiveness of the cinematic apparatus was analyzed as deriving from a number of factors – the cinematic situation (immobility, darkness), the enunciatory mechanisms of the image (camera, optical projections, monocular perspective) – all of which induce the subject to project him or herself *into* the representation. Picking up on the cues provided by the earlier work of Edgar Morin, 1970s theorists like Jean-Louis Baudry, Christian Metz, and Jean-Louis Comolli saw the question of the impression of reality as inseparable from the question of spectatorial positioning and identification. Baudry was the first to draw on psychoanalytic theory to characterize the cinematic apparatus as a technological, institutional, and ideological machine with strong "subject-effects." In "Ideological Effects of the Basic Cinematic Apparatus" (1971) Baudry argued that the apparatus flattered infantile narcissism by exalting the spectatorial subject as the center and origin of meaning. Baudry postulated an unconscious substratum in identification, in the sense that cinema, as a simulation apparatus, not only represents the real but also stimulates intense "subject-effects."

In "The Apparatus" (1975) Baudry explored the oft-cited similitude between the scene of Plato's cave and the apparatus of cinematic projection, arguing that the cinema constituted the technical realization of a perennial dream of a perfect, total simulacrum. The shadowy images on the screen, the darkness of the movie theater, the passive immobility of the spectator, the womb-like sealing off of ambient noises and quotidian pressures, all foster an artificial state of regression, generating "archaic moments of fusion" not unlike those engendered by dream. Thus a kind of double whammy operates in the cinema: extremely strong visual and auditory stimuli inundate us at a moment when we are predisposed toward passive reception and narcissistic self-absorption. The film, like a dream, tells a story – a story rendered in images and therefore resonant with the logic of a primary process which "figures itself forth in images." Specifically cinematic techniques such as superimposition and the lap-dissolve "mime" the condensations and displacements through which the primary-process logic of dreams works over its phantasized objects.

The cinema, for Baudry, constitutes the approximate material realization of an unconscious goal perhaps inherent in the human psyche: the regressive desire to return to an earlier state of psychic development, a state of relative narcissism in which desire could be satisfied through a simulated, enveloping reality where the separation between one's body and the exterior world, between ego and non-ego, is not clearly defined. In apparatus theory the cinema becomes a very powerful machine which transforms the embodied, socially situated individual into a spectatorial subject. In effect, Baudry put a negative spin on Bazin's positively connoted "myth of total cinema." The film as window-on-the-world became barred, like a prison.

For 1970s psychoanalytic theory, Lacan's notion that desire is not a matter of desiring the other but of "desiring the *desire* of the other" seemed a marvelously apt description of the processes of identification in the cinema. Psychoanalytic theory largely absorbed the Lacanian vision of the deluded subject of the cinema. Given an initial lack of being (*manque à être*), the initial loss of an originary plenitude linked to a dual relation with the mother, human beings were seen as constitutively alienated, split from themselves, with psychic "identity" consisting of a flimsy *bricolage* of ephemeral identifications. These ephemera congealed into a kind of identity only during the phase Lacan called the mirror stage, the stage in the child's development where hyperactive perception coincides with a low level of motor activity. Lacan describes how the infant ego is constituted by the child's identification with and misrecognition of the lure of the mirror image, which offers an imaginary picture of his own autonomous self-presence. Both Metz and Baudry compared the spectator's situation to the mirror stage, with Metz pointing out that the mirror analogy was only partially accurate; the cinema, unlike the mirror, does not reflect back the spectator's own image.

From a feminist perspective, this theory was now seen as giving expression to a masculinist denial of sexual difference. The self-deluded, ideologically coherent subject constructed by dominant cinema, for these feminist theorists, was gender-specific. Taking a term coined by Marcel Duchamp and elaborated by Michel Carrouges, feminist critic Constance Penley (1989) later compared the Baudry model of the apparatus to a "bachelor machine," i.e. as a closed, self-sufficient, frictionless machine controlled by a knowing overseer subject to a fantasy of closure and mastery, ultimately as a compensatory pleasure and consolation for male lack and alienation. Joan Copjec (1989) argued that apparatus theory constructed a paranoid anthropomorphic machine producing only male subjects, as a "delusional defense against the alienation that the elaboration of cinema as a language opened in theory."

In "The Imaginary Signifier" Metz argued that the doubly imaginary nature of the cinematic signifier – imaginary in what it represents and imaginary by the nature of its signifier – heightens rather than diminishes the possibilities of identification. The signifier itself, even before coming to form part of a fictive imagined world, is marked by the duality of presence/absence typical of the Lacanian imaginary. The impression of reality is stronger in film than in theater because the weak phantom-like figures on the screen virtually invite us to invest them with our phantasies and projections. The cinema spectator identifies, first of all, with his or her own act of looking, with "himself as a pure act of perception (as wakefulness, alertness); as condition of possibility of the perceived and hence as a kind of transcendental subject" (Metz, 1982, p. 51). What Metz calls primary identification, then, is not with the events or characters de-

164

picted on the screen but rather with the act of perception that makes these secondary identifications possible, an act of perception both channeled and constructed by the anterior look of the camera and the projector that stands in for it, granting the spectator the illusory ubiquity of the "all-perceiving subject." The spectator is caught in a play between regression and progression. The images received come from without, in a progressive movement directed toward external reality; yet due to inhibited mobility and the processes of identification with camera and character, the psychic energy normally devoted to activity is channeled into other routes of discharge.

Metz had especially interesting observations about the question of pleasure and displeasure in the cinema. Some films, for example pornographic films, might generate displeasure by touching too closely on the spectator's repressed desires, thus triggering a defensive reaction. Building on Melanie Klein's analysis of the role of objects in the infant's fantasy life – the child's tendency to project libidinal or destructive feelings onto certain privileged objects such as the breast – Metz spoke of the critical tendency to confuse the actual film as a sequence of images and sound with the film experience such as it has pleased or displeased, in function of the phantasies, pleasures, and fears triggered in specific spectators by the film. Thus spectators–critics misconstrue an aesthetic question – the quality of the film – with a psychoanalytic question: Why did this film please or displease *me*? (A classic example of this confusion occurred with Woody Allen's *Stardust Memories*, which critics, many of them former admirers of Allen, took as an attack on themselves (rather than as a witty and self-mocking exercise in intertextuality) and which they therefore condemned in the most violent possible bad-object language as "vicious," "mean-spirited," and "poisonously bad.") Metz also put the theorist on the couch, since film theorists were not immune to such projections. Thus Metz analyzed the various forms of "love" for the cinema, ranging from the fetishism of the collector to the critic–theorist who sees most films as "bad objects" yet maintains a "good object relation" with the cinema as a whole. Metz became the psychoanalyst of the film theorists, much as Lévi-Strauss had been the ethnologist of the anthropologists.

On a more positive note, cinema can also mean the rupture of solitude. The material existence of filmic images, for Metz, creates the feeling of a "little miracle," a sharing of phantasies not unlike that "temporary rupture of solitude" called love: "This is the specific joy of receiving from the external world images that are usually internal . . . of seeing them inscribed in a physical location (the screen), of discovering in this way something almost realizable in them" (Metz, 1977, pp. 135–6).

Metz's analysis explains what might otherwise be a conundrum: the pleasures generated even by films which at first glance seem to be dystopian, threatening, even repulsive. Disaster films, for example, play on our most elemental insecurities about nature, yet such films often become monstrous hits. Such films, despite their superficial disagreeableness, ultimately reassure, in a Metzian perspective, because they give material form to our fears, thus reminding us that we are not alone. We are not crazy to feel such anxieties, such films seem to be telling us, since our fears are so palpably present there on the screen, inscribed in images and sounds, recognized and felt by other spectators as well.

Psychoanalytic criticism also prolonged earlier work on the relation between film and dream. Hugo Mauerhofer had suggested in "The Psychology of Cinematic Experience" (1949) that what he called the "cinema situation" shares a good deal with the dream situation, notably passivity, comfort, and withdrawal from reality. Suzanne Langer (1953) argued that film exists in a "dream mode," in that it creates a "virtual present conjoined with a feeling of immediacy, an impression of reality." It was only with the special issue of *Communications* on "Psychoanalysis and the Cinema," however, that the film–dream analogy was explored in depth. In "The Fiction Film and its Spectator" Metz offered the most systematic exploration yet of the analogies and disanalogies between film and dream, much as he had earlier explored the analogies between film and language. For Metz, the impression of reality offered by film derives from a cinematic situation that encourages feelings of narcissistic withdrawal and dreamy self-indulgence, a regression into primary process conditioned by circumstances similar to those which underlie the illusion of reality in dream. The conventional fiction film invokes a lowering of wakefulness that triggers a state close to that of sleep and dreaming. This lowering of wakefulness implies a withdrawal of concern from the external world and a heightened receptivity to phantasized wish-fulfillment. In the cinema, unlike dream, we do not literally confuse our phantasies with perceptions, since here we are dealing with an *actual* perceptual object – the film itself. While dream is a purely internal psychic process, film involves real perception, potentially common to other viewers, of actual images recorded on film. The dream, as Metz points out, is doubly illusion: the dreamer believes more than the spectator, and what he or she "perceives" is less real. The continuing perceptual stimulation of the cinema prevents unconscious wishes from taking a completely regressive path, therefore, and what is illusion of reality in dream is merely an impression of reality in film. Yet the parallels between the conditions of film viewing and those of dreams help explain the quasi-hallucinatory degree of this impression of reality that films can achieve.

The view of Hollywood as a dream factory suggested that the dominant industry promoted escapist fantasy. Screen theory, similarly, stressed the negative, exploitative dimension of film dream. But while theory was right to denounce the alienations provoked by dominant cinema, it is also important to recognize the desire that brings spectators to the movie theater. The perennial comparison of film and dream points not only to film's potential for alienation but also to its central utopian thrust. Dreams are not merely regressive; they are vital to human well-being. They are, as the Surrealists emphasized, a sanctuary for desire, an intimation of the possible transcendence of dichotomies, the source of kinds of knowledge denied cerebral rationality.

Psychoanalytic questions, while not on the surface political, could also be easily pushed in a political direction. What is the "libidinal economy" of the cinema? How does Hollywood, for example, exploit the spectator's voyeuristic and regressive tendencies in order to maintain itself as an institution? In "The Imaginary Signifier" Metz distinguished two "machines" operating within the cinematic institution: first, the cinema as industry, producing commodities whose sale as tickets provides a return on investment; second, the mental machine, which spectators have internalized and which adopts them for the consumption of films as pleasurable "good objects." One economy, involving the generation of profit, is intimately linked to the other, involving the circulation of pleasure (the third "machine" is critical discourse about the cinema). Metz in this context psychoanalyzed and institutionalized the underlying springs of cinematic pleasure: identification (first with the camera and then with characters); voyeurism (observation of others from a protected position); fetishism (the play of lack and disavowal); and narcissism (self-aggrandizing sensations of being an all-perceiving subject). Metz thus tried to answer a very important question: Why do spectators go to the cinema if they are not forced? What pleasure are they seeking? And how do they become part of an institutional machine that both delights and deludes them? Answering such questions about the imbricated functions of the real, the imaginary, and the symbolic in film reception might even have a feedback effect, yielding a new contribution to psychoanalysis itself.

The psychoanalytic critics also deployed the notion of the Oedipus Complex in the analysis of the cinema. In a Lacanian perspective, the Law catalyzes Desire. The cinema is oedipal not only in its stories – usually stories about a male protagonist overcoming his problems with the paternal Law – but also in its incorporation of the processes of disavowal and fetishism, whereby the spectator is aware of the illusory nature of the cinematic image and yet believes in that image nevertheless. This belief, furthermore, is premised on the spectacle being placed at a safe distance, and in this sense depends on voyeurism (with sadistic overtones). The cinema was clearly founded on the pleasure of looking, conceived since its origins as a place from which one could "spy on" others. What Freud called scopophilia, the impulse to turn the other into the object of a curious gaze, is one of the primordial elements in cinematic seduction. Indeed, the titles of some of the earliest films bear witness to this fascination: *As Seen Through a Telescope* (1900), *Ce que l'on voit de mon sixieme* (What one sees from my sixth floor, 1901), *Through the Keyhole* (1900), and *Peeping Tom in the Dressing Room* (1905). The cinematic apparatus, for Metz, combines visual hyperperception with minimal physical mobility; it virtually demands an immobile secret viewer who absorbs everything through the eyes. The precise mechanism of gratification "rests on our knowing that the object being looked at does not know it is being looked at" (Metz, 1977). The voyeur is careful to maintain a gulf between the object and the eye. The voyeur's *invisibility* produces the visibility of the objects of his or her gaze. It is the breaking down of these processes, the shattering of an illusory voyeuristic distance, that is allegorically staged in Hitchcock's *Rear Window*, where the protagonist is caught in the act through a series of scopic inversions which turn him into the object of the gaze. Psychoanalysis, as we shall see later, formed part of many subsequent movements such as film feminism and post-colonialism, and certainly inflects the work of later figures such as Kaja Silverman, Joan Copjec, and Slavoj Zizek.

The Feminist Intervention

At its height, the left wing of semiotic film theory hoped for a creative amalgam of the projects of the "Holy Trinity" (or Sinister Triumvirate, depending on one's point of view) of Althusser, Saussure, and Lacan. In an amicable division of labor, Marxism would provide the theory of society and ideology; semiotics would provide the theory of signification; and psychoanalysis would provide the theory of the subject. But in fact it was not an easy task to synthesize Freudian psychoanalysis with Marxist sociology, or historical materialism with a largely ahistorical structuralism. Indeed, the post-1968 period witnessed an overall decline in the prestige of Marxism and the emergence of the new politics of social movements such as feminism, gay liberation, ecology, and minority empowerment. The decline of Marxism had to do not only with the transparent crisis of socialist societies (a point sometimes exploited to obscure the fact that global capitalism was also in crisis), but also with increasing skepticism about all totalizing theories. Gradually, the focus of radical film theory shifted away from questions of class and ideology toward other concerns.

The move away from Marxism did not necessarily mean the abandonment of oppositional politics; it meant, rather, that the oppositional impulse now animated a different set of practices and concerns. Whereas class and ideology had dominated analysis in the 1960s, 1970s, and 1980s it began to disappear in favor of the simultaneously diminished (because classless) and expanded "mantra" of race, gender, and sexuality. Much of the discussion now revolved around feminist issues. The feminist goal was to explore the power arrangements and psycho-social mechanisms undergirding patriarchal society, with the ultimate aim of transforming not only film theory and criticism but also hierarchically gendered social relations in general. Film feminism was in this sense linked to the activism of consciousness-raising groups, to theme conferences and political campaigns which raised diverse issues of special importance to women: rape, spousal abuse, child care, the right to abortion, and so forth, in an atmosphere where the "personal is political."

Feminist theory, as has often been pointed out, is not single but plural. Feminism has millennial roots going back to mythical figures like Lilith, to the fighting Amazons, and to classical plays like *Lysistrata*. But during the century of cinema there have been at least two waves of feminist activism (in the West), the first linked to the struggle for universal suffrage, and the second emerging from the liberationist political movements of the 1960s. The Women's Liberation movement was named in the 1960s on the model of the Black Liberation movement, just as the coinage "sexism" was modeled on "racism." (Black liberationist and anti-colonialist women of color also did feminist work, but not necessarily in the context of film theory.) Many feminists built their analysis of sexism on previous understandings of racism, a move that recalled the earlier parallelism between the first-wave feminist critique of paternalism and the abolitionist critique of slavery. Film feminism, like feminism generally, built on "early fem-inist" texts like Virginia Woolf's *A Room of One's Own* and de Beauvoir's *The Second Sex*. De Beauvoir's title implied a rejection of Freud's sexual monism, the idea that there

170

was a single, essentially masculine, libido that defined all sexuality. De Beauvoir saw both women and blacks as in the process of emancipation from a paternalism that would keep them in their "place" (the formulation overlooked the fact that some of the women were black). Women, she argued, "are made not born"; patriarchal power deploys the brute fact of biological difference in order to manufacture and hierarchize gender difference. There was no "women's problem" but only a men's problem, just as there was no "black problem" but only a white one. (Three feminist classics from the late 1960s, Ti-Grace Atkinson's *Amazon Odyssey*, Shulamith Firestone's *Dialectic of Sex*, and Kate Millett's *Sexual Politics*, were all dedicated to de Beauvoir.) Feminists also built on Betty Friedan's *The Feminine Mystique* (1963) and the work of later feminists like Nancy Chodorow, Sandra Gilbert, Susan Gubar, Adrienne Rich, Audre Lorde, Kate Millett, Hélène Cixous, and Luce Irigaray. The founding in the United States of the National Organization of Women in 1966 and of *Ms* magazine in 1972 were also key events.

The feminist wave in film studies was first heralded by the emergence of women's film festivals (in New York and Edinburgh) in 1972, as well as by popular early 1970s books like Molly Haskell's *From Reverence to Rape*, Marjorie Rosen's *Popcorn Venus*, and Joan Mellon's *Women and Sexuality in the New Film*. Molly Haskell's cautiously feminist book, for example, rejected melioristic assumptions about women's progress in the cinema, tracing instead a zigzagging trajectory from chivalric "reverence" in the silent era, to the "rape" of 1970s Hollywood, with the zenith formed by the spunky heroines of screwball comedies in the 1930s. Haskell criticized both Hollywood anti-feminist backlash films and phallocentric European art films, while crediting the "woman's picture" with giving some voice to women suffering under patriarchy. These books generally stressed questions of representations of women, especially through negative stereotypes – madonnas, whores, vamps, scatterbrains, bimbos, gold diggers, schoolma'ams, nags, sex kittens – which infantilized women, or demonized them, or turned them into rampant sex objects. They showed that filmic sexism, like sexism in the three-dimensional world, was protean: it could involve idealizing women as morally superior beings, inferiorizing them as castrated and asexual, hyperbolizing them as horrifically powerful *femmes fatales*, envying them for their reproductive capacities, or fearing them as the incarnations of nature, age, and death. The cinema confronted women with a kind of Catch-22. As novelist Angela Carter put it, "In the celluloid brothel of the cinema, where the merchandise may be eyed endlessly but never purchased, the tension between the beauty of women, which is admirable, and the denial of the sexuality which is the source of that beauty but is also immoral, reaches a perfect impasse" (Carter, 1978, p. 60).

Feminism provides a large-scale methodological and theoretical grid which has implications for every facet of thinking about film. In terms of authorship, feminist film theory critiqued the boys'-club masculinism of auteurism while also facilitating the "archeological" recovery of female auteurs such as Alice Guy-Blache (arguably the first professional filmmaker in the world), Lois Weber, and Anita Loos in the United States, Aziza Amir in Egypt, Maria Landeta in Mexico, and Gilda de Abreu and Carmen Santos in Brazil. Theorists thus revisited the question of auteurism from a feminist perspective. Sandy Flitterman-Lewis (1990) examined the "search for a new cinematic language capable of expressing female desire," embodied by such female auteurs as Germaine Dulac and Agnes Varda. Feminist film theory also sparked new thinking about style (the question of *écriture feminine*), about industrial hierarchies and production processes (the historical relegation of women to jobs like editing, a kind of "sewing," and "scriptgirl," a kind of tidying up), and about theories of spectatorship (the female gaze, masochism, masquerade).

Early film feminism focused on practical goals of consciousness-raising, on denunciation of negative media imagery of women, as well as on more theoretical concerns. As the "Womanifesto" of the 1975 New York Conference of Feminists in the Media put it: "We do not accept the existing power structure and we are committed to changing it by the content and structure of our images and by the ways we related to each other in our work and with our audience" (Rich, 1998, p. 73). Partly reworking and reinvoicing the pre-existing amalgam of Marxism, semiotics, and psychoanalysis deployed by earlier (largely male) critics, theorists such as Laura Mulvey, Pam Cook, Rosalind Coward, Jacqueline Rose, Kaja Silverman, Mary Ann Doane, Judith Mayne, Sandy Flitterman-Lewis, Elizabeth Cowie, Gertrud Koch, Parveen Adams, Teresa de Lauretis, and many others criticized the naive essentialism of early feminism, moving the focus from biological sexual identity, seen as tied to "nature," to "gender," seen as a social construct shaped by cultural and historical contingency, variable and therefore reconstructable. Rather than focus on the "image" of women, feminist theorists transferred their attention to the gendered nature of vision itself, and the role of voyeurism, fetishism, and narcissism in the construction of a masculinist view of women. This discussion took the debates beyond the simple corrective task of pointing out misrepresentations and stereotypes, in order to examine the way dominant cinema engenders its spectator. In "Women's Cinema as Counter Cinema" – an essay first written for the Women's Event at the Edinburgh Film Festival in 1976 – Claire Johnston called for an analytic focus not only on image but also on the textual iconographic and narrative operations that maneuvered women into subordinate positions. Male characters in film, Johnston pointed out, tend to be active, highly individualized figures, while female figures seem like abstract entities from a timeless world of myth. At the same time, Johnston called for a feminist filmmaking that would mingle both reflexive distancing and the play of female desire.[1]

Theorists such as Johnston, and journals like *Camera Obscura*, called for a radical deconstruction of patriarchal Hollywood cinema, and the elaboration of an avant-garde feminist cinema exemplified by the work of Marguerite Duras, Yvonne Rainer, Nelly Kaplan, and Chantal Akerman. Film feminism was especially strong in Britain, the United States, and Northern Europe. (Despite the importance of women theorists in France – Cixous, Irigaray, Wittig – and despite the importance of French women filmmakers, feminist film theory was not a strong presence there.)

Feminism was also impacted by diverse currents from within psychoanalysis. In *Psychoanalysis and Feminism* (1974) Juliet Mitchell argued that although Freud certainly reflected the patriarchal attitudes of his time, he also provided the theoretical instruments for transcending those attitudes by showing how patriarchy affected his patients. The inaugural text for feminist film theory, at least in its psychoanalytic incarnation, was Laura Mulvey's seminal 1975 essay "Visual Pleasure and Narrative Cinema." The essay enlisted (the non-feminist) Lacan and (the equally non-feminist) Althusser into the feminist project by arguing for the gendered nature of narrative and point of view in classical Hollywood cinema. For Mulvey, the cinema choreographs three kinds of "gaze:" that of the camera, that of the characters looking at one another, and that of the spectator, induced to voyeuristically identify with a masculinist gaze at woman. Dominant cinema reinscribes patriarchal conventions by privileging the male in terms of both narrative and spectacle. "Interpellation," for Mulvey, is gendered. The male is made the active subject of the narrative and the female the passive object of a spectatorial gaze defined as male. The man is the driver of the narrative vehicle, while the woman is the passenger. Visual pleasure in the cinema thus reproduced a structure of male looking and female to-be-looked-at-ness, a binary structure which mirrored the asymmetrical power relations operative in the real social world. Women spectators had the Hobson's Choice of identifying either with the active male protagonist or with the passive, victimized female antagonist. The cinema could be voyeuristic *à la* Hitchcock – where the spectator identified with the male gaze at an objectified female – fetishistic *à la* Sternberg, where the beauty of the female body was deployed to stop the narrative in its tracks through close-ups exuding magical, erotic power. While Claire Johnston had argued for the release of the collective fantasies of women, Mulvey argued for the strategic rejection of filmic pleasure.

Mulvey was subsequently criticized (and criticized herself) for forcing the female spectator into a masculinist mold. In 1978 Christine Gledhill questioned the exclusively textual nature of film feminism: "under the insistence of the semiotic production of meaning, the effectivity of social, economic and political practice threatens to disappear altogether" (Gledhill, in Doane et al., 1984). Elizabeth Cowie, in "Fantasia" (1984), called for multiple and cross-gender identifications. David Rodowick (1991) argued that Mulvey's theory failed to allow for historical variability. A special issue of *Camera Obscura* (1989) featured some fifty responses to Mulvey's essay. Mulvey's model was now regarded as overly deterministic, blind to the diverse ways in which women could subvert, redirect, or undermine the male gaze.

Many feminists pointed to the ideological limitations of Freudianism, with its privileging of the phallus, of male voyeurism, and of an oedipal scenario which left little place for female subjectivity, quite apart from such subtly gendered concepts as "analytic neutrality." Freud, it was pointed out, was concerned with the oedipal trajectory only of the male child. Mary Ann Doane argued that the overwhelming presence to itself of the female body made it impossible for women to establish the distance from the image necessary for voyeuristic pleasure and control. The whole concept of fetishism, Doane pointed out, had little to do with a female spectator "for whom castration cannot pose a threat" (see Doane, in Doane et al., 1984, p. 79). Furthermore, there were other options available. The female spectator, Doane argued, could identify, transvestite-like, with the male gaze, thus paradoxically empowering herself while disempowering her gender; or identify in a masochistic way with her own stigmatization as lack (ibid.). In her study of the woman's film, Doane (1987) distinguished three subgenres – maternal, medical, and paranoid – emplotted by scenarios of masochism and hysteria.

In her study of the woman's films, *The Desire to Desire* (1987), Doane argues that these films, although they foreground women characters, ultimately circumscribe and frustrate their desire, leaving them with nothing to do but "desire to desire." The various subgenres within this larger field work in parallel but different ways to achieve this effect. In those films revolving around illness, female desire is coopted by the institutional relation between doctor and patient. In family melodramas, it is sublimated into motherhood. In romantic comedy, it is channeled into narcissism. And in gothic horror films, desire is undone by anxiety.

Gaylyn Studlar, meanwhile, countered Mulvey (along with Baudry and Metz) by suggesting that the key to spectatorship might lie less in voyeurism and fetishism than in a masochism rooted in the archaic memory of a powerful mother. The male reaction to the spectacle of sexual difference, for example, might be more masochistic than sadistic: "The cinematic apparatus and the masochistic aesthetic offer identificatory positions for male and female spectators that reintegrate psychic bisexuality, offer the sensual pleasures of polymorphous sexuality, and make the male and female one in their identification with and desire for the pre-Oedipal mother" (Studlar, 1988, p. 192). Books like Carol Clover's *Men, Women and Chain Saws* shifted the ground of debate by suggesting that spectatorial positions can oscillate between the active and the passive, the sadistic and the masochistic. Contemporary horror films, she suggested, do not position the male spectator toward sadism; rather, they prod male spectators to identify with the female victim (Clover, 1992). Rhona J. Berenstein (1995) further complicated the analysis of spectatorship in the horror film by advancing a performative view of a genre marked by role playing and disguise, and where spectators adopt and discard fixed gender and sexual roles. Teresa de Lauretis, for her part, argued that the spectator was positioned bisexually, since the daughter never fully relinquishes her desire for the mother. Calling for an "Oedipus Interruptus" which opted out of masculinist models, de Lauretis suggested that the cinema should move beyond sexual difference to explore differences among women. Gender, de Lauretis (1989) argued, was produced by various social technologies, including that of the cinema. Complex social technologies – institutions, representations, processes – model individuals, assign them a role and function and place. Men and women are solicited differentially by these technologies, and have conflicting investments in the discourses and practices of sexuality.

In the wake of all the criticism, Mulvey made a kind of auto-critique in her "Afterthoughts on Visual Pleasure," where she acknowledged that she had neglected two important issues: melodrama and the "woman in the audience." In her later work, Bakhtinian hybridism offered a way out of the binaries of Lacanianism. Kaja Silverman (1992), meanwhile, turned her attention to "perverse," non-phallic, para-oedipal masculinities that say "no" to power, while arguing that the concept of ideology remained an "indispensable tool not only for Marxist, but for feminist and gay, studies." Psychoanalytic feminist theory argued for an understanding of femininity and masculinity as cultural constructs, the result of processes of discursive and cultural production and differentiation. Identification, once seen as monolithic, was dispersed across a broad, changing field of positionalities. An exclusive concern with sexual difference gave way to ramifying differences among women. De Lauretis spoke of the "productive heterogeneity of feminism" and asked feminists to think about issues of enunciation and address: "who is making films for whom, who is looking and speaking, how, where, and to whom?"[2]

The period of feminist film theory has also been the heyday of filmmaking by women. In an attempt at schematizing this variegated production, Ruby Rich (1998) proposed an experimental taxonomy of descriptive categories:

1 Validative (legitimating films about women's struggles, e.g. *Union Maids*).
2 Correspondence (avant-garde films such as *Film About a Woman Who . . .* , which inscribe their author into the text).
3 Reconstructive (formally experimental films such as Sally Potter's *Thriller* that reinvoice conventional genres).
4 Medusan (films like Nelly Kaplan's *A Very Curious Girl* which celebrate the potential of feminist texts to "blow up the law").
5 Corrective realism (feminist features aimed at a wide audience, such as von Trott's *The Second Awakening of Christa Klages*).

Many of the films by women had a feminist-theoretical thrust, as in the films of Laura Mulvey and Peter Wollen, Yvonne Rainer, Marleen Gooris, Su Friedrich, Sally Potter, Julie Dash, Chantal Akerman, Jane Campion, Mira Nair, Lizzie Borden, and many others.

At the same time, in the 1980s and 1990s, feminists began to be more respectful of the *pleasures* of mainstream cinema. In *The Women Who Knew Too Much* Tania Modleski pointed to the remarkable ambivalence of Hitchcock's regard on/for women, arguing that male characters in his work project their own suffering onto the women characters in a "dialectic of identification and dread." Feminists also turned their attention to popular genres, as in Kaplan's (1998) anthology on film noir and Christine Gledhill's (1987) work on the melodrama. Some feminists lauded the carnivalesque incarnations of the "unruly woman," who proudly makes a spectacle of herself as a way of negotiating invisibility in the public sphere. Drawing on Bakhtin and Mary Douglas, Kathleen Rowe (1995) lamented the focus on melodrama and female victimization, and lauded instead the comedic transgressions of excessive women – "too fat, too funny, too noisy, too old, too rebellious" – who unsettle social hierarchy. (Molly Haskell had partly anticipated this move by her valorization of the feisty heroines of screwball comedies.)

Feminist film theory was also criticized for being normatively "white" and for marginalizing lesbians and women of color. Alice Walker found the term "feminism" unattractive for blacks and coined the term "womanist" to designate black women's writing and criticism. Black feminists complained that the "Woman as Nigger" formulation failed to acknowledge that "niggers" could also be women. As Barbara Christian put it, "If defined as black, her woman nature was often denied; if defined as woman, her blackness was often ignored; if defined as working class, her gender and race were muted" (quoted in Young-Bruehl, 1996, p. 514).

Poet Adrienne Rich (1979) acknowledged the critique by excoriating "white solipsism," the "tunnel-vision which simply does not see nonwhite experience or existence as precious or significant, unless in spasmodic, impotent guilt-reflexes, which have little or no long-term, continuing momentum or political usefulness." Ella Shohat in "Gender and the Culture of Empire" pointed to the colonial undertext of some of Freud's writings[3] and lamented the limitations of mainstream feminist analysis when dealing with Euro-colonialist films like *Black Narcissus*, which provisionally grant the power of the gaze to white female characters but only as part of a colonial civilizing mission (Shohat, in Bernstein and Studlar,1996). Jane Gaines also pointed to the ethnocentrism of some feminist theory. bell hooks argued that black female spectators were almost necessarily oppositional in ways that went beyond the critical gaze of black male spectators (see hooks, 1992, pp. 115–31).

The achievements of feminist film theory retroactively exposed the masculinist underpinnings of theory itself: the eroticized misogyny of the Surrealists; the heroic (oedipal) masculinism of auteur theory, the supposedly genderless "objectivity" of semiotics. Feminists discerned sexism in the subliminal tropes that undergirded such theories. Tania Modleski pointed out the ways that Frankfurt School theory, for example, feminized mass culture by linking it to qualities stereotypically associated with women – passivity and sentimentality. Through a gendered division of symbolic labor, women are held accountable for the pernicious effects of consuming mass-culture, while men shoulder the responsibility for generating a socially critical high culture.[4]

The Poststructuralist Mutation

In the late 1960s the Saussurean model and the structuralist semiotics derived from it came under attack – most notably from Derridean deconstruction – and thus led to poststructuralism. The poststructuralist movement shares the structuralist premise of the determining, constitutive role of language, and shares the assumption that signification is based on difference, but it rejects structuralism's "dream of scientificity," its hopes of stabilizing the play of difference within an all-encompassing master-system.

Drawing on the work of Friedrich Nietzsche and the phenomenology of Husserl and Heidegger, poststructuralism saw that the drive toward systematicity typical of structuralism should be confronted by everything that it excluded and repressed. Indeed, many of the seminal texts of poststructuralism (for example, Derrida's *Of Grammatology*, *Writing and Difference*, and *Speech Phenomenon*, all published originally in 1967) comprised explicit critiques of the central figures and cardinal concepts of structuralism. Derrida's paper at the 1966 "Languages of Criticism and the Sciences of Man" Con-

179

ference at Johns Hopkins University, Baltimore (a conference which established the broad interdisciplinary base for the introduction of deconstructionist theory into the American academy), for example, was a critique of the notion of "structure" in the structuralist anthropology of Lévi-Strauss. Derrida called for a "decentering" of structures, suggesting that "even today the notion of a structure lacking any center represents the unthinkable itself" (Derrida, 1978, p. 279).

Poststructuralism has been variously described as a shift of interest from the signified to the signifier, and from the utterance to enunciation. The poststructuralist movement, which along with Derrida includes among others Foucault, Lacan, Kristeva, and the later Roland Barthes, demonstrated a thoroughgoing distrust of any centered, totalizing theory. ("Deconstruction" tends to refer specifically to the work of Derrida, while "poststructuralism" is the broader, more inclusive term, although one used more in North America than in Europe.) Deconstruction thus gave voice to a radical skepticism about the possibility of constructing an overarching meta-language, since the signs of the meta-language itself are themselves subject to slippage and indeterminacy, as unstable signs move ceaselessly outward within a proliferation of allusion spiraling from text to text. If structuralism assumed stable, homeostatic structures, poststructuralism looked for moments of rupture and change. In this sense, deconstruction forms part of the anti-foundationalist wave going back to Nietzsche, Freud, and Heidegger, and notably to the "hermeneutics of suspicion" (Paul Ricoeur) that interrogates the inevitable slips that corrode attempts to fix and stabilize meaning. For this reason the poststructuralist lexicon tends to favor a vocabulary that undermines any sense of grounded stability: words like "fluidity," "hybridity," "trace," "slippage," and "dissemination." Echoing Voloshinov's and Bakhtin's critique of Saussure in *Marxism and Philosophy of Language* (1929), but probably unaware of that text, deconstruction critiques the concepts of the stable sign, the unified subject, and identity and truth. (As Julia Kristeva already noted in the late 1960s, Bakhtin uncannily foreshadowed major poststructuralist topoi: the denial of univocal meaning, the infinite

180

spiral of interpretation, the negation of originary presence in speech, the unstable identity of the sign, the positioning of the subject by discourse, the untenable nature of inside–outside oppositions, and the pervasive presence of intertextuality.)[1] Derrida adopts keywords in the Saussurean vocabulary – especially "difference," "signifier," and "signified" – but redeploys them within a transformed framework. The structuralist emphasis on binary contrasts as the source of linguistic meaning gives way to Derrida's view of language as a multivalent place of "play," an indeterminate field of slippages and substitutions. Saussure's notion of the differential relation between signs is reinscribed by Derrida as a relation *within* signs, whose constitutive nature is one of constant displacement or trace. Language for Derrida is thus always inscribed in a network of relays and differential "traces" beyond the grasp of the individual speaker. Without rejecting the semiotic project or denying its historical importance, Derrida proposes a "grammatology" which would study the science of writing and textuality in general.

Perhaps because it was so intimately linked to language-based disciplines (literature and philosophy), Derridean poststructuralism has been a quiet but hardly overwhelming presence within film theory. Often that presence has been lexical, as terms and concepts at least partially derived from Derrida – "trace," "dissemination," "logocentrism," "excess" – have circulated widely within film-critical discourse. Julia Kristeva, a writer associated with the journal *Tel Quel*, a group which regarded modernist literary–textual practices (Lautréamont, Mallarmé, Artaud, etc.) as prototypes of a revolutionary *écriture*, was a key influence. As absorbed within film-theoretical milieu (in such film journals as *Cahiers du cinéma* and especially *Cinetique*), Tel Quelism led in the 1970s to a radical rejection of all conventional mainstream films, and even of aesthetically conventional left militant films, in favor of films which provoked a dramatic rupture with conventional practices – films such as Jean Daniel Pollet's *Mediterranée*, the experimental films of the Dziga Vertov group (Jean-Luc Godard and Jean-Pierre Gorin), and even the reflexive farces of Jerry Lewis. At times film form was fetishized, as theorists forgot the historicity of forms themselves. Mere style was made to bear a heavy burden of political disruption. While grammar was disrupted, power relations were left intact.

Metz's theories in *Language and Cinema*, meanwhile, were at times clearly inflected by the poststructuralist literary currents associated with Derrida and Kristeva. Metz tended to oscillate between a more neutral "structuralist" notion of text as any finite, organized discourse, on the one hand, and the more programmatic avant-garde deconstructionist sense of text on the other. Unlike the Tel Quelists, Metz does not generally use the word "text" as an honorific reserved for radical avant-garde films. For him, all films are texts and have textual systems. Yet there exists a clear tension in *Language and Cinema* between a static, taxonomic, structuralist–formalist view of textual systems, and a more dynamic poststructuralist Barthesian–Kristevan view of text as "productivity," "displacement," and "*écriture*." Influenced by the Kristevan critique of the Saussurean paradigm (a critique indebted not only to the Derridean critique of the sign but also to Bakhtin's translinguistic critique of Saussure), Metz describes the moment of filmic *parole* as the dissolution of the very systematicity he has elsewhere emphasized:

The system of the text is the process which displaces codes, deforming each of them by the presence of the others, contaminating some by means of others, meanwhile replacing one by another, and finally – as a temporarily "arrested" result of this general displacement – placing each code in a particular position in regard to the overall structure, a displacement which thus finishes by a positioning which is itself destined to be displaced by another text. (Metz, 1974a, p.103)

It is this latter view of the text as a "non-finalized" perpetual displacement that constitutes the more dynamic pole in *Language and Cinema*. A film's text is not the additive "list" of its operative codes, then, but rather the labor of restructuration by which the film "writes" its text, modifies and combines its codes, playing some codes off against others, and thus constitutes its system. The textual system, then, is the instance which displaces the codes so that they come to inflect and substitute one another. While film language can be seen as an ensemble of codes, filmic *écriture* is an active operation, the writerly process which displaces the codes.

The Marxists of *Cinetique* and *Cahiers du cinéma* gave a distinct left–Brechtian slant to the Derridean notion of deconstruction, using it to name the process of exposing the subliminal ideological underpinnings of the cinematic apparatus and of dominant cinema. In this reading the deconstructive text referred less to the complex philosophical maneuvers of Derrida and more to films which made visible the operative codes and ideologies of dominant cinema. (Most poststructuralist film theory and analysis, for reasons already explained, has been based more on Lacan's "return to Freud" than on Derridean deconstruction.)

Deconstruction has made its presence felt in film theory and analysis especially as a method of reading. The emphasis on reading skeptically, of calling attention to the repressions and contradictions and aporias of film texts (or texts about film), the assumption that no text takes a position that it does not at the same time undermine, the idea that all texts are constitutively contradictory, now permeate film studies. Poststructuralism destabilized textual meaning, shaking early semiology's scientistic faith that analysis might definitively capture the totality of a film's meaning by delineating all its codes. In film theory the implications of deconstruction have been explored by such analysts as Marie-Claire Ropars, Michael Ryan, Peter Brunette, David Wills, and Stephen Heath (via Kristeva). Marie-Claire Ropars, in a number of texts published only in French, has extra-polated into film analysis an expansive Derridean notion of *écriture* – understood as a "theoretical hypothesis" which replaces the notion of "sign" with "trace" as part of a differential process of signification whose terms are unassignable and unfixable. Ropars sees cinematic montage, especially as practiced by Eisenstein, as the means of transcending mimetic representation in favor of creating an abstract conceptual space. Eisenstein's "writerly" texts reveal the processes of their own *écriture* and thus generate instability of meaning. In *Le Texte divesé* (1981), perhaps the most sophisticated of the Derridean analyses of the cinema, Ropars turns the hieroglyph, as a superimposed set of signifying systems, into a figure for the "scriptural vocation of the cinema" as a kind of "writing machine." Through exemplary readings of films like *M* and *India Song*, Ropars explodes and disperses filmic signification rather than "taming" it. For Ropars, film texts potentially put into play active, unsynthesizable "structural conflicts." The disjunctive capacity of montage, especially, can dismantle the sign by playing on the "differences" between material signifiers. Films are fissured by two forces, écriture and counter-écriture, one tending toward a disseminating scriptural energy, and the other toward sense and representation. (Bakhtin would have said between "centrifugal" and "centripetal" forces.)

Brunette and Wills (1989) deploy Derridean categories in order to interrogate various totalizing notions which they see as surreptitiously informing film theory and analysis: the notions of narrative film; Hollywood as a self-identical coherent system; the primacy of the visual, seen as analogous to the primacy of speech over writing in the logocentric tradition. (Many of these notions had already been questioned without recourse to Derrida, of course.) Calling for a move beyond totalizations, the authors invoke the possibilities of an "anagrammatical" reading practice that sees cinema as writing, text, "an interplay of presence and absence, of the seen and not seen, in relations not reducible either to totalization or transcendence" (ibid., p. 58).

Deconstruction has also influenced film theory and analysis indirectly, through certain writers themselves influenced by deconstruction, who rarely write about film but who are frequently cited by film theorists. Thus Judith Butler's work on gender becomes a key reference for queer film theory, while Gayatri Spivak's work on the subaltern subject and Homi Bhabha's work on "hybridity" and "nation and narration" become frequent (although often ornamental) references in film-theoretical writing. In political terms deconstruction has been seen as progressive, in that it systematically undermines certain binary hierarchies – male/female, West/East, black/white – that have historically buttressed oppression. Derrida has aligned himself with the feminist critique of Lacanian phallocentrism, for example. On the other hand, critics of deconstruction have complained that it is easily co-optable by academic elitists (as, for example, in the Yale School of literary deconstruction) and that its grand claims of "subversion" tend to be merely rhetorical. At times, in hyper-deconstructionist discourse, essentialism becomes the equivalent of original sin, resulting in a less-essentialist-than-thou sweepstake. Deconstruction also shifts political valence depending on who or what is the object of its critique. Progressive when it interrogates historically rooted social hierarchies (Man over Woman, West over East), deconstruction becomes regressive when it runs after the chimera of a completely de-essentialized thinking, handing over to language and discourse the collective agency rightfully belonging to human subjects.

Textual Analysis

The question of the text was at the very heart of Derrida's work, and Derrida himself performed textual analyses (of Rousseau, Saussure and others). Deconstruction was on one level a form of textual exegesis, an "unpacking" of texts, a way of interrogating their unspoken premises while being alert to their discursive heterogeneity. And although textual analysis traces its long-term antecedents to biblical exegesis, nineteenth-century hermeneutics and philology, the French pedagogical method of close reading (*explication de texte*), and American New Criticism's "immanent" analysis, its more immediate antecedents include Lévi-Strauss's work on myth, Umberto Eco's study of the "open work," Roland Barthes's distinction between "work" and "text," Althusser's and Macharey's (Freudian) notion of "symptomatic reading" and "structuring absences," and Derrida's work on *differance* and dissemination.

The emergence of the "film text" was thus rooted in multiple problematics and intertexts. The term transferred from literature to film the respect traditionally accorded the sacred word (first religious and then literary) and thus served to garner prestige for a maligned medium. In religious terms, film, too, has its quantum of "revelation." When films are texts rather than movies they become worthy of the same serious attention normally given to literature. Textual analysis is also a logical corollary to auteurism: What would "authors" write, after all, if not texts? At the same time, the film text is a function of semiology's focus on film as the site of systematically organized discourse rather than as a random "slice of life." The presumption of textual analysis that film as a medium deserves serious study distinguishes it not only from literary elitist writing but also from a journalistic criticism which sees film as mere entertainment. If Pauline Kael's boast that she would never see a film more than once before writing about it had been made by a literary critic with regard to *Hamlet* or *Ulysses* it would have been taken as a sign of laziness or incompetence. Literary criticism, as Barthes pointed out, was always a matter of "rereading."

The concept of "text" – etymologically "tissue" or "weave" – conceptualizes film not as an imitation of reality but rather as an artifact, a construct. In "From Work to Text" Barthes made two distinctions. "Work" was defined as the phenomenal surface of the object, for example the book one holds in one's hand, i.e. a completed product conveying an intended and pre-existent meaning. "Text" was defined as a methodological field of energy, a production absorbing writer and reader together. "We now know," Barthes wrote, "that the text is not a line of words releasing a single 'theological' meaning (the 'message' of an Author-God) but a multi-dimensional space in which a variety of writings, none of them original, blend and clash" (Barthes, 1977, p. 146). In *S/Z* Barthes further distinguished between the "readerly" and the "writerly" text or, better, between readerly and writerly *approaches* to texts. The readerly approach privileges those values sought and assumed in the classic text – organic unity, linear sequence, stylistic transparency, conventional realism. It posits authorial mastery and readerly passivity, turning the author into a god and the critic into "the priest whose task is to decipher the Writing of the god" (Barthes, 1974, p. 174). The writerly approach, in contrast, fashions an active reader, sensitive to contradiction and heterogeneity, aware of the work of the text. It turns its consumer into a producer, foregrounding the process of its own construction and promoting the infinite play of signification.

186

Building on his own background in literary theory, Raymond Bellour addressed some of the difficulties in extending literary models to film in his essay "The Unattainable Text." Whereas literary criticism emerges from centuries of reflexion, film analysis is of recent date. More important, the film text, unlike the literary text, is not "quotable" (Bellour was writing prior to the existence of Cine-Scans, VCRs, laser-disks, and cable television, a time when the very scarcity contributed to the mystique of film analysis). Whereas literature and literary criticism share the same medium of words, film and film analysis do not. While the film medium deploys Metz's five tracks (image, dialogue, noise, music, written materials), the analysis of film consists of words. Critical language is therefore inadequate to its object; the film always escapes the language that attempts to constitute it. Bellour then compares film to other artistic texts in terms of their coefficient of "quotability." The painterly text is quotable, and can be taken in at a glance. The theatrical text can be rendered as written text, but with a loss of "accent." Bellour then analyzes the uneven susceptibility of the five tracks of cinematic expression to verbal rendering. Dialogue can be quoted, but with a loss in tone, intensity, timbre, and the simultaneity of bodily and facial expression. In the case of noise, a verbal account is always a translation, a distortion. The image, finally, cannot possibly be rendered in words. Individual frames can be reproduced and quoted, but in stopping the film, one loses what is specific to it – movement itself. The text escapes at the very moment one tries to seize it. Given this obstacle, the analyst can only try, in "principled despair," to compete with the object he or she is attempting to understand.

Metz distinguished between two complementary tasks, a kind of shot–reverse shot dialogue, as it were, between (1) film theory (the study of film language *per se*) and (2) film analysis. While cinematic language is the object of cine-semiological *theory*, the text is the object of filmolinguistic *analysis* (in practice, as we shall see, the distinction is not always so clear). In *Language and Cinema* Metz developed the notion of the textual system, i.e. the undergirding structure or network of meaning around which the text coheres, even in cases, such as *Un Chien Andalou*, where the structure is one of willed incoherence. The structure is a configuration arising from the choices made from the diverse codes available to the filmmaker. The textual system does not inhere in the text; it is constructed by the analyst. In *Language and Cinema* Metz was not concerned with providing a "how-to" book for textual analysis, but rather with determining its theoretical "place." Textual analysis, for Metz, explores the mesh of cinematic codes (camera movement, off-screen sound) and extra-cinematic codes (ideological binarisms of nature–culture, male–female), either across a number of texts or within a single text. All films, for Metz, are mixed sites; they all deploy cinematic and non-cinematic codes. No film is constructed uniquely out of cinematic codes; films always speak of something, even if, as in the case of many avant-garde films, they speak only about the apparatus itself, or about the film experience, or about our conventional expectations concerning that experience.

Metz's formulations had the advantage of socializing, as it were, the artistic process of creation. By foregrounding *écriture* as the re-elaboration of codes, Metz envisions film as a signifying practice not dependent on obscure romantic forces like inspiration and genius but rather as a reworking of socially available discourses. However, in some respects Metz's socialization did not go far enough. In this sense, the Bakhtin–Medvedev critique of the Formalists in *The Formal Method in Literary Scholarship* can be extrapolated so as to apply to the Metzian view of textual systems. The Formalists described textual contradiction in terms redolent of social struggle, in metaphors evoking combat, struggle, and conflict. Shklovsky, for example, compared the advent of a new school of literature to a revolution, "something like the emergence of a new class."[1] However, even the Formalists retreated from the implications of their own metaphor – it was "only an analogy" – and literary contradiction remained in a hermetically sealed world of pure textuality. Bakhtin and Medvedev, in contrast, took the Formalist metaphors seriously, especially those terms evocative of class struggle and insurrection: revolt, conflict, struggle, destruction, and even "the dominant" – but made them apply equally to the text and to the social itself (Pechey, 1986).

The Metzian and the Formalist views of the text might be usefully complemented, then, by the Bakhtinian concept of heteroglossia, i.e. a notion of competing languages and discourses as they operate within both "text" and "context." The role of the artistic text, within a Bakhtinian perspective, is not to represent real-life "existents" but rather to stage the conflicts inherent in heteroglossia, the coincidences and competitions of languages and discourses. A social semiotic of the cinema would retain the Formalist and the Metzian notion of *textual contradiction*, but rethink it through heteroglossia. The languages of heteroglossia, Bakhtin argues (in words that echo Metz's affirmations about mutually displacing filmic codes), may be "juxtaposed to one another, mutually supplement one another, contradict one another and be interrelated dialogically."[2] James Naremore's essay on *Cabin in the Sky*, for example, takes this "discursive" approach, seeing the film as relaying distinct discourses (rural–folklorist, Afro-urban–modernist, etc.).

The publication of Metz's *Language and Cinema* was followed by an international deluge of textual analyses of films in journals such as *Screen* and *Framework* in Britain, *Iris, Vertigo*, and *Ça* in France, *Camera Obscura*, *Wide Angle*, and *Cinema Journal* in the United States, *Contracampo* in Spain, and *Cadernos de Crítica* in Brazil. (Roger Odin focused on essays in French and found 50 analyses of this type by 1977.) Such analyses investigated the formal configurations of textual systems, isolating a small number of codes and then tracing their interweavings across a film. Among the more ambitious textual analyses were Kari Hanet's analysis of *Shock Corridor*, Stephen Heath's analysis of *Touch of Evil*, Pierre Baudry's analysis of *Intolerance*, Thierry Kuntzel's analysis of *The Most Dangerous Game*, and *Cahiers'* analysis of *Young Mr Lincoln*.

What, then, was *new* in the semiotic approach to textual analysis? First, the new method demonstrated a heightened sensitivity to the filmic signifier and to specifically cinematic formal elements, as opposed to the traditional emphasis on character and plot. Second, analyses tended to be methodologically self-aware; they were at once about their subject – the film in question – and about their own methodology. Each analysis became an exemplum of a possible approach. In contrast to journalistic criticism, the analysts cited their own theoretical presuppositions and critical intertext (many analyses began with quasi-ritual invocations of the names of Metz, Barthes, Kristeva, or Heath). Third, these analyses also presupposed a radically different emotional stance toward films, one characterized by a kind of Brechtian distantiation, an oscillation between passionate love and critical distance. The analyst was supposed to adopt a schizophrenic attitude, both loving and not loving the film. Rather than a single screening, the analyst scrutinized the film shot-by-shot (the development of VCRs has since that time democratized the practice of close analysis). Analysts such as Marie-Claire Ropars and Michel Marie developed elaborate schemata for notation, registering such codes as angle, camera movement, movement in the shot, off-screen sound, and so forth.

Given the closeness of attention of such analyses it became impossible to try to say everything about a film. As a result, many analyses focused on synecdochic fragments of films. Thus Marie-Claire Ropars devoted 40 pages to the initial shots of Eisenstein's *October* and Rocha's *Antonio das Mortes*, while Thierry Kuntzel dedicated long analyses to the *ouverture* sequences of films such as *M*, *King Kong*, and *The Most Dangerous Game*, seen as condensed matrices of meaning. The dedication of many pages of critical writing to a brief segment also indirectly demonstrated to high-art elitists that the same medium despised by others was actually the scene of veritable cornucopias of meaning. The analyses also varied widely in scale. The limits of the text might be defined by a single image (for example, Ronald Levaco's and Fred Glass's analysis of the MGM logo), by a single segment (Bellour on *The Birds*), by an entire film (Heath on *Touch of Evil*), by the entire oeuvre of a filmmaker as examples of a "plurifilmic textual system" (René Gardies on Glauber Rocha), or even by a vast corpus of films (Michele Lagny, Marie-Claire Ropars, and Pierre Sorlin on the French cinema of the 1930s, and Bordwell, Staiger, and Thompson, from a largely non-semiotic perspective, on classical Hollywood cinema).

Textual analyses rejected the traditional evaluative terms of film criticism in favor of a new vocabulary drawn from structural linguistics, narratology, psychoanalysis, Prague School aesthetics, and literary deconstruction. In what was perhaps an over-reaction against traditional film criticism, textual analysts often completely ignored issues traditionally central to film analysis: elements like character, acting, performance. Although most of the analyses generated by this wave belonged, broadly speaking, to the general semiotic current, not all of them were rigorously based on Metzian categories. Marie-Claire Ropars Wuilleumier's extremely intricate analyses of such films as *India Song* and *October* synthesized semiotic insights with a more personal project inspired by Derridean grammatology. Many textual analyses were influenced by literary textual analyses, for example Julia Lesage's extrapolation of Barthes's "five codes" to Renoir's *Rules of the Game* (in Nichols, 1985). Some textual analyses were inspired by Proppian narratological methods (e.g. Peter Wollen on *North by Northwest*), by Lacan's "return to Freud (e.g. Bellour on *North by Northwest*), or by other theoretical currents.

While some textual analyses sought to construct the system of a single text, others studied specific films as instances of a general code informing cinematic practice. Here, too, the distinction is not always clear, however; Raymond Bellour's analysis of *The Birds* offers both a microcosmic textual analysis of the Bodega Bay sequence of the Hitchcock film and an interrogation of broader narrative codes shared by a larger body of films; to wit, the constitution of the couple as the *telos* of Hollywood narrative. In two books, Kristin Thompson (1981; 1988) offered a programmatic alternative neo-Formalist method of textual analysis, performed both with and against the grain of semiotics. Alfred Guzzetti (1981), meanwhile, offers a blow-by-blow account of the Godard film in terms of sound, image, and intertextual reference.

The theoretical discourse concerning the cinema that developed in France in the 1960s was taken up in the 1970s by the British journal *Screen* and subsequently migrated to the United States and to many other countries with the growth of cinema studies programs, many of them with a strong Parisian link. (The Centre Americain d'Études Cinématographiques, which sent American students to Paris to study with leading French semioticians, was crucial in this regard.) Left-leaning versions of semiotics favored a

191

subversive work of denaturalization by scrutinizing social and artistic productions in order to discern the cultural and ideological codes operative in them. Film theory generally, in fact, developed a discourse to the left of many other more traditional disciplines, not only because of a strong "French connection" – the French subsequently moved dramatically rightward – but also because of its simultaneous emergence alongside such counter-cultural disciplines as women's studies, ethnic studies, and popular culture studies. As a result, film studies was never plagued in the same way by the "mouldy figs," entrenched conservatives who dominated more traditional fields like literature and history.

The emergence of film theory as a growth industry also had institutional causes: the inauguration of cinema studies as a discipline in major universities in France, Britain, the USA, Australia, Italy, Brazil, and elsewhere. Sophisticated versions of theory testified to the intellectual seriousness of film study, and thus indirectly provided a rationale for the creation of cinema studies departments. Just as film had to legitimate itself as an art, so film studies had to legitimate itself as a discipline. With its institutional home base in the academy and the publishing industry, film theory acquired considerable prestige and dissemination. The snobbism of traditional literary academics, with their scorn for popular culture and for film as a medium supposedly inferior to consecrated arts like literature, painting, and music, inadvertently prodded film studies to demonstrate its own seriousness, and at times to over-compensate by virtuoso displays of theoretical prowess.[3]

Interpretation and its Discontents

In the 1980s textual analysis as conceived by film semiotics came under attack from a number of directions. On the one hand, poststructuralist currents both inspired and destabilized textual analysis, shaking early semiology's scientific faith that analysis might definitively capture a film's meaning by exhaustively delineating all its

192

codes. On the other hand, the emerging field of cultural studies was not terribly invested in textual analysis. Its attitude was summed up later in the words of Cary Nelson, Paula Treichler, and Lawrence Grossberg in their introduction to *Cultural Studies* (1992), where they state that "although there is no prohibition against close textual readings in cultural studies, they are also not required, [since] textual analysis in literary studies carries a history of convictions that texts are properly understood as wholly self-determined and independent objects."

Jacques Aumont and Michel Marie (1989) outline four possible critiques of textual analysis:

1 Its relevance is limited to narrative cinema.
2 It "murders to dissect," ignoring the organic unity of the text.
3 It reductively "mummifies" film by reducing it to its systemic skeleton.
4 It elides film's context, its conditions for production and reception.

The first of these critiques misfires (since textual analysis is applicable to any object), while the second seems rooted in hostility to analysis *per se*, especially when performed in relation to an "unworthy" medium. But the last two have some force, and are in fact interrelated. When textual analyses are reductive, it is precisely because they *are* ahistorical and therefore fail to take production and reception into account. And the charge of ahistoricism is not answered satisfactorily by Aumont and Marie's suggestion that analysts "also" do history. The roots of the "decontextualization" of some textual analysis lie in the ahistoricism of two of the source movements of semiotics: Saussurean linguistics – particularly its tendency to cut off language from history – and Russian Formalism, with its preference for a purely intrinsic analysis. When analysts within the filmolinguistic tradition recommend that film scholars should *also* study – within a kind of amicable division of labor – history, economics, sociology, and so forth, they recapitulate the approach taken by the Formalists themselves, who also recommended *first* the immanent study of the literary text and only *then* the study of the relation between the literary series and the other historical series. For a truly "historical poetics," in contrast, all artistic languages, given their inherently dialogical quality and the fact that they are addressed to socially situated interlocutors, are "always already" social and historical.

Film analysis is, above all, an open-ended and historically shaped practice oriented by diverse goals. Analysis tends to find what it is looking for. While the New Critics in literature looked for (and found) "organic unity" and "image clusters" and "irony," deconstructionist critics looked for tensions and fissures and aporias. Film analysis is a method rather than an ideology; it is a genre of film writing open to diverse influences (from Barthes to Jameson to Deleuze), to diverse grids (psychoanalysis, Marxism, feminism), to diverse "schemata" (reflexivity, excess, carnival), and to diverse principles of pertinence, both cinematic (camera movement, editing) and extra-cinematic (representation of women, blacks, gays and lesbians). A film like *Rear Window*, for example, can be seen in terms of diverse grids: auteurism (its relation to Hitchcock's oeuvre as a whole); marks of enunciation (Hitchcock's "deictic" self-inscription through style and cameo appearance); music (the Franz Waxman score); mise-en-scène (the spatial restriction of the apartment complex setting); reflexivity (allegorical references to film spectatorship); the gaze (the play of looks and eyeline matches between Jeffries, Lisa, Stella, and Thorwald); psychoanalysis (a symptomatic reading of the protagonist's voyeurism); gender (the sexual politics of looking); class (the tensions between the hardworking photojournalist and upscale fashion-plate); period resonances (allusions to McCarthyism), to mention just a few of the "schemata" (Bordwell), "codes" (Metz), and "socio-ideological discourses" (Bakhtin) relevant to the film.

David Bordwell (1989) offers a densely informative and multidimensional account of the evolution of the field of cinema studies, and mounts an attack on "interpretation." While cultural studies advocates saw textual analysis in literary studies as *under*-politicized, Bordwell seemed to regard textual analysis in film as *over*-politicized. In post-1968 "symptomatic criticism," Bordwell argues, "The theme of fate is replaced by the duality power/subjection. Love is replaced by desire, or law/desire. Instead of the individual there is subject/ object or phallus/lack. Instead of art there is signifying practice. Instead of society there is nature/culture or class struggle" (Bordwell, 1989, p. 109). Bordwell laments, in quasi-elegiac terms, the shift from the "individualist perspective" to "an analytical, almost anthropological detachment that sees sexuality, politics, and signification" as the key areas of meaning. Film interpreters root out symbolic meanings by bringing into play "semantic fields" and "heuristics" assumed in advance rather than emerging inductively from the analysis itself. While claiming to do theory, interpreters merely "apply" it in a "piecemeal, ad hoc, and expansionist manner" (ibid., p. 250). Bordwell critiques the predominance in film criticism of two tendencies linked to textual analysis in the semiotic tradition: thematic explanation and symptomatic reading (usually *politically* symptomatic reading). According to Bordwell, both tendencies share an interpretative logic and rhetoric, when in fact "the great days of interpretation-centered criticism are over." The epidemic of interpretation "attests to the powerful role of literature departments in transmitting interpretative values and skills. Academic humanism's omnivorous appetite for interpretation rendered cinema a plausible text" (ibid., p. 17).

Bordwell deploys two Formalist schemata: (1) the demand for specificity, here *disciplinary* specificity (film studies should not borrow from literature departments); (2) Formalist estrangement, the critique of the "routinization" of symptomatic reading. (The role of art for the Formalists, we recall, was to challenge automatized perceptions.) If reading means the ascription of symptomatic meanings, Bordwell concludes, it would be better *not* to "read" films at all. (Bordwell's own method, ironically, itself performs a symptomatic reading of a vast and variegated corpus of textual analyses, here seen as symptomatic of theoretical and analytical sloppiness.)

In *Making Meaning* Bordwell argues that film analysis in the semiotic tradition often tends to do little more than illustrate preconceived ideas. Using the example of Hitchcocks's *Psycho*, he suggests that interpretation is predetermined by *a priori* conceptual schemata. Bordwell sets up a polarity between his idea of "historical poetics" – a phrase Bakhtin had used in a subtitle to his "Chronotope" essay in the 1930s – and "interpretation," associated for Bordwell with the ascription of implicit and symptomatic meanings by interpretative communities, usually filtered through SLAB theory (Saussure/Lacan/Althusser/Barthes).[1] This polarization of historical poetics and interpretation is misleading, however. The opposite of his-torical poetics is not interpretation but *ahistorical* poetics. There is no reason why interpretation cannot be historicized. Prestigious traditions such as hermeneutics and philology, for example in the work of Erich Auerbach or Leo Spitzer, have always historicized interpretation. Rejecting interpretation in general just because *some* interpretations are inept seems rather like saying we should abandon film theory in general because some theories have been clumsily developed.

Bordwell (in Palmer, 1989) proposes his project of historical poetics as an alternative to the interpretative tradition. He explicitly grounds his neo-Formalism in three explanatory schemas: a rational agent model, an institutional model (i.e. the social and economic system of filmmaking), and a perceptual–cognitive model (see Bordwell, in Palmer, 1989). Historical poetics studies "how, in determinate circumstances, films are put together, serve specific functions, and achieve specific effects" (Bordwell, 1985, pp. 266–7). In Bordwell's constructivist approach the spectator uses filmic cues, constructed by the filmmaker, to "execute determinable operations, of which the construction of all sorts of meanings will be a part" (ibid., p. 270). Bordwell's professed (and laudable) goal in *Making Meaning* is not to repudiate interpretation completely but rather to place it "within a broader historical inquiry" (ibid., p. 266). But by dichotomizing referential, explicit readings on the one hand (seen as manageable and responsible matters of comprehension), and symptomatic, implicit readings on the other (seen as irresponsible and anarchic, a pseudo-knowledge based on whims of interpretation), Bordwell undercuts his own project. In a sense he repeats the strategy of the Formalists by appealing to its misleading spatial metaphor of intrinsic meaning (the "inside" of the text) as opposed to the "outside" of imposed institutional schemata. But in fact there is a

permeable membrane between inside and outside, as there is between, for example, comprehension and interpretation. While there
are some cognitive commonalities, how specific audiences comprehend and interpret a given film also depends on historical moment,
community affiliations, political ideology, and so forth. It could even
be argued that comprehension implies an interpretation, and even a
critical position. Adorno argued (in *Aesthetic Theory*) against the
scientistic divorce of comprehension and interpretative value; aesthetic comprehension *requires* interpretative value judgments. The
Gus and Flora rape sequence in *Birth of a Nation* was understood,
and interpreted, very differently depending on whether one was a
member of the Ku Klux Klan or an African American. A racist was
likely to comprehend and interpret what he or she was seeing as a
realistic depiction of the typical behavior of black men, while African Americans were more likely to see a white man in blackface
enacting a vicious stereotype. While one spectator might feel enraged by the behavior of the character in the fiction, another spectator might feel enraged by those who devised and shaped the fiction.
While both might agree that they were seeing the representation of
a rape, their understanding and interpretation of that representation
would hardly be identical.

Bordwell's historical poetics proposes to study film style in historical context, certainly a more than worthy endeavor. It studies
history in order to understand style. But would it not be equally
legitimate to do the reverse, i.e. to study style in order to understand history? For Bakhtin and Medvedev form and structure are
just as historically and ideologically shaped as theme and content. A
deeply historical poetics would examine not only the local, institutional determinations of film style, but also the back-and-forth reverberations between history and style, the interplay of historical
and artistic chronotopes, without reducing one to a mere backdrop
for the other. A deep examination of what Bordwell calls the "con-
structional principles" of film would bring up questions of economics, ideology, and ethics. To reduce history in the broad sense to
mere context or material for the history of style is to unduly restrict
the field. It is to ignore what Bakhtin would call the historicity of

forms themselves, i.e. forms as themselves historical events which both refract and shape a multi-faceted history at once artistic and trans-artistic. The aggressive technological exhibitionism of block-buster action films, within this perspective, can be seen as mirroring the agressivity of their narrative content. The jiggly hand-held cameras and impulsive swish-pans of the New Wave, seen from the perspective of the historicity of forms, might be seen to resonate *simultaneously* with technological developments (recently developed lightweight equipment), film-intertextual developments (cinema verité), film-critical developments (the decades of literary discussion of urban wandering and *flânerie*), philosophical developments (phenomenology), artistic-theoretical developments (the romantic expressivism of auteurism), and even biographical developments (Truffaut's oedipal revolt against the academic style of the "cinéma de papa"). Like the Formalists, Bordwell sees art as an "aggregate of formal/linguistic possibilities" when it is more illuminating to see it as part of a larger field of social and discursive contradiction.

Historical contradiction impacts film in very concrete and often dramatic ways. The rise of Nazism forces progressive directors to flee to Hollywood. A *coup d'état* in Brazil leads not only to film censorship but also to the disruption of leftist film productions like Coutinho's *Cabra Marcado para Morrer*. Patricio Gusman's *Battle of Chile* has to be smuggled out of Chile after the *coup d'état*. The Indian film *Fire* triggers riots because it includes lesbian scenes. Film history is not just a *combinatoire* of formal possibilities. It also has to do with what issues (and style) are declared off-limits, with the role of economics in deciding who makes or distributes films, with racial conventions that decide who can perform in films, with power differentials in distribution that determine that while films in some countries can be *made* they are unlikely to be *exhibited* because of the Hollywood stranglehold on exhibition circuits. Of course, Bordwell is well aware of all this, and he is among those calling for a more historical approach, but the formalist aspects of his own theory indirectly discourage attention to these larger issues.

While Bordwell occasionally cites Bakhtin favorably, as in his critique of Colin MacCabe on realism, he seems not to have absorbed the import of the Bakhtin–Medvedev critique of Formalism. Paraphrasing *The Formal Method in Literary Scholarship*, we could easily affirm that *film* is "an inseparable part of culture and it cannot be understood outside the total context of the entire culture of a given epoch [and] … the socio-cultural life that generates the ideological horizons of an epoch." Style, ideology, and history are inextricably linked. Even referential meaning cannot be cordoned off from history and communities of interpretation. Spectatorial "schemata" are historically shaped. History reverberates in film, and not just contemporary history but the entire weight of the past is "embedded" in the film text. As Ira Bhaskar (Miller and Stam, 1999) argues in her wide-ranging critique, Bordwell's "technicist" and "detectivist" notions of narrative fail to see the ways that narrative embodies culture, and the ways that it shapes, and is shaped by, history. While Bordwell is right to mock the more irresponsible interpretations filtered through SLAB theory, it would be better to call for a deep, millennial historicization to "ground" interpretation rather than to reject interpretation altogether. Bordwell develops what Bhaskar sees as a narrow, institutionalized constructivism based on textual cues (operations) and filtered through schemata, while Bhaskar, following Bakhtin, sees both understanding and interpretation as a negotiation between the languages and socio-ideological discourses of the text and those of the reader. Narratives are powerful not only because they cue inferences, but also because they resonate with a multiplicity of historical associations. A truly historical approach, as Bhaskar puts it,

demands a view of narrative as culturally and historically rooted, as embodying within it the life-world of its times; in other words, as embodying the forms of cultural life, the life processes, the ideologies, the values; in fact as embodying the very conceptual schemes that Bordwell sees as the subject of interpretation. If narrative were to be understood in this way, as encoding within its fabula *and* syuzhet, *its form and style, the vision of its world, then the interpretative act would not be schismatically separated from the interpretative one, and explicit, referential meanings would carry within them the implicit, symptomatic ones. (Miller and Stam, 1999)*

The historicizing impetus of Bordwell's "historical poetics" thus runs up against the ahistoricity of Formalism. The substantive "poetics" overwhelms the merely adjectival "historical." And here Bordwell undermines the richness of his own work elsewhere, his tremendous contribution to the history of film style and his analysis of specific filmmakers (Ozu, Eisenstein, Godard) as well as of Hollywood's "excessively obvious" cinema.[2]

Bordwell's work also displays a certain hostility to the play of interpretation. He quotes Laura Mulvey's 1970s project of "taking the pleasure out of film viewing" and adds that it is now time to "take the pleasure out of film interpretation." To which one can only respond: Why? Why is pleasure, including the pleasure of Bordwell's own analyses, something to be shunned? In a Bakhtinian perspective, humor and pleasure can be productive of knowledge; Rabelais was at his most brilliant when he was laughing most boisterously. There is no reason that interpretation too should not be playful, free, even erotic.

The announced death of textual analysis and interpretation therefore seems decidedly premature. Any perusal of the pages of *Screen*, *Camera Obscura*, *Cinema Journal*, or *Jump Cut* reveals scores of close analyses of films, and major publication series, like the BFI Classics, or the Rutgers Film Analysis Series, or the "Étude Critique" (Nathan) series in France, will guarantee the role of film analysis well into the future. (Fredric Jameson has joked that "interpretation" is for undergraduates, "theory" for graduates.) Nor has interpretation been definitively discredited. Even a "cognitivist" like Noël Carroll entitled a recent book *Interpreting the Moving Image* (1998). The digital age, moreover, has given new impetus to the practice of textual analysis. We now have CD-ROMs not only on film analysis in general (the work of Henry Jenkins and Ben Singer) but also on analyses of specific films such as Hitchcock's *Rebecca* and Peixoto's *Limite*. While we might lament the more delirious textual analyses, we cannot impose law and order on the anarchy of interpretation. We all bring our interpretative standpoints to film. To ban interpretation is indirectly to ban politics, since it is with interpretation that the political stakes of film analysis become clear.

Films are open to our desires and projections, even when these desires are sublimated into an apparatus of positivist objectivity. It is therefore hard to imagine that we will ever get completely "beyond" interpretation. While one can critique the more predictable and derivative analyses, and suggest that there is much to do *besides* analysis, that does not mean that analysis (and its inevitable fellow-traveler, interpretation) is not worth doing. That textual analysis can be flat, stale, and derivative does not discredit the enterprise *in toto*.

From Text to Intertext

In one sense, the decline of the text as an object of study in the 1980s coincided with the ascendance of the intertext. Rather than focus on specific films or single genres, intertextuality theory saw every text as related to other texts, and thus to an intertext. Like "genre," "intertextuality" is a venerable idea, implicit already in Montaigne's observation that "more books are written about other books than about any other subject," and in T. S. Eliot's notion of "tradition and the individual talent." By speaking of texts (etymologically "tissue" or "weave") semiotic analysts prepared the way for a notion of intertextuality that went beyond the old philological conception of "influence."

Since genre theory always runs the double risk of taxonomism and essentialism, genre might be more productively regarded as a specific aspect of the broader and more open question of intertextuality. The term "intertextuality" was first introduced in the 1960s as Kristeva's translation of Bakhtin's "dialogism," coined in the 1930s, a translation which loses some of the philosophical and human overtones of Bakhtin's term. Dialogism refers to the necessary relation of any utterance to other utterances. (An utterance, for Bakhtin, can refer to any "complex of signs," from a spoken phrase, to a poem, or song, or play, or film.) The concept of dialogism suggests that every text forms an intersection of textual surfaces. All texts are tissues of anonymous formulae embedded in the language, variations on those formulae, conscious and unconscious quotations, conflations and inversions of other texts. In the broadest sense, intertextual dialogism refers to the infinite and open-ended possibilities generated by all the discursive practices of a culture, the entire matrix of communicative utterances within which the artistic text is situated, and which reach the text not only through recognizable influences but also through a subtle process of dissemination. The cinema, in this sense, inherits (and transforms) millennia of artistic tradition. It "embeds," as it were, the entire history of the arts. A film like Scorsese's *Cape Fear*, for example, embeds the literature of apocalypse, going at least as far as the Book of *Revelation* in the Bible. Mel Brooks's *History of the World* not only claims to tell the history of the world, but also embeds very ancient comic stategies. The "Last Supper" sequence, for example, inherits the tradition of *parodia sacra* of which Bakhtin speaks in *Rabelais and His World*. When we recall that Christ's Last Supper was originally a Passover Seder, which referenced Jewish oppression in Egypt, we see that such references spiral back far into the mists of time.

The concept of intertextuality is not reducible to matters of influence or sources of a text in the old philological sense. The intertext of Altman's *Nashville* could be said to consist of all the genres and discourses to which the film refers, for example the Hollywood-on-Hollywood film, the documentary, the musical, and extending to the entire canon of Altman films, Haven Hamilton films, Eliot Gould films, along with gospel music, country music, populist political discourse, and so forth. The intertext of the work of art, then, may be taken to include not just other artworks in the same or comparable form, but also all the "series" within which the singular text is situated. Any text that has slept with another text, to put it more crudely, has necessarily slept with all the texts the other text has slept with.

Intertextuality theory is best seen as an answer to the limitations both of textual analysis and of genre theory. The term "intertextuality" has a number of advantages over "genre." First, genre has a circular, tautological quality: a film is a western because it has the characteristics of a western. Intertextuality is less interested in taxonomic essences and definitions than in the processual interanimation of texts. Second, genre seems a more passive principle: a film "belongs" to a genre as an individual "belongs" to a family, or a plant "belongs" to a genus. Intertextuality is more active; it sees the artist as dynamically orchestrating pre-existing texts and discourses. Third, intertextuality does not limit itself to a single medium; it allows for dialogic relations with other arts and media, both popular and erudite.

Intertextuality is a valuable theoretical concept in that it relates the singular text principally to other systems of representation, rather than to an amorphous "context." In order to even discuss the relation of a work to its historical circumstances, we are obliged to situate the text within its intertext and then relate both text and intertext to the other systems and series which form its context. But intertextuality can be conceived in a shallow or a deep manner. Bakhtin spoke of what he called the "deep generating series" of literature, i.e. the complex and multidimensional dialogism, rooted in social life and history, comprising both primary (oral) and secondary (literate) genres, which engendered literature as a cultural phenomenon. In "The Problem of Speech Genres," Bakhtin provides extremely suggestive concepts susceptible to extrapolation for the analysis of cinema. Bakhtin calls attention to a wide gamut of "speech genres," both oral and written, simple and complex, which range all the way from "the short rejoinders of ordinary dialogue" through everyday narration, to all the literary genres (from the proverb to the multi-volume novel) and other "secondary (complex) speech genres," such as major genres of social–cultural commentary and scientific research. Many individuals who have an excellent general command of a language, Bakhtin points out, feel painfully inadequate in particular spheres of communication because they lack mastery of the requisite generic forms. Juzo Itami's *The Funeral*, in this sense, treats the genre of the "funeral speech." The film chronicles the attempt by an upscale Japanese couple to cope with the discursive challenge engendered by the funeral and burial of the man's father. Out of touch with Shinto tradition and with contemporary funeral decorum, they master the genre with the help of a video cassette: "The ABCs of the Funeral."

203

A translinguistic approach to speech genres in the cinema might correlate the primary speech genres – familial conversation, dialogue among friends, boss–worker exchange, classroom discussion, cocktail party banter, military commands – with their secondary cinematic mediation. It would analyze the etiquette by which the classical Hollywood film, for example, deals with typical speech situations such as two-person dialogue (usually by the conventional ping-pong of shot–counter shot), dramatic confrontations (the verbal stand-offs of the western and the gangster film), as well as with the more avant-gardist subversions of that etiquette (e.g. Godard).

The Bakhtinian reformulation of the problem of intertextuality must be seen as an "answer" both to the purely intrinsic formalist and structuralist paradigms of linguistic theory and literary criticism, and to sociologistic paradigms interested only in extrinsic class-bio-graphical and ideological determinations. Bakhtin's notion of the chronotope (literally "time–space") is also relevant to our discussion of filmic genre. The chronotope refers to the constellation of distinctive temporal and spatial features within a genre defined as a "relatively stable type of utterance." The chronotope addresses the warp that history enters the time and space of artistic fiction. In "Forms of Time and Chronotope in the Novel" Bakhtin suggests that time and space in the novel are intrinsically connected, since the chronotope "materializes time in space." The chronotope mediates between two orders of experience and discourse: the historical and the artistic, providing fictional environments where historically specific constellations of power are made visible. The chronotope is multi-leveled; it has to do with a text's representation of historical processes, with the relations of space and time within the diegesis, and with the spatiotemporal articulations of the text itself. The chronotope offers specific settings where stories can "take place" (the atemporal other-worldly forest of romance, the "nowhere" of fictional utopias, the roads and inns of the picaresque novel). In the cinema one thinks, for example, of the relations between character and environment, whether in synch (the cowboy ambling along the wide-open spaces), out-of-synch (Monica Vitti lost and disoriented against the backdrops of Antonioni's *Red Desert*), or comically deterministic (characters commandeered by architect-ure in Tati's *Play-time*).

Through the idea of the chronotope Bakhtin shows how concrete spatiotemporal structures in literature limit narrative possibility, shape characterization, and mold a discursive simulacrum of life and the world. And although Bakhtin does not refer to the cinema, his category seems ideally suited to it as a medium where "spatial and temporal indicators are fused into one carefully thought-out concrete whole." Bakhtin's description of the novel as the place where time "thickens, takes on flesh, becomes artistically visible," and where "space becomes charged and responsive to the movements of time, plot and history," seems in some ways even more appropriate to film than to literature, for whereas literature plays itself out within a virtual, lexical space, the cinematic chronotope is quite literal, played out concretely across a screen with specific dimensions and unfolding in literal time (usually 24 frames per second), quite apart from the fictive time–space specific films might construct. Film illustrates Bakhtin's idea of the inherent relationality of time and space, because in the cinema any modification on one register entails changes on the other: a closer shot of a moving object increases the apparent speed of that object, the presence of the temporal medium of music alters our impression of space, and so forth.

A number of analysts, notably Vivian Sobchack, Arlindo Castro, Kobena Mercer, Maya Turovskaya, Michael Montgomery, Paul Willemen, Paula Massood, and Robert Stam, see the chronotope as a means for historicizing the discussion of filmic genre. Turovskaya (1989) deploys the concept of the chronotope in relation to Andrei Tarkovsky's idea of cinema as "imprinted time." Massood uses the chronotope to clarify the historical dynamics of the "ghettocentric" film. Michael Montgomery, in *Carnival and Common Places* (1993), cites the "shopping mall" films of the 1980s as chronotopes. More productive than searching for cinematic equivalents to Bakhtin's literary chronotopes, perhaps, is the construction of specifically filmic chronotopes. For purposes of illustration, one might imagine films belonging to such categories as the "between four walls" chronotope, i.e. those films which restrict their action to a single space (e.g.

205

Hitchcock's *Rear Window* and *Rope*, Jabor's *Tudo Bem*, Fassbinder's *Bitter Tears of Petra von Kant*); the "TV-mediated film chronotope" (e.g. *Adieu Phillipine, Medium Cool, The China Syndrome*), where a television milieu brings with it the presence of multiple TV monitors, which have the effect of multiplying and linking diegetic spaces;[1] the "dystopian banquet chronotope" (*Exterminating Angel, Don's Party, Who's Afraid of Virginia Woolf?*, and *The Celebration*).

Vivian Sobchack extends chronotopic analysis to the spatiotemporal features of film noir as a cinematic space–time in which the postwar crises in cultural values and in economic and sexual identity found vernacular expression. Chronotopes, Sobchack argues, are not merely the spatiotemporal backdrop for narrative events but also the literal and concrete ground from which narrative and character emerge as the temporalization of human action. The diacritical contrast which structures film noir is between the impersonal, discontinuous, rented space of cocktail lounge, nightclub, hotel, and roadside café, on the one hand, and the familiar, unfragmented secure space of domesticity on the other. The characters generated by this chronotope are transient, without roots or occupation, in a world where murder is more natural than death. (See Sobchack in Brown, 1997.)

Dialogism operates within all cultural production, whether literate or non-literate, verbal or non-verbal, highbrow or lowbrow. The film artist, within this conception, becomes the orchestrator, the amplifier of the ambient messages thrown up by all the series – literary, painterly, musical, cinematic, publicitary, and so forth. Even TV commercials display generic features: headache remedies (Excedrin in the 1980s) evoked the deep-focus stylistics of Orson Welles; Taster's Choice coffee commercials in the 1980s evoked romantic melodrama; jean commercials have affinities with porn; while perfume commercials seek an effect of Daliesque fantasy. As John Caldwell points out, film history becomes a trampoline for TV stylists. *Moonlighting* "did" film noir, MTV, Orson Welles, Frank Capra. The 1989 "Here's Looking at You Kid" was designed around replications of *The Sheik* and *Casablanca* (see Caldwell, 1994, p. 91). A number of films – Bruce Conner's *A Movie*, Mark Rappaport's *The Journals of Jean Seberg* – literalize the notion of intertextuality by incorporating pre-existing texts. Woody Allen's *Zelig*, in this sense, can be seen as the site of intersection of innumerable intertexts, some specifically filmic (newsreels, archival material, home movies, television compilation films, "witness" documentaries, cinema verité, film melodrama, psychological case-study films like *Spellbound*, "fictive documentaries" like *F for Fake*, and more immediate fiction-film predecessors like Warren Beatty's *Reds*); others literary (the Melvillean "anatomy"); and some broadly cultural (Yiddish theater, Borscht-Belt Comedy). *Zelig*'s originality, paradoxically, lies in the audacity of its imitation, quotation, and absorption of other texts.

Even a cinematic technique can constitute an intertextual allusion: the iris-in to an informer in *Breathless*, or the use of Griffith-style masking in *Jules et Jim*, allude by their calculatedly archaic nature to earlier periods of film history, while the subjectivized camera movements and point-of-view structurings in Brian de Palma's *Body Double* allude to the strong intertextual influence of Alfred Hitchcock. (Generic intertext here carries its own affect; the formal structures themselves encode memories and trigger fears.) Indeed, specific camera movements have even generated their own "post-texts," as in the long line that connects the various virtuoso long-take *ouvertures* from *Touch of Evil* through *The Player*, *Boogie Nights*, and *Snake Eyes*.

Building on Bakhtin and Kristeva, Gérard Genette in *Palimpsestes* (1982) proposed the more inclusive term "transtextuality" to refer to "all that which puts one text in relation, whether manifest or secret, with other texts." Genette posits five types of transtextual relations. He defines intertextuality, more restrictively than Kristeva, as the "effective co-presence of two texts" in the form of quotation, plagiarism, and allusion. Although Genette restricts himself to literary examples – the only film he mentions is *Play It Again, Sam* – it is easy to imagine filmic instances of the same procedures (see Stam, 1992). Quotation can take the form of the insertion of classic clips into films, for example Peter Bogdanovich's quotation of Hawks's *The Criminal Code* in *Targets*. Films like *Mon Oncle d'Amérique*, *Dead Men Don't Wear Plaid*, and *Zelig* make the citation of pre-existing film sequences a central structuring principle. Allusion, meanwhile, can take the form of a verbal or visual evocation of another film, as an expressive means of commenting on the fictional world of the alluding film. Godard in *Contempt* alludes, through a title on a movie theater marquee, to Rossellini's *Voyage in Italy*, a film which recounts, like *Contempt* itself, the slow undoing of a couple. Even an actor can constitute an allusion, as in the case of the Boris Karloff character in *Targets*, seen as the embodiment of old-style gothic horror, the essential dignity of which Bogdanovich contrasts with anonymous contemporary mass-murder.[2]

"Paratextuality," Genette's second type of transtextuality, refers to the relation, within the totality of a literary work, between the text proper and its "paratext," i.e. the accessory messages and commentaries which come to surround the text, for example prefaces, dedications, illustrations, and even book jacket designs. It is intriguing to speculate about the relevance of such a category to film. One thinks of posters, previews, publicity t-shirts, TV ads, and even the marketing of subsidiary products such as toys and models. Widely reported information about the budget of a film, similarly, can inflect critical reception, as in the case of Coppola's *Cotton Club*, where reviewers found that the filmmaker had achieved very little given the enormous budget. Program notes distributed at press screenings, by the same token, often orient journalistic responses to commercial films. Reports of censorship anxieties, as in the case of Adrian Lyne's *Lolita*, also have impact on a film's reception. All these matters, operating on the margins of the official text, impinge on the issue of a film's paratext.

"Metatextuality," Genette's third type of transtextuality, consists of the critical relation between one text and another, whether the commented text is explicitly cited or only silently evoked. Genette cites the relation between Hegel's *Phenomenology of Mind* and the text that it constantly evokes without explicitly mentioning: Diderot's *Le Neveu de Rameau*. The avant-garde films of the New American Cinema offer metatextual critiques of classical Hollywood cinema. The multiple refusals of Hollis Frampton's *nostalgia* – of plot development, of movement in the shot, of closure – suggest a mocking critique of the expectations triggered by conventional narrative films.

Even *Thelma and Louise*, by putting its women characters literally in the driver's seat, implicitly critiques the masculinism of the road movie genre.

"Architextuality," Genette's fourth category of transtextuality, refers to the generic taxonomies suggested or refused by the titles or infratitles of a text. Architextuality has to do with a text's willingness or reluctance to characterize itself directly or indirectly in its title as a poem, essay, novel, film. Some film titles, for example, align a text with literary antecedents: *Sullivan's Travels* evokes Swift's *Gulliver's Travels* and, by extension, the satiric mode. The title of Woody Allen's *Midsummer Night's Sex Comedy* begins by alluding to Shakespeare and ends with a comic fall into prurience, all the while echoing Bergman's *Smiles of a Summer Night*.

"Hypertextuality," Genette's fifth type of transtextuality, is extremely suggestive for film analysis. Hypertextuality refers to the relation between one text, which Genette calls "hypertext," to an anterior text or "hypotext," which the former transforms, modifies, elaborates, or extends. In literature, the *Aeneid*'s hypotexts include the *Odyssey* and the *Iliad*, while the hypotexts of Joyce's *Ulysses* include the *Odyssey* and *Hamlet*. All the texts in the series operate transformations on pre-existing texts. The term "hypertextuality" is rich in potential application to the cinema, and especially to those films which derive from pre-existing texts in ways more precise and specific than those evoked by the term "intertextuality." Hypertextuality evokes, for example, the relation between filmic adaptations and their source novels, now seen as hypertexts derived from pre-existing hypotexts, transformed by operations of selection, amplification, concretization, and actualization. The diverse filmic adaptations of *Madame Bovary* (Renoir, Minnelli, Chabrol, Mehta) can be seen as variant hypertextual "readings" triggered by an identical hypotext. Indeed, the diverse prior adaptations can form part of the hypotext available to a filmmaker coming relatively "late" in the series.

Recent discussions of filmic adaptations of novels have moved from a moralistic discourse of fidelity and betrayal to a less judgemental discourse of intertextuality. Adaptations are by definition caught up in the ongoing whirl of intertextual transformation, of texts generating other texts in an endless process of recycling, transformation, and transmutation, with no clear point of origin. Let us take as an example Defoe's *The Adventures of Robinson Crusoe* (1719), one of the seminal source novels of a specific tradition, the realistic novel supposedly based on "real life" and written in such a way as to generate a strong impression of factual reality. Yet this "realistic" novel is itself rooted in various intertexts: the Bible, religious homilies, journalistic texts about Crusoe's prototype Alexander Selkirk, and sensationalist travel literature, to mention just a few. The original novel, rooted in this complex and variegated intertext, also generated its own textual afterlife or post-text. Already by 1805, less than a century after the publication of the Defoe novel, a German encyclopedia (*Bibliothek der Robinsone*) offered a comprehensive guide to all the works inspired by *Robinson Crusoe*. The *Crusoe* post-text also ramifies into the world of film, where a long pageant of adaptations rings the changes on the themes of the original. *Miss Crusoe* (1919) performs a variation in gender; *Little Robinson Crusoe* (1924) changes the protagonist's age; *Mr Robinson Crusoe* (1932) supplies Crusoe with a feminine companion, not "Friday" but "Saturday"; *Swiss Family Robinson* (1940) permutates the number and social status of characters; the Laurel and Hardy film *Robinson Crusoeland* (1950) shifts genre from colonial adventure story to slapstick comedy; *Robinson Crusoe on Mars* (1964), similarly, turns the novel into science fiction; and in *Lieutenant Robinson Crusoe* the transformation is both professional and zoological, as Defoe's protagonist becomes the sailor played by Dick van Dyke, while Crusoe's parrot becomes a chimpanzee.

Hypertextuality calls attention to all the transformative operations that one text can operate on another text. Travesty, for example, irreverently devalorizes and "trivializes" a pre-existing "noble" text. Many Brazilian comedies, such as *Bacalhau* (Codfish) – a parody of *Jaws* – parodically re-elaborate Hollywood hypotexts whose production values they both resent and admire. Other hypertextual films simply update earlier works while accentuating specific features of the original. The Morissey/Warhol collaboration *Heat* (1972) transposes the plot of Wilder's *Sunset Boulevard* (1950) to 1970s Holly-wood, filtering the original through a gay-camp sensibility. Else-where the transposition is not of a single film but of an entire genre. Kasdan's *Body Heat* (1981) evokes the corpus of 1940s film noir in terms of plot, character, and style in such a way that a knowledge of film noir becomes a privileged hermeneutic grid for the cine-literate spec-tator (see Carroll, 1982, pp. 51–81). A more expansive con-ception of hypertextuality might include many of the films gener-ated by the Hollywood combinatory: remakes like *Invasions of the Body Snatchers* (1978), *The Postman Always Rings Twice* (1981), and *Twelve Monkeys*; Pierre Menard-like replicas such as van Sant's *Psycho* (1998); revisionist westerns like *Little Big Man* (1970); generic reworkings like Scorsese's *New York, New York* (1977); and parodies like Mel Brooks's *Blazing Saddles* (1974). Most of these films assume spectatorial competence in diverse generic codes; they are calculated deviations meant to be appreciated by discerning connoisseurs.

Theories of literary intertextuality, then, can yield benefits for film theory and analysis. Another literary theorist whose work is ripe for extrapolation for film analysis is Harold Bloom. In *The Anxiety of Influence* Bloom argues that literary art develops out of an interper-sonal and generational struggle with strong oedipal overtones. Thus Milton wrestles with the ghost of Shakespeare over the mantle of "greatest English writer." This view has been rightly critiqued by feminists as masculinist (exclusively concerned with oedipal strug-gles between men), leaving no place for the quilt-like intertextuality of women's dialogue with their literary mothers. It can also be seen as Darwinian (literary survival of the fittest) and Eurocentric, and certainly lacks the amiable generosity of Bakhtinian dialogism. None-theless, Bloom's approach does at least bring desire, and even pas-sion, into the question of intertextuality. Thus Bloom speaks of diverse strategic maneuvers that artists make in relation to their pred-ecessors: *clinamen* – attaining maturity by swerving away from one's predecessors (one thinks of Truffaut's relation to the cinéma de papa); *tessera* – completing the work of one's predecessor (one thinks of Brian de Palma's relation to Hitchcock); *kenosis* – breaking with one's antecedents (Godard's relation to Hollywood); *daemonization* – mythifying one's predecessors (Tarantino and Godard, Paul Schrader and Bresson); *askasis* – radical rejection, the purging of all links (a certain avant-garde in relation to entertainment cinema); and *apophrades* – assuming the place of, inheriting the mantle of (Truffaut as the heir of Renoir).

Some less Eurocentric versions of intertextuality theory also have relevance to film. Giving a new twist to the old trope of "eating" the text (Quintilian, Montaigne, Rabelais), the 1920s modernists in Brazil and their Tropicalist heirs in the 1960s posited the ideal of "anthropophagy," i.e. the cannibalistic devouring of European texts as a way of absorbing their force without being dominated by them, just as the Tupinamba Indians reportedly devoured Europeans in order to appropriate their strength. Henry Louis Gates in *Signifying Monkey*, similarly, offers a specifically African American theory of intertextuality, tracing the "signifying" of black literature to the Yoruba trickster figure Exu-Legba, the spirit of the crossroads and a hermeneutic figure for what Bakhtin calls "double-voiced" discourse. Intertextuality, in this case, becomes inseparable from culture.

The Amplification of Sound

The semiotic project, broadly conceived, had room not only for the study of genre and intertextuality but also for precise work on specific codes. Metz's definition of the cinema's "matter of expression" as the "five tracks" (image, dialogue, noise, music, written materials), of which three were aural, certainly stimulated research into sound by undermining the formulaic view of the cinema as an "essentially visual" medium. The new interest in sound occurred in concert with a revolution both in sound technology and in the ways sound in the cinema was theorized. Film historians and technicians spoke of a "second sound revolution," as innovations in sound recording in film and in the music industry began to impact film and tele-vision. With Dolby Sound (optical stereophonic sound on film, conveyed through speakers dispersed around the theater), first used in 1975 in conjunction with music documentaries, and in such films as *Star Wars, Close Encounters,* and *Grease,* the sound system became the "star." For Michel Chion, Dolby added "three octaves" to what had been a five-octave piano. In the 1970s, filmmakers like Francis Ford Coppola, in films such as *Apocalypse Now, Rumble Fish,* and *The Conversation,* began to spend as much time mixing the soundtrack as in actually shooting the film (Chion, 1994, p. 153). On *Apocalypse Now* Walter Murch used 160 separate tracks. In the opening sequence where Willard (Martin Sheen) is lying in a room in a Saigon Hotel, Murch combines Willard's interior monologue with a shift from objective to subjective noises: the hotel fan gives way to a remembered helicopter, car horns transmute into birds, and a fly into a mosquito.

The sound revolution, then, was theoretical as well as technological. Analysts such as Christian Metz, Rick Altman, Elizabeth Weiss, John Belton, Claudia Gorbman, Kaja Silverman, Arthur Omar, Alan Weiss, Mary Ann Doane, Alan Williams, Jeff Smith, Kathryn Kalinak, Michel Marie, Royal Brown, Michel Chion, Daniel Percheron, Dominique Avron, David Bordwell, Kristin Thompson, Marie-Claire Ropars-Wuilleumier, and Francis Vanoye began to give to the soundtrack the kind of precise attention previously accorded only to the image track. An important catalyst was the groundbreaking special issue in 1980 of *Yale French Studies* entitled *Cinema/Sound,* which included important work by key French and American scholars.

Nevertheless, one is struck by the "lateness" of the study of sound in the cinema. Film music, for example, has been present since film's beginnings, yet it has been rigorously analysed only in the 1980s and 1990s (with rare exceptions like Eisler and Adorno's *Composing for the Film* in 1944). Some of this "retardation" has to do, perhaps, with the conventional view of sound as a mere addendum or supplement to the image. It might even have to do with a religious iconophobic substratum inherited from the Judaic prohibition against graven images and from Protestant iconoclasm, as well as with the traditional hierarchy that positions word-based arts like literature "above" image-based arts like the cinema. The assumption that film is essentially visual, as Rick Altman points out in his introduction to *Cinema/Sound*, is embedded in our habitual ways of speaking about film. The very names for the cinema – the movies, motion pictures, cinema – stress the inscription of visible phenomena, destined for spectators (not auditors) who go to see (not hear) a film. The critical meta-language used to speak about film, similarly, is better equipped to speak about such things as eyeline matches and point-of-view editing than it is about sound.

A number of theorists have analyzed the differences between the imagistic and the acoustic analogon in terms of the relation between "original" and "copy." The reproduction of sound, unlike the reproduction of three-dimensional visual phenomena, involves no *dimensional* loss – both original and copy involve mechanical radiant energy transmitted by pressure waves in the air; thus we perceive sound as three-dimensional. While a filmed object loses a dimension in the recording, recorded sound maintains its dimensions; it begins as an airy vibration and continues to function in the same way as a recording. Sound goes around corners, while light rays are blocked; we can hear the soundtrack of a film playing in a neighboring room, but we cannot see its images. As Michel Chion (1994) puts it, "Light propagates (at least apparently) in a linear manner, but sound spreads out like a gas. The equivalent of light *rays* is sound *waves*. The image is bounded in space, but sound is not." Since sound penetrates and pervades space, it molds a heightened sense of presence. Indeed, watching a film without sound creates an uncanny feeling of flatness.

Recorded sound thus has a higher coefficient of "reality" than the image, in that it can be measured in decibels and can even damage the eardrum. Recorded sound, as the famous Memorex commercial suggested, can *literally* break glass. At the same time, this reality effect of sound does not mean that sound is not also mediated, constructed, and codified through choice of microphones, angle of microphone, recording equipment, recording tape, sound reproduction systems, and post-production sound re-editing. Nor is even realistic sound necessarily mimetic. While real-life punches are often noiseless, Michel Chion points out, in the cinema the sound of impact is virtually obligatory (ibid., p. 60).

214

Altman (1992) speaks of four fallacies in relation to sound. The first *historical* fallacy suggests that the historical precedence of the image renders sound as historically less important; because sound came second, it is therefore secondary. But cinema never really was silent. Even in the nickelodeon period there were competing sound paradigms drawn from diverse exhibition traditions. Even if early cinema *had* been silent, Altman further argues, no definition of a medium should be tethered to a specific period of its history; a comprehensive definition must allow for technological change. The second, *ontological* fallacy, advanced by pro-silent film theorists like Arnheim and Bálázs, sees film as essentially and constitutively founded by the image, with sound as necessarily subordinate. But the fact that cinema has historically privileged the visual, Altman argues, does not mean that it must always do so. Even the defenders of sound, he adds, sometimes indirectly devalue sound by associating it with precapitalist times (Adorno and Eisler) or with the archaic and amniotic (as in some feminist–psychoanalytical accounts). A third *reproductive* fallacy asserts that while the image is creatively unfaithful, sound is automatically faithful. But in actuality, sound recording is also creative; rather than simply reproduce sound, it manipulates and reshapes it. A fourth *nominalist* fallacy, by stressing the material heterogeneity of sound, downplays a common ground of sound recognition.

Many sound theorists have explored the phenomenology of sound "auditorship." Chion has coined the term *synchresis* (a combination of synchronism and synthesis) to evoke the "spontaneous and irresistible weld produced between a particular auditory phenomenon and visual phenomenon when they occur at the same time" (Chion, 1994, p. 63). This welding is what makes dubbing, post-synchronization, and sound-effects possible; an infinity of voices could conceivably be welded to a single performer on screen. Often the image "absorbs" the sound in ways that transcend literal mimesis; a shot of a train, for example, when "covered" by the tick-a-tack of typewriters, will be read as the clackity-clack of a moving train. Chion speaks of *trompe-l'oreille* (trick the ear) on the analogy of *trompe-l'oeil* painting.

215

Building on the basic distinctions concerning filmic sound – "on-screen/off-screen" (a question of framing, whether we literally see the source of the sound); "diegetic/non-diegetic" (a question of whether a sound is constructed as issuing from the fictive world of the story or not); "synchronous/non-synchronous" (a question of the exact correlation between moving lips and heard speech, for example); and "direct/post-synchronized" (a question of the technical procedures of the production itself) – analysts have sought a more precise account of the relation between filmic sound and story. The notion of the diegesis as the posited world of the film's fiction facilitated a more sophisticated analysis of the diverse possible relationships between the sound and story. In the case of verbal dialogue within film, for example, Metz distinguished between fully diegetic speech (that spoken by characters as voices in the fiction), non-diegetic speech (commentary "off" by an anonymous speaker), and semi-diegetic speech (voice-over commentary by one of the characters of the action). Daniel Percheron distinguished between films with an unmarked diegesis, i.e. films which dissemble the narrative activity, and those, such as *Jules et Jim*, with a marked diegesis, i.e. films which foreground the act of narration.

Another analytic question is to what extent the language usually deployed for visuals can be transferred to sound. We can recognize a sound "scale" – close or far – and a sound "focus," for example the acoustic isolation of a group within a crowd (a feature of the sound-obsessed film *The Conversation*). Both sound and image can "fade" and "dissolve," and sound edits, like shot edits, can be "visible" or "invisible" (or better, "audible" or "inaudible"). Chion speaks of *phonogenie*, by analogy to *photogenie*, to refer to the propensity of some voices to sound euphonious when recorded. The classical approach to sound entailed a highly codified set of conventions which implied selectivity (only diegesis-relevant voices and sounds should be heard); hierarchy (dialogue trumps background music or noise); invisibility (the sound boom is not to be seen); seamlessness (no abrupt changes in volume); motivation (only motivated distortion, for example a character's disturbed hearing); and readability (all sound elements should be intelligible). (See Gorbman, 1987, on "inaud-

216

ible" music in classical scoring of films.) Gaps in the soundtrack are taboo, since spectators might infer that the sound equipment is not working. There should be no sound without its accompanying image, and no image without sound, whence the disorientation provoked by soundless shots of scenes that would normally produce noise. Cinematic sound, in sum, has been highly codified, constructed, hemmed in by restrictions, the product of myriad protocols and prohibitions.

Filmic sound, for Chion (1982; 1985; 1988; 1994), is multi-track, and has diverse origins. The synchronous voice can be traced back to the theater; film music derives from opera; and voice-over commentary goes back to commented-on projections such as magic lantern shows. For Chion, both film practice and film theory/criticism have been "vococentric," i.e. they privilege the voice *vis-à-vis* the other acoustic tracks (music and noise). The sound-production process in the classical cinema was designed to showcase the human voice and make it audible and comprehensible; other forms of sound (music, noise) were subordinated to dialogue and image.

For French psychoanalytic theorists Guy Rosalto and Didier Anzieu sound plays an essential role in the constitution of the subject. Wrapped in the sonorous envelope of the womb, the child conflates self with other, inside with outside. For Rosalto, music triggers the auditory imaginary in conjunction with the pre-oedipal language of sound. Chion borrows from Pierre Schaeffer the term "acousmatic" to refer to those sounds without a visible source, a situation which Schaeffer sees as typical of a media-saturated environment where we constantly hear the sounds of radio, telephone, CDs, etc., without seeing their literal sources. The term also evokes highly personal intra-familial associations. The voice of the mother for the child still within the womb is strangely acousmatic. Within the history of religion, the term evokes the voice of the Divine entity which mere mortals were *forbidden* to see. The acousmatic voice, Chion suggests, unsettles the spectator because of its capacity (1) to be everywhere (ubiquity), (2) to see everything (panopticism), (3) to know everything (omniscience), and (4) to do everything (omnipotence). The omnipresence of Hal the Computer in *2001: A Space Odyssey* illustrates the capacity of the acousmatic voice to be everywhere, while the "voice-of-God" narration of the canonical documentary illustrates its capacity to know everything. The voice of the wizard in *The Wizard of Oz* evokes the voice as all-knowing and all-seeing, although the film also culminates in an ironic "de-acousmatization," i.e. the process by which a bodiless voice is finally given a body, as the Grand Oz is discovered behind the curtain.

While analysts have spent considerable energy on the clarification of issues concerning point of view, they have paid little attention to what Chion calls point of hearing (*point d'ecoute*), i.e. the positioning of sound in terms of placement during the production, placement within the diegesis, and spectatorial apprehension. Often, there is no strict coincidence between aural and visual point of view/hearing, for example when distant human figures are heard as if in close-up, or as in the musical, where cabaret-style sound maintains a constant (ideal) level of fidelity and proximity despite differences in visual scale. Chion also cites examples of aural point of view, as in Abel Gance's *Un Grand Amour de Beethoven*, where the director makes us empathize with the composer's growing deafness by depriving us of the sounds engendered by the visual objects and activities on the screen. Such effects work always in tandem with and not independently of the image; close shots of the composer "anchor" our impression that the aural effects evoke the protagonist's handicap.

The theorization of sound has also been inflected by feminist currents. Some feminist theory contrasts the voice as fluid and continuous expression with the rigid linearity of writing. Julia Kristeva especially speaks of a pre-languaged vocal freedom, close to the marvelous original language of the mother, a language which would be incarnated purely in the form of voice. Luce Iragaray claims that patriarchal culture has a heavier investment in seeing than in hearing. Kaja Silverman argues that dominant cinema "contains" the female voice in order to facilitate the male viewer's own disavowal of his own insufficiency (Silverman, 1988, p. 310). Feminist filmmakers can trigger a "phallic divestiture" by evoking the "choric scene," i.e. the moments when the mother's voice addresses the child, in a premonition of cinematic voice-over. They can do this through the voice-over narration of mothers, as in the Mulvey/Wollen film *Riddles of the Sphinx*, or through the deliberate misalignment of a female voice with a male on-screen body, as in Marjorie Keller's *Misconception*.[1]

Pursuing Bakhtin and Medvedev's insight that "all manifestations of ideological creativity are bathed by, suspended in, and cannot be entirely segregated or divorced from the element of speech" (Volosinov, 1976, p. 15), we might argue that even the non-verbal tracks, for example the music and noise tracks, can also embrace linguistic elements. Recorded music is often accompanied by lyrics, and even when it is not it can evoke them. Purely instrumental versions of popular songs often elicit in the spectator the mental presence of the words. (Kubrick exploits remembered lyrics in *Dr Strangelove* when he superimposes the well-known melody of "Try a Little Tenderness" on shots of nuclear bombers.) Even apart from lyrics, music itself is permeated with semantic and discursive values. Musicologist J. J. Nattiez (1975), for example, sees music as deeply embedded in social discourses, including verbal discourses. Nor are recorded noises necessarily "innocent" of language. In some cultures, music is literally discursive, as in the case of the "talking drums" in *Daughters of the Dust*; those fluent in the code will "hear" the message, others will not. Speech can also become noise. The stylized murmur of conversing voices in the restaurant sequences of classical Hollywood films renders human speech as background noise, while Jacques Tati films give voice to an international esperanto of aural effects – vacuum cleaners that wheeze and vinyl suits that go "poof" – characteristic of the postmodern environment.

A number of scholars have examined the varying coefficients of mimeticism in the image as opposed to music. The "realistic" effect of music is paradoxical precisely because music, despite occasional "anecdotal" musical scores such as *Peter and the Wolf* and *Till Eulenspiegel*, is *not* directly representational. Nevertheless, music can be indirectly representational (see Brown, 1994, pp. 12–37; Gorbman, 1987, pp. 11–33). Royal Brown (1994) argues that music, as a non-iconic medium, when accompanying the other tracks of film, can have a generalizing function, encouraging the spectator to receive the scene on the level of myth, while also triggering a "field of association" likely to foster emotional identification. Claudia Gorbman (1987) traces the function of music back to the silent film, where it covered the noise of the projector, promoted an emotional interpretation of the narrative, and provided historical or cultural atmosphere. The music of the pianists and organists who accompanied silent film thus "managed" spectatorial response, underscoring the screen events with sound elements adapted to their mood and rhythm. Music provided an emotional "beat" for the film, compensating for the cold, voiceless, ghost-like image. Conventional film music has always worked to efface the instruments of production of the cinematic illusion, channeling and directing the audience's emotional response. Although in the sound film these two functions have been integrated into the filmic text and rendered more subtle, their purpose has not changed.

Music in films has classically taken a number of forms: (1) music performed in the film (whether literally synchronous or post-synchronized); (2) pre-existing recorded music; and (3) music specifically scored for the film (for example, Bernard Herrmann for *Psycho*, *Vertigo*, and *Taxi Driver*, Franz Waxman for *Rear Window*). Music can be literally diegetic (performed or played within what is posited as the story-world of the film) or it can be extra-diegetic, autonomous, and call attention to itself as music (for example, Giovanni Fusco's music for *Hiroshima Mon Amour*). Music can begin as non-diegetic (for example, the use of the theme from Grieg in Fritz Lang's *M*) and yet become diegeticized (when the same tune is whistled by the murderer). A number of directors deploy a kind of comic, surprise diegeticization, as when Fellini uses the "Ride of the Valkyrie" as what seems to be (non-diegetic) commentative music, yet suddenly reveals the orchestra performing the piece at the spa (Woody Allen achieves a similar effect in *Bananas* when he reveals the harpist in the closet).

Music is polysemic, suggestive, open to infinite association. As the "tonal analogue of feeling" (Suzanne Langer), music engages the psyche, substituting for literal, visual mimesis the realism of subjectivity and the sensuous feel of thought. Within an illusionist aesthetic, images and music mutually anchor and reinforce each other. Music carries the spectator over the rough spots of the diegesis – whence the importance of music during the opening credits, where the presence of written text and the citation of the production personnel might call undue attention to the film's process of fabrication. Film music, like montage, is one of those devices that at first glance seems anti-naturalistic, but which is ultimately recuperable by a naturalist aesthetic. On superficial examination, all music not immediately anchored in the image (i.e. whose source is neither present nor implied to be present in the image) would seem by definition to be anti-illusionistic. Conventional cinema, however, often substitutes for the superficial realism of visual appearance the ultimately more persuasive realism of subjective response. The musical scores of Hollywood dramatic films lubricate the spectator's psyche and oil the wheels of narrative continuity; music goes for the emotional jugular. Rather like aesthetic traffic cops, film music directs our emotional responses; it regulates our sympathies, extracts our tears, excites our glands, relaxes our pulses, and triggers our fears, usually in strict conjunction with the image.

The style of film music which dominated Hollywood studios during the 1930s and 1940s may be succinctly described as the symphonic style of late nineteenth-century European romanticism (see Bruce, 1991). The most influential composers – for example, Max Steiner, Dimitri Tiomkin, Franz Waxman, Miklós Rózsa – tended to be European immigrants steeped in a specific tradition of musical composition. Given their European education, these film composers were inclined to favor the lush sounds of rich orchestral scoring, with long-spanned melodies based on Wagnerian leitmotifs. The concept of the *Gesamtkunstwerk* was transmuted into a canonical aesthetic for film music; one which wedded music to action and character, dialogue, and sound-effects by furnishing the appropriate musical "color" and environment.

Without slighting the brilliance of these composers, one can question the inevitability of their aesthetic as the only appropriate one for such an open and discontinuous medium as film. Their ideas, in lesser hands, became subject to vulgarization and standardization. The leitmotif became a rather mechanical device for allying particular themes to particular characters, themes which were returned to with minimal variation during the course of the film. Film scores tended to be redundant, subliminal, hackneyed, and comfortably tonal. They were redundant because hyper-explicit: cheerful images redoubled with cheerful sounds, tragic moments underlined with "tragic" harmonics, and narrative climaxes carefully matched to swells and crescendos. The image was over-stuffed with a pleonastically high coefficient of representation. Such scores were subliminal in that they were meant to be felt emotionally rather than heard intellectually. They were hackneyed because they appealed to a series of petrified associations – flutes for meadows, Mendelsohn for weddings, ominous chords for danger. The scores are reassuringly tonal, finally, in being spiritually descended from the late romantic period. Returning the public to the lost paradise of tonality, melody, and final resolution, the scores rigorously avoided modernist dissonance and tension.

Since music is closely tied to communitarian culture and "structures of feeling," it can tell us where a film's emotional heart is. The choice of European symphonic music rather than African music in films set in Africa (for example *Out of Africa* and *Ashanti*) suggests that the film's heart is with the European protagonists and that Africa is merely background decor. On the other hand, the African music on the soundtracks of *beur* films (i.e. films made by North African Arabs in France) such as *Bye Bye* and *Salut Cousin* layer an African acoustic feeling over European cityscapes. Music tracks can also "locate" us within time, a technique which goes at least as far back as *American Graffiti*, *Coming Home*, and *The Big Chill*, but which is continued in period films like *The Dead Presidents* and *The Ice Storm*, where period pop songs become a kind of shorthand for evoking a historical period.

Music obviously can also play a role in alternative aesthetics. A number of African and Afro-diasporic films, such as *Faces of Women* (1985), *Barravento* (1962), and *Pagador de Promessas* (1962), deploy drum *ouvertures* in ways that affirm African cultural values. Films

222

by African and Afro-diasporic directors like Sembene, Cisse, and Faye not only use African music but celebrate it. Julie Dash's *Daughters of the Dust* (1990) deploys an African "talking drum" to drive home, if only subliminally, the Afrocentric thrust of a film dedicated to the diasporic culture of the Gullah people.

Arthur Jafa speaks of the cinematic possibilities of "Black visual intonation," whereby "irregular, nontempered (nonmetronomic) camera rates and frame replication . . . prompt filmic movement to function in a manner that approximates black vocal intonation," forging the filmic equivalent of the tendency in black music to "treat notes as indeterminate, inherently unstable sonic frequencies rather than as fixed phenomena" (quoted in Dent, 1992). What might be the filmic equivalent, one wonders, of call and response, melisma, and a suspended beat? Clearly the theoretical ramifications and aesthetic possibilities of sound have only begun to be explored.

The Rise of Cultural Studies

While film semiotics was concerned with specifically cinematic codes such as sound, the movement which came to be known as cultural studies was more interested in embedding media like the cinema in a larger cultural and historical context. Cultural studies traces its roots to the 1960s and is conventionally seen as beginning with such British leftists as Richard Hoggart (*The Uses of History*), Raymond Williams (*Culture and Society*), E. P. Thompson (*The Making of the English Working Class*), and Stuart Hall. Hall, together with Dick Hebdige, Richard Johnson, Angela McRobbie, and Larry Grossberg, is associated with the Birmingham Centre for Contemporary Cultural Studies. Conscious of the oppressive aspects of the British class system, the members of the Birmingham Centre, many of whom were associated with adult education projects, looked for aspects of ideological domination and for new agents of social change. A more diffuse and international genealogy for cultural studies might be traced to the work of such figures as Roland Barthes in France,

Leslie Fiedler in the United States, Frantz Fanon in France and North Africa, and C. R. L. James in the Caribbean, all going back to the 1950s.

Cultural studies draws on diverse intellectual sources; initially Marxism and semiotics, and later, feminism and critical race theory. Cultural studies has variously absorbed and reconfigured a constellation of concepts: Raymond Williams's definition of culture as a "whole way of life;" Gramsci's concept of "hegemony" and "war of position;" Michel de Certeau's concept of "poaching;" Volosinov's ideas about ideology and language as coterminous with the "multi-accentual" sphere of language; Clifford Geertz's notion of culture as a narratological ensemble; Foucault's reflexions on knowledge and power; Bakhtin's notion of carnival as social inversion; and Bourdieu's notions of "habitus" and the "cultural field." While film semiotics began in France and Italy and then spread to the English-speaking world, cultural studies began in the English-speaking world and then spread to Europe and Latin America (volumes on German, Spanish, and Italian cultural studies have recently been published).

The Italian Marxist Antonio Gramsci was a key influence on cultural studies. In his *Prison Notebooks*, written between 1929 and 1935, Gramsci questioned the primacy in Marxist thought of the economic base over ideological superstructure. According to Gramsci, only a reconfigured analysis of base–superstructure relations would enable the left to account for the stalling of revolution in Western Europe, in situations where economic conditions would seem to favor revolution. Ideologies, Gramsci argued, cut across class lines; conversely, the same individual can be inflected by diverse, even contradictory, ideologies. The left needed to expose social "common sense," that amalgam of contradictory ideas drawn from multiple time periods and traditions, as an impediment to the coming-to-consciousness of the working class.

Cultural studies is notoriously difficult to define due to its deliberately eclectic and open-ended method. Fredric Jameson speaks of "the desire called cultural studies." The "culture" in cultural studies is at once anthropological and artistic. One can define cultural studies in terms of its democratizing notion (inherited from semiotics) of all cultural phenomena as worthy of study. The authors of *Cultural Studies* define cultural studies, somewhat imperialistically, as a kind of disciplinary omnivore: "Cultural studies is thus committed to the study of the entire range of society's arts, beliefs, institutions and practices" (Nelson, Treichler, and Grossberg, 1992, p. 4). Alternatively, one can define cultural studies in terms of its relation to traditional disciplines. In this sense it marks the end of any one master discipline in the humanities. Cary Nelson calls cultural studies a counter-disciplinary "cluster of disciplines under erasure," a response to the repressions of overly specific and overly traditional disciplines.

In terms of its object of study, cultural studies is less interested in "media specificity" and "film language" than it is in culture as spread out over a broad discursive continuum, where texts are embedded in a social matrix and where they have consequences in the world. Transformalist, cultural studies calls attention to the social and institutional conditions under which meaning is produced and received. It represents a shift from interest in texts *per se* to an interest in the processes of interaction between texts, spectators, institutions, and the ambient culture. It radicalizes classical semiotics' interest in all texts – not just high-art texts – highlighting moments of both hegemonic manipulation and political or ideological resistance. Despite Nelson, Treichler, and Grossberg's denial of the legitimacy of textual analysis, however, it is a misnomer to assume that cultural studies never does textual analysis. It does do textual analysis, but the "text" in question is no longer Keats's *Grecian Urn* or Hitchcock's *Vertigo*, but rather Madonna and Disneyworld, shopping malls and Barbie dolls.

Offering itself as an alternative to what it sees as the ahistoricity of both structuralism and psychoanalysis, cultural studies explores culture as a site where subjectivity is constructed. For cultural studies, contemporary subjectivity is inextricably interwoven with media representations of all sorts. The subject is constructed not only in terms of sexual difference but also in terms of many other kinds of difference, in a permanent and multivalenced negotiation between material conditions, ideological discourses, and social axes of stratification based on class, race, gender, age, locale, sexual orientation, national origin. In this sense, cultural studies tries to open up space for marginalized voices and stigmatized communities, participating in what Cornel West later called "the cultural politics of difference."

In the realm of film, cultural studies was a reaction both against screen theory and against quantitative (number crunching) mass communications audience studies. (It was also a way for English departments to incorporate film study without worrying about film history or film specificity.) Unlike screen theory, cultural studies does not focus on any one medium such as film, but rather on the larger spectrum of cultural practices. Indeed, at times, an insufficient attention on the part of adherents of cultural studies to media specificity leads to neglect of the ways that diverse media (film, MTV, video) generate *specific* pleasures and effects. In this sense, recent film studies has retrofitted apparatus theory to account for film viewing not only in the classical movie theater or Cineplex but also on VCRs at home, in airports, on planes, and so forth. The kind of concentrated attention paid to a high-definition image in a darkened theater – the conditions assumed in the analyses of a Baudry or a Metz – differs radically from the kind of dispersed reception of film viewing on a moving airplane.

The precise relation between film studies and cultural studies is also a contested topic. Does cultural studies complete and enrich film studies or threaten to dilute it? Some film theorists welcome cultural studies as a logical extension of work already being done in film studies, while others see it as a treasonous betrayal of cinema studies' founding principle of medium specificity. While the name of one discipline – cinema studies – designates a medium, the name of the other – cultural studies – transcends medium specificity. For some film scholars, cultural studies is to be despised because it no longer studies a high art (the cinema) but rather low, vulgar, popular arts like TV sitcoms – a rather ironic claim in the light of film studies' long struggle to establish the dignity of its own despised object of study. If 1970s film theory developed a neurotic distance from, even antipathy toward, its object of study, cultural studies has sometimes been accused of not being critical enough, of falling under the spell of mass-culture.

David Bordwell (Bordwell and Carroll, 1996) argues that earlier "subject-positioning" theory and cultural studies have many features in common, namely a shared group of practitioners as well as basic bibliographies (Saussure, Lévi-Strauss, Barthes as common references). More important, Bordwell argues, there are common "doctrines" – the word is deliberately used to evoke sterile orthodoxy and ritualistic adherence – notably beliefs that (1) human practices and institutions are in all significant respects socially constructed; (2) the understanding of spectatorship requires a theory of subjectivity; (3) spectatorial response to the cinema depends upon identification; (4) verbal language supplies and appropriates an adequate analogue for film. The two movements also share similar protocols or "reasoning routines:" (1) a top-down, doctrine-driven inquiry; (2) argument as *bricolage*; (3) associational reasoning; and (4) the hermeneutic interpretative impulse. While Bordwell's argument has a grain of truth, it also ignores the heated polemics that separated the two movements, especially in Britain, where the cultural studies group at the Birmingham Centre critiqued the *Screen* group as elitist and apolitical, as overly concerned with the productivity of signifying systems and not concerned enough with social production in general. Overall, cultural studies distinguished itself from screen theory by being more interested in the uses of texts than in texts *per se*, by being more enamored of Gramsci than of Althusser, by being less interested in psychoanalysis than in sociology, and by being more optimistic about the audience's capacity to read "against the grain." One can also question the prejudicial formulations that suggest that semioticians and cultural studies advocates are "doctrine-driven" while their non-semiotic opponents are presumably neutral and objective. The derisive term "doctrine-driven" in this sense has a function analogous to the "p.c." slur in right-wing attacks on "tenured radicals."

A key issue in cultural studies is the question of agency: whether resistance and change are possible in a mass-mediated world. Despite the decline of leftist politics, cultural studies has tended to be more sanguine about possibilities for resistance than Althusserian apparatus theory. Cultural studies was less interested in top-down ideological manipulation by apparatuses and elites than in bottom-up subcultural resistances. Its emphasis on digging out "moments" of subversion provides continuity to the "gaps and fissures" analysis of 1970s Marxist semiotics, but introduces a new vocabulary of "negotiation" and "contestation" which come from a Gramscian framework. At the same time, cultural studies adopted a less militant approach toward cultural products, one that reflects the general decline of political radicalism, and the entangled social positioning of contemporary radicals themselves, who no longer boycott the system but rather work to various degrees within it. Key to cultural studies is the idea that culture is the site of conflict and negotiation within social formations dominated by power and traversed by tensions having to do with class, gender, race, and sexuality. In Britain cultural studies began by being more oriented toward issues of class; it came to engage issues of gender and race relatively "late." In 1978 the Women's Study Group lamented the "absence from CCCS of a visible concern with feminist issues." And in the 1980s cultural studies was challenged to pay more attention to race, partly under the influence of US cultural studies, which has tended to focus more on gender and race than on class.

At its best, cultural studies locates moments of subcultural subversion and resistance; at its worst, it celebrates fandom and consumerism as exercises in untrammeled freedom. It often has an ambivalent attitude toward its mass-mediated objects of study, an ambivalence in some ways reminiscent of film semiology's simultaneous love for and distance from classical cinema. It is fond of oxymoronic responses like "complicitous critique" (Linda Hutcheons), finding mass-culture, as Eve Sedgewick has put it, always "sort of transgressive, and sort of hegemonic." The articulations of these complexities at times become formulaic. Meeghan Morris (in Mellencamp, 1990, p. 20) laments the fact that "thousands of versions of the same article about pleasure, resistance, and the politics of consumption are being run off under different names with minor variations." At the Urbana Cultural Studies Conference, Tony Bennett mocked the "consumer pleasure as resistance" school which consists of "sleuthing for subversiveness where one would least expect to find it."

Cultural studies becomes depoliticized when it loses sight, as it sometimes does, of the unequal power relations within which spectators engage with texts, at which point it lapses into what David Morley (1992) calls the "don't worry, be happy" American school of cultural studies. Morley's comment implies that Americans have depoliticized the insights of the founders of cultural studies. (One senses here a left version of the old European lament about the history-less barbarians on the other side of the Atlantic.) Within the United States, ironically, these same cultural studies scholars are demonized by neo-conservatives as "tenured radicals" who have "politicized" the university and corrupted youth. It is also ironic that a certain strand of cultural studies, best exemplified by John Fiske, emphasizes the freedom and resistance in the sphere of consumption just when the field of production is more and more concentrated, more and more subject to the power of vast corporations like Viacom and of megamoguls like Rupert Murdoch, a time when most alternative productions, including even European art cinema, are being frozen out by blockbuster films and media mega-conglomerates.

The Birth of the Spectator

In the late 1960s Roland Barthes had prophesied the "death of the author" and the "birth of the reader." Yet in a sense it is a misnomer to speak of the birth of the spectator in film theory, since film theory has *always* been concerned with spectatorship. Whether in Munsterberg's idea that film operates in the mental sphere, or in Eisenstein's faith in the epistemological leaps triggered by intellectual montage, or in Bazin's view of the spectator's democratic freedom to interpret, or in Mulvey's concern with the male gaze, virtually all film theories have implied a theory of spectatorship.

In the 1970s theory psychoanalyzed the pleasures of the cinematic situation as such. In the 1980s and 1990s analysts became more interested in socially *differentiated* forms of spectatorship. This move gave expression to a shift that had already taken place in literary studies, variously called reader response theory (Stanley Fish, Norman Holland) or reception theory (associated especially with the Constance School of Reception Aesthetics). Hans Robert Jauss's historicizing approach, a synthesis of Formalism and Marxism, was complemented by Wolfgang Iser's examination of the interaction between the reader and a "virtual" text which requires readerly "concretization." The emphasis in reception theory on "filling in the gaps of the text" can be seen, in retrospect, as ideally suited to a medium like the cinema where the spectator is necessarily active, obliged to compensate for certain lacks – the lack of a third dimension, for example – and literally sees darkness much of the time.

The spectator was now seen as more active and critical, not the passive object of "interpellation" but rather at once constituting and constituted by the text. *Contra* earlier apparatus theory, it was now argued that the strong subject-effects produced by narrative cinema were not automatic or irresistible, nor could they be separated from the desire, experience, and knowledge of historically situated spectators, constituted outside the text and traversed by sets of power relations such as nation, race, class, gender, and sexuality. Stuart Hall, borrowing from Umberto Eco and Frank Papkin, anticipated and concretely shaped this shift in his influential essay "Decoding and Encoding" (1980). For Hall, mass-media texts do not have a univocal meaning but can be read differently by different people, depending not only on their social location but also on their ideologies and desires. Rejecting the tradition which sees the subject of the media as simply "spoken" by ideological structures and discourses, Hall sees texts (in this case televisual texts) as susceptible to diverse readings based on political–ideological contradiction. Hall posits three broad reading strategies in relation to dominant ideology: (1) the *dominant* reading produced by a viewer situated to acquiesce in the dominant ideology and the subjectivity it produces; (2) the *negotiated* reading produced by the viewer who largely acquiesces in dominant ideology, but whose real-life situation provokes specific "local" critical inflections; and (3) the *resistant* reading produced by those whose social situation and consciousness place them in a directly oppositional relation to dominant ideology. Resistant reading on one axis (e.g. class), I would add, might go hand-in-hand with a dominant reading on another axis (e.g. race), along all the permutations of social identity and affiliation. David Morley, complicating Hall's tripartite schema, argued for a discursive approach that would define spectatorship as the "moment when the discourses of the reader meet the discourse of the text" (Morley, 1980).

Text, apparatus, discourse, and history, in sum, are all in play and in motion. Neither text nor spectator is a static, pre-constituted entity; spectators shape and are shaped by the cinematic experience within an endless dialogical process. Cinematic desire is not only intra-psychic; it is also social and ideological. Any truly comprehensive ethnography of spectatorship must distinguish multiple registers: (1) the spectator as fashioned by the text itself (through focalization, point-of-view conventions, narrative structuring, mise-en-scène); (2) the spectator as fashioned by the (diverse and evolving) technical apparatuses (Cineplex, IMAX, domestic VCR); (3) the spectator as fashioned by the institutional contexts of spectatorship (social ritual of moviegoing, classroom analysis, cinémateque); (4) the spectator as constituted by ambient discourses and ideologies; (5) the actual spectator as embodied, raced, gendered, and historically situated. The analysis of spectatorship must therefore explore the gaps and tensions among the different levels, the diverse ways that text, apparatus, history, and discourse construct the spectator, and the ways that the spectator as subject–interlocutor also shapes the encounter.

In the 1880s and 1990s, film scholars paid increasing attention to the historically conditioned nature of spectatorship. The history of cinema, in this sense, is not just the history of films and filmmakers, but also the history of what meanings successive publics have attributed to film. Thus we find studies of the demographics of the movie audience in terms of age and class. The special issue of *Iris* (1990) on "Early Cinema Audiences" provides a good example of this tendency, where diverse authors (Richard Abel, Janet Staiger, Elena Degrado) discuss such diverse issues as the class composition of the audience, urbanization and the growth of the moviegoing public, and the development of a cinematic "imaginary." In *Babel and Babylon: Spectatorship in American Silent Film* (1991), Miriam Hansen examines the role of the "fan," and specifically the cult of Valentino. In *Interpreting Films* (1992), finally, Janet Staiger overviews contemporary reception theory in film, subdividing the field into (1) text-activated; (2) reader-activated; and (3) context-activated theories. Within an approach she calls "historical–materialist," Staiger explores the reception of a wide range of films (from *Uncle Tom's Cabin* to *Zelig*) to demonstrate the historical/contextual shaping of interpretation.

Although film theory had known since Mulvey that spectatorship was gendered, 1980s theory was also beginning to recognize that spectatorship was also sexualized, classed, raced, nationed, regioned, and so forth. The culturally variegated nature of spectatorship derives from the diverse locations in which films are received, from the temporal gaps of seeing films in different historical moments, and from the conflictual subject-positionings and community affiliations of the spectators themselves. In its quasi-exclusive focus on sexual as opposed to other kinds of difference, and in its privileging of the intra-psychic as opposed to the intersubjective and the discursive, psychoanalytic film theory often elided questions of culturally inflected spectatorship. In an essay on black spectatorship Manthia Diawara stressed the racial dimension of spectatorship, arguing that black spectators cannot "buy into" the racism of *Birth of a Nation*. They disrupt the functioning of Griffith's film, rebelling against the "order" imposed by its narrative. For black spectators, the character Gus, as a blackface incarnation of lust and violence, clearly cannot represent blacks but only white prejudice toward blacks. bell hooks, meanwhile, spoke of the "oppositional gaze" of black female spectators. That blacks under slavery and segregation were punished for the very act of looking, hooks argues, generated a "traumatic relationship to the gaze." The existence of black women within white supremacist culture, she continues, problematizes and complexifies the issue of female identity, representation, and spectatorship. Critical black female spectators implicitly construct a theory of looking relations where "cinematic visual delight is the pleasure of interrogation" (hooks, 1992, p. 115).

At the same time, there is no racially, culturally, or even ideologically circumscribed essential spectator – *the* white spectator, *the* black spectator, *the* Latino/Latina spectator, *the* resistant spectator. These categories repress the heteroglossia within spectators themselves. Spectators are involved in multiple identities (and identifications) having to do with gender, race, sexual preference, region, religion, ideology, class, and generation. Moreover, socially imposed epidermic identities do not strictly determine personal identifications and political allegiances. It is not only a question of what one is or where one is coming from, but also of what one desires to be, where one wants to go, and with whom one wants to go there. Within a complex *combinatoire* of positions, members of an oppressed group might identify with the oppressing group (Native American children rooting for the cowboys against the "Indians"; Africans identifying with Tarzan; Arabs with Indiana Jones), just as members of privileged groups might identify with the struggles of oppressed groups. Spectatorial positioning is relational: communities can identify with one another on the basis of a shared closeness or on the basis of a common antagonist. Spectatorial positions are multiform, fissured, schizophrenic, unevenly developed, culturally, discursively, and politically discontinuous, forming part of a shifting realm of ramifying differences and contradictions (Shohat and Stam, 1994).

If spectatorship is on one level structured and determined, on another it is open and polymorphous. The cinematic experience has a ludic and adventurous side as well as an imperious one; it fashions a plural, "mutant" self, occupying a range of subject positions. One is "doubled" by the cinematic apparatus, at once in the movie theater and with the camera/projector and the action on screen. And one is further dispersed through the multiplicity of perspectives provided by even the most conventional montage. Cinema's "polymorphous projection-identifications" on a certain level transcend the determinations of local morality, social milieu, and ethnic affiliation (see Morin, 1958). Spectatorship can become a liminal space of dreams and self-fashioning. Through the psychic chameleonism of spectatorship, ordinary social positions, as in carnival, are temporarily bracketed.

Building on Michel de Certeau's notion of reading as poaching,

Henry Jenkins in *Textual Poachers* analyses the phenomenon of fan culture. Fans, Jenkins notes, "rewrite" their favorite shows through a panoply of techniques: recontextualization, expansion of timeline, refocalization, moral realignment, genre shifting, crossovers, character dislocation, personalization, emotional intensification, and eroticization. Fandom, then, has an element of empowerment: "Fans are poachers who get to keep what they take and use their plundered goods as the foundations for the construction of an alternative cultural community" (Jenkins, 1992, p. 223).

But if 1970s theory was unduly pessimistic and defeatist, current theory has perhaps swung a bit too far in the opposite direction. Media theorists have stressed spectatorial agency and freedom, ironically, just as media production and ownership have become ever more centralized. Resistant readings, moreover, depend on a certain cultural or political preparation that "primes" the spectator to read critically. In this sense one might question the more euphoric claims of theorists such as John Fiske, who see TV viewers as mischievously working out "subversive" readings based on their own popular memory. Fiske rightly rejects the hypodermic-needle model of media influence that sees TV viewers, for example, as passive drugged patients getting their nightly fix, reduced to "couch potatoes" and "cultural dupes." He rightly suggests that minorities, for example, "see through" the racism of the dominant media. But if disempowered communities can decode dominant programming through a resistant perspective, they can do so only to the extent that their collective life and historical memory have provided an alternative framework of understanding. In the case of the Gulf War, for example, the majority of American viewers lacked any alternative grid to help them interpret events, specifically a view rooted in an understanding of the legacy of colonialism and its particular complexities in the Middle East. Primed by the sheer inertia of orientalist discourse, they gave credence to whatever views the Administration chose to present.

Cognitive and Analytic Theory

Much of the 1980s and 1990s were devoted to revising, if not dismantling, the premises of 1970s screen theory. During this period theorists like Noël Carroll and David Bordwell attacked with iconoclastic glee and "the-emperor-has-no-clothes" irreverence virtually all its major tenets. (The targets of these provocations reacted with olympian hauteur, rarely deigning to respond.) Representing the "postanalytic" tradition, meanwhile, Richard Allen and Murray Smith criticized the philosophical overreaching of screen theory:

What is striking about the Continental philosophy that has been taken to the cinema is the way in which extraordinarily sweeping claims that pertain to the end of epistemology, the construction of the subject, or theses concerning the ultimate constituents of reality, are all rooted in one aspect of the cinema – the causal or indexical nature of the photographic image – as if within this feature of cinematic representation somehow lies an answer to every question we might seek to ask about the cinema (and even modern-ity or knowledge in general!). (Allen and Smith, 1997, p. 22)

The postanalytic thinkers accused screen theory of a number of dubious argumentative strategies: deferential appeals to authoritative figures; the misleading use of examples and analogies; the refusal to submit arguments to empirical test: the strategic use of willful obscurity (ibid., p. 6). The "Continentals," in turn, saw analytic philosophy and its cinematic offshoots as arid, trivial, apolitical, and narrowly technical, a professionalist evasion of social and intellectual responsibility.

The "cognitive theory" movement, which loosely includes such diverse figures as Gregory Currie, Torben Grodal, Edward Branigan, Trevor Ponech, Murray Smith, Noël Carroll, and David Bordwell, began – if one sets aside "proto-cognitivists" like Munsterberg and the filmolinguists – gains force in the 1980s. Cognitivism looks for more precise alternative answers to questions raised differently about film reception by semiotics and psychoanalytic theory. Cognitivism has been a continuing thread, although by no means the *only* thread,

235

in the work of David Bordwell. It surfaces in "The Viewer's Activity" section of *Narration in the Fiction Film*, in the polemics against psychoanalysis in *Making Meaning*, in the 1989 essay "A Case for Cognitivism," and in *Post-Theory*, where Bordwell and Carroll characterize cognitivism not as a theory but as a stance which "seeks to understand human thought, emotion, and action by appeal to processes of mental representation, naturalistic processes, and (some sense of) rational agency" (Bordwell and Carroll, 1996, p. xvi). Cognitivists stress the physiological and cognitive systems "hard-wired" into all human beings, what Bordwell calls the "contingent universals" prior to particularities of history, culture, and identity: the assumption of a three-dimensional environment, the assumption that natural light falls from above, and so forth. These contingent universals make possible artistic conventions which seem natural because they accord with the norms of human perception.

In *Narration and the Fiction Film* (1985), Bordwell offers a cognitive alternative to semiotics to explain how spectators make sense of films. For Bordwell, narration is a process whereby films furnish cues to spectators who use interpretative schemata to construct ordered, intelligible stories in their minds. From the point of view of reception, spectators entertain, elaborate, and sometimes suspend and modify their hypotheses about the images and sounds on the screen. From the point of view of the film, it operates on two levels: (1) what the Russian Formalists called *syuzhet*, i.e. the actual form, however fragmented and out-of-sequence, in which events are recounted; and (2) the *fabula*, i.e. the ideal (logically and chronologically ordered) story which the film suggests and which the spectator reconstructs on the basis of the film's cues. The first instance, *syuzhet*, guides the narrative activity of the spectator by offering various forms of pertinent information having to do with causality and with spatiotemporal relations. The second is a purely formal construct characterized by unity and coherence.

Cognitivists have been critical of what they regard as the hermetic, inflated, and tautological discourse of film theory and especially psychoanalytic film theory. (For the cognitivists, to put it somewhat crudely, a cigar really is sometimes just a cigar.) These theorists therefore bypass psychoanalytic film theory, drawing instead on the most cogent theories of perception, reasoning, and information-processing to understand how films are received and followed in terms of cause–effect narrative, space–time relations, and so forth. The cognitivist research program by now has generated studies of classical Hollywood cinema (Bordwell, Thompson, Currie, Smith), the avant-garde (Carroll, Peterson), the documentary (Carroll, Plantinga), and horror (Carroll, Freeland). A symposium on Cognitivism in Copenhagen (May 1999) featured papers on a wide spectrum of issues: nonfiction film and emotion (Carl Plantinga); the social psychology of the horror film (Dolf Zillman); a cognitive approach to film acting (Johannes Riis); cinema's psychology of perception (Revor Ponech); film history and the cognitive revolution (Casper Tybjerg); lighting styles in Lubitsch (Kristin Thompson); and Caligari and cognition (Wayne Munson). As Noël Carroll (1996, pp. 321–2) points out, cognitivism is difficult to define because it is not a unified theory. First, it is not a single theory but rather a constellation of small-scale theories. Second, these various small-scale theories conceptualize the issues differently. Third, the theories, taken together, do not form a single framework. Gregory Currie (in Miller and Stam, 1999) also points out that there are few specific doctrines to which all cognitivists subscribe. Cognitivism tends to be eclectic, wary of systematic thinking, with cognitivists tending to "cut 'n' mix" their cognitivism with other theories. Richard Allen combines cognitivism with both psychoanalysis and postanalytic philosophy; David Bordwell melds cognitivism with Prague School Formalism. Cognitivists also dis-agree with one another; for example, Carroll versus Currie on empathy and simulation; Allen versus Carroll on "illusion" and so forth. Most cognitivists, however, would agree that (1) the processes of film spectatorship are best understood as rationally motivated attempts to make visual or narrative sense out of the textual materials; and (2) that these processes of making sense are not dissimilar to those we deploy in our everyday life experience.

Cognitivism recapitulates – in a non-linguistic register – first-phase film semiology's attempt to understand "how films are understood." Cognitivism bypasses the linguistic model and focuses instead on formal elements of film which "match" the norms of human perception. In fact, cognitivists tend to reject the notion of film language. Thus Noël Carroll asserts that "cinema is not a language," while he acknowledges that language does play "an intimate role in several of the symbolic structures used in cinema" (Carroll, 1996, p. 187). Virginia Brooks (1984) finds film semiology untestable and unverifiable and therefore unscientific; she describes Christian Metz's filmolinguistic work as "devoid of any experimental content or even any suggestion as to how decisions might be reached as to the rightness or wrongness of its assertions" (ibid., p. 11). Gregory Currie (1995) rejects the suggestion that linguistics can help us explain how we use, interpret, or appreciate the cinema. Film, he argues, lacks the salient features of natural language: it lacks productivity (the capacity to utter and comprehend an infinity of sentences) and conventionality, i.e. no set of conventions operates to confer meaning on cinematic images in anything like the way in which conventions confer literal meaning on language. Film syntax, furthermore, cannot be compared to language. "While a few kinds of shot-combinations have acquired the status of recurrent and familiar patterns (e.g. point-of-view editing), these in no sense constitute or even approach the status of meaning-determining rules" (Currie, in Miller and Stam, 1999).

Some of these critiques seem rather ungenerous. Metz himself had already implicitly made them when he said that cinema was not a *langue* (language system), and acknowledged that "meaning-determining rules" like the Grand Syntagmatique were historically time-bound (just a codification of editing in a certain period). Metz always stressed the disanalogies as well as the analogies between film and language, never equating analogy with identity. It is therefore somewhat gratuitous to inventory all the ways in which film is *not* a language system when Metz had already said as much. The cognitivist rejection of filmolinguistics partially derives from the sensitivity, typical of analytic and ordinary-language philosophy, to the possible abuses of metaphor, here the metaphor of film as language (or later dream). For cognitivists, metaphor is not necessarily a cognitive, exploratory instrument, but rather a kind of category mistake (although one might perform a cognitive study of metaphor itself). Cognitivists tend to be suspicious of the playful, punning, metaphorical, and analogical modes of some screen theory; they react to it as Samuel Johnson reacted to Shakespeare's puns, as a "fatal Cleopatra" to be shunned. (Nonetheless, writers like Noël Carroll are themselves fond of using witty analogies, a kind of metaphor, as a strategy in argument.) However, metaphors are not wrong or right; they are suggestive and illuminating, or they are not. It is one thing to say that a metaphor such as "film language" has given us all it can give us and that we should move on or change tack; it is a very different thing to say that it is simply "wrong."

Cognitivists do not completely deny the usefulness of psychoanalysis, but they see that usefulness as limited to the emotive and irrational aspects of film. Cognitivism, Carroll writes, looks for "alternative answers to many of the questions addressed by or raised by psychoanalytic film theories, especially with respect to film reception, in terms of cognitive and rational processes rather than irrational or unconscious ones"(Bordwell and Carroll, 1996, p. 62), Bordwell, similarly, acknowledges that psychoanalytic theories are better equipped than cognitivism for issues of sexuality and fantasy (Bordwell, 1985, p. 336). But there is "no reason," as Bordwell puts it, "to claim for the unconscious any activities which can be explained on other grounds" (ibid., p. 30).

Using a cognitive/analytic approach, Allen (1995) tried to recuperate psychoanalytic theory through a critical reassessment that would cleanse it of "ambiguity and equivocation." Distinguishing between mere "sensory deception" and "epistemic deception," Allen argued that psychoanalysis can help us understand the ways that the spectator actively contributes to "projective illusion." We know that what we are seeing is only a film, yet we experience that film as a "fully realized world." Allen proposes a tripartite division for the question of belief in the cinema. Using George Romero's horror film *Night of the Living Dead* as an example, he distinguishes between a first level realist reading, a second level of "reproductive" illusion, and a third level of "projective illusion" (Allen, 1993).

Cognitivism, in sum, explicitly rejects some of the first principles of screen theory. It rejects, first of all, the axiomatic base of filmolinguistics, that film is a "language-like" entity that can be apprehended through a linguistic–semiological approach. Second, it rejects the founding abstraction of psychoanalytic film theory – the Unconscious – in favor of conscious and preconscious operations. Third, unlike the semiotic and Althusserian tradition, it tends to be supportive rather than suspicious of "common sense" – the aggregate of common opinion derisively labeled "doxa" by Roland Barthes – and in some versions offers a populist endorsement of what Currie calls "folk psychology" or "folk theoretic wisdom." Fourth, cognitivism disdains grand theoretical claims – the author is dead! the spectator is born! the apparatus lures! – in favor of the time-tested pragmatism of "problem solving." Fifth, it tends to reject the political claims made for Brechtian–modernist reflexivity. Sixth, it rejects, if only implicity, the postmodern notion of the end of meta-narratives, specifically the rejection of the meta-narrative of scientific progress. For cognitivism, film theory should approximate the condition of science by progressing through empirical investigation and rational debate. Seventh, despite the very diverse political affiliations of its practitioners, cognitivism prefers what it sees as a stance of objective, apolitical neutrality to what it sees as the "agenda-driven" politicizing of theory. In this sense, it distances itself from political and cultural radicalism. In the background is the ideal of a peaceful combat of competing hypotheses in a kind of free market-place of ideas, where the "best theories" will win out through the processes of meritocratic competition.

While cognitivism claims to be the "latest thing," it can be viewed as a nostalgic move backward to a world prior to Saussurean differentialism, prior to the Frankfurt School indictment of "instrumental reason," prior to Lacan's destabilized ego, prior to Marxist and Freudian critiques of "common sense," prior to Foucault's power–knowledge nexus and the mutually constitutive relation between reason and madness. Cognitivism shows a touching faith in reason (after Auschwitz) and science (after Hiroshima). It keeps its faith with science, even though "science" had not so recently

240

"proved" black, Jewish, and Native American inferiority. The question, of course, is to what end is science being used, and who gets to decide.

Currie's concept of "folk theoretic wisdom," meanwhile, ignores the question of heteroglossic contradictions both within and between "folks." In the contemporary era, is there any unalloyed "folk" consensus that joins rich and poor, black and white, male and female? Most black folk in the United States seem to feel that whites have been collectively racist toward them; many whites are reluctant to agree. Does the notion of common folk wisdom help us in such situations? While a white suburbanite moviegoer who has never been victimized by the police and an inner-city resident who has been brutalized by the police might share a common recognition that what they are seeing on screen is a white policeman, their affective response, the historical associations, the socio-ideological "intonation" they bring to that figure, might well be different. For German anti-semites in the 1930s, anti-semitic films like *The Jew Suss* resonated with their "common sense," but not for Jews or their sympathizers.

Cognitive theory allows little room for the politics of location, or for the socially shaped investments, ideologies, narcissisms, and desires of the spectator, all of which seem too irrational and messy for the theory to deal with. Why do some spectators love, and others hate, the *same* films? There is little room in cognitive theory for the potential homophobic reaction of the spectator of *Cruising*, or the potential anti-Arab/Muslim reaction of the spectator of *The Siege*, or the potential misogynistic reaction of the spectator of *Fatal Attraction*. In cognitive theory, a raceless, genderless, classless understander/interpreter encounters abstract schemata. But why do we go to films? Is it to make inferences and test hypotheses? While that is admittedly part of the process, we also go to films for other reasons: to confirm (or question) our prejudices, to identify with characters, to feel intense emotions and "subject-effects," to imagine another life, to enjoy kinaesthetic pleasure, to taste glamor, eroticism, charisma, passion.

The critique I deploy here does not imply cultural relativism, as some imagine, but rather the historical study of multifaceted relations between cultural formations. A focus on cognitive commonalities across all cultures exists below the threshold of cultural and social difference, and therefore discourages analysis of tensions rooted in history and culture. What is missing in cognitive theory's notion of the spectator is a sense of social and ideological contradiction, a notion of the heteroglossia, the stratified and conflictual "many-languagedness" within and between social formations. Even single individuals are conflicted, torn between their charitable and selfish impulses, their progressive and regressive tendencies. The social formation as a whole is even more riven. And why does cognitivism insist that our responses to film are largely rationally motivated? Couldn't spectatorial response intertwine the rational and the irrational? Is our response to TV commercials, or to political "attack-ads," rational? Were pro-Nazi responses to *Triumph of the Will* rational? Were white responses to *Birth of a Nation* rational? Can spectatorship be reduced to a matter of making inferences from the cues provided by a text? Why do we enjoy certain films, such as *Rear Window*, long *after* we have mastered their inferential cues? What about the contradictory desires engaged by film – for eroticism, for beauty, for aggression, for community, for law and order, for rebellion?

The cognitive approach downsizes, as it were, the ambitions of theory, concentrating instead on manageable research problems. In reaction against subject-positioning and apparatus theory, which made grand claims about the cinema's alienating role *in general*, Noël Carroll proposes a more modest and local project: not the operations of *all* discourse, but rather "the rhetorical organization of *some* discourse" (Carroll, 1998, p. 391). Within this project cognitivists have done substantial and productive work on issues of spectatorial engagement not with the apparatus in general, not with narrative in general, but with characters in film, a subject long rendered off-limits by theoretical anti-humanism. A number of theorists, for example Murray Smith (1995), Ed Tan (1996), and contributors to *Passionate Views: Thinking about Film and Emotions* (1999), have explored the contribution of cognitivism in accounting for emotional responses to film. In *Moving Pictures: A*

New Theory of Film Genres, Feelings and Cognition, Torben Kragh Grodal pays attention to the very physiology of film reception, that aspect of the cinematic experience which makes us say that a film "sent chills up our spine" or made our "heart sink." As Grodal puts it:

> *The film experience is made up of many activities: our eyes and ears pick up and analyze image and sound, our minds apprehend the story, which reso- nates in our memory; furthermore, our stomach, heart, and skin are activated in empathy with the story situations and the protagonists' ability to cope. (Grodal, 1997, p. 1)*

Grodal rejects Bordwell's contention that comprehension of film is theoretically separable from emotional response, arguing that "feel- ings and emotions are just as much 'objective' aspects of the internal constructions of the fabula as cognitions are" (ibid., p. 40). Grodal also disputes the idea that cognitive film theory is only suited to rational processes, while psychoanalytic methods are better suited to explaining non-rational responses such as emotions. Emotions, he rightly points out, "are not irrational forces" but rather "motivators for cognition and possible resulting actions." Grodal discriminates an ascending hierarchy of responses, each with emotion-producing potential: (1) visual perception of lines and figures; (2) memory matching within the cerebral archives; (3) the construction of a diegesis; and (4) identification with characters, resulting in diverse possible reactions: (a) voluntary telic (goal-oriented) responses; (b) paratelic (semi-voluntary responses); and (c) autonomic involuntary responses (laughing, crying).

Cognitive theory's turn to scientific methods was motivated by its fatigue with high-flying theoretical speculation, with bold assertions unsupported by evidence, and with the relentless politicization of Screen theory. As part of this scientific turn, Cognitive theory favors a distinct vocabulary featuring words like "schemata," "visual data," "neuropsychological coordinates," "image-processing," "evolution- ary perspectives," "physiology of response," and the "cognitive– hedonic relabeling of arousal" (Grodal, 1997, p. 102). But in its

243

revolt against intellectual inflation, cognitivism sometimes runs the opposite risk of reductivism, of suggesting that the film experience is "nothing but" physiological response and cognitive processing.

Murray Smith (1995) replaces the psychoanalytic concept of identification (developed by Metz, Mulvey, Heath, and many others) with the concept of engagement. Smith usefully distinguishes three levels of engagement. Building on Richard Wollheim's distinction in *The Thread of Life* (1984) between "central" and "acentral" imagining, and rejecting what he sees as the false dichotomy of the cognitive and the emotive, he argues for three levels of imaginative engagement which together form a "structure of sympathy:" (1) recognition (the spectatorial construction of characters as individuated and continuous agents); (2) alignment (the process by which spectators are placed in congruent relation in terms of access to a character's actions, knowledge, and feelings); and (3) allegiance (the cognitive and affective adherence to a character's values and moral point of view). Theorists have often conflated (2) and (3), Smith argues, under broad terms like "identification" and "point of view."

By focusing on emotion, Smith corrects the more rationalist and constructivist Bordwellian emphasis on "hypothesis-testing" and "inferential cues," but his main target is the Brechtian emphasis on rational and ideological distantiation and screen theory's emphasis on the subjected and positioned spectator. Smith reasserts spectatorial agency but without making larger Fiskean claims of subversion and resistance: "Spectators, I will argue, are neither deceived with respect to the status of representations, nor entirely caught within the cultural assumptions of those representations" (Smith, 1995, p. 41). Smith rejects what he calls the "incarceration" of the spectator, seen as benighted, spellbound in ideological darkness, and in this sense his move parallels that of others. But he goes too far in depoliticizing the cinema when he argues that schema theory can substitute for "ideology." The spectator, I would argue, both is constructed and him or herself constructs, within a kind of constrained or situated freedom. In a Bakhtinian perspective the reader/spectator exercises agency, but always within the force-fields of contradiction characteristic both of the social field and of the individual psyche. Cognitive theory, by focusing on mental processes, must work in complementarity with more socially and historically minded methods, otherwise it runs the risk of its own form of incarceration, i.e. of driving complex historical processes into the monadic perceptual prison of the individual psyche. Smith's disastrous substitution of the word "moral" for the word "ideological," for example, throws out the collective achievements of the Frankfurt School, screen theory, and cultural studies, leaving a social void which the word "moral," with its Victorian associations, cannot possibly fill.

Noël Carroll (1998) takes a more nuanced position on ideology, proposing an expanded definition which allows not only for class domination but for any system of oppression. Carroll rejects what he sees as an overly broad definition of ideology which would equate it with perception (Althusser), language (Volosinov), or discourse (Foucault). Picking up on decades of work on gender, race, and sexuality, Carroll proposes dropping exclusive references to class oppression, instead defining ideology as epistemically defective propositions with "contextually grounded implications favorable to some practice of social domination" (ibid., p. 378). Such a definition has the advantage of emphasizing the effects of ideology in the world, but has the disadvantage of grounding the operations of ideology in "propositions" rather than in the asymmetrical power arrangements that structure everyday life and consciousness. What is missing in Smith, as opposed to Carroll, is a notion of a social vantage point, of spectatorial *investments* in representation, notions of ideological grids and cultural narcissisms that reflect the social channeling of emotional engagement. British spectators at the height of imperialism felt flattered by representations of their empire spreading order and progress around the world; the imperialized, meanwhile, protested such representations. Many American spectators, similarly, enjoy *Indiana Jones*-style images which flatter their sense of America's mission in the world. It is not an accident that Hollywood returns incessantly to World War II, the "good war" where Americans were liberating heroes. Many Americans are quite accepting of stereotypical representations of Muslim Arabs in films like *The Sheik, Ishtar,*

Aladdin, and *The Siege* because they are not personally invested in positive representations; their ox is not being gored. Arab and Muslim spectators, on the other hand, react with hurt and outrage to incendiary stereotypes of all Arabs and Muslims (the two terms are usually confused) as terrorists. An innocuous notion of folk beliefs lacks the strength to account for *differential* reactions, rooted in distinct histories. There is thus a kind of complacency in one strand of cognitive theory that assumes we live in a well-ordered cosmos, where good spectators align with good characters in a common-sense world where everyone agrees about the nature of good and evil. But what happens when the cinema idealizes certain figures who might have historically played a fairly sinister role – for example, FBI agents during the Civil Rights movement in *Mississippi Burning* – and presents them as heroes? What happens when action blockbusters encourage adolescents to indulge in dreams of "infantile omnipotence" by identifying with the sadistic violence of law-and-order figures fighting diabolical evil, even if, indeed *especially* if, those characters are presented as exercising violence in a putatively "good" cause?

A simplistic view of cognitive theory as simply the antithesis of screen theory also obscures shared terrain. The work of Murray Smith, like that of Edward Branigan, activates a dialogue between cognitive theory and the narratology of theorists like Gérard Genette and François Jost. Smith's "alignment," for example, is in some ways akin to Genette's notion of "focalization." Filmolinguistics and cognitive theory also share a common appeal to scientific standards, even if the master-sciences and jargons in question (linguistics versus cognitive psychology) are not identical. Eco and Metz, after all, also talked about codes of perception and cognition. Both cognitivism and semiology downplay issues of evaluation and ranking, moreover, in favor of probing the ways texts are understood. Both movements refuse a normative, belletristic approach; they share a democratizing impulse uninterested in lauding individual filmmakers as geniuses or specific films as masterpieces. For Carroll (1998) as for Metz, all mass art is art. In any intellectual movement questions are more important than answers, and cognitivism shares many of its questions with screen theory: What is the nature of cinematic illusion? How are films understood? What is the nature of narrative comprehension? What are the schemata and semantic fields (Bordwell), the extra-cinematic codes (Metz), the disciplinary paradigms of knowledge (Foucault), the bodies of (largely unarticulated) knowledge and belief, that we bring to bear on our understanding of film? How does the viewer locate him or herself in the space of the action? How do audiences construct meaning? What accounts for emotional, empathic responses to films?

The polemics between the cognitivists and the semioticians, then, mask substantial commonalities: the appeal to scientificity, the search for rigor, the refusal of impressionism in favor of painstaking work on precise theoretical problems. Ironically, both Metz and Carroll deploy the same metaphor of the sausage-machine to mock the kind of sterile, epigonic film analysis they dislike. The two movements also share certain blindspots. Both cognitivism and Metzian semiotics have been critiqued for their lack of attention to race, gender, class, and sexuality, their quiet presumption of a white, middle-class, heterosexual spectator. The two schools differ, of course, in the master disciplines to which they appeal – linguistics and psychoanalysis in the case of semiotics; cognitive psychology, Prague School aesthetics, and more generally an appeal to the protocols of scientific rationalism (inference, proof, demonstration, induction, deduction, abduction, verifiability) in the case of cognitivism. The two movements also differ in style and rhetoric. While a certain strand of Barthesian semiotics has been playful, at best ludically experimental and at worst pretentiously vapid in its fondness for punning and word play, the cognitive school, and its distant cousin the "postanalytic school," show a certain squeamishness about unconstrained association and the free play of interpretation. But a search-and-destroy mission against all ambiguities of meaning can be just as silly as the willful inflation of "undecidabilities." If one side can be accused of willful inflation, the other can be accused of short-sighted reductionism.

Semiotics Revisited

What was known as screen theory, conceived in a broad sense, for a long time set the terms of debate in film theory. It formed the matrix, and provided much of the vocabulary, for approaches which mingled linguistic, psychoanalytic, feminist, Marxist, narratological, and translinguistic approaches. As the result of internal evolution and external attack, screen theory in the 1980s lost its former arrogance. Nevertheless, what Guy Gauthier calls the "semiotic diaspora" remains a strong, dynamizing presence within reflexion on film. (It is interesting, in this sense, that relatively new fields such as queer theory, in order to establish disciplinary pedigree, end up by reaching for a paradoxical "cutting-edge respectability" by asserting a strong link with semiotic or poststructuralist theory.)

Here I will concentrate on both the prolongations of semiotic work and the ruptures and emerging fields. In the United States, Nick Browne (1982) and Edward Branigan (1984; 1992) analyzed filmic point-of-view. In France, meanwhile a number of theorists have provided continuity to the Metzian semiological enterprise through very precise studies of the status of the image (Aumont, 1997), textual analysis (Aumont and Marie, 1989), narratology (Gaudreault and Jost, 1990; Vanoye 1989), enunciation (Marc Vernet), and film sound (Michel Chion). Much of the work has had to do with filmic "enunciation," i.e. the ensemble of discursive operations which turn an authorial intention into a textual discourse, instantiating the film text as being "by" a producer and "for" a spectator. A special issue (38) of *Communications* (1983), co-edited by Jean-Paul Simon and Marc Vernet, was devoted to the subject of "Enunciation and the Cinema." There scholars addressed such issues as "who sees?" and "who speaks?" in a film, and how narrators place themselves in relation to the story told. Within this same current, we have Francesco Casetti's (1986 in Italian, 1990 in French) work on film as discourse (in Benveniste's sense), and which therefore employs deictics, i.e. those indices or traces which refer back to the speaker of a discourse; for example, in language the pronouns that indicate the speaker or the adverbs that indicate time or location. Casetti associates the filmic enunciator with the pronoun "I," the filmic addressee with the pronoun "you," and the narrated utterance, the story itself, with the pronoun "he" (or "she"). Casetti distinguishes three areas of research within enunciation theory: (1) the examination of the enunciatory signals which mark the presence of the spectator in the film; (2) the examination of the positioning of the spectator as determined by diverse configurations (objective shots, subjective shots, direct interpellation, objective but "unreal" shots); (3) the tracing of the trajectory of the spectator "across" the film, through direct and indirect hints, suggestions, and instructions.

Christian Metz (1991) argues against Casetti that film is not discourse but *histoire*. (Here Metz returns to his earlier position that film became a discourse *by* telling stories.) The theoretical search for the equivalent of the deictics of verbal language, he argues, is useless, since what theorists should really be looking for are instances of authorial reflexivity, such as direct visual address to the camera, verbal direct address, the frame-within-the-frame, the display of the apparatus, and so forth. In an ironic turnabout, Metz criticizes Casetti for relying too much on purely linguistic entities such as pronouns. The work of Andre Gaudreault and François Jost, meanwhile, synthesizes enunciation theory with theories of narration. Gaudreault, for example, argues that films are both "diegetic" and "mimetic" in Plato's sense: they "show," like the theater, and "tell" (like a novel). If the film as such is the product of an enunciation, the discursive realization of a communicative intention, the film as story is the product of a narration. In this context, Gaudreault speaks of the diverse narrative agents of film, specifically calling attention to the presence of the "mega-narrator" who combines the functions of the theatrical and the novelistic narrators. In another joint essay, the two authors speak of the heterogeneity if the filmic narrator. Using examples such as *Citizen Kane* they distinguish between the great image-maker or the mega-narrator (the instance "behind" the film's images and sounds as a whole), and explicit narrators and subnarrators. The diversity of the materials of expression makes it possible for diverse forms of play between these diverse modalities

249

of narration (see Gaudreault and Jost in Miller and Stam, 1999).

Casetti (1999) usefully schematizes the strengths as well as the dangers inherent in these three distinct approaches, which might be labeled post-semiotics, cognitivism, and pragmatics. For post-semiotics, cinematic representation is located in the internal dynamics of the text, specifically through enunciation as giving shape to the film, and narration as engendering the story. The danger here is that of all formalisms, of making the text autonomous and self-sufficient. For cognitivism, cinematic representation is rooted in the mental activities of the spectator who uses mental schemata to process the audio-visual data in order to construct a narrative meaning. The danger here is the opposite one, not of reifying the text but rather of eliding it altogether. Cognitivism, for Casetti, runs the risk of reducing the text to the stimuli – sonorous materials and luminous tones – which trigger cognitive procedures and mental activities, some innate and some acquired. Not *Citizen Kane* but a mental construction called *Citizen Kane*. A pragmatic approach, finally, mingles "intrinsic" and "extrinsic" approaches. The text forms part of a social continuum of representations. Both text and context impact each other mutually and reciprocally.

Recent years have also brought strong revisionist currents of feminist psychoanalytic theory, as exemplified by the ongoing work of Teresa de Lauretis, Kaja Silverman, Elizabeth Cowie, and many others. At the same time there are new inflections of Lacanian theory by such figures as Joan Copjec and Slavoj Žižek. While critical of apparatus theory, these theorists recuperate psychoanalytic theory in other respects. Copjec builds on Lacan's Seminar XI to develop a symbolic theory of the look. The subject, in this perspective, can never acquire the transcendental status attributed to it by apparatus theory, since the subject is never visible to itself: "Semiotics, not optics, is the science that clarifies for us the structure of the visual domain" (Copjec, 1989, pp. 53–71).

Slavoj Žižek, meanwhile, in a veritable avalanche of books (e.g. Žižek 1992; 1993), reads films "symptomatically" in ways that go beyond Althusser. As suggested by the subtitle of his *Looking Awry: An Introduction to Jacques Lacan through Popular Culture*, Žižek

(1991) performs a reciprocally illuminating interface between Lacanian theory and specific films (*Psycho, Strangers on a Train, Jaws, The Crying Game*). Indeed, on one level Žižek's view of cinema is quite instrumental; he uses the cinema to demonstrate the validity of Lacan's ideas. Just as for the believer everything proves the truth of the scriptures, so for Žižek everything (or at least the most symptomatic cultural artifacts) demonstrates the truth of Lacan. In this sense, Žižek is a brilliant exegete. But he is also more than this. First of all, he shows that some films, such as *Psycho*, stage and illuminate Lacan's ideas in ways that go beyond Lacan himself. And while previous Lacanian theory tended to privilege the Imaginary and the Symbolic, Žižek recuperates "the Real." The "real," in the Lacanian idiom, has little to do with the positivist materially existing real; it is rather the psychic real of unconscious desire and phantasy, the heterological, irrecuperable real of the psyche. More precisely, Žižek focuses on the "sublime object of ideology" as the kernel of the real, i.e. that in life or art which is projected as precisely the attribute dolorously missing in the subject. Just as mathematics is structured around nothing – the zero – and just as some African polyrhythmic music is structured precisely around the beat which is *not* heard, so psychic life is structured around an object of desire believed to be in the possession of the Other, a compensation for the void at the center of being, the irreducible lack which prevents subjectivity from achieving full identity. Unlike Mulvey's subjectivized, diegeticized male gaze, Žižek's gaze is unmoored from characterological or authorial subjectivity. The Lacanian gaze is an impersonal, non-human "Thing" (*das Ding*):

What lies beyond is not the Symbolic order but a real Kernel, a traumatic core. To designate it, Lacan uses a Freudian term: das Ding, *the Thing as an incarnation of the impossible jouissance (the term Thing is to be take here with all the connotation it possesses in the domain of horror science fiction: the "alien" from the film of the same name is a pre-symbolic maternal Thing* par excellence. (Žižek, 1989, p. 132)

Recasting one of the topoi of Hitchcock criticism, Žižek argues that Hitchcock's films are structured around impossible "nothings" or

MacGuffins – the cigarette lighter in *Strangers on a Train*, or the middle initial (O) of Roger Thornhill's name in *North by Northwest* – which function as fragments of the Real. Modernist art, Žižek (1996) argues, installs this nothing, this openness, this lack in the symbolic order, this "abyss beyond identification," at the center of its textuality. The "ultimate lesson" of *Psycho*, for Žižek,

is that the Beyond is itself hollow, devoid of any positive content: there is no depth of "soul" in it (Norman's gaze is utterly "soulless," like the gaze of monsters and the living dead) – as such, the Beyond coincides with the gaze itself ... a depthless void of pure Gaze which is nothing but a topological reverse of the Thing. (Žižek, 1992, pp. 257–8)

On another level, Žižek continues the dialogue between Marxism and psychoanalysis begun by thinkers from the Frankfurt School (Fromm, Reich, Marcuse) – for whom both capitalist productivism and Nazi authoritarianism depended on sexual repression – and further developed by Sartre and Fanon, on the one hand, and Althusser on the other (for example, in his "Freud and Lacan" essay). While Foucault replaces "ideology" with "discourse," Žižek retains the former term. But instead of Lacan's anti-Americanism, stigmatized as the deluded land of "ego psychology," Žižek embraces Hollywood and popular culture. Indeed, his prose "enacts," as it were, the leveling of high and low culture.

Unlike many of those who address film from an outside perspective, Žižek pays extraordinary attention to the cinematic signifier. In a way, he performs a further Lacanian twist on the famous Narboni–Comolli "category e" as referring to those mainstream Hollywood films which open up gaps and fissures in their illusionism. And it is here that Žižek sees Hitchcock as a "subversive" director. Hitchcock's falsely happy endings, for Žižek, unmask the "radical contingency of the enchainment of narration, the fact that, at every point, things might have turned out otherwise" (Žižek, 1991, p. 69). Žižek stresses those directors who "disturb" Hollywood's protocols over those who reject them outright. He contrasts Hitchcock's subversive strategies, for example, with those of the avant-garde:

Rather than directly breaking [the] rules which guarantee the consistency of a narrative space (the usual strategy of the avant-garde authors), Hitchcock's subversion of it consists in dispelling the lure of its false "openness" – in rendering visible the closure as such. He pretends to comply fully with the rules of closure – in Psycho *for example . . . yet the standard effect of closure remains unfulfilled. (Žižek, 1992, pp. 243–4)*

Hitchcock's films do not show us truth (in Lacanian terms an impossibility); rather, they use specifically cinematic procedures such as the subjective tracking shot to demonstrate the fictional, constructed nature of the very filmic truth in which Hitchcock himself has earlier persuaded us to believe. (The technique is epistemologically analogous, on some levels, to the technique analyzed by Stanley Fish in relation to Milton's *Paradise Lost*, where the reader is continually "surprised in sin.")

Other theorists have extended the linguistic rather than the psychoanalytic strand of semiotics. While one group of cognitivists (Bordwell, Branigan, Carroll) saw themselves as working against linguistics-based structuralist and poststructuralist film theory, another group, notably Dominique Chateau, Michel Colin, and Warren Buckland, worked in tandem with semiotics, cognitive science, and linguistic pragmatics, although at this point Chomsky was just as likely to be an inspiration as Saussure. In "The Grand Syntagmatique Revisited" Michel Colin deployed Chomskian categories to redefine Metz's syntagmatic types as the epiphenomena of something more important: fundamental generative processes. In these movements a number of currents combine: (1) Chomskian generative grammar and cognitive science (in the work of Michel Colin, 1985, and Dominique Chateau); (2) the work on enunciation and narration (e.g. Metz, 1991; Francesco Casetti, 1986; and Gaudreault in Miller and Stam, 1999); and (3) pragmatics (e.g. Roger Odin, in Buckland, 1995).

The goal of "semio-pragmatics," a movement especially associated with the names of Francesco Casetti and Roger Odin, was to study the production and reading of films insofar as they constitute programmed social practices. In linguistics, pragmatics is that branch of linguistics concerned with what transpires between a verbal or written performance and its reception, i.e. the ways in which language produces meaning and influences its interlocutors. Semio-pragmatics prolongs Metz's speculations in "The Imaginary Signifier" concerning the active role of the spectator whose look brings the film, as it were, into existence. Semio-pragmatics is less interested in a sociologistic study of actual spectators than in the psychic disposition of the spectator during the film experience; not spectators as they are in life, but spectators as the film "wants" them to be. The goal of semio-pragmatics, according to Roger Odin, is to show the mechanisms of producing meaning, to understand how a film is understood. Within this perspective, both the production and the reception of film are institutional acts involving roles shaped by a network of determinations generated by the larger social space.

Semio-pragmatics pursues the Metzian project of studying how filmic meaning is produced, but places this production within a more social and historical "space." Casetti speaks of "the communicative pact" and of "communicative negotiation," i.e. the pragmatic interacting and cooperating that takes place between texts and spectators. For Odin (1983), the "space of communication" constituted by producer and spectator of film together is highly diverse, ranging from the pedagogic space of the classroom, through the familial space of the home movie, to the fictional-entertainment space of mass-mediated culture. Along its history, the cinema has tried to perfect the technique, language, and conditions of reception to suit the requirements of "fictionalization." In western societies, and increasingly in non-western societies, the space of fictional communication is becoming the dominant space. "Fictionalization," for Odin, refers to the process by which the spectator is made to resonate to the fiction, the process which moves us and leads us to identify with, love, or hate the characters. Odin divides this process into seven distinct operations:

1 *Figurativization,* the construction of audiovisual analogical signs.
2 *Diegetization,* the construction of a fictive world.

3   *Narrativization*, the temporalization of events involving antagonistic subjects.

4   *Monstration*, the designation of the diegetic world, be it actual or constructed, as "real."

5   *Belief*, the split regime whereby the spectator is simultaneously aware of being "at the movies" and experiencing the film "as if" it were real.

6   *Mise-en-phase* (literally, the "placing-in-phase" or "phasing in" of the spectator), the operation which enlists all the filmic instances in the service of the narration, mobilizing the rhythmic and musical work, the play of looks and framing, to make the spectator vibrate to the rhythm of the filmic events.

7   *Fictivization*, the intentional modality which characterizes the status and the positioning of the spectator, who sees the enunciator of the film not as an originary self but as fictive. The spectator knows that he or she is witnessing a fiction which will not reach him or her personally, an operation which has the paradoxical result of allowing the film thus to touch the spectator in the very depths of the psyche. The non-fiction film, in this perspective, refers to those films which block some or all of the fictionalizing operations.

Casetti (1986) explores the ways that films signal the presence and assign a possible position to the spectator, coaxing him or her to follow an itinerary. While early film semiotics saw the spectator as at best a relatively passive decoder of pre-established codes and at worst a dupe of an overwhelming ideological machine, Casetti sees the spectator as active interlocutor and interpretant. The film offers the spectator a specific position and role, but the spectator can negotiate that position in function of personal taste, ideology, and cultural context. Odin also speaks of a new kind of spectator shaped by the postmodern communications environment. Taking as an example Giorgio Moroder's musical "actualization" in 1984 of Fritz Lang's *Metropolis* (1926), Odin foregrounds processes such as colorization which "de-realize" the film, rendering it as surface. (Odin's analysis is easily extrapolable for music video.) Instead of

255

the usual tertiary structure of film, narration, and spectator, we find a dual structure in which the film acts directly on the spectator, who vibrates not to a fiction but rather to variations of rhythm, intensity, and color, to what Baudrillard calls "plural energies" and "fragmentary intensities." This mutation of social space generates a new "spectatorial economy," product of the crisis of the "grand narratives of legitimation"(Lyotard, 1984), the "end of the social" (Baudrillard, 1983), and a new spectator less alert to "stories" than to the energetic discharge of the flux of music and images. Communication gives way to communion.

Just in Time: The Impact of Deleuze

Film theory has also been feeling the positively corrosive impact of the writings of Gilles Deleuze, and especially of two ambitious books from the 1980s: *Cinema I, l'image-mouvement* (Deleuze, 1986) and *Cinema II, l'image-temps* (Deleuze, 1989). Prior to his specific film writing Deleuze, together with Félix Guattari, had already been indirectly influential on film theory through his critique of psycho-analysis in *Anti-Oedipus: Capitalism and Schizophrenia* (1972), where the two authors condemned the "analytic imperialism" of the Oedipus Complex as a form of "colonialism pursued by other means." Building on the Freudian Marxism of Wilhelm Reich, Deleuze and Guattari set out to destroy two major pillars of film semiotics: Saussure and Lacan. They attacked the former by moving from language-based metaphors for addressing culture to a lexicon of flows, energies, and desiring machines. They attacked the latter by arguing that the Freudian Oedipus story has served as a mechanism of repression, rooted in absence and lack of access to the forbidden mother, a mechanism useful to patriarchal capitalism because it represses all undisciplined, polymorphous desires (and not only *sexual* desires) deemed to be in excess of capitalistic rationality. In contrast to Lacan's dystopian version of the deluded oedipal subject, Deleuze and Guattari proposed an unashamedly utopian politics of polyvalent desire, where schizophrenia is seen not as pathology but as a subversive disordering of bourgeois thought processes.

Long a subterranean current, Deleuze's influence is now becoming more visible within film theory, as evidenced by a special issue of *Iris*, the first book-length study in English (Rodowick, 1997), a Deleuze-inspired monograph (Shaviro, 1993), and a proliferation of Deleuze-inflected dissertations. Like the cognitivists, Deleuze attacks Grand Theory, but from a completely different direction. He sets out, as David Rodowick puts it, to "critique and demolish the Saussurean and Lacanian foundations on which, coincidentally, most contemporary cultural and film theory has been based" (Rodowick, 1997, p. xi). Deleuze deploys Peirce's theory of signs against Metzian filmolinguistics and against the Lacanian system which makes cinematic desire orbit around the "lack" rooted in the gap between an imaginary signifier and its signified. For Deleuze, film is neither *langue* nor language *à la* Metz, but a semiotic, *à la* Peirce. While Metz argues that cinema is a language but not a language system, Deleuze asserts that "the language system only exists in its reaction to a non-language material that it transforms" (Deleuze, 1989, p. 29). He calls this non-language material the *enoncable* or "that which can be uttered," a "signaletic material" which includes verbal elements but which is also kinetic, intensive, affective, rhythmic, a "plastic mass prior to language, an a-signifying and a-syntactic material, a material not formed linguistically even though it is not amorphous and is formed semiotically, aesthetically, and pragmatically" (ibid., p. 19).

Although for Deleuze the relation between cinema and language remains "the most pressing problem," he is critical of the reductionist, code-seeking Saussure-based film semiology that empties the cinema of its vital, blood-like, circulating substance – movement itself. In this sense, he is close to Bakhtin and Volosinov's (1928) position which rejects the Saussurean couplets (synchrony–diachrony; signifier–signified) in favor of a constantly changing *parole*. Deleuze thus foregrounds precisely what was left out of linguistic accounts of the cinema – the encounter of perception and matter called "movement" – precisely that aspect of the text which made it "unattainable." Following Bergson, Deleuze equates "the infinite set of all images" as parallel to the ceaseless movements of matter in a "world of universal variation, of universal undulation, universal rippling" (Deleuze, 1989, p. 58). Deleuze is drawn to Bergson as a philosopher of becoming, for whom being and matter are never stable. Within Deleuze's Bergsonian conception, matter and movement are imbued with and inseparable from consciousness as itself material. Bergson's *Matter and Memory* (1896), for Deleuze, anticipated the multiple temporalities and superimposed *durées* of the cinema itself. What interests Deleuze are not images *of* something which would constitute a diegesis, but rather images caught up in the Heraclitan flux of time, film as event rather than representation. He is interested in the ways that cinema can convey multiple and contradictory "sheets of time." In *Citizen Kane*, for example, we are "carried away by the undulations of a great wave, time gets out of joint, and we enter into temporality as a state of permanent crisis" (Deleuze, 1989, p. 112).

Deleuze worked out his ideas as a kind of parallel montage between two disciplines: film theory and philosophy. In Deleuze, concepts drawn from the two fields inter-fecundate and are in the process changed. Bypassing the tired question of "film art," Deleuze sees the cinema as itself a philosophical instrument, a generator of concepts and a producer of texts which render thought in audiovisual terms, not in language but in blocks of movement and duration. Both film and philosophy articulate a conception of time, for example, but film does it not through discursive abstraction but through light and movement. A theory of cinema, for Deleuze, is not "about" the cinema but about the concept that the cinema itself triggers, the ways in which it fabricates new connections between fields and disciplines. Deleuze not only theorizes the cinema in new ways but also cinematizes philosophy. While Metz was interested in the analogies and disanalogies between film and language, or between film and dream, Deleuze is interested in commensurabilities between the history of philosophy and the history of cinema, the conceptual moves which link Eisenstein to Hegel, for example, or modern cinema to

Nietzsche or Bergson. At the same time, Deleuze's disconcerting style mingles philosophical speculation and literary excursions, along with quick, sharp analyses of specific films and filmmakers: the "interval" in Vertov, the free indirect style in Pasolini, the slow time-images of Ozu.

To elaborate his conceptual machine, Deleuze draws on philosophers like Bergson and Peirce, novelists like Balzac and Proust, filmmakers like Godard and Bresson, and film theorists like Bazin and Metz. Deleuze picks up some of the perennial themes of film theory – realism, modernism, the evolution of film language – but recasts and revitalizes them. Realism, for example, no longer refers to a mimetic, analogical adequation between sign and referent, but rather to the sensate feel of time, to the intuition of lived duration, the mobile slidings of Bergsonian *durée*. Film restores the real rather than represent it. The frame, for Deleuze, is unstable, dissolvable into the flux of time; time leaks out through the borders of the frame.

When reading Deleuze one hears frequent echoes of other theorists – Bazin on neo-realism, Kracauer on contingency, Brecht on autonomous scenes, Bordwell on classical cinema, Pasolini on free indirect discourse – but filtered through a philosophical sensibility and recast in neologistic language. Jon Beasley-Murray points out Deleuze's many affinities with Bazin: a shared predilection for the long take, a concern with mimesis and ontology, and the idea that "the specificity of the cinema remains its unfolding of the image in the real time that becomes the lived time of thought and the body." Deleuze also inherits a heroic version of auteurism which emphasizes filmmakers themselves, surprising in a philosopher who always distanced himself from any notion of an empirical or transcendental "subject." In *Cinema I* he contrasts the "masterpieces" of the pantheon of great high modernist directors – "comparable not only to painters, architects, and musicians but also to thinkers" – with the "vast proportion of rubbish in cinematic production" (Deleuze, 1986, p. xiv).

Deleuze's approach is self-proclaimedly taxonomic in that it attempts to classify images and sounds, but his analysis is not static in the manner of structuralist taxonomies. He theorizes the transition from classical ("movement-image") to modern cinema ("time-image"). Indeed, the rupture between the two volumes stages, as it were, the movement from one mode to the other, a rupture which Deleuze associates with the immediate postwar moment that ultimately generates both Italian neo-realism and the various New Waves around the world:

The fact is that in Europe, the post-war period has greatly increased the situations which we no longer know how to react to, in spaces which we no longer know how to describe. . . . [These] situations could be extremes, or, on the contrary, those of everyday banality, or both at once: what tends to collapse is the sensory–motor schema which constituted the action-image of the old cinema. And thanks to this loosening . . . it is time, "a little time in the pure state," which rises us to the surface of the screen. Time ceases to be derived from the movement, it appears in itself. (Deleuze, 1989, p. xi)

The transition from movement-image to time-image is multi-dimensional, at once narratological, philosophical, and stylistic. While the movement-image as used in mainstream Hollywood presents a unified diegetic world conveyed through spatiotemporal coherence and rational cause–effect editing – the cinematic equivalent of the teleological drive toward synthesis that so repels Deleuze in Hegel – the time-image is based on discontinuity as performed by the "irrational cuts" of Godard's jump-cuts or the elegant mismatches of Resnais's *faux raccords*. Instead of Kuleshov's linkage, then, we have systematic de-linkage. The movement-image is associated with classical cinema (whether Soviet or American, Eisenstein or Griffith), with its clear exposition of a situation which sets up a fundamental conflict to be resolved by the progress of the narrative. The movement-image and especially its most representative form, the "action-image," is based on cause and effect, on organic linkages and teleological development, and on protagonists plowing purposefully through the narrative space. (Here we are close to the Bordwell–Thompson–Staiger emphasis on characters' projects and chains of causality.) The time-image associated with modern cinema, in contrast, is less concerned with linear cause–effect logic. While the movement-image involves the exploration of physical space, the time-image conveys the mental processes of memory, dream, and the imaginary. The narratively shaped action image gives way to a dispersive, aleatory cinema of "optical-sound situations." Central to Deleuze's conception is the idea that the shot faces in two directions: toward parts within the frame, and toward a larger developing whole outside the frame. Film, like consciousness itself, thus slices up perceptual phenomena, re-arranges them, and forms new, provisional wholes or totalities. If the classic movement-image relates part to whole as an organic to-tality, in this sense, the time-image engenders autonomous shots with uncertain or absent causality within a non-totalized process where the continuity bridges have broken down, a process exempli-fied by films like Marguerite Duras's *India Song* (1975).

The time-image, according to Deleuze, can be delivered up by four kinds of montage (organic, dialectical, quantitative, and inten-sive–extensive), each associated with a different national tradition (respectively the American, Russian, French, and German expres-sionist). This cinema produces *mnemosignes* (memory-images) and *onirosignes* (dream-images). The "crystal image" presents the fun-damental operations of time as a fleeting, unseizable border between the immediate past which is no more and the immediate future which is not yet. (The account is reminiscent of the Sid Ceaser sketch where the standup-comic tries to physically seize the present, which once you grab, "it's gone.") With the time-image, a cinema of the agent transmutes into a "cinema of the seer," a movement that resonates, I would suggest, with literary-critical accounts of the transition from the static ontologized descriptions of a Balzac to the mobilized gaze of a Flaubert. For Deleuze, digital technologies augment the poss-ibilities of a "nomadic" cinema. The panoramic organization of space loses its thrust and gives way to the screen as palimpsestic memory.

Many critics have questioned Deleuze's originality or disputed his conclusions. Analysts have pointed to Deleuze's debts to ante-cedent film theory, history, and analysis (to be fair, Deleuze himself acknowledges many of these debts). Deleuze's account of the move-ment-image draws on work by Bazin, Heath, Bordwell, and Burch on classical cinema. Bordwell points out that Deleuze builds his own account of film history on the mistaken assumptions of orthodox versions of the historiography of style, and that Deleuze's fundamental distinction between classical (movement-image) and modern (time-image) cinema goes back to Bazin (Bordwell, 1997, pp. 116–17). Paisley Livingston calls Deleuze's general approach an example of "irrational interdisciplinarity," and also contests specific analyses. For Livingston, Deleuze overstates the dispersal and fractured causality of neo-realist classics. Films like *Ladri di Biciclette* and *I Vitelloni* do not do what Deleuze claims they do. They have their own recognizable agents, their purposeful activities, and their forms of linkage. Deleuze's claim that aspects of these films "shatter" the narrative, for Livingston, "is akin to saying that the dramatic pauses 'shatter' the melodies in Beethoven's Ninth Symphony." While one can acknowledge the brilliance of Deleuze's analyses, and while one can dialogue with Deleuze, try to philosophize like Deleuze, or do with other philosophers something analogous to what Deleuze does with Bergson, it seems somewhat more problematic to "apply" Deleuze, to simply "translate" analysis into a Deleuzian language.

The Coming Out of Queer Theory

Feminist theory in the 1980s was both riven and energized by tensions around race, class, and sexual orientation. While "radical feminists" focused on gender inequality, "cultural feminists" focused on innate biological differences between men and women, but this time to the advantage of women, now seen as innately gentle, dialogic, ecological, and nurturing. There was also tension between straight and lesbian feminism, with some applauding Ti-Grace Atkinson's 1970s declaration that "feminism is the theory, lesbianism is the practice." If film theory was revealed in the 1980s to have been normatively white and European, it was also revealed to have been normatively heterosexual. Psychoanalysis had been blind to class,

262

Marxism had been blind to race and gender, but both psychoanalysis and Marxism had been blind to sexuality. In its exclusive attention to sexual difference, some argued, psychoanalytic/feminist theory spoke of "the other" but itself "otherized" gays and lesbians. Indeed, "queerness" seemed retroactively to have been the blindspot common to virtually *all* the theories. Building on the achievements of gay and lesbian activism in the wake of the 1968 Stonewall rebellion, when gays, lesbians, and transvestites resisted routine harassment by the New York police, many theorists developed a gay and lesbian approach to culture generally, and to film in particular. The movement was first called Gay Liberation, on the model of Black and Women's Liberation. Subsequently, through a kind of lexical ju-jitsu, gay and lesbian theorists reappropriated the formerly pejorative "queer" as a positive term and a "proud, get-used-to-it" assertion of difference. Queers were no longer a subculture, but a "nation" with its own proud history, its founding texts, and its public rituals.

The concept of gender replaced the idea of binary anatomical difference with a more plural concept of culturally and socially constructed "identity." Within the essentialism–anti-essentialism debate, queer studies generally sided with the anti-essentialist faction, emphasizing sexuality and gender as social constructs shaped by history and articulated together with a complex set of social, institutional, and discursive relations. Perhaps because queer theory took as its point of departure an already highly theoretical and anti-essentialist feminism, and because it also absorbed the insights of poststructuralism and postmodernism, it began as one of the most "constructivist" and "anti-essentialist" of disciplinary formations. (This was complicated later by the political usefulness of scientists' claims that homosexuality was genetic and therefore not a matter of choice.) Building on Butler's Foucauldian account of gender not as an essence or even a symbolic entity but rather as a practice, queer theorists criticized the coercive binarism of sexual difference, favoring instead hybrid permutations of gay and straight, lesbian and bisexual.

In the late 1970s and early 1980s the field of gender studies, which emerged together with women's studies, also eased the way for gay and lesbian studies (subsequently "queer studies"). Many theorists associated with these fields emphasized the idea that the borders between gender identity were highly permeable and artificial. Theorists began to argue that all gender was "performative," an imitation rather than an essence. "What happens to the subject and to the stability of gender categories," Judith Butler asked, "when the epistemic regime of presumptive heterosexuality is unmasked as that which produces and reifies these ostensible categories of ontology?" (Butler, 1990, p. viii). For Butler, drag constitutes "the mundane way in which genders are appropriated, theatricalized, worn, and done; it implies that all gendering is a kind of impersonation and approximation." Sexualizing Baudrillard's account of the simulacrum, Butler adds that gender is an imitation "for which there is no original; in fact, it is a kind of imitation that produces the very notion of the original as an *effect* and consequence of the imitation itself" (Butler, in Fuss, 1991). Similarly emphasizing the constructedness of gender categories, Teresa de Lauretis (1989) spoke of the "technologies" of the "sex/gender system." This new formation examined all gender formations, whether heterosexual, homosexual, or what Eve Sedgewick called "homosocial." Sedgewick (1985) spoke of the "homosocial cast" of a "triangulated" male desire modeled on another male's desire. Sedgewick (1991) observes that "it is the paranoid insistence with which the definitional boundaries between the 'homosexual' (minority) and the 'heterosexual' majority are charged up, in this century, by nonhomosexuals, and especially by men against men, that most saps one's ability to believe in 'the homosexual' as an unproblematically discrete category of persons." Sedgewick argued that our "coarse axes of categorization" flatten out and homogenize a vast range of sexualized identities and identificatory practices.

In film studies the power of queer theory is attested to by innumerable conferences, film festivals, special issues of journals (e.g. *Jump Cut*), and the publication of a burgeoning number of anthologies and monographs devoted to queer cinema and theory. Lesbian and gay research, as Julia Erhart points out, enlivened feminist criticism generally, and feminist film criticism specifically, at the moment when heterosexual feminists were bumping up against the constraints of straight feminist theory.[1] Queer theory in film, as practiced by such theorists as Teresa de Lauretis, Judith Mayne, Alexander Doty, Richard Dyer, Martha Gever, Ruby Rich, Chris Straayer, Jacquie Stacey, Andrea Weiss, Patricia White, and many others, critically extended and critiqued the feminist intervention. Queer theory was almost inevitably suspicious of theoretical feminism's affiliation with psychoanalysis, given the lamentable record of the psychoanalytic movement in branding gay and lesbian practices as deviant. Queer theorists pointed to the "heterosexedness" of psychoanalytic theory. Despite Freud's acknowledgment of the principle of bisexuality, his sexual monism, and the Freudian–Lacanian fetishization of sexual difference left little room for differences between women, or for gay or lesbian spectatorship.

Psychoanalytically inflected film theory, in this sense, had participated in what Adrienne Rich called "compulsory heterosexuality." Jackie Stacey pointed out that the binary oppositions (masculinity–femininity; activity–passivity) underpinning psychoanalytic theory "masculinized" female homosexuality (Stacey, in Erens, 1990, pp. 365–79). Teresa de Lauretis corrected Laura Mulvey by suggesting that film narrative was not only sexed but "heterosexed," in that narrative usually involves the active movement of a male hero through a female-gendered space, much as the imperial hero plows through "virgin land." Theorists like de Lauretis in a sense "queered" psychoanalytic theory by revising its notions of fetishism, castration, and the oedipal narrative by pointing out the ways in which such categories became insufficient when seen through a gay or lesbian grid.

Building on the earlier (largely pre-theoretical) achievements of Parker Tyler's *Screening the Sexes* and Vito Russo's *The Celluloid Closet* (1998), queer analysts delineated the typical homophobic archetypes populating dominant cinema: the limp-wristed sissy, the gay psychopath, the lesbian vampire. Like feminist film theory before it, and race theory after it, but much more quickly, queer theory moved from the corrective analysis of stereotypes and distortions to more theoretically sophisticated models. In "Stereotyping" (1977)

Richard Dyer analyzed the ways that gay and lesbian stereotypes functioned to normativize straight masculine sexuality while marginalizing and rendering invisible alternative forms. The goal for Dyer was not just to denounce stereotypes, nor to create positive images, but rather to achieve a self-representation which is complex, diverse, and nuanced.

Queer theory also recuperated and "decloseted" mainstream gay and lesbian auteurs. Ruby Rich, for example, analyzed *Mädchen in Uniform* in terms of historical attitudes toward gender and sexuality. Judith Mayne reinvigorated a moribund auteur theory by showing the lesbian dimension to the work of Hollywood director Dorothy Arzner, especially focusing on the relations between and among women in her films. Queer theory also read popular texts like *Sylvia Scarlet* and *Gentlemen Prefer Blondes* against the heterosexual grain. Harry Benshoff, in *Monsters in the Closet*, explored the association between monstrousness and homosexuality in the horror film. Queer film theory also extended and interrogated the premises of Mulvey-style feminist film theory. Chris Straayer, first in her "She/Man" essay, and later in *Deviant Eyes, Deviant Bodies* (1996), called attention to the ways that figures manifesting traits of both sexes (for example, the "She-man") destabilized biological–sexual binarism. The co-presence of seemingly exclusive body parts and accoutrements (women with mustaches, men in drag) undermined conventional understanding and empowered both performers and viewers. Sexual performance undid, as it were, the rigidities of sexual identity.

Many of these film theorists focused on queer spectatorship, on the lesbian appeal of stars like Marlene Dietrich and Greta Garbo, on the homoerotic appeal of Marlon Brando and Tom Cruise, on the appeal for gay men of "excessive" figures like Carmen Miranda and Judy Garland. They explored the gay subtext in Hitchcock films like *Rope* and *Strangers on a Train*, and in popular icons like Batman and Pee Wee Herman (Doty, 1993), while also detecting what Patricia White called "the ghostly presence of lesbianism." Queer film theory was also concerned with representations of masculinity and the male body, the ways in which males, even in heterosexually themed films, could be posited as erotic object. In his 1982 essay on

266

the male pin-up, Richard Dyer showed that corporalized men too could be the object of the gaze. Queer theory was also concerned with the gay sensibility behind "camp" as a popular phenomenon which estranges and denormalizes categories like femininity and masculinity.

Lesbian theorists insisted on certain specificities in the challenge of doing lesbian theory. While gay men might unearth gay material, Ruby Rich argued, lesbians have to conjure it up in what she calls the "Great Dyke rewrite." Where the "boys are archeologists, the girls have to be alchemists" (Rich, 1992, p. 33). Just as homosexual theory criticized psychoanalysis for its homophobia, lesbian theorists pointed out that psychoanalytic film theory

is not only fundamentally antagonistic to lesbian existence, but utterly unable (by definition) to incorporate "lesbians" into thinking about discursive/textual production, construction or consumption without implicit reproduction of hegemonic doctrines of homophobia/heterosexism. (Tamsin Wilton, 1995, p. 9)

Queer film theory was also enlivened by a constant dialogue with a growing body of queer features, documentaries, and videos, themselves often influenced by queer theory, from early directors like Kenneth Anger, Jean Genet, Andy Warhol, and Jack Smith, to later directors like Lizzie Borden, Barbara Hammer, Su Freidrich, Cheryl Dunne, Isaac Julien, Rosa von Praunheim, John Greyson, Marlon Riggs, Thomas Allen Harris, Richard Fung, Prathibha Parmar, Tom Kalin, Derek Jarman, Gus van Sant, Gregg Araki, Karim Ainouz, Sergio Bianchi, and Nick Deocampo.

Multiculturalism, Race, and Representation

Parallel to the feminist concern with gender, the queer concern with sexuality, and the third-worldist concern with colonialism, empire, and nationality, theorists began in the 1980s to take up issues of race. The very language which we use to address race and racism comes to us from distinct discursive traditions: (1) the tradition of anti-colonialist and anti-racist writing; (2) postwar analyses of anti-semitism and Nazism; (3) Sartrean existentialism and the language of authenticity; and (4) the Women's Liberation movement (see Young-Bruehl, 1996, pp. 23–5). What is the relation between all these distinct axes of social representation? Is one of the axes primordial, the root of all the others? Is class the foundation of all oppressions, as canonical Marxism had suggested? Or is patriarchy ultimately more fundamental to social oppression than classism and racism, as some versions of feminism might suggest? Can one "allegorize" one kind of oppression, say racism, through another form of oppression, such as sexism? Are there "analogical structures of feeling" which would lead one oppressed group to identify with another? What are the analogies between anti-semitism, anti-black racism, sexism, and homophobia? Watch out for the anti-semites, Fanon warned his black brothers, because you can be sure that they hate you too. Yet Fanon himself was quite blind, as Third World feminists and queer theorists have pointed out, and as Isaac Julien illustrates in his film *Black Skin, White Mask*, to both sexism and homophobia. Certainly "haters" of all stripes can try to "coalitionize" their prejudices, as in the slogan that "Feminism is a Jew–Dyke conspiracy against the White Race." Both homophobia and anti-semitism have in common a penchant for projecting enormous power on to their targeted victims: "they" control everything, or "they" are trying to take over. But what is unique and specific to each of these forms of oppression? Persons can be the victims of homophobia within their own family, for example, something far less likely in the case of anti-semitism or anti-black racism. To what extent can one "ism" buddy up, as it were, with other isms? Sexism, racism, and classism can all be tinged with homophobia, for example. What is most important, many theorists would suggest, is not to ghettoize these axes of representation, but to realize that race is classed, that gender is raced, and so forth.

In the 1980s "multiculturalism" became one of the buzzwords to evoke these debates. Although neo-conservatives caricature multiculturalism as calling for the violent jettisoning of European classics and of "western civilization as an area of study,"[1] multiculturalism is actually an assault not on Europe (in the broad sense of Europe and its affiliates spread around the world) but on Eurocentrism – on the procrustean forcing of cultural heterogeneity into a single paradigmatic perspective in which Europe is seen as the unique source of meaning, as the world's center of gravity, as ontological reality to the rest of the world's shadow. As an ideological substratum or discursive residue common to colonialist, imperialist, and racist discourse, Eurocentrism is a form of vestigial thinking which permeates and structures contemporary practices and representations even after the formal end of colonialism. Eurocentric discourse is complex, contradictory, historically unstable. But in a kind of composite portrait, Eurocentrism as a mode of thought might be seen as engaging in a number of mutually reinforcing intellectual tendencies or operations. Eurocentric thinking attributes to the West an almost providential sense of historical destiny. Like Renaissance perspective in painting, it envisions the world from a single privileged point. It bifurcates the world into the "West and the Rest"[2] and organizes everyday language into binaristic hierarchies implicitly flattering to Europe: *our* "nations," *their* "tribes"; *our* "religions," *their* "superstitions"; *our* "culture," *their* "folklore."[3] Eurocentric discourse projects a linear historical trajectory leading from the Middle East and Mesopotamia to classical Greece (constructed as "pure," "western," and "democratic"), to imperial Rome, and then to the metropolitan capitals of Europe and the US. In all cases Europe, alone and unaided, is seen as the "motor" for progressive historical change: democracy, class society, feudalism, capitalism, the industrial revolution. Eurocentrism appropriates the cultural and material production of non-Europeans while denying both their achievements and its own appropriation, thus consolidating its sense of self and glorifying its own cultural anthropophagy.

A multicultural view critiques the universalization of Eurocentric norms, the idea that any race, in Aimé Cesaire's words, "holds a monopoly on beauty, intelligence, and strength." Needless to say, the critique of Eurocentrism is addressed not to Europeans as individuals but rather to dominant Europe's historically oppressive relation to its external and internal "others" (Jews, Irish, Gypsies, Huguenots, peasants, women). It does not suggest, obviously, that non-European people are somehow "better" than Europeans, or that Third World and minoritarian cultures are inherently superior. That there exists an "underside" of European history does not cancel out an "overside" of scientific, artistic, and political achievement. And since Eurocentrism is a historically situated discourse and not a genetic inheritance, Europeans can be anti-Eurocentric, just as non-Europeans can be Eurocentric. Europe has always spawned its own critics of empire: de las Casas, Montaigne, Diderot, Melville.

On one level, the multicultural idea is very simple; it refers to the multiple cultures of the world and the historical relations between them, including relations of subordination and domination. The multiculturalist *project* (as opposed to the multicultural *fact*) sees world history and contemporary social life from the perspective of the radical equality of peoples in status, intelligence, and rights. In its more co-opted version, it can easily degenerate into a state or corporate-managed United Colors of Benetton pluralism whereby established power promotes ethnic "flavors of the month" for commercial or ideological purposes, but in its more radical variants it strives to decolonize representation, not only in terms of cultural artifacts but also in terms of power relations between communities.

The word "multiculturalism" has no essence; it simply points to a debate. While one is aware of its ambiguities, it can perhaps be prodded in the direction of a radical critique of power relations, a rallying cry for a substantive and reciprocal intercommunalism. A radical or polycentric multiculturalism calls for a profound restructuring and reconceptualization of the power relations between cultural communities. It sees issues of multiculturalism, colonialism, and race not in a ghettoized way, but "in relation." Communities, societies, nations, and even entire continents exist not autonomously but rather in a densely woven web of relationality. This relational, dialogical approach is in this sense profoundly anti-segregationist. Although segregation can be temporarily imposed as a socio-politi-

270

cal arrangement, it can never be absolute, especially on the level of culture.

It is possible to distinguish between a co-optive liberal pluralism, tainted at birth by its historical roots in the systematic inequities of conquest, slavery, and exploitation,[4] and a more radical *polycentric multiculturalism*. The notion of polycentrism globalizes multiculturalism. It envisions a restructuring of intercommunal relations within and beyond the nation-state according to the internal imperatives of diverse communities.[5] Within a polycentric vision, the world has many dynamic cultural locations, many possible vantage points. The emphasis in polycentrism is not on points of origin but on fields of power, energy, and struggle. The "poly" does not refer to a finite list of centers of power but rather introduces a systematic principle of differentiation, relationality, and linkage. No single community or part of the world, whatever its economic or political power, is epistemologically privileged.

Polycentric multiculturalism differs from liberal pluralism in the following ways. First, unlike a liberal–pluralist discourse of ethical universals – freedom, tolerance, charity – polycentric multiculturalism sees all cultural history in relation to social power. It is not about "sensitivity" but about empowering the disempowered. Polycentric multiculturalism calls for changes not just in images but in power relations. Second, polycentric multiculturalism does not preach a pseudo-equality of viewpoints; its sympathies are clearly with the under-represented and the marginalized. Third, whereas pluralism is grudgingly accretive – it benevolently "includes" other voices within a pre-existing mainstream– polycentric multiculturalism is celebratory, seeing so called minoritarian communities as active, generative participants at the very core of a shared, conflictual history. Fourth, polycentric multiculturalism rejects a unified, fixed, and essentialist concept of identities (or communities) as consolidated sets of practices, meanings, and experiences. Rather, it sees identities as multiple, unstable, historically situated, the products of ongoing differentiation and polymorphous identifications.[6] Polycentric multiculturalism goes beyond narrow definitions of identity politics, opening the way for informed affiliation on the basis of shared social

271

desires and identifications. Fifth, polycentric multiculturalism is reciprocal, dialogical; it sees all acts of verbal or cultural exchange as taking place not between essential, discrete, bounded individuals or cultures but rather between permeable, changing individuals and communities (see Shohat and Stam, 1994).

Various subcurrents mingle in the larger stream of what might be called "multicultural media studies:" the analysis of "minority" representation; the critique of imperialist and orientalist media; work on colonial and postcolonial discourse; the theorizing of "Third World" and "Third Cinema"; work on "indigenous media"; work on "minority," "diasporic," and "exilic" cinemas; "whiteness" studies; and work on anti-racist and multicultural media pedagogy.

What is most striking about "official" film theory's relation to race and multiculturalism is that theory sustained for so long such a remarkable silence on the subject. European and North American film theory for most of this century seems to have had the illusion of being raceless. There are few references to racism in the film theory of the silent period, for example, even though that period coincided with the heights of European imperialism and of scientific racism, and with myriad colonialist films like *King of the Cannibals* and *Le Musulman Rigolo*. When European and North American theorists of the silent period refer to race, they tend to mean European nationalities. The commentary of theorists on films like *The Birth of a Nation*, similarly, tended not to focus on the film's racism but rather on its status as a "masterpiece." Eisenstein was an exception to the rule, since he spoke in "Dickens, Griffith, and the Film Today" of the "repellent" nature of Griffith's "celluloid monument to the Ku Klux Klan." We have also mentioned the 1929 issue of *Close Up* dedicated to the treatment of the "Negro" in the cinema. But most of the protesting was left to the community newspapers of racialized communities, and to organizations such as the NAACP. In retrospect it seems quite astonishing that critics and theorists did not notice until 1996, when Michael Rogin (1996) pointed it out, that "the four transformative moments in the history of American film [*Uncle Tom's Cabin* in 1903, *Birth of a Nation* in 1915, *The Jazz Singer* in 1927, and *Gone with the Wind* in 1939] – moments that combine box-office success, critical recognition of revolutionary significance, formal innovations, and shifts in the cinematic mode of production – all organized themselves around the surplus symbolic value of blacks, the power to make African Americans represent something beside themselves."

Over the past few decades important work has been done on issues of ethnic/racial/cultural representation within Hollywood cinema. A key early text (first written in Spanish but widely translated), Ariel Dorfman and Armand Mattelart's *How to Read Donald Duck: Imperialist Ideology in the Disney Comic* (1975), exposed the imperialist racism that permeated Disney cartoons:

Disney visits . . . distant regions in the same way his characters do with their bodies; that is, lacking any notion of former reprehensible historical relations, almost as if they were only recent arrivals to the distribution of land and wealth. . . . Just as Disney plunders all folklore, fairy tales and nineteenth and twentieth century literature . . . so he proceeds with world geography. He feels no obligation to avoid the caricature, and rebaptizes each country as if it were a can on the shelf, an object of infinite fun, always good for a laugh. Disney starts with a clearly identifiable nucleus (a part of the original name or something that sounds like it, a supposedly typical characteristic) and then adds certain North American traces or endings: Azteclano, Chiliburgeria, Brutopia, Volcanovia, Inca Blinca, Hondorica and Sana Banandor in Latin America; Kachanooga, the Oasis of Nolssa, Kooko Coco, and Foola Zoola in Africa; the provinces of Jumbostan, Backdore, Footsore, and Howdoyustan in India . . . a disheartening panorama of the majority of mankind as viewed by a minority that happens to have a monopoly on the concoction of postcards and package tours. (Dorfman, 1983, p. 24)

Much of the work has had to do with the filmic representations of US communities of color. For much of Hollywood's history, it was virtually impossible for African Americans or Native Americans to represent themselves. Racism was inscribed in official regulations (e.g. the Hayes Code's prohibition of representations of miscegenation) and in unofficial practices practices (Louis B. Mayer's injunction that blacks be shown only as bootblacks or porters). Native American critics such as Vine Deloria, Ralph and Natasha Friar (1972), Ward Churchill (1992), and many others discussed the binaristic splitting that turned Native Americans into bloodthirsty beasts or noble savages. Other scholars, notably Daniel Leab, Thomas Cripps (1979), Donald Bogle (1989), James Snead (1992), Mark Reid, Clyde Taylor (1998), Ed Guerrero (1993), Jim Pines, Jacquie Jones, bell hooks (1992), Michelle Wallace, and Pearl Bowser, have explored anti-black stereotypes. Bogle (1989) surveys representations of blacks in Hollywood cinema, especially foregrounding the unequal struggle between black performers and the stereotypical roles offered them by Hollywood. For Bogle, the history of black performance is one of battling against confining types and categories, a battle homologous to the quotidian struggle of three-dimensional blacks against the imprisoning conventions of an apartheid-style system. At their best, black performances undercut stereotypes by individualizing the type or slyly standing above it. McDaniel's "flamboyant bossiness," her way of looking Scarlett right in the eye, within this project, translated aggressive hostility toward a racist system. Throughout, Bogle emphasizes the resilient imagination of black performers obliged to play against script and studio intentions, their capacity to turn demeaning roles into resistant performance by revealing some unique quality of voice or personality that audiences immediately responded to, whether in the form of Bojangle's "urbanity," Rochester's "cement-mixer voice," Louise Beaver's "jollity," or Hattie McDaniel's "haughtiness" (ibid., p. 36). Performance itself intimated liberatory possibilities.

Apart from work on Native Americans and African Americans, important work has also been done on the stereotypes of other "minoritized" groups such as Latinos (see Pettit, 1980; Woll, 1980; Fregoso, 1993). Woll (1980) points to the substratum of male violence common to Latino male stereotypes – the bandido, the greaser, the revolutionary, the bullfighter. Latina women, meanwhile, call up the heat and passionate salsa evoked by the titles of the films of Lupe Velez: *Hot Pepper* (1933), *Strictly Dynamite* (1934), and *Mexican Spitfire* (1940). Pettit (1980) traces the intertext of such imagery to the Anglo "Conquest fiction" of writers like Ned Buntline and Zane Grey. Already in conquest fiction, Pettit argues, the Mexican is defined negatively, in terms of "qualities diametrically opposed to an

Anglo prototype." Anglo conquest authors transferred to the mestizo Mexicans the prejudices previously directed toward the Native American and the black. Morality, in such works, is color-coordinated; the darker the color, the worse the character (ibid., p. 24).

Stereotype analysis, the critical dissection of repeated, ultimately pernicious constellations of character traits, made an indispensable contribution by (1) revealing oppressive *patterns* of prejudice in what might at first glance have seemed random and inchoate phenomena; (2) highlighting the psychic devastation inflicted by systematically negative portrayals on those groups assaulted by them, whether through internalization of the stereotypes themselves or through the negative effects of their dissemination; (3) signaling the social *functionality* of stereotypes, demonstrating that stereotypes are not an error of perception but rather a form of social control, intended as what Alice Walker calls "prisons of image" (Alternative Museum, 1989). The call for positive images, in the same way, corresponds to a profound logic which only the representationally privileged can fail to understand. Given a dominant cinema that trades in heroes and heroines, minority communities rightly ask for their fair share of the pie as a simple matter of representational parity.

Subsequent to this very important "image studies" work, objections were raised to its methodological and theoretical limitations. Drawing on psychoanalysis and poststructuralism, Steve Neale (1979–80) outlined a number of problems with stereotype analysis: overemphasis on character; naive faith in "reality;" and the failure to reveal racism as a social practice. Some of the revisionist work appeared in *Screen*, beginning with a 1983 special issue on "Colonialism, Racism, and Representation," with an introductory essay by Robert Stam and Louise Spence, and essays by Robert Crusz, Rosie Thomas, and others, followed in 1985 by an issue on "Other Cinemas, Other Criticisms," edited by Julianne Burton, and culminating in the ironically titled "Last 'Special Issue' on Race," edited by Isaac Julien and Kobena Mercer in 1988. Analysts called for a move similar to that from "image of woman" studies in feminist analysis to the more sophisticated analyses grounded in semiotics, psychoanalysis, and deconstruction. While recognizing the importance of stereotypes and distortions analysis, these critics raised methodological questions about the underlying premises of such approaches. While stereotypes and distortions analyses posed legitimate questions about social plausibility and mimetic accuracy, about negative stereotypes and positive images, they were often premised on an exclusive allegiance to an aesthetic of verisimilitude.[7] An obsession with realism cast the question as simply one of "errors" and "distortions," as if the "truth" of a community were unproblematic, transparent, and easily accessible, and "lies" about that community easily unmasked.

The stereotype and distortions approach entails a number of pitfalls from a theoretical–methodological standpoint.[8] The exclusive preoccupation with images, whether positive or negative, can lead to a kind of *essentialism*, as less subtle critics reduce a complex variety of portrayals to a limited set of reified formulae. Such reductionist simplifications run the risk of reproducing the very racism they were designed to combat. This essentialism generates in its wake a certain *ahistoricism*; the analysis tends to be static, not allowing for mutations, metamorphoses, changes of valence, altered function; it ignores the historical instability of the stereotype and even of language. Stereotypic analysis is likewise covertly premised on *individualism*, in that the individual character, rather than larger social categories (race, class, gender, nation, sexual orientation), remains the point of reference. Individual morality receives more attention than the larger configurations of power. The focus on individual character also misses the ways in which whole cultures, as opposed to individuals, can be caricatured or misrepresented without a single character being stereo-typed. The flawed mimesis of many Hollywood films dealing with the Third World, with their innumerable ethnographic, linguistic, and even topographical blunders, which have Brazilians wearing Mexican sombreros as they dance a tango, for example, has less to do with stereotypes *per se* than with the tendentious ignorance of colonialist discourse.

A moralistic and individualistic approach also ignores the contradictory nature of stereotypes. Black figures, in Toni Morrison's words, come to signify polar opposites: "On the one hand, they signify benevolence, harmless and servile guardianship and endless love," and on the other "insanity, illicit sexuality, chaos." A moralistic ap-

276

proach also sidesteps the issue of the relative nature of morality, eliding the question "positive for whom?" It ignores the fact that oppressed people might not only have a *different* vision of morality, but even an *opposite* vision. What is seen as positive by the dominant group, e.g. the acts of those "Indians" in westerns who spy for the whites, might be seen as treason by the dominated group. The taboo in Hollywood was not on positive images but rather on images of racial equality, images of anger and revolt. The privileging of positive images also elides the patent differences, the social and moral heteroglossia, characteristic of any social group. A cinema of contrivedly positive images betrays a lack of confidence in the group portrayed, which usually itself has no illusions concerning its own perfection. Nor can one assume an automatic connection between control over representation and the production of positive images. Many African films, such as *Laafi* (1991) and *Finzan* (1990), do not offer positive images of African society; rather, and more importantly, they offer *African* perspectives on African society. Rather than heroes, they offer subjects. "Positive images," in this sense, can be signs of insecurity. Hollywood, after all, has never worried about sending films around the world which depicted the US as a land of gangsters, rapists, and murderers.

A privileging of social portrayal, plot, and character often leads to a slighting of the specifically cinematic dimensions of films; often the analyses might as easily have been of novels or plays. A thoroughgoing analysis has to pay attention to "mediations:" narrative structure, genre conventions, cinematic style. Eurocentric discourse in film may be relayed not by characters or plot but by lighting, framing, mise-en-scène, music. The cinema translates correlations of social power into registers of foreground and background, on-screen and off-screen, speaking and silent. To speak of the "image" of a social group we have to ask precise questions about images themselves: How much space do the representatives of different social groups occupy in the shot? Are they seen in close-ups or only in distant long shots? How often do they appear compared with the Euro-American characters and for how long? Are they allowed to relate to one another, or do they always require mainstream "mediation?" Are they active, desiring characters or decorative props? Do the eyeline matches identify us with one gaze rather than another? Whose looks are reciprocated, whose ignored? How do character positionings communicate social distance or differences in status? How do body language, posture, and facial expression communicate social hierarchies, arrogance, servility, resentment, pride? Is there an aesthetic segregation whereby one group is haloed and the other villainized? What homologies inform artistic and ethnic/ political representation?

The critique of stereotypes approach is implicitly premised on the desirability of "rounded" three-dimensional characters within a realist–dramatic aesthetic. Given the cinema's history of one-dimensional portrayals, the hope for more complex and "realistic" representations is completely understandable, but should not preclude more experimental, anti-illusionistic alternatives. Realistic positive portrayals are not the only way to fight racism or to advance a liberatory perspective. Within a Brechtian aesthetic, for example, (non-racial) stereotypes can serve to generalize meaning and demystify established power, in a situation where characters are presented not as role models but as the sites of contradiction. Parody of the kind theorized by Bakhtin, similarly, favors decidedly negative, even grotesque images to convey a deep critique of societal structures. Satirical or parodic films may be less concerned with constructing positive images than with challenging the stereotypical expectations an audience may bring with them. On the other hand, what one might call the generic defense against accusations of racism – "It's only a comedy!" "Whites are lampooned too!" "All the characters are caricatures!" – is highly ambiguous, since it all depends on the modalities and the objects of the lampooning, on who is the butt of the joke. (For more on the critique of positive images see Friedman, 1982; Shohat and Stam, 1994; Diawara, 1993; Wiegman, 1995; Taylor, 1998.)

While on one level film is mimesis, representation, it is also utterance, an act of contextualized interlocution between socially situated producers and receivers. It is not enough to say that art is constructed. We have to ask: Constructed for whom and in conjunction with which ideologies and discourses? In this sense, art is a representation in not so much a mimetic as a political sense, as a delegation of voice.[9] Within this perspective it makes more sense to say of *First Blood (Rambo)* (1983), not that it "distorts" reality, but rather that it "really" represents a rightist discourse designed to flatter and nourish the masculinist fantasies of omnipotence characteristic of an empire in crisis. One methodological alternative to the mimetic stereotypes and distortions approach is to speak less of images than of voices and discourses. The very phrase "image studies" symptomatically elides the oral and the voiced. A more nuanced discussion of race in the cinema would emphasize less a one-to-one mimetic adequacy to sociological or historical truth than the interplay of voices, discourses, and perspectives, including those operative within the image itself. The task of the critic would be to call attention to the cultural voices at play, not only those heard in aural "close-up" but also those distorted or drowned out by the text. The question is not of pluralism but of multi-vocality, an approach that would strive to cultivate and even heighten cultural difference while abolishing socially generated inequalities.

The 1980s and 1990s witnessed an attempt to move beyond ghettoized studies of isolated groups – Native Americans, African Americans, Latinos – in favor of a relational and contrapuntal approach (see Freidman, 1991; also Shohat and Stam, 1994). The period also witnessed the emergence of whiteness studies. This movement responds to the call by scholars of color for an analysis of the impact of racism not only on its victims but also on its perpetrators. Whiteness scholars questioned the quiet yet overpowering normativity of whiteness, the process by which "race" was attributed to others while whites were tacitly positioned as unmarked norm. Although whiteness (like blackness) was on one level merely a cultural fiction without any scientific basis, it was also a social fact with all-too-real consequences for the distribution of wealth, prestige, and opportunity (Lipsitz, 1988, p. vii). In the wake of historical studies by Theodor Allen and Noel Ignatiev of how diverse "ethnics" (for example, the Irish) became "white," whiteness studies "outed" whiteness as just another ethnicity, although one historically granted inordinate privilege. It can be hoped that this movement signals the end of "the innocent white subject," and an end to the venerable practice of unilaterally racializing the Third World or minority "others," while casting whites as somehow "raceless."

Toni Morrison, bell hooks, Coco Fusco, George Lipsitz, and Richard Dyer are among the many who have problematized normative notions of whiteness. Dyer (1997) focuses on the representation of white people in western culture. The term "people of color" as a designation for "non-whites," Dyer points out, implies that whites are colorless and thus normative: "Other people are raced, we are just people" (ibid., p. 1). Even lighting technologies, and the specific mode of movie lighting, Dyer points out, have racial implications, and the assumption that the "normal" face is the white face runs through most of the manuals on cinematography.

Whiteness studies at its best denaturalizes whiteness as unmarked norm, calling attention to the taken-for-granted privileges (e.g. not to be the object of media stereotypes) that go with whiteness. At its most radical it calls for "race treason" in the John Brown tradition, for an opting out of white privilege. At the same time whiteness studies runs the risk of once again recentering white narcissism, of changing the subject back to the assumed center – a racial version of the show-business dictum: "speak ill of me but speak." Whiteness studies also needs to be seen in a global context where black and white are not always the operative categories, but rather caste or religion. The important thing is to maintain a sense of the hybrid relationality and social co-implication of communities, to see the blackness of whiteness and the whiteness of blackness, without falling into a facile discourse of easy synthesis. And in a globalized world, it is perhaps time to think in terms of *comparative* multiculturalism, of relational studies which do not always pass through the putative "center." What are the relationalities between Indian and Egyptian cinema, or between Chinese and Japanese cinema? How are issues of race and caste formulated in other national contexts? What discourses are deployed? Such studies would go a long way to deprovincializing a discussion that has too often focused only on American issues and Hollywood representations.

Third Cinema Revisited

For a long time the various "Third World" and "Third Cinemas" which collectively form the majority cinema in the world were largely ignored by standard film histories as well as by Eurocentric film theory. When not ignored, Third World cinema was treated with condescension, as if it were merely the subaltern shadow of the real cinema of North America and Europe. In the 1980s and 1990s, however, there was a veritable explosion of theory and scholarship on Third World cinema, resulting in a cornucopia of texts in English: Teshome Gabriel's pioneering *Third Cinema in the Third World: The Aesthetics of Liberation* (1982), Roy Armes's *Third World Filmmaking and the West* (1987), Manthia Diawara's *African Cinema* (1992), and Frank Ukadike's *Black African Cinema* (1994); full-length books on Cuban cinema, Mexican cinema (Mora, 1988), Argentine cinema, Brazilian cinema (Xavier, 1998), Israeli cinema (Shohat, 1989), and Indian cinema; valuable collections by Jim Pines and Paul Willemen (1989), John Downing (1987), Michael Chanan (1983), Julianne Burton (1985; 1990), Mbye Cham and Claire Andrade-Watkins (1988), Michael Martin (1993; 1997); plus the ongoing work of those journals regularly featuring work on Third World cinema (notably *Cineaste, Jump Cut, Film Quarterly, Framework, Screen, The Independent, Black Film Review, Quarterly Review of Film Studies, Cinemaya, East–West Film Journal, Cinemais, Imagems*, and many others).

But if cinematic third-worldism is thriving, political third-worldism is in crisis. The "third-worldist euphoria" of the revolutionary 1960s has long given way to the disenchantment triggered by the collapse of communism, the frustration surrounding the hoped-for "tricontinental revolution," the realization that the "wretched of the earth" are not unanimously revolutionary (nor necessarily allied to one another), and the recognition that international geopolitics and the global economic system have obliged even socialist regimes to make their peace with transnational capitalism. (One of the Brazilian framers of the radical "dependency theory," Fernando Henrique Cardoso, is now Brazil's neo-liberal president.)

This disenchantment brought with it a rethinking of political, cultural, and aesthetic possibilities. The rhetoric of revolution began to be greeted with a certain skepticism. As a result of external pressures and internal self-questioning, the cinema, too, gave expression to these mutations, as the anti-colonial thrust of earlier films gradually gave way to more diversified themes. Filmmakers who had denounced Hollywood hegemony began to seek deals with Warners, on HBO. Cultural and political critique took on a new "post-third-worldist" form by taking for granted the fundamental legitimacy of the anti-colonialist movement, while also probing the social and ideological fissures within the Third World nation.[1] In cinematic–industrial terms, theorist–filmmakers became more aware of the need to theorize the mass media in less Manichean ways and to create a cinema which engendered not only political awareness and aesthetic innovation but also the kind of spectatorial pleasure which could enable a viable film industry to flourish.

This same period also witnessed a terminological crisis swirling around the term Third World itself, now seen as an inconvenient relic of a more militant period. Arguing from a Marxist perspective, Aijaz Ahmad argues that Third World theory is an "open-ended ideological interpellation" that papers over class oppression in all three worlds, while limiting socialism to the now non-existent "second world" (see Ahmad, 1987; Burton, 1985). Whereas Jameson defines the first capitalist and the second socialist worlds actively, in terms of their systems of production, Ahmad points out, the Third World is defined passively, as having had a certain "experience," as having "suffered" and "undergone" colonialism. Three-worlds theory not only flattens heterogeneities, masks contradictions, and elides differences, but also obscures similarities. In terms of the media, the concept of the Third World, as Geoffrey Reeves puts it, homogenizes "markedly different national histories, experiences of European colonialism and extent of incorporation into capitalist production and exchange relations, levels and diversity of industrialization and economic development . . . and ethnic, racial, linguistic, religious, and class differences" (Reeves, 1993, p. 10). The term forces into an uneasy – and often purely theoretical – alliance hugely

productive industries (India, Mexico) with intermittently productive industries (Brazil), with those countries that produce very few
films (Zimbabwe, Madagascar, Costa Rica).

Third-worldism might even hinder Third World cinema's chances
in the world. The kinds of critical generalizations made about "Third
World Cinema," as Anthony Guneratne points out, would be unthinkable for "First World Cinema." These generalizations are made,
furthermore, in a situation of patronizing non-reciprocity, with negative consequences for Third World film: "ignoring the audiences in
'Third World' societies, [scholars working in developed countries]
have tended to project their own political agendas as a moral requirement upon films from the 'Third World' without, however,
insisting on a similar requirement for First World cinema."[2] Thus
Third World (and "minority") filmmakers are supposed to speak for
the oppressed; no such demand is made of Tarantino or Scorsese.
The concept of Third World Cinema has thus led to a kind of didac-
tic pressure on films from Asia, Africa, and Latin America to fulfill
the criteria for Third Cinema. A kind of miserabilist exoticism means
that Third World films about middle-class people in Iran, for example, are not "really" Third World. Third-worldist film ideology also
risks installing a formula for a correct cinema, but one which ignores
the concrete conditions, needs, and traditions of particular countries.

The concept of the Third World also elides the presence of a
"Fourth World" existing within all of the other worlds, comprising
those peoples variously called "indigenous," "tribal," or "first nations"; in sum, the still-residing descendants of the original inhabitants of territories subsequently taken over or circumscribed by alien
conquest or settlement. As many as 3,000 native nations, representing some 250 million people, according to some estimates, function
within the 200 states that assert sovereignty over them.

Fourth World peoples more usually appear in "ethnographic films,"
which of late have attempted to divest themselves of vestigial
colonialist attitudes. While in the old ethnographic films self-
confident "scientific" voice-overs delivered the "truth" about subject peoples unable to answer back (while sometimes prodding the

"natives" to perform practices long abandoned), the ethnographic filmmakers theorize their own practice by questioning their own authority, while striving for "shared filmmaking," "participatory filmmaking," "dialogical anthropology," "reflexive distance," and "interactive filmmaking," as artists experience a salutary self-doubt about their own capacity to speak "for" the other.[3] This new modesty on the part of filmmakers reflects the impact of anti-colonialist and anti-orientalist theory, as filmmakers and theorists discard the covert elitism of the pedagogical or ethnographic model in favor of an acquiescence in the relative, the plural, and the contingent. (Anthropology, as one *boutade* has it, has become "Anthro-Apology.") The question, ideally, is no longer how one represents the other, but rather how one collaborates with the other. The goal, rarely realized, is to guarantee the effective participation of the "other" in all phases of production, including *theoretical* production.

Indigenous people, meanwhile, have undertaken to represent themselves, with little or no mediation. We now have the first independent narrative fiction feature film written, produced, directed, and acted by Native Americans: *Smoke Signals* (1998). Adapted from a book by Sherman Alexie (Spokane) called *The Lone Ranger and Tonto Fistfight in Heaven*, and directed by Chris Eyre (Cheyenne), its coming-of-age story about two young Coeur d'Alene men often pokes fun at the media. ("If there's anything more pathetic than watching Indians on television," says one of the men, "it's *watching* Indians watching Indians on television.") In New Zealand Lee Tamahori's *Once Were Warriors* (1994) was the first Maori feature to become an international hit. The most remarkable recent development has been the emergence of "indigenous media," i.e. the use of audiovisual technology (camcorders, VCRs) for the cultural and political purposes of indigenous peoples. The phrase "indigenous media," as Faye Ginsburg points out, is oxymoronic, evoking both the self-understanding of aboriginal groups and the vast institutional structures of TV and cinema.[4] Within indigenous media the producers are themselves the receivers, along with neighboring communities and, occasionally, distant cultural institutions or festivals such as the Native American film festivals held in New York and San Francisco. (The three most active centers of indigenous media production are Native North American (Inuit, Yup'ik), Indians of the Amazon Basin (Nambiquara, Kayapo), and Aboriginal Australians (Warlpiri, Pitjanjajari). At their best, indigenous media become an empowering vehicle for communities struggling against geographical displacement, ecological and economic deterioration, and cultural annihilation.[5]

The question of indigenous media brings up a number of complex theoretical issues. Indigenous film and video-makers confront what Ginsburg calls a "Faustian dilemma:" on the one hand, they use new technologies for cultural self-assertion, on the other they spread a technology that might ultimately only foster their own disintegration. The leading analysts of indigenous media, such as Ginsburg and Terence Turner, do not see such work as being locked into a bound traditional world, but rather as concerned with "mediating across boundaries, mediating ruptures of time and history," and advancing the process of identity construction by negotiating "powerful relationships to land, myth and ritual."[6] At times the work goes beyond merely asserting an existing identity to become "a means of cultural invention that refracts and recombines elements from both the dominant and minority societies."[7] Rather than a mere adaptation of western visual culture, as Faye Ginsberg argues, we are dealing with a "new form of collective self-production" (Ginsberg, in Miller and Stam, 1999). At the same time, indigenous media should not be seen as a magical panacea, either for the problems faced by indigenous peoples or for the aporias of anthropology. Such work can provoke factional divisions within indigenous communities, and can be appropriated by international media as tokens of the facile ironies of the postmodern age.[8]

Despite the imbrication of "First," "Third," and "Fourth" worlds in the age of globalization, the international distribution of power still tends to make the First World countries (now redubbed "the North") cultural transmitters and to reduce most Third World countries (now "the South") to the status of receivers. One byproduct of this situation is that First World minorities such as African Americans have the power to project their cultural productions around

285

the globe. (The *beur* films made by North Africans in France, for example, betray the pervasive influence of black hiphop culture.) On one level, the cinema inherits the structures laid down by the communication infrastructure of empire, the networks of telegraph and telephone lines and information apparatuses which literally wired colonial territories to the metropole, enabling the imperial countries to monitor global communications and shape the image of world events. While the world generally is inundated with North American films, TV series, popular music, and news programs, the First World receives precious little of the vast cultural production of the Third World, and what it does receive is usually mediated by transnational corporations. These processes are not entirely negative, of course. The same multinational corporations that disseminate inane blockbusters and canned sitcoms also spread Afro-diasporic music such as reggae and rap around the globe. The problem lies not in the exchange but in the unequal terms on which the exchange take place.

At the same time, "media imperialism" theses, as Tomlinson (1991) and others have argued, need drastic retooling in the age of globalization. By assuming western omnipotence, media imperialism theses reproduce the very Eurocentric perspective they are critiquing. First, as Tomlinson points out, it is simplistic to imagine an active First World simply injecting its products into unsuspecting and passive Third World victims. Second, global mass-culture does not so much replace local culture as coexist with it, providing a cultural lingua franca marked by a "local" accent. Third, there are powerful reverse currents as a number of Third World countries (Mexico, Brazil, India, Egypt) dominate their own markets and even become cultural exporters. Hindi cinema is exported throughout South Asia, and in much of Africa. The Indian TV version of the *Mahabharata* won a 90 percent domestic viewer share during a three-year run and Brazil's Rede Globo now exports its *telenovelas* to more than 100 countries internationally. Fourth, these issues are media specific; a nation can be strongly resistant in relation to one medium but dominated in relation to another. Brazilian popular music and television, for example, domi-

286

nate the domestic market; it is only in the cinema that media imperialism is the norm.

Finally, we must distinguish between the ownership and control of the media – an issue of political economy – and the specifically cultural issue of the implications of this domination for the people on the receiving end. The hypodermic needle model is as inadequate for the Third World as it is for the First: everywhere spectators actively engage with texts, and specific communities both incorporate and transform foreign influences. For Appadurai the global cultural situation is now more interactive; the US is no longer the puppeteer of a world system of images, but only one mode of a complex transnational construction of "imaginary landscapes." In this new conjuncture, he argues, the invention of tradition, ethnicity, and other identity-markers becomes "slippery, as the search for certainties is regularly frustrated by the fluidities of transnational communication." Appadurai posits five dimensions of these global cultural flows: (1) ethnoscapes (the landscape of persons who constitute the shifting world in which people live); (2) technoscapes (the global configuration of technologies moving at high speeds across previously impermeable borders); (3) financescapes (the global grid of currency speculation and capital transfer); (4) mediascapes (the distribution of the capabilities to produce and disseminate information and the large complex repertoire of images and narratives generated by these capabilities; and (5) ideoscapes (ideologies of states and counter-ideologies of movements, around which nation-states have organized their political cultures).[9] Now the central problem becomes one of tension between cultural homogenization and cultural heterogenization, in which hegemonic tendencies, well-documented by Marxist analysts like Mattelart and Schiller, are simultaneously "indigenized" within a complex, disjunctive global cultural economy. At the same time, Appadurai's metaphor of "flows" risks naturalizing the forces of stratification; discernible patterns of domination still channel the fluidities even of a multipolar world; the same hegemony that unifies the world through global networks of circulating goods and information also distributes them according to hierarchical structures of power, even if those hegemonies are now more subtle and dispersed.

Another salient phrase in this discussion is "national allegory." For Fredric Jameson all Third World texts are "necessarily allegorical," in that even those invested with an apparently private or libidinal dynamic "project a political dimension in the form of national allegory: the story of the private individual destiny is always an allegory of the embattled situation of the public third-world culture and society."[10] It is difficult to endorse Jameson's somewhat hasty totalization of *all* Third World texts; no single artistic strategy can be seen as uniquely appropriate to the cultural productions of an entity as heterogenous as the Third World. Allegory, furthermore, is equally relevant to cultural productions elsewhere. In his essay "Allegory and Nation" Ismail Xavier links allegory to historical moments of "cultural shock, slavery, repression, and violence," pointing to such diverse films as Griffith's *Birth of a Nation* (1916), Eisenstein's *October* (1927), Fritz Lang's *Metropolis* (1927), Gance's *Napoleon* (1928), Renoir's *La Marseillaise* (1936), and Wajda's *Danton* (1982) as all having a national-allegorical dimension (Xavier, in Miller and Stam, 1999). Despite these objections the concept of national allegory, here conceived in a broad sense as any kind of oblique or synecdochic utterance soliciting hermeneutic completion or deciphering, is a productive category for dealing with many Third World films. Nor is allegory an entirely new phenomenon in Third World cinema. In the 1930s and 1940s in India, the female star "fearless Nadia" rescued oppressed peoples from foreign tyrants, in ways which were read at the time as anti-British allegories.[11] But in the more recent history of Third World cinema we find at least three major strands of allegory. First, we have the teleological Marxist-inflected nationalist allegories of the early period (e.g. *Black God White Devil*), analyzed by Xavier, where history is revealed as the progressive unfolding of an immanent historical design. Second, we have the modernist self-deconstructing allegories of the later period (e.g. *Red Light Bandit*), where the focus shifts from the "figural" signification of the onward march of history to the fragmentary nature of the discourse itself, and where allegory is deployed as a privileged instance of language-consciousness in the context of the felt loss of larger historical purpose.

A third variant of allegory, indifferently teleological or modernist, might be found in those films (e.g. de Andrade's *The Conspiradores*) where allegory serves as a form of protective camouflage against censorious regimes, where the film uses the past to speak of the present, or treats a microcosmic power situation (for example, fraternity hazing in Mike de Leon's *Batch '81* (1982)) to evoke a macrocosmic structure (the Philippines under Marcos). The allegorical tendency available to all art is strengthened in the case of intellectual filmmakers profoundly shaped by nationalist discourse, who feel obliged to speak for and about the nation as a whole, and becomes even more exacerbated in the case of repressive regimes.

Early third-worldist film theory was often premised on nationalism, and often assumed that "nation" was an unproblematic term. As the products of national industries, produced in national languages, portraying national situations and recycling national intertexts (literatures, folklores), all films are of course national, just as *all* films (whether Hindu mythologicals, Mexican melodramas, or third-worldist epics) project national imaginaries. First World filmmakers seem to float "above" petty nationalist concerns only because they can take for granted the projection of a national power that facilitates the making and the dissemination of their films. Third World filmmakers, on the other hand, cannot assume a substratum of national power. Rather, relative powerlessness generates a constant struggle to create an elusive "authenticity" to be constructed anew with every generation.

Third-worldist filmmakers saw themselves as part of a national project, but their concept of the national was itself discursively overdetermined and contradictory. Some of the early Third World discussions of nationalism took it as axiomatic that the issue was simply one of expelling the foreign to recover the national, as if the nation were a kind of "heart of the artichoke," to be found by peeling away the outer leaves, or as if, to change the metaphor, the nation were the ideal sculpted form lurking within the unworked stone. Schwarz (1987) calls this view the "national by subtraction," i.e. the assumption that the simple elimination of foreign influences will automatically allow the national culture to emerge in its native glory. There are a number of problems with this notion. First, the *topos* of a unitary nation often covers and camouflages the existence of indigenous nations within them. Some nation-states might better be called "multi-nation states" (Kymlycha). Second, the exaltation of the national provides no criteria for distinguishing exactly what is worth retaining in the national tradition. A sentimental defense of patriarchal social institutions simply because they are "ours" can hardly be seen as progressive. Third, all countries, including Third World countries, are heterogenous, at once urban and rural, male and female, religious and secular, native and immigrant, and so forth. The unitary nation muffles the polyphony of social and ethnic voices within heteroglot cultures. Third World feminists especially have highlighted the ways in which the subject of the Third World nationalist revolution has been covertly posited as masculine. Fourth, the precise nature of the national "essence " to be recuperated is elusive and chimerical. Some locate it in the pre-colonial past, or in the country's rural interior (e.g. the African village), or in a prior stage of development (the pre-industrial), or in a non-European ethnicity (e.g. the indigenous or African strata in the nation-states of the Americas). But often even the most prized national symbols are indelibly marked by the foreign. Fifth, scholars have emphasized the ways in which national identity is mediated, textualized, constructed, "imagined," just as the traditions valorized by nationalism are "invented." The nation, like a film, is a "projected image," partly phantasmatic in nature. Any definition of filmic nationalism, then, must see nationality as partly discursive and intertextual in nature, must take class and gender into account, must allow for racial difference and cultural heterogeneity, and must be dynamic, seeing "the nation" as an evolving, imaginary, differential construct rather than an originary essence.

The centrifugal forces of the globalizing process, and the global reach of the media, virtually oblige the contemporary media theorist to move beyond the restrictive framework of the nation-state. The cinema, for example, is now, and arguably always has been, a thoroughly globalized medium. In terms of personnel, we have only to think of the role of German émigrés in Hollywood, of Italians in Brazil's Vera Cruz, or of the Chinese in Indonesian film. Globalization has also been aesthetic. India's "Bollywood" borrows and spices up Hollywood plots, while Brazilian comedies parody American blockbusters; thus *Jaws* becomes *Bacalhau* ("Codfish"). Moreover, Hollywood has by now been internalized as an international lingua franca which inhabits, as it were, virtually all cinemas, if only as constant temptation or demonized other. But it is not only Hollywood that has international influence. In the 1940s neo-realism became an influence in India (Ray) and Egypt (Chahine) and all around Latin America (dos Santos, Birri). The French New Wave and cinema verité cast their spell over the African francophone countries. Nor is the influence unidirectional. Herzog, Coppola, and Scorsese express admiration for Brazil's Cinema Novo; Quentin Tarantino registers the impact of Hong Kong action films. Formerly Third World filmmakers are no longer strictly limited to Third World locations. Mexican filmmakers like Alfonso Arau and Guilhero del Toro, for example, work in the United States, while the Chilean Raul Ruiz is based in France but also works elsewhere.

As long as they are taken, not as "essential" pre-constituted entities, but rather as collective projects to be forged, and terms "under erasure," both "Third World Cinema" and "Third Cinema" retain some tactical and polemical use for a politically inflected cultural practice. It is useful, furthermore, to distinguish between the Third World as a geopolitical location, and third-worldist as referring to a discourse and ideological orientation (see Shohat and Stam, 1994).

If Third World cinema is in some ways an anachronistic label, it at least has the virtue of reminding us that what we used to call the Third World, taken in a broad sense, far from being a marginal appendage to First World cinema, actually produces *most* of the world's feature films. Third World cinema includes the major traditional film industries of countries like India, Egypt, Mexico, Brazil, Argentina, and China, as well as the more recent post-independence or post-revolution industries of countries like Cuba, Algeria, Senegal, Indonesia, and scores of others. Third World and postcolonial cinema are not, therefore, poor relatives of Hollywood; rather, they are an integral part of world cinema, a fact which film theory needs to take into account more fully.

Film and the Postcolonial

What was once called Third World theory has now largely been absorbed into the field of the postcolonial. Postcolonial discourse theory refers to an interdisciplinary field (including history, economics, literature, the cinema) which explores issues of the colonial archive and of postcolonial identity, often in highly theoretical work inflected by the poststructuralism of Lacan, Foucault, and Derrida. Gauri Viswanathan defines postcolonial studies as the "study of the cultural interaction between colonizing powers and the societies they colonized, and the traces that this interaction left on the literature, arts, and human sciences of both societies" (Bahri and Vasudeva, 1996, pp. 137–8).

Postcolonial theory is a complex amalgam fed by diverse and contradictory currents: studies of nationalism (for example, Benedict Anderson's *Imagined Communities*), the literature of "Third World allegory" (Xavier, Jameson, Ahmad), the work of the "Subaltern Studies Group" (Guha, Chatterjee), and the work of the postcolonials *per se* (Edward Said, Homi Bhabha, and Gayatri Spivak). Postcolonial theory built on and assumed earlier anti-colonial theory (Cesaire, Fanon, Memmi, Cabral, Dorfman and Mattelart) and dependency theory (Gunder-Frank, Amin, Wallerstein). Although Fanon never spoke of orientalist discourse *per se*, for example, his critiques of colonialist imagery in the 1950s and early 1960s provided proleptic examples of anti-orientalist critique. Using words which might have described countless colonialist films, Fanon points in *The Wretched of the Earth* to the colonial binarism whereby "the settler makes history; his life is an epoch, an Odyssey," while against him "torpid creatures, wasted by fevers, obsessed by ancestral customs, form an almost inorganic background for the innovating dynamism of colonial mercantilism."

Postcolonial theory recombined Fanon's insights with Derridean poststructuralism. Within the academy the foundational text for postcolonial theory was Edward Said's *Orientalism* (1978), where Said used Foucauldian notions of discourse and the power–

knowledge nexus to examine the ways that western imperial power and discourse constructed a stereotypical "Orient." Representations of East and West were mutually constitutive, Said argued, locked together within asymmetrical power relations. The ideological production of European "rationality" went hand in hand with the production of Oriental "irrationality." (Subsequent analysts criticized Said for homogenizing both West and East, and for ignoring the various forms of resistance to western domination, a criticism "answered" in Said's subsequent book *Culture and Imperialism*.)

Foucault, partly via Said, was also a major influence on postcolonial theory. Foucault replaced the concept of ideology with "discourse," seen as more pervasive, variegated, less tethered to Marxist concepts of class and production. More than a set of statements, discourse for Foucault has social materiality and efficacity and is always imbricated with power. For Foucault, power is, like God, everywhere and nowhere. Rather than emanating outward from a hierarchical center, "power is everywhere; not because it embraces everything but because it comes from everywhere." Stuart Hall has criticized the vagueness of Foucault's conception of power, arguing that Foucault saves himself for the "political" through his insistence on power, but denies himself a *politics* by having no idea of "relations of force" (Hall, in Morley and Kuan-Hsing, 1996, p. 136). Other critics have pointed out the relentless Eurocentrism of Foucault's work, not only in terms of its focus – European modernity – but also in its failure to discern the relations between modernity lived in Europe and as lived in the colonized world. The "individuation of subjects that took place in Europe, for example, was denied colonized people." In the colonies, Europeans relied on brutally coercive power rather than the euphemistic "productive" exercise of power more typical of the metropole (see Loomba, 1998, p. 52).

Homi Bhabha has also been a major influence on postcolonial studies, and terms associated with Bhabha ("ambivalence," "hybridity," "third space of negotiation") are widely disseminated in postcolonial studies. In a series of essays, Bhabha drew on semiotic theories of language and Lacanian theories of subjectivity to call attention to the equivocal, hybrid nature of colonial exchange. What at first glance looks like colonial servility ("mimicry") on closer inspection is re-vealed to be a sly form of resistance. (Bhabha's own "mimicry" of the style of Derrida and Lacan, within this perspective, could itself be seen as a sly form of subversion, although one no longer required in a postcolonial era.) Appealing to a lexicon of "slippage" and "flu-idity," Bhabha usefully destabilized theory by focusing on the fail-ure of colonialism to produce fixed identities. Yet critics were quick to note that Bhabha, in his fondness for the slips and slides of "sly civility," had in some ways depoliticized the anti-colonial insights of Cesaire and Fanon, for whom the Manichean nature of colonialism was decreed not by nature but by the binaristic colonial power struc-ture. Sly subversion, in this sense, could be seen as a rather pathetic consolation prize for oppressed people, as if to say: "Certainly you've lost your land, your religion, and they torture you, but look on the bright side – you're hybrid!" It was also pointed out that "hybridity" had long been given a positive valence by the literary modernisms of Latin America and the Caribbean.

The widespread adoption of the term "postcolonial" to designate work thematizing issues emerging from colonial relations and their aftermath, in the late 1980s, clearly coincided with the eclipse of the older "Third World" paradigm. The "post" in "postcolonial" sug-gests, as Ella Shohat points out, a stage after the demise of colonial-ism, and it is therefore imbued with an ambiguous spatiotemporality. "Postcolonial" tends to be associated with Third World countries that gained independence after World War II, yet it also refers to the Third World diasporic presence within First World metropolises. The term "postcolonial" blurs the assignment of perspectives. Given that the colonial experience is shared, albeit asymmetrically, by (ex-) colonizer and (ex-)colonized, does the "post" indicate the perspect-ive of the ex-colonized (Algerian, for example), the ex-colonizer (in this case, French), the ex-colonial-settler (*pied noir*), or the displaced hybrid in the metropole (Algerian in France)? Since most of the world is now living "after" colonialism, the "post" neu-tralizes significant differences between France and Algeria, Britain and Iraq, the US and Brazil. By implying that colonialism is over, furthermore, "postcolonial" risks obscuring the deformative traces

Film and the Postcolonial

of the colonial hangover in the present, while at the same time delegitimizing research into the pre-colonial past (see Shohat, 1992).

If the nationalist discourse of the 1960s drew sharp lines between First World and Third World, oppressor and oppressed, postcolonial discourse replaces such binaristic dualisms with a more nuanced spectrum of subtle differentiations, in a new global regime where First World and Third World are mutually imbricated. Notions of ontologically referential identity metamorphose into a conjunctural play of identifications. Purity gives way to contamination. Rigid paradigms collapse into sliding metonymies. Erect, militant postures give way to an orgy of positionalities. Once secure boundaries become more porous; an iconography of barbed-wire frontiers mutates into images of fluidity and crossing. A rhetoric of unsullied integrity gives way to miscegenated grammars and scrambled metaphors. Colonial tropes of irreconcilable dualism give way to complex, multi-layered identities and subjectivities, resulting in a proliferation of terms having to do with various forms of cultural mixing: religious (syncretism); biological (hybridity); linguistic (creolization); and human–genetic (*mestizaje*).

Black Skin, White Masks, Isaac Julien's highly theorized post-third-worldist documentary about Frantz Fanon, gives voice to these discursive shifts. While accepting the basic anti-colonialist thrust of third-worldist discourse, the film also interrogates the limits and tensions within that discourse, especially in terms of infra-national differences having to do with race, gender, sexuality, and even religion.

Although postcolonial theory absorbs and develops the insights of poststructuralism, it in some ways has an adversary relation to postmodernism, forming, in a sense, its reverse field. If postmodernism is Eurocentric, narcissistic, flaunting its "latest thingedness," postcoloniality argues that the West's models cannot be generalized, that the East is in the West and vice versa, that "we are here because you were there." The emphasis on "mixedness" in postcolonial writing calls attention to the multiple identities, already present under colonialism, but now further complicated by the geographical displacements characteristic of the post-independence era, and presupposes a theoretical framework, influenced by anti-

295

essentialist poststructuralism, that refuses to police identity along purist either–or lines. But while reacting against the colonialist phobias and the fetish of racial purity, contemporary hybridity theory also counterposes itself to the overly rigid lines of identity drawn by third-worldist discourse. The celebration of hybridity (through a switch in valence for what were formerly negatively connoted terms) gives expression, in the era of globalization, to the new historical moment of the post-independence displacements which generated dually or even multiply hyphenated identities (Franco-Algerian, Indo-Canadian, Palestinian-Lebanese-British, Indo-Ugandan-American, Egyptian-Lebanese-Brazilian).

Often displacements are piled on to displacements. A number of recent postcolonial films – Stephen Frears's *Sammy and Rosie Get Laid* (1989), Gurinder Chada's *Bhaji on the Beach* (1994), and Isaac Julien's *Young Soul Rebels* (1991) – bear witness to the tense postcolonial hybridity of former colonials growing up in what was once the "motherland." In the multicultural neighborhood of *Sammy and Rosie Get Laid* the inhabitants have "lines out," as it were, to the formerly colonized parts of the globe. Many "postcolonial hybrid" films focus on diasporas in the First World: the Indian diaspora in Canada (*Masala*, 1991) and the US (*Mississippi Masala*, 1991); the Iranian diaspora in New York (*The Mission* (1985), *The Suitors* (1988)); Ghanaians in Britain (*Testament*, 1988); Turks in Germany (*Farewell to False Paradise*, 1988); North Africans in France (*Le The du Harem d'Archimede* (Tea in the Harem, 1985)); Chinese in the US (*Full Moon over New York*, 1990). Such films also reflect a real-world situation where Mexican and Pakistani "immigrants" to the US, for example, keep in close touch with their home communities thanks to cheap flights, and technologies such as VCRs (on which to see films from home), e-mail, satellite television, and faxes, not to mention local cable stations featuring programs in Spanish or Urdu. Old-style assimilation gives way to the active maintenance of multiple loyalties, identities, and affiliations.

Postcolonial theory deals very effectively with the *cultural* contradictions and syncretisms generated by the global circulation of peoples and cultural goods in a mass-mediated and interconnected world,

296

resulting in a kind of commodified or mass-mediated syncretism. The culinary metaphors typical of postcolonial discourse often imply a fondness for this kind of *mélange*. Significantly, Indian filmmakers speak of blending the masalas – literally, Hindi for "spices," but metaphorically evoking the creation of "something new out of old ingredients" – as a key to their recipe for making films (see Thomas, 1985). Indeed, the word masala forms part of the titles of two Indian diasporic films, one Indian–Canadian (*Masala*) and the other Indo-American (*Mississippi Masala*). In the former film the god Krishna, portrayed as a gross hedonist, appears to a nostalgic Indian grandmother thanks to an interactive VCR. While mocking the official multiculturalism of Canada, the filmic style itself serves up a kind of masala, where the language of the Hindu "mythological" mingles with the language of MTV and the mass media.

The postcolonial critique also borders on gender issues. Largely produced by men, third-worldist film theory was not generally concerned with a feminist critique of nationalist discourse. Gender contradictions were subordinated to anti-colonial struggle: women were expected to "wait their turn." The postcolonial discourse of the 1980s and 1990s, by contrast, does not so much reject the nation as interrogate its repressions and limits. Thus feminists of color call for an "intersectionality" (Kimberly Crenshaw) of axes of analysis. A number of films influenced by theory, films like Mona Hatoum's *Measures of Distance* (1988), Tracey Moffat's *Nice Coloured Girls* (1987), Gurinder Chada's *Bhaji on the Beach* (1994), and Isaac Julien's *Black Skin, White Masks* (1997), suggest that a purely nationalist discourse cannot apprehend the layered, dissonant identities of diasporic or postcolonial subjects. The "post-third-worldist" theory of the 1980s and 1990s displays a certain skepticism toward meta-narratives of liberation, but does not necessarily abandon the notion that emancipation is worth fighting for. But rather than flee from contradiction, it installs doubt and crisis at the very core of theory.

Postcolonial theory has been critiqued for (1) its elision of class (not surprising, given the elite origins and status of many of the theorists themselves); (2) its psychologism (the tendency to reduce large-scale political struggles to intra-psychic tensions); (3) its elision of questions of political economy in an age where economic neo-liberalism is the driving force behind the globalized cultural changes registered by postcolonial theory; (4) its ahistoricity (its tendency to speak in the abstract without specifying historical period or geographical location); (5) its denial of the pre-colonial past of non-European societies; (6) its ambiguous relation, in the academy, to ethnic studies, where postcolonial theory is projected as sophisticated (and unthreatening) while ethnic studies is seen as militant and crude (see Shohat, 1999); and (7) its ambiguous relation to indigenous peoples. While postcolonial thought stresses de-territorialization, the artificial, constructed nature of nationalism and national borders, and the obsolescence of anti-colonialist discourse, Fourth World indigenous peoples emphasize a discourse of territorial claims, symbiotic links to nature, and active resistance to colonial incursions.

The Poetics and Politics of Postmodernism

The phenomenon called postmodernism consecrates, on a certain level, the decline of the radicalism of the 1960s, in the First World and the Third, gradually gave way in the 1980s and 1990s to "business as usual" and an acquiescence in capitalist market values. The idea that Marxism was the only legitimate theoretical horizon soon gave way to monumental political realignments and startling ideological reversals. In France, as one critic put it, "the entire left bank changed course like a school of dolphins" (see Guillebauden, in Ory and Sirinelli, 1986, p. 231). *Cahiers du cinèma*, after its period of intricate Marxist analyses (for example, of *Young Mr Lincoln*), largely reverted to its pre-1968 auteurism. The denunciations of an oppressive apparatus and Hollywood alienation gave way in the 1980s to Baudrillard's strangely melancholic celebration of a postmodernity best exemplified by a previously excoriated American mass-culture.

The theoreticians of *Tel Quel* moved from a modernist (cum pseudo-Maoist) vaunting of the European avant-garde in the 1970s to a postmodern celebration of American-style liberalism. (Deleuze and Guattari were among the few French intellectuals who didn't deny the legacy of May 1968.) Common to many of these currents was an anti-systemic impulse, a predilection for the plural, the multiple, a valorization of everything that had been suppressed by earlier systematicity, everything that had been left out or relegated to the margins. Everything that suggested mastery or meta-narrative came to be seen as suspect, potentially totalizing, and even totalitarian.

Globalization and the decline of revolutionary utopian hopes over the last few decades have led to a remapping of political and cultural possibilities, a downsizing of political hopes. Since the 1980s one finds a self-reflexive and ironic distance from revolutionary and nationalist rhetoric. The right proclaims the "end of history" and universal access to capitalism and democracy, seen, in their eyes, as inevitable companions. On the left, meanwhile, a language of revolution has been eclipsed by an idiom of resistance, indicative of a crisis in totalizing narratives and a shifting vision of the emancipatory project. Substantive nouns like "revolution" and "liberation" transmute into a largely adjectival opposition: "counter-hegemonic," "subversive," "adversarial." Instead of a macro-narrative of revolution, there is now a decentered multiplicity of localized "micro-political" struggles. While not disappearing completely from view, class and nation lose their privileged position, as they are both supplemented and challenged by counter-hegemonic resistances based on such categories as race, gender, and sexuality. Instead of socialist revolution, the implicit goal, more and more, seems to be capitalism with a human face.

Contemporary film theory has of necessity to confront the phenomena summed up in the slippery and polysemic term "postmodernism," a term which implies the global ubiquity of market culture, a new stage of capitalism in which culture and information become key terrains for struggle. The term "postmodernism" itself has a long prehistory in studies of painting (John Watkins Chapman in 1870 spoke of postmodern painting), in literary study (Irving Howe in 1959 spoke of postmodern fiction), and in architecture (Charles Jencks). Postmodernism was anticipated (without the term) in Guy Debord's *Society of the Spectacle* (1967), where the French situationist argued that everything that had once been directly lived had in the contemporary world transmuted into a representation. By shifting attention away from the political economy *per se* to the economy of the sign and the spectacularization of everyday life, Debord clearly anticipated similar moves by Jean Baudrillard.

Postmodernism is on one level not an event but a discourse, a conceptual grid which has by now been "stretched" to the breaking-point. As Dick Hebdige (1988) points out, postmodernism has shown a protean capacity to change meaning in different national and disciplinary contexts, coming to designate a host of heterogeneous phenomena, ranging from details of architectural decor to broad shifts in societal or historical sensibility. Hebdige discerns three "founding negations" within postmodernism: (1) the negation of totalization, i.e. an antagonism to discourses which address a transcendental subject, define an essential human nature, or prescribe collective human goals; (2) the negation of teleology (whether in the form of authorial purpose or historical destiny); and (3) the negation of utopia, i.e. a skepticism about what Lyotard calls the *grands recits* of the West, the faith in progress, science, or class struggle. (A *boutade* summed up this position as: "God is dead, so is Marx, and I'm not feeling too well myself.") The empty sequentiality of "post" corresponds to a preference for words which begin with the prefixes *de* or *dis* – *de*centering, *dis*placement – and which suggest the demystification of pre-existing paradigms. Postmodernism is fond of terms which connote openness, multiplicity, plurality, heterodoxy, contingency, and hybridity.

In Jameson's paradoxical formulation, postmodernism is "a unified theory of differentiation," torn between an impulse to unify its fields with totalizing assertions and a contrary impulse to proliferate differences (Jameson, 1998, p. 37). In general, postmodernism foregrounds the fragmented and heterogenous nature of socially constituted identity in the contemporary world, where subjectivity becomes "nomadic" (Deleuze) and "schizophrenic" (Jameson).

Other leitmotifs in postmodernist writing (some shared with post-structuralism) are (1) the dereferentialization of the real, whereby the linguistic referent is bracketed (Saussure), the psychoanalytic patient's actual history is substituted by an imaginary history (Lacan), where "there is no outside-the-text" (Derrida), and where no history exists without "prior textualization" (Jameson) or rhetorical "emplotment" (Hayden White); (2) the desubstantialization of the subject: the transmutation of the old, stable ego into a fractured, discursive construct fashioned by the media and by social discourses; (3) the dematerialization of the economy: the shift from the production of objects (metallurgy) to the production of signs and information (semiurgy); (4) the breakdown of the high art–low art distinction (Huyssens) evidenced in the commercial co-optation of high modernism and "the surrealist takeover of the pop sensibility" (Sontag); for example, Daliesque perfume commercials; (5) an atrophied historical sense (Jameson's "depthlessness" and the "waning of affect"); and (6) dissensus rather than consensus, as diverse communities endlessly negotiate their differences.

How we see postmodernism, and its relation to film theory, depends very much on whether we see it as (1) a *discursive/conceptual grid*; (2) a *corpus of texts* (both those which theorize postmodernism – Jameson, Lyotard, etc. – and those which are theorized by it – *Blade Runner*, for example); (3) a *style or aesthetic* (characterized by self-conscious allusiveness, narrational instability, and nostalgic recycling and pastiche); (4) an *epoch* (roughly the post-industrial, transnational information age); (5) a *prevailing sensibility* (nomadic subjectivity, historical amnesia); or (6) a *paradigm shift*: the end of Enlightenment meta-narratives of Progress and Revolution. (Some theorists, such as Fredric Jameson, take a multidimensional approach which sees postmodernism as *simultaneously* a style, a discourse, and an epoch.) How we feel about all these definitions *politically* depends partly on who we feel is the butt of the postmodernist joke: High modernists who look down on popular culture? Frankfurt School cultural pessimists? Nostalgic avant-gardists? Political activists?

The term "postmodernism" has been mobilized almost in oppo-

site political senses. One such mobilization retools "ideology critique" for a new era, thus enabling the critical demystification of
media texts. Some see postmodernism as decreeing the death of utopian alternatives, while using a utopian language to describe "actually existing capitalism." For some, postmodernism is seen as the
aging of Aquarius, a symptom of the battle fatigue of tenured leftists, a signal of the obsolescence of left politics, now seen as uptight
and puritanical. Since everyone now participates in the system, the
system is no longer visible qua system. Hal Foster (1983) discerns
contradictory political tendencies within postmodern discourse, distinguishing between neo-conservative, anti-modernist, and critical
postmodernisms, and argues finally for a postmodern "culture of
resistance" as a "counter-practice not only to the official culture of
modernism but also to the 'false narrativity' of a reactionary postmodernism" (ibid., p. xii).

A foundational (and in many ways quite problematic) text for the
theory of the postmodern was Jean-François Lyotard's *The
Postmodern Condition* (published in French in 1979 and in English
in 1984). The point of departure for Lyotard's book was the epistemology of the natural sciences in the academy, a subject about which
Lyotard confessed that he knew very little. The book became dis-
proportionately influential because of its uncanny timing and title.
For Lyotard, postmodernism represented a crisis of knowledge and
legitimation, one which led to a historically conditioned skepticism
toward the *grands récits*, i.e. the meta-narratives of the Enlightenment concerning scientific progress and political liberation. Echoing Adorno on the impossibility of poetry after Auschwitz, Lyotard
questioned whether any thought could "sublate Auschwitz in a general process toward universal emancipation" (Lyotard, 1984, p. 6).

While many of the postmodernists were lapsed radicals like
Baudrillard and Lyotard, Fredric Jameson theorized postmodernism
from within an unabashedly neo-Marxist framework. As the title of
his essay "Postmodernism, or the Cultural Logic of Late Capitalism"
implies, for Jameson postmodernism is a periodizing concept. Building on Ernest Mandel's account of the three phases of capitalism (market, monopoly, and transnational), and borrowing from the

terminology of the Russian Formalists, Jameson posited postmodernism as the "cultural dominant" of late capitalism. Positions on postmodernism, for Jameson, carry with them a specific stance on transnational capitalism. While many postmodern critics stress the aesthetic, Jameson shows the inextricable connections between the economic and aesthetic in an era where specters of free-floating capital vie against each other "in a vast world-wide disembodied phantasmagoria," where electronic capital transfers abolish space and time, and where capital achieves its ultimate dematerialization in a globalized cyberspace (Jameson, 1998, pp. 142, 154).

In the postmodern era the conflation of the economic with the cultural results in the "aestheticization of everyday life" (ibid., p. 73). Postmodern art tends to be reflexive, ironic. One might speak, in this context, of the postmodern reflexivity of commercial television, which is often reflexive and self-referential, but whose reflexivity is, at most, politically ambiguous. Films like *Pulp Fiction*, or TV programs like *The David Letterman Show* and *Beavis and Butthead*, are relentlessly reflexive, but almost always within a pervasively ironic stance which looks with bored distaste at all political position-taking. The mass media thus seem to have cannibalized reflexivity theory for their own "culinary" purposes. Many of the distancing procedures characterized as reflexive in Godard's films now typify many television shows: the designation of the apparatus (cameras, monitors, switches), the "disruption" of narrative flow (via commercials); the juxtaposition of heterogenous genres and discourses; the mixing of documentary and fictive modes. Yet, rather than triggering alienation effects, television often simply alienates. The self-referentiality of commercials that deconstruct themselves or parody other commercials serves only to signal to the spectator that the commercial is not to be taken seriously, and this relaxed state of expectation renders the viewer more permeable to the commercial message. Indeed, advertisers have such faith in this lucrative self-mockery that ABC took to denouncing its own programming as bad for the viewer: "8 hours a day, that's all we ask," reads one panel, and the next: "Don't worry, you've got billions of brain cells."

The most typical aesthetic expression of postmodernism is not parody but pastiche, a blank, neutral practice of mimicry, without any satiric agenda or sense of alternatives, nor for that matter, any mystique of "originality" beyond the ironic orchestration of dead styles, whence the centrality of intertextuality and what Jameson calls the "random cannibalization of all the styles of the past." TV programs like *The Daily Show*, where the news of the day – famine in the Sudan, massacres in Bosnia, Bill Clinton and Monica Lewinsky – becomes the trampoline for smirky humor, offers evidence for Jameson's point. Here irony becomes not only "blank" but auto-telic, a self-satisfied "yeah, whatever" response to history.

Postmodernism as a discursive–stylistic grid has enriched film theory and analysis by calling attention to a stylistic shift toward a media-conscious cinema of multiple styles and ironic recyclage. Much of the work on postmodernism in film has involved the positing of a postmodern aesthetic, exemplified in such influential films as *Blue Velvet* (1982), *Blade Runner* (1987), and *Pulp Fiction*. Jameson discerns in such neo-noir films as *Body Heat* a "nostalgia for the present." Films like *American Graffiti* for Americans, *Indochine* for the French, and the "raj nostalgia" films (*Heat and Dust*, *A Passage to India*) for the British convey a wistful sense of loss for what is imagined as a simpler and grander time. For this stylistically hybrid postmodern cinema, both the modernist avant-garde modes of analysis – with the cinema as the instigator of epistemological breakthroughs – and the modes of analysis developed for classical cinema, no longer quite "work." Instead, libidinal intensities compensate for the weakening of narrative time, as the older plots are replaced by an "endless string of narrative pretexts in which only the experiences available in the sheer viewing present can be entertained" (Jameson, 1998, p. 129).

Strategies of allusion are central to postmodern popular culture. As Gilbert Adair put it, "the postmodernist always rings twice." Thus commercials for Diet Coke feature long-deceased Hollywood actors, updating and commercializing the Kuleshov experiments in montage. The music video for Madonna's *Material Girl* encodes *Gentlemen Prefer Blondes*, even though some of Madonna's contemporary fans might not be aware of the fact. What Noël Carroll calls the "cinema of allusion," meanwhile, works with spectators assumed to be knowledgable about film history. The point is to combine references to the most diverse sources possible in a ludic game with the spectator, whose narcissism is flattered not through old-fashioned secondary identification with characters but rather through the display of cultural capital made possible by the recognition of the references. Thus the titles of postmodern films themselves pay homage to this strategy of recycling (e.g. *Pulp Fiction*, *True Romance*). Here we find a recombinant, replicant cinema, where the end of originality goes hand-in-hand with the decline of utopias. In an era of remakes, sequels, and recyclings, we dwell in the realm of the already said, the already read, and the already seen; been there, done that.

The work of Jean Baudrillard both extends and revises semiotic and Marxist theory, while incorporating the provocations of the situationists and the anthropological theories of Marcel Mauss and Georges Bataille. Baudrillard argues that the contemporary world of mass-mediated commodification entails a new economy of the sign, and consequently an altered attitude toward representation. (Baudrillard (1975) had already argued against the productivist logic of Marxism, with its tendency to valorize the economy *per se* while ignoring the more subtle economies of the sign.) The new era, for Baudrillard, is characterized by semiurgy, i.e. the process by which the production of objects as the motor of social life has given way to the production and proliferation of mass-mediated signs. Baudrillard (1983) posited four stages through which representation had passed on its way to unqualified simulation: a first stage where the sign "reflects" a basic reality; a second stage where the sign "masks" or "distorts" reality; a third stage where the sign masks the *absence* of reality; and a fourth stage where the sign becomes mere simulacrum, i.e. a pure simulation bearing no relation whatsoever to reality. With hyperreality, the sign becomes more real than reality itself. The disappearance of the referent and even of the signified leaves in its wake nothing but an endless pageant of empty signifiers. Los Angeles becomes a bad copy of Disneyworld, presented as imaginary in order to convince us that the rest is real. The photo is cuter than the baby. John Hinkley recapitulates Travis Bickle's rescue fantasy in *Taxi Driver*, while Reagan confounds his real life with his reel life.

The masses, in an era of the death of the social, become an implosive force that can no longer be spoken for, articulated, or represented.

Baudrillard's critics, such as Douglas Kellner and Christopher Norris, accuse him of fake, risk-free radicalism, blasé nihilism, and "sign fetishism." For Kellner, Baudrillard is a "semiological idealist" who abstracts signs from their material underpinnings, while Norris (1990) describes Baudrillard's project as resulting in an "inverted Platonism," a discourse that systematically promotes what for Plato were negative terms (rhetoric, appearance) over their positive counterparts. The descriptive fact that we currently inhabit an unreal world of mass-media manipulation and hyperreal politics, as evidenced by the Gulf War and as mocked in the film *Wag the Dog*, does not mean that no alternative is possible. One cannot so easily jump from a descriptive account of contemporary conditions to a blanket rejection of all truth claims and political agency. Baudrillard has only provided a meta-narrative in reverse, a negative teleology of the progressive emptying out of the social.

On another level, Baudrillard's work is a symptom of Parisian provincialism, the assumption that when Paris sneezes, the whole world catches a cold. Indeed, Third World critics have argued that postmodernism in general was merely another way for the West to repackage itself, to pass off its provincial concerns as universal conditions. "For the African," writes Denis Epko, "the celebrated postmodern condition [is] nothing but the hypocritical self-flattering cry of overfed and spoiled children" (Epko, 1995, p. 122). Latin American intellectuals, meanwhile, pointed out that neologistic Latin American culture (for example, Brazilian modernism and Mexican *mesticaje* in the 1920s), in its precocious embrace of hybridity and syncretism, had been postmodern *avant la lettre*. This global synchronicity was missed even by such a generally acute cultural theorist as Fredric Jameson, who in his unguarded moments seems to conflate the terms of political economy (where he projects the Third World into a less developed, less modern frame) and those of aesthetic and cultural periodization (where he projects it into a "premodernist" or "pre-postmodernist" past). A residual economism or "stagism" here leads to the equation of late capitalist/postmodernist and precapitalist/pre-modernist, as when Jameson speaks of the "belated emergence of a kind of modernism in the modernizing Third World, at a moment when the so-called advanced countries are themselves sinking into full postmodernity" (Jameson, 1992, p. 1). Thus the Third World always seems to lag behind, not only economically but also culturally, condemned to a perpetual game of catch-up in which it can only repeat on another register the history of the "advanced" world.

How we see postmodernism aesthetically depends on how we see its relation to modernity (the move beyond feudal structures provoked by the interrelated operations of colonialism and capitalism in the fifteenth century and industrialism and imperialism later) and to modernism (the movement beyond conventional mimetic representation in the arts), all of which varies depending on which art or medium is being discussed, in relation to which national context, and which discipline. Dominant cinema, for example, despite its technological razzle-dazzle, i.e. its modernity, largely adopted a pre-modernist aesthetic (see Stam, 1985; Friedberg, 1993). Television, video, and computer technologies, in contrast, seem like postmodern media *par excellence* and they are very avant-garde in aesthetic terms. But when *Pee-Wee's Playhouse* "so comprehensively fulfills the aberrant ideals of avant-garde radicality it is worth examining why such shows fail to threaten or disrupt dominant culture" (Caldwell, 1995, p. 205).

The important point that postmodernism makes is that virtually all political struggles take place nowadays on the symbolic battleground of the mass media. Instead of the 1960s slogan "the revolution will not be televised" it seems in the 1990s that the *only* revolution will be televisual (or cybernetic). The struggle over representation in the realm of the simulacra homologizes that of the political sphere, where questions of representation slide into issues of delegation and voice. At its worst, postmodernism reduces politics to a passive spectator sport where the most we can do is react to pseudo-events (but with real-world effects) like the "Bill and Monica show" through polls or call-in tabloid news programs. At its best, postmodernism alerts us that new times demand new strategies.

307

The Social Valence of Mass-Culture

The issue of postmodernism must also be seen against the backdrop of longstanding debates about the political valence of popular and mass-mediated culture. Within certain Marxist and third-worldist discourses, "popular culture" evokes the culture of "the people" as a proleptic sign of social transformation, while "mass-mediated culture" evokes capitalist consumerism and the machine of commodification for which "the people" are mere objects of manipulation. While "mass-culture" evokes Frankfurt School cultural pessimism and an atomized audience of narcoleptic monads, "popular culture" evokes cultural studies optimism and the insurgent energies of Bakhtin's carnival. But both "popular culture" and "mass-culture" are far from being unitary sites. The former risks populist idealization, while the latter risks elitist condescension. Do we refer "popular" to the point of consumption, i.e. to the box-office and Nielsen sense of culture consumed by the people? Or do we refer "popular" to its point of production, as culture produced by and for the people? The word "culture" itself, as Raymond Williams (1985) warns us, also embeds ideological minefields. Do we mean it in the honorific sense of monuments and masterpieces, or in the anthropological sense of how people live their lives?

Left political culture has historically displayed a schizophrenic attitude toward mass-mediated culture. As the "children of Marx and Coca-Cola" – to cite Godard's *Masculin, Féminin* – the left participates in a mass-culture that it often theoretically condemns. But even apart from any split between personal tastes and political stance, the left has shown theoretical ambivalence about the political role of the mass media. On the one hand, a certain left with roots both in the Frankfurt School (Theodor Adorno, Max Horkheimer, Herbert Schiller, Armand Mattelart) and in the theorists of May 1968 (Jean-Louis Baudry, Louis Althusser) excoriates the mass media as the unredeemed voice of bourgeois hegemony and the instrument of capitalist reification. In this more pessimistic phase, the left laments the media's manipulation of "false needs" and "false desires" and practices, as a didactic/theoretical corollary, a kind of pedagogy of media displeasure, and thus concedes a crucial area to the enemy. Another left, in contrast, salutes the revolutionizing impact of modern reproduction techniques (Benjamin) or the mass-mediated subversion of the traditional class privileges of the literary elite (Enzensberger), detecting progressive potential in mass-mediated cultural products, finding inklings of empowerment in the negotiated pleasures of mass-mediated entertainment.

Thus the left has oscillated between melancholia and euphoria, alternately playing the nudnik and the Pollyanna. Meeghan Morris, in "Banality in Cultural Studies," contrasts the "cheerleaders" with the "prophets of doom." Any number of analysts, fortunately, have sought to go beyond this ideological manic-depression by stressing the contradictions lurking just below the apparently unperturbed surface of the mass media. Many theorists have amplified a tendency already present in some thinkers loosely associated with Critical Theory (notably Kracauer, Benjamin, Ernst Bloch, and even Adorno), i.e. a dialectical approach that discerns a utopian strain within mass-culture, the view that the media contain the antidote to their own poison. Building on this tradition, Enzensberger (1974) spoke of the media as "leaky," corporately controlled but pressured by popular desire and dependent on "politically unreliable" creative talent to satisfy its inexhaustible appetite for programming. More important, Enzensberger took exception to the manipulation theory of the media as mass-deception, emphasizing instead their address to what Jameson called "the elemental power of deep social needs." Also working out of the Critical Theory tradition, filmmaker–theorist Alexander Kluge stressed the notion of an "oppositional public sphere" characterized by democratic openness, freedom of access, political reflexivity, and communicative reciprocity.[1]

Far from being essentially regressive and alienating, the social space of media is politically ambivalent. The theories of the apparatus and of dominant cinema first developed in the 1970s, as we have seen, were rightly critiqued as being monolithic, even paranoid, failing to allow for progressive redeployments of the apparatus, or for subversive textuality, or for "aberrant readings." The very word "apparatus" evoked an overwhelming cinema-machine, imagined as a monstrous operation or *engrenage*, in which the spectator is denied even a Chaplinesque *Modern Times*-style subterfuge. But real-life spectatorship is more complex and overdetermined. Certain films, such as *Thelma and Louise*, *Do the Right Thing*, or *Bulworth*, catalyze the Zeitgeist, trigger its faultlines, provoking seismic reactions of debate, adulation, resentment, backlash, and so forth.

Nor are even the most mainstream Hollywood films monolithically reactionary. Even Hollywood-style market research implies an attempt to negotiate diverse community desires. As Jameson, Enzensberger, Richard Dyer, and Jane Feuer have all argued, to explain the public's attraction to a text or medium one must look not only for the "ideological effect" that manipulates people into complicity with existing social relations, but also for the kernel of utopian fantasy reaching beyond these relations, whereby the medium constitutes itself as a projected fulfillment of what is desired and absent within the status quo. Symptomatically, even imperialist heroes like Indiana Jones and Rambo are posited not as the oppressors but as the liberators of subject peoples. In the musical comedy, Richard Dyer argues, the oppressive structures of everyday life are not so much overturned as they are stylized, choreographed, and mythically transcended. Through an artistic "change of signs" the negatives of social existence are turned into the positives of artistic transmutation (Dyer, in Altman, 1981). Films can nourish dreams of upward mobility or encourage struggle for social transformation. Altered contexts (for example, alternative films screened in union halls and community centers) also generate altered readings. The confrontation is not simply between individual spectator and individual author/film – a formulation that recapitulates the individual-versus-society trope – but between and among diverse communities within diverse contexts viewing diverse films in diverse ways.

The mass media form a complex network of ideological signs situated within multiple environments – the generating mass-media en-vironment, the broader generating ideological environment, and the generating socio-economic environment – each with its own specificities. Television, in this sense, constitutes an electronic microcosm which reflects and relays, distorts and amplifies, the ambient heteroglossia.[2] Television's heteroglossia is of course in some ways severely compromised, truncated; many social voices are never heard or severely distorted. But as a matrix in which centripetal–dominant and centrifugal–oppositional discourses do battle, the mass media can never completely reduce the antagonistic dialogue of class voices to what Jameson calls the "reassuring hum of bourgeois hegemony." There are patterns of ownership, and clear ideological tendencies, but domination is never complete, for television is not only its owners and industrial managers, but also its creative participants, its workers, and the audience that can resist, pressure, and decode.

Bakhtin and Medvedev's notion of "speech tact" can be useful here. They define "speech tact" as the "ensemble of codes governing discursive interaction," which is "determined by the aggregate of all the social relationships of the speakers, their ideological horizons, and, finally, the concrete situation of the conversation" (Bakhtin and Medvedev, 1985, p. 95). The notion of "tact" is extremely suggestive for film theory and analysis, applying literally to the power relations implicit in the verbal exchanges within the diegesis, and figuratively to the dialogue of genres and discourses within the text, as well as the dialogue between film as historically situated "utterance" and the spectator as historically situated receiver.[3]

Within this approach there is no unitary text, no unitary producer, no unitary spectator, but rather a conflictual heteroglossia pervading producer, text, context, and reader/viewer. Each category is traversed by the centripetal and the centrifugal, the hegemonic and the oppositional. The proportion might vary within each category. In contemporary American television, the owner–producer category is likely to incline toward the hegemonic, yet even here the process is conflictual, involving an orchestration of the diverse "voices" responsible for the assemblage of the text, a process which leaves traces and discordances in the text itself. The texts produced, given the conflictual nature of the creative process as well as the socially generated needs of the audience, are likely to feature a certain proportion of resistant messages or at least to make possible resistant readings. The role of a critical hermeneutics of the mass media would be to heighten awareness of all the voices relayed by the mass media, to point both to the "off-screen" voices of hegemony and to those voices muffled or suppressed. The goal would be to discern the often distorted undertones of utopia in mass media, while pointing to the real structural obstacles which make utopia less realizable and at times even less imaginable. It is a question of bringing out the text's muffled voices, rather like the work of a sound-studio mixer who re-elaborates a recording to tease out the bass, or clarify the treble, or amplify the instrumentation.

Rather than a schizophrenic careening between optimism and despair, then, it is possible to adopt a complex attitude toward the mass media, one involving a whole spectrum of moods and attitudes and strategies. The "tact" of American television, in this perspective, might be analyzed as a product of the relations between all the interlocutors (on and off-screen), the concrete situation of the conversation, and the aggregate of social relationships and the ideological horizons informing the discourse. Take, for example, the television talk show. At the center of such shows we find the dialogical interplay of speaking subjects, of persons in literal or metaphorical dialogue. In the wings, meanwhile, there are the unheard participants in the dialogue: the network managers and the corporate sponsors who "speak" only through the commercial messages. And facing the celebrities in the literal space of the studio, the in-the-flesh surrogate audience, an ideally participatory version of the invisible audience at home with whom host and guest also dialogue, an audience which is itself a cross-section of a populace traversed by contradictions involving class, gender, race, age, and politics.

In the world of the talk show the corporate sponsors wield the ultimate discursive power; they have the right to suspend or even terminate the conversation. A cold cash nexus, as well as an ideological filter, severely compromises what appears to be the warm exchange of an "ideal speech situation" (Habermas) based on "free and familiar contact" (Bakhtin). The "joke," in Martin Scorsese's *The King of Comedy*, consists in having its protagonist try to "collect" on the implicit promise of television's "warmth"; Rupert Pupkin literally believes the talk-show host Jerry Langford (modeled on

Johnny Carson) is his "friend." The communicative utopia is compromised, furthermore, not only by corporate getting and spending but also by the obsession with ratings, by the search for ever-more sensational victims or mind-numbing absurdities, by the peripheralization of any truly alternative discourse, and by the insistent success trope which underlies the shows and fosters vicarious identification with the ephemeral triumphs of "stars." The discourse is further marred by other hidden and not-so-hidden agendas having to do with the promotion of books, films, and shows. The conversation, in sum, is neither free nor disinterested; the discourse is bound by the innumerable restraints of corporate and social "tact."

Mass and popular culture are conceptually distinguishable but also mutually imbricated; it is the tense and lively dynamic between the two that defines the contemporary moment. The appeal of the mass media derives, on a certain level, from their capacity to commodify the popular memory and hope for a future egalitarian *communitas*. The media thus try to substitute the canned applause of simulacral festivities for the deep belly laugh of carnival, but which only retain innocuous traces of the original subversive energy. Whatever its political orientation, popular culture is now fully imbricated in transnational globalized technoculture. It makes sense, then, to see it as plural, as negotiating among diverse communities involved in a conflictual process of production and consumption.

Contemporary mass media constantly serve up the simulacra of carnival-style festivity. Television often implicitly offers the possibility of universal Andy Warhol-style stardom, an updating of carnival's erasure of the line between the spectator and the spectacle. This kind of participation takes countless forms. The spectator might get a call from a talk-show host, be thanked on the telethon, get interviewed by *Eyewitness News*, ask a question on the *Oprah Show*, be mocked by a superimposed title on *Saturday Night Live*, appear on *People's Court* or the *Jerry Springer Show*. In all these instances, as Elayne Rapping puts it, the people literally "make a spectacle of themselves," thus abolishing, *à la* carnival, the barrier between performer and audience. In this sense, we can account for the appeal of many mass-mediated products as relaying, in a compromised manner, the distant cultural memory and imagery of carnival. The American mass media are fond of weak or truncated forms of carnival which capitalize on the frustrated desire for a truly egalitarian society by serving up distorted versions of carnival's utopian promise: Fourth of July commercial pageantry, jingoistic singalongs, authoritarian rock concerts, festive soft-drink commercials. What emerge from such analyses are profoundly mixed situations, mingling the crassest kind of manipulation with subliminally utopian appeals and modestly progressive gestures. (Indeed, we badly need analytical categories, such as those of Bakhtin, which subvert Manichean evaluations by allowing for the fact that a given utterance or discourse can be progressive and regressive *at the same time.*)

As suggested earlier, left theory has often been schizophrenic, sometimes endorsing entertainment uncritically and sometimes lamenting the delight that mass audiences take in alienated spectacles. Too often a puritanical left throws out the baby of pleasure with the bathwater of ideology. This refusal of pleasure has at times created an immense gap between cultural critique and those it purports to serve. Indeed, the political consequences of left puritanism have been enormous. An austere super-egoish left that addresses its audience in moralistic terms, while advertising and mass-culture speak to its deepest desires and fantasies, is theoretically and pragmatically handicapped. The point is that the consciousness industry and capitalism cannot ultimately satisfy the real needs which they exploit. "Anticipatory" readings, in this sense, can show mass-media texts as inadvertently predictive of possible alternative forms of social life.

Post-Cinema: Digital Theory and the New Media

The current of cinema in its much-vaunted specificity now seems to be disappearing into the larger stream of the audiovisual media, be they photographic, electronic, or cybernetic. Losing its hard-won privileged status as "king" of the popular arts, the cinema must now compete with television, video games, computers, and virtual reality. Just one, relatively narrow band on a wide spectrum of simulation apparatuses, film is now seen as on a continuum with television, rather than as its antithesis, with a good deal of cross-fertilization in terms of personnel, financing, and even aesthetics.

There have been a number of theoretical responses to this changed situation, where both disciplines and media seem to lose their established "place." We find one response in the emerging field of "visual culture," an interdisciplinary formation situated at the frontiers of such diverse disciplines as art history, iconology, and media studies. Visual culture names a variegated field of concerns having to do with the centrality of vision and the visual in producing meanings, channel-ing power relations, and shaping fantasy in a contemporary world where visual culture is "not just part of your everyday life, it *is* your everyday life" (Mirzoeff, 1998, p. 3). In the wake of film theory's explorations, visual culture explores the asymmetries of the gaze, asking such questions as: How is vision gendered and sexualized (Waugh, in Gever and Greyson, 1993)? What are the visual codes by which some are allowed to look, others to hazard a peek, and still others are forbidden to look altogether (Rogoff, in Mirzoeff, 1998, p. 16)? Even war can affect the field of vision. In such books as *War and Cinema* (1989) and *The Vision Machine* (1994) Paul Virilio argues that war has been a major engine of change not only in visual technologies but also in our notions of the visual, as "the visual field was reduced to the line of fire" (Virilio, 1994, pp. 16–17). In *Screening the Body* Lisa Cartwright makes another linkage, between the cinema and "the long history of bodily analysis and surveillance in medicine and science" (Cartwright, 1995). On one level, of course, the importance of visual culture is old news for film theory, since almost all the earliest film theorists valorized the visual; the challenge was to avoid its hegemony, to also remember the role of language and sound in film.

Visual theorists have also drawn on Foucault's concept of the panoptic regime, i.e. a regime of synoptic visibility designed to facilitate a "disciplinary" overview of a prison population, best exemplified in

Bentham's "panoptical prisons," where rings of backlit cells encircle a central observation tower. Since the panopticon installs a unidirectional gaze – the scientist or warden can see the inmates but not vice versa – it has been frequently compared to the voyeuristic situation of the film spectator. L. B. Jeffries, at the beginning of *Rear Window*, overseeing the world from a sheltered position, subjecting his neighbors to a controlling gaze, becomes the warden–spectator, as it were, in a private panopticon, where he observes the wards ("small captive shadows in the cells of the periphery") of an imaginary prison. Foucault's description of the cells of the panopticon – "so many cages, so many small theatres, in which each actor is alone, perfectly individualized and constantly visible" – in some ways describes the scene exposed to Jeffries's gaze.

Dan Armstrong (1989) uses a Foucauldian framework to show how the documentarian Frederick Wiseman explores in his oeuvre a continuum of social institutions spreading out from the prison to the larger society, demonstrating "an extensive rationality and economy of power at work shaping, normalizing and objectifying subjects for the purposes of social utility and control." Wiseman's works investigate the dynamics of the panoptical gaze in the diverse institutions making up the "carceral archipelago:" confinement and punishment in *Titicut Follies* and *Juvenile Court*; social assistance in *Hospital* and *Welfare*; and the "productive" disciplines of school, the military, re-ligion, and work in *High School, Basic Training, Essene*, and *Meat*.

Implicit in the notion of visual culture as developed by such figures as W. J. T. Mitchell, Irit Rogoff, Nick Mirzoeff, Anne Frielberg, and Jonathon Crary is a rejection of the aestheticism of conventional art history (including modernist art history), with its emphasis on masterpieces and geniuses, and its consequent failure to place art in relation to other practices and institutions. Gary suggests in *Technique of the Observor* (1995) that vision is always linked to questions of social power. Visual culture also tries to rescue the visual from the opprobrium to which it has been subjected, for example by those such as Neil Postman who seem to regard media imagery as inherently corrosive of thought and rationality. Some theorists also placed apparatus theory within an "ocularphobic" intertext. For Martin Jay (1994) apparatus theory forms part of a longer history of the "denigration of vision" in western thought. Whereas the Enlightenment saw sight as the noblest of the senses, the twentieth century showed hostility to vision, whether in Sartre's paranoid view of *le regard d'autrui*, Guy Debord's demonization of the "society of the spectacle," Althusser's "anti-ocular critique of ideology," Comolli's attack on the "ideology of the visible," or Foucault's critique of the panopticon.

While cultural studies has been fascinated by "technologies" in the metaphorical, Foucauldian sense ("technologies" of gender, surveillance, and the body), John Caldwell has pointed out, it has tended to ignore technology in the more concrete sense of technological innovations. Caldwell's own work focuses on the impact of new technologies, such as the video-assist, electronic non-linear editing, digital effects, T-grain film stocks, and Rank-Citel, on television production and aesthetics. Caldwell demonstrates on a technical level what others have called the blurring of boundaries between the mainstream and the avant-garde, to the point that by the 1980s the real avant-garde was to be found in primetime television commercial production, with commercials "one of the most dynamic sites for visual experimentation" (ibid., p. 93).

Any contemporary analysis of the processes of spectatorship, furthermore, must deal not only with the fact of new venues (films seen in planes, in airports, bars, etc.) but also with the fact that new audiovisual technologies have generated not only a new cinema but also a new spectator. A new blockbuster cinema, made possible by huge budgets, sound innovations, and digital technologies, favored a "sound and light show" cinema of sensation. What Laurent Julier calls "concert films" foster a fluid, euphorical montage of images and sounds reminiscent less of classical Hollywood than of video games, music video, and amusement park rides. (George Lucas made the comparison explicit in a *Time* interview in 1981.) Cinema of this kind becomes "immersive," in Biocca's expression; the spectator is "in" the image rather than confronted by it. Sensation predominates over narrative, and sound over image, while verisimilitude

317

is no longer a goal; rather, it is the technology-dependent production of vertiginous, prosthetic delirium. The spectator is no longer the deluded master of the image but rather the inhabitant of the image.

In a certain sense recent developments in commercial film relativize *both* cognitive and classical semiotic approaches, revealing them as relevant only to classical forms of cinema. Lately we find a slackening of narrative time, a kind of postmodern picaresque stringing of narrative non-events. Here a critique of linear narrative, exploitative spectacle, and the dominating gaze becomes irrelevant. In the face of such a cinema, both semiotic–psychoanalytic accounts based on identification, suture, and the gaze, and cognitive approaches based on cause–effect inferences and "hypothesis-testing," seem somewhat obsolescent.[1] In the postmodern "allusionist" (Carroll) cinema of a Tarantino, causality and motivation are trivialized; here, characters kill not out of any "project" but rather through accident (*Pulp Fiction*) or due to a fleeting impulse or momentary irritation (*Jackie Brown*). Neither type of cinema quite fits into the neat schemata of semiotic *or* cognitive theory.

In a cybernetic update of Walter Benjamin's seminal essay, Henry Jenkins, in "The Work of Theory in the Age of Digital Transformation" (1999), addresses the emerging body of "digital theory:"

Digital Theory may address anything from the role of CGI special effects in Hollywood blockbusters to new systems of communication (the Net), new genres of entertainment (the computer game), new styles of music (techno) or new systems of representation (digital photography or virtual reality). (Jenkins, in Miller and Stam, 1999)

Although many speak apocalyptically of the end of cinema, the current situation uncannily recalls that at the beginning of cinema as a medium. "Pre-cinema" and "post-cinema" have come to resemble each other. Then, as now, everything seemed possible. Then, as now, film "neighbored" with a wide spectrum of other simulation devices. And now, as then, film's pre-eminent position among media arts seemed neither inevitable nor clear. Just as early cinema neighbored with scientific experiments, burlesque, and sideshow, new forms of post-cinema neighbor with home-shopping, video games, and CD-ROMs.

Changing audiovisual technologies dramatically impact virtually all of the perennial issues engaged by film theory: specificity, auteurism, apparatus theory, spectatorship, realism, aesthetics. Just as Umberto Eco suggested in *Foucault's Pendulum* that literature would be changed by the existence of word processors, so film, and film theory, will be irrevocably changed by the new media. As Jenkins puts it,

E-mail poses questions about virtual community; digital photography about the authenticity and reliability of visual documentation; virtual reality about embodiment and its epistemological functions; hypertext about readership and authorial authority; computer games about spatial narrative; MUDs about identity formation; webcams about voyeurism and exhibitionism. (Jenkins, in Miller and Stam, 1999)

The new media blur media specificity; since digital media potentially incorporate all previous media, it no longer makes sense to think in media-specific terms. In terms of auteurism, purely individual creation becomes even less likely in a situation where multimedia creative artists depend on an extremely diversified network of media producers and technical experts.

Digital imaging also leads to the de-ontologization of the Bazinian image. With the dominance of digital image production, where virtually any image becomes possible, "the connection of images to solid substance has become tenuous . . . images are no longer guaranteed as visual truth" (Mitchell, 1992, p. 57). The artist need no longer search for a pro-filmic model in the world; one can give visible form to abstract ideas and improbable dreams. (Peter Greenaway (1998) prefers to speak of virtual *irreality* rather than virtual reality.) The image is no longer a copy but rather acquires its own life and dynamism within an interactive circuit, freed of the contingencies of location shooting, weather conditions, and so forth. But the simulacral advantage is also a disadvantage; since we know that images can be created electronically, we are more skeptical about the image's truth value.

In stylistic terms the new technologies offer new possibilities both for realism and for *irrealism*. On the one hand, they facilitate more dizzyingly persuasive and "engulfing" forms of "total cinema" such as IMAX spectacles. With virtual reality, whereby users don helmets in order to interface with three-dimensional computer-generated environments, the impression of the real reaches vertiginous proportions. Within the cybernetic paraspace of virtual reality, the flesh-and-blood body lingers in the real world while computer technology projects the cybersubject into a terminal world of simulations. For cyber-enthusiasts, virtual reality expands the reality effect exponentially by switching the viewer from a passive to a more inter-active position. Within this more interactive position, the raced, gendered, sensorial body could be implanted, theoretically, with a constructed virtual gaze, becoming a trampoline for identity play. Such media transform us all into what Walter Mitchell (1992) calls "morphing cyborgs capable of reconfiguring ourselves by the minute."

These possibilities have led to a euphoric discourse of the new, reminiscent in some ways of that which greeted the cinema a century earlier. An enormous ideological load gets attached to new technologies. The new media, it is argued, inherently encourage collaborative behavior and cancel out the stratifying effects of physical embodiment: gender, age, race, and so forth. But the idea that the new media can make possible such social transcendence ignores the historical inertia of these socially generated stratifications. Disproportionate power, furthermore, still rests with those who build, disseminate, and commercialize these new apparatuses. The Internet, for example, privileges English to the detriment of other languages. Nor are the new apparatuses epistemologically subversive. For Sally Pryor and Jill Scott, virtual reality rests on "an unstated foundation of conventions such as Cartesian space, objective realism, and linear perspective" (Pryor and Scott, in Hayward and Wollen, 1993, p. 168). The film *Strange Days* offers a dystopian extrapolation of future possibilities of such media, showing a world where participants get "wired" with VR headgear directly connected to the cerebral cortex, and who are thus able to plug into and vampirize other people's lives for their own entertainment. Cybernetic pimps make the life worlds of others, for example of rape victims, available for sale and replay.

The new technologies clearly impact spectatorship in ways that make apparatus theory seem even more obsolescent. Whereas the classical viewing situation presumed a darkened movie theater where all eyes were directed toward the screen, the new media often involve small screens in well-lit situations. It is no longer a question of Plato's cave in which the spectator is trapped, but the information superhighway on which the spectator travels, presumably toward freedom. In "Archeology of the Computer Screen" Lev Manovich (1994) argues that the cinema's classical screen (three-dimensional perspectival space on a flat surface) is replaced by "the dynamic screen" where multiple, mutually relativizing, images evolve over time. While the classical film was a well-oiled machine for producing emotions, one which obliged the spectator to follow a linear structure which provoked a sequenced set of emotions, the new interactive media allow the participant – the word "spectator" seems too passive – to forge a more personal temporality and mold a more personal emotion. The screen becomes an "activity center," a cyber-chronotope where both space and time are transformed. While it makes sense to ask the length of a film, it is meaningless to ask the same question of an interactive narrative, game, or CD-ROM. The participant decides the duration, the sequence, the trajectory. CD-ROMs such as *Myst* and *Riven* use high-definition image and stereo sound to bring the participant into a film-like diegetic world with multiple byways, exits, and endings. Now the key word is "interactivity" rather than enforced passivity, whence the obsolescence of the Baudry–Metz style analyses of spectatorship. Rather than the subject-effect of suture theory, the interactive participant is "recognized" by the computer, which is informed about his or her whereabouts in material space and in social space. At the same time, this "freedom" is reversible, as the cyber-participant becomes vulnerable to surveillance, thanks to the data trail left by credit transactions, tax and income records, as well as the record of World Wide Web sites visited (Morse, 1998, p. 7).

The new technologies also have clear impact on production and aesthetics. The introduction of digital media has led to the use of computer animation in *Toy Story* and of CGI special effects in *Jurassic Park*. Morphing is used to interrogate essentialist racial differences (for example, in Michael Jackson's *Black or White*), in an aesthetic that emphasizes similarities across difference rather than the graphic conflicts of Eisensteinian montage (Sobchack, 1997). The seven-minute Swiss film *Rendezvous à Montreal* (1987) offered an entirely computer-generated film which stages a threshold romance between Marilyn Monroe and Humphrey Bogart. In mainstream film, computer-generated sequences appeared in *Star Trek II* (1983), while computer-generated characters appeared in *Terminator II* (1991). The cyber-fetishist journal *Wired* spoke in 1997 of "Hollywood 2.0," implicitly comparing the film industry's transformation to the frenzied production of obsolescence implicit in the recurrent upgradings of computer software .

At the same time, digital cameras and digital editing (AVID) not only open up montage possibilities but also facilitate low-budget filmmaking. And in terms of distribution, the Internet makes it possible for a community of strangers to exchange texts, images, and video sequences, thus enabling a new kind of international communication, one, it is hoped, that is more reciprocal and multi-centered than the old Hollywood-dominated international system. Thanks to fiber-optics we can look forward to "dial-up cinema," the capacity to see, or download, a vast archive of films and audiovisual materials. The shift to the digital makes for infinite reproducibility without loss of quality, since the images are stored as pixels, with no "original." We are also promised computer-generated actors, desktop computers that can produce feature films, and creative collaborations across geographically dispersed sites.

We also find an uncanny affinity between the new media and what used to be regarded as avant-garde practices. Contemporary video and computer technologies facilitate media ju-jitsu and the recycling of media detritus as "found objects." Rather than the 1960s "aesthetic of hunger," low-budget video-makers can deploy a kind of cybernetic minimalism, achieving maximum beauty and effect at minimum expense. Video switchers allow the screen to be split, divided horizontally or vertically, with wipes and inserts. Keys, chromakeys, mattes and fader bars, along with computer graphics, multiply audiovisual possibilities for fracture, rupture, polyphony. An electronic quilting can weave together sounds and images in ways that break with linear character-centered narrative. All the conventional decorum of dominant cinema – eyeline matches, position matches, the 30 degree rule, cutaway shots – is superseded by proliferating polysemy. The centered perspective inherited from Renaissance humanism is relativized, the multiplicity of perspectives rendering identification with any one perspective difficult. Spectators have to decide what the images have in common, or how they conflict; they have to effect the syntheses latent in the audiovisual material.

The obvious fact that mainstream cinema has largely opted for a linear and homogenizing aesthetic where track reinforces track within a Wagnerian totality in no way effaces the equally salient truth that the cinema (and the new media) is infinitely rich in polyphonic possibilities. The cinema has always been able to stage temporalized contradictions between the diverse tracks, which can mutually shadow, jostle, undercut, haunt, and relativize one another. Jean-Luc Godard anticipated these possibilities with his 1970s video-research films like *Numéro Deux* and *Ici et Ailleurs*, and Peter Greenaway pushed them in new directions in films like *Prospero's Books* and *The Pillow Book*, where multiple images mold an achronological multiple-entry "narrative." The new media can combine synthesized images with captured ones. The digitalized culture industry can now promote "threshold encounters" between Elton John and Louis Armstrong, or allow Natalie Cole to sing with her long-departed father. They are capable of chameleonic blendings *à la Zelig* and digital insertions *à la Forest Gump*. The capacity for palimpsestic overlays of images and sounds facilitated by electronics and cybernetics opens the doors to a renovated, multi-channel aesthetic. Meaning can be generated not through the drive and thrust of individual desire as encapsulated by a linear narrative, but rather through the interweaving of mutually relativizing layers of sound, image, and language. Less bound by canonical institutional and aesthetic traditions, the new media make possible what Arlindo Machado (1997) calls the "hybridization of alternatives."

Contemporary theory needs to take new audiovisual and computer technologies into account, not only because the new media will inevitably generate new forms of audiovisual intertextuality, but also because a number of theorists have posited a kind of "match" between contemporary theory itself and new media and computer technologies. To explore the first point, electronic or virtual textuality is necessarily different from print or celluloid textuality. To read Moulthrope describing hypertext as "not a definable artifact like a bound volume" but rather a "dynamic, expandable collection of writings" is to hear the echoes of Barthes on the distinction between "work" and "text." "Hypermedia" combines sound, graphics, print, and video, allowing for extraordinary new combinations. For one thing, some films now come accompanied by parallel digital texts. The CD-ROM that accompanies Isaac Julien's documentary on Fanon, *Black Skin, White Masks*, for example, provides a digital version of the film's paratext, with source materials on Fanon, Algeria, psychoanalysis, and so forth. Those parts of the interviews not included in the film proper can now be seen in their entirety on the CD-ROM. Second, theorists have pointed out that the hypertext and multimedia discourse of links, networks, and interweaving is shared with Barthesian semiotics, Bakhtinian dialogics, and Derridean deconstruction. For hypertext theorists like Landow and Lanham this connection between the new technologies and recent literary theory emerged from dissatisfaction with "the related phenomena of the printed book and hierarchical thought" (Landow, 1994, p. 1). Designers of computer software, Landow argues, recognize themselves in the split-writing of Derrida who, when he spoke of a new kind of writing, did not realize he was speaking of cybernetic *écriture*. Hypertext, for Landow, offers an open-bordered text, like Barthes's virtual space of writing. The interactive nature of computers turns their users into producer–*bricoleurs*. Conceivably, cybernetically aware hypertexters could take a well-known novel like *Madame Bovary*, turn it from print to a hypertext version, then add music and graphics to create a kind of hybrid adaptation, a quasi-film. As Gregory

Ulmer points out, electronic culture allows diverse cultural formats – oral, written, and electronic – to coexist interactively, facilitating the technological realization of Walter Benjamin's dream of a book composed entirely of quotations.[2]

The shift from the author–work–tradition triad to the text–discourse–culture triad, and the digital theorists' openness to mixed modes and miscegenated technologies, both remind us of Bakhtinian dialogism. The decentering of the culture of the book promoted by hypertext would seem to buttress the critique of the literacy–orality hierarchy, while the emphasis on multi-authorial textuality subverts the romantic individualism of auteurism. Replacing single-entry linear texts by fluid texts with multiple points of entry, as well as hypertext's openness to multiple temporalities and perspectives, also has positive implications for a polycentric, polychronic view of film, one that substitutes an image of infinite passageways and pathways for the exclusivist logic of the "final word." Since hypertext, meanwhile, is ultimately about "linking," in a world where everything is potentially "next to" everything else, the new media can help make relational connections across space and time: (1) temporal links between diverse periods; (2) spatial links across different regions; (3) disciplinary links between usually compart-mentalized fields; and (4) discursive intertextual links between different media and discourses.

Any discussion of the new media has to speak of their uses and potentialities in specific times and spaces, suggesting both their advantages and their limitations. Even what qualifies as "new" or as high-tech is relative; in the US or Europe it might be IMAX or the World Wide Web; in the Amazon it might be camcorders, VCRs, and satellite dishes. Despite the gravity-defying prowess of cyberdiscourse, physical location still does matter. Surfing the Net from a Third World location, for example, is often slowed by inadequate phone systems.[3] There are also differences in the progressive potential of the new media. On the one hand, we find spectacular IMAX-style immersive media, where technological razzle-dazzle is wedded to a time-worn illusionistic project. And despite all the talk of democratization and interactivity, techno-futurist discourse often resorts to gendered tropes rooted in colonial domination or conquest: "trailblazing," "home-steading of the electronic frontier," "wide-open spaces," a "pioneer/settler philosophy." The 1993 *Newsweek* cover story on interactive technologies invoked "virgin territory," literally "there for the taking." But facile talk about democratization, as Stuart Moulthrop warns, "does not exonerate [the new media] of their complicity in military/entertainment/information culture." The danger is that multimedia democratization will be limited to a tiny privileged sphere, that cybernetic democracy will resemble other partial democracies, like that of the slaveholding democracies of ancient Athens and the American revolution. Given the *realpolitik* issues of political economy and differential access, the progressive uses of the new media could still be relegated to the off-ramps of the Infobahn. Islands of information-affluence might neighbor with what Mitchell calls "electronic Jakartas" for the "bandwidth disadvantaged." All of these complexities induce the theorist to adopt a nuanced position; roughly speaking, my own is – to paraphrase Gramsci – "pessimism of the hardware; optimism of the software."

Despite the social ambiguities of the new technologies, they do open up intriguing possibilities for both film and film theory. Interestingly, some contemporary theorists now "do" theory through the new electronic and cybernetic media. Semioticians like Umberto Eco, film theorists like Henry Jenkins, filmmakers like Peter Greenaway, Chris Marker, and Jorge Bodansky, video artists like Bill Viola, have all turned to the new media. We are now seeing CD-ROMs of film analysis by Henry Jenkins and Marsha Kinder in the United States, by Jurandir Noronha and Zita Caravalhosa in Brazil. The medium of film analysis might no longer be exclusively verbal, as at the time of Bellour's "unattainable text," now it is available, copyable, downloadable, revisable. Chris Marker's CD-ROM *Immemory* contrasts cinema, which is "bigger than us," with TV, where one "can see the shadow of a film, the trace of a film, the nostalgia, the echo of a film – but never a film." Marsha Kinder deconstructs race and gender in her computer game *Runaways* (1998). A special issue of *Postmodern Culture*, edited by Robert Kolker, provided a forum for cyber essays on films like *Casablanca*

326

and *Prospero's Books*, some of which included clips. Jorge Bodanksy, who made films in the Amazon in the 1970s, is now creating what amounts to a kind of cybernetic updating of Hales Tours, a CD-ROM which allows the "voyager" to visit the Amazon, to click on a tree which reveals the animals inside it, to trigger a fire or deforestation and see its ecological consequences.

While being aware of the dangers of cyber-authoritarianism, it would be short-sighted to ignore the progressive potential of digital media. Stone (1996) invokes the Native American myth of Coyote, the shapeshifter, to laud digital media as subverting fixed social identities and stable configurations of power. Digital media have been linked both to the military–industrial complex and to the counter-culture. Henry Jenkins (in Miller and Stam, 1999) speaks of the "surprisingly comfortable fit" between the hacker subculture battling media conglomerates and cultural studies' concepts of "poaching" and "resistance." Can multimedia, as Janet Murray implies in *Hamlet on the Holodeck* (1997), turn mute, inglorious nerds into "cyberbards?"

The Pluralization of Film Theory

Recent theory manifests a certain backlash against excesses of structuralism and poststructuralism. Both structuralism and poststructuralism had in common the habit of "bracketing the referent," i.e. insisting more on the interrelations between signs than on any correspondence between sign and referent. In its critique of verism, poststructuralism occasionally went to the extreme of detaching art from all relation to a social and historical context. The adepts of screen theory sometimes confused history with historicism and empirical research with empiricism. But not all theorists accepted the pan-semiotic vision of what Edward Said called "wall-to-wall text." The constructed, coded nature of artistic discourse, they argued, does not preclude all reference to reality. Even Derrida, whose writing sometimes became the alibi for a wholesale rejection of all truth claims, protested that his view of text and context "embraces and does not exclude the world, reality, history . . . it does not suspend reference" (Norris, 1990, p. 44). Filmic and literary fictions inevitably bring into play everyday assumptions not only about space and time but also about social and cultural relationships. If language structures the world, the world also structures and shapes language; the movement is not unidirectional. To the texting of the world corresponds the worlding of the text.

Theory is currently undergoing a kind of re-historicization, partly as a corrective to the elision of history by the Saussurean and Freudian–Lacanian models, and partly to answer the multiculturalist call to place film theory within larger histories of colonialism and racism. In literary studies the "new historicists" saw texts as part of complex symbolic negotiations that reflected power relations understood in Foucauldian as well as Marxist terms. Film theory and film history, long assumed to be antipodal activities, have now begun to dialogue more seriously. An emerging consensus calls for the historicization of theory and the theorization of history. The film historians, with the aid of theory, have begun to reflect on their own practices and discourses. Incorporating some of the insights of the "metahistorians" such as Hayden White, film theorists–historians have censured a number of features of conventional film history: the privileging of films and filmmakers at the expense of the larger history of technologies and cultural formations, the impressionism of many histories, the failure of the discipline to reflect on its own instruments and procedures, its conceptions of periodization (for example, the substratal teleologies, often relayed through metaphors, that pervade the field, such as biological notions of birth, development, and decline), and the corollary cult of "firsts" whereby history becomes the teleological unfolding of progressive gestures leading toward a normative form of cinema.

This is hardly the place to examine all of the multiple interventions in the field of film history; here we can only touch on a few highlights and subgenres. First, there are the theorized analytical film-centered histories of large corpusses of film: Lagny, Ropars, and Sorlin (1986) on French films of the 1930s; Phil Rosen (1984) and Bordwell, Staiger, and Thompson on classical American cinema (1985); Musser (1991), Burch (1990), Hansen (1991), Elsaesser (1990) Gaudreault and Gunning on early silent cinema; and the vast body of work on third world, postcolonial, and minority cinemas. Second, there are the economic–industrial–technological–stylistic histories of the cinema (Wasko, 1982; Allen-Gomery, 1985; Bordwell, Staiger, and Thompson, 1985; Salt, 1995). Third, there are the texts which concentrate on representations of history within film (Ferro, 1977; Sorlin, 1977, 1991; Rosenstone, 1993).

The larger theoretical movement arising out of structuralism and semiotics has been critiqued internally and externally. Internally, it was asked why film semiology, for example, had limited itself to one kind of linguistics – Saussurean structuralist linguistics – while ignoring sociolinguistics, translinguistics, conversation analysis, and "transformational" linguistics which looked at issues of social class, translation, grammar, and other forms of language. It was also asked why psychoanalytic film theory had been inspired only by Lacan's "return to Freud," while ignoring D. W. Winnicott, Melanie Klein, Jessica Benjamin, Nancy Chodorov, and Erik Erikson. Why had psychoanalytic theory focused so narrowly on fetishism, voyeurism, masochism, and identification, while bypassing other promising categories such as fantasy, the family romance, and so forth? Psychoanalysis, it was pointed out, pretended to identify psychic processes common to humanity as a whole, but in fact its oedipal analyses tended to universalize a particular guilt-ridden and time-bound culture: Christian, patriarchal, occidental, and based on the nuclear family.

Theory was questioned externally, meanwhile, by critical race theory, radical multiculturalism, and queer theory. Partisans of these grids questioned film theory's relentless focus on sexual difference, on the erotic gaze, and the oedipal story of "Daddy, Mommy, and Me," as opposed to other differences within the social and psychic formation. Why had film theory been so blithely ethnocentric, they asked, why so uncritical of cinema's complicity with imperialism, so blind to issues of race and ethnicity, so quietly and normatively "white?"

Under the combined pressure of radical feminism, cultural studies, multiculturalism, queer theory, postcoloniality, Bakhtinian dialogism, Derridean deconstruction, cognitive theory, neo-formalism,
post-analytic philosophy, and Baudrillardian postmodernism, film
theory as a project of methodological unification is now in eclipse.
But to reject theory *in toto*, as if it were the serpent in the garden of
film analysis, is on one level simply to reject the major intellectual
currents of our epoch. As Jameson puts it, to cast out theory would
be to ignore Nietzsche's "shattering discovery of the aggressivity
that seethed through all the old ethical injunctions," to bypass Freud's
"disarticulation of the conscious subject and its rationalizations,"
and to forget Marx's "flinging all the old individual ethical categories up to a new dialectical and collective level" (Jameson, 1998,
p. 94). But as a result of all these questionings, theory now is a
little less grand, a little more pragmatic, a little less ethnocentric,
masculinist, and heterosexist, and a little less inclined toward overarching systems, drawing on a plurality of theoretical paradigms.
While exciting on one level, the pluralization of film theory also
carries with it the danger of fragmentation. What is necessary, I think,
is for the diverse theories to be more aware of one another, so that
psycho-analytically oriented theorists read cognitive theory, and cognitive theorists read critical race theory, for example. The question is
not one of relativism or mere pluralism, but rather of multiple grids
and knowledges, each of which sheds a specific light on the object
studied. It is not a question of completely embracing the other theoretical perspective, but rather of acknowledging it, taking it into
account, being ready to be challenged by it.

Notes

The Antecedents of Film Theory

1   I place "West" in quotation marks here because classical Greece is often constructed as the point of origin of an idealized West, when in fact classical Greece was an amalgam of African, Semitic, and (what later became known as) European cultures. See Shohat and Stam (1994).
2   For more on Hitchcock as modernist, see my "Hitchcock and Buñuel" in *Hitchcock's Rereleased Films*. For more on the problematic nature of seeing Hollywood as modernism's "other," see Morrison (1998).

Film and Film Theory: The Beginnings

1   See H. Magdoff, *Imperialism: From the Colonial Age to the Present* (New York: Monthly Review Press, 1978), p. 108.
2   See Shohat (1991, p. 42).

Early Silent Film Theory

1   Quoted in Barnouw and Krishnaswamy (1980, p. 5).
2   Quoted in Mora (1982, p. 6).
3   Walter M. Fitch, "The Motion Picture Story Considered as a New Literary Form," *Motion Picture World* (February 19, 1910), p. 248; quoted in Hansen (1991, pp. 80–1).
4   Another issue of *Motion Picture World* (July 10, 1911), entitled "Indians Grieve over Picture Shows," reports on protests by Native American groups from California concerning Hollywood portrayals of them as bloodthirsty warriors when in fact they were peaceful farmers.

331

5 *Cinearte*, Rio de Janeiro (June 18, 1930).
6 This aesthetic stance existed on a continuum with elite attitudes in everday social life. Writer Monteiro Lobato, for example, writing in 1908, expressed repulsion at seeing Cariocas on their way home from work: "How can we fix these people? What terrible problems the poor African negro, in his unconscious vengeance, has created for us here. Perhaps salvation will come from São Paulo and other zones with higher injections of European blood. The Americans saved themselves from miscegenation by creating the barrier of racial prejudice. That barrier exists here as well, but only among certain classes and in certain areas. In Rio it doesn't exist" (Monteiro Lobato, *A Barca da Gleyre*). Together with the endorsement of conventional Aryanist notions of beauty goes a class-conscious insistence on social hierarchy, both of which would tend to exclude Brazilian blacks. (The euphemistic insistence on "good appearance" anticipates the 1950s' use in want ads of phrases like "person of good appearance" as a polite euphemism for "white.")
7 *Cinearte* (December 11, 1929), p. 28.
8 Munsterberg (1970, p. 74). The volume was originally published under the title *The Photoplay: A Psychological Study* (New York: D. Appleton, 1916).
9 Language-related citations from Canudo and Delluc can be found in a number of classical anthologies: Lapierre (1946), L'Herbier (1946), and L'Herminier (1960).
10 See Bálázs (1930), ideas later taken up in Bálázs (1972).
11 Louis Feuillade, "L'Art du vrai," *Ciné-journal* (April 22, 1911); quoted in Jeancolas (1995, p. 23).

The Essence of Cinema

1 Jean Epstein, "De Quelques conditions de la photogenie," in *Cinea-cinne-pour-tous* (August 15, 1924); included in Abel (1988, Vol. I, p. 314).
2 Riccioto Canudo, *L'Usine aux aimages* (Paris: Etienne Chiron, 1926); in Abel (1988, p. 59).
3 Quoted in Jeancolas (1995, p. 31).
4 Louis Delluc, "La Beaute au cinéma," in *Le Film 73* (August 6, 1917); in Abel (1988, Vol. I, p. 137).
5 Epstein, "Magnification," in Epstein (1977, p. 9).
6 Jean Epstein, "Une Conversation avec Jean Epstein," *L'Ami du peuple* (May 11, 1928), in Annette Michelson's introduction to Vertov (1984, pp. xliv–xlv).
7 Germaine Dulac, "L'Essence du cinéma: l'idee visuelle," *Cahiers du moi* (1925) in Abel (1988, Vol. I, p. 331).
8 Jean Epstein, quoted in Kracauer (1997, p. 178).
9 Ibid., p. 179.

Notes

The Soviet Montage-Theorists

1   See Eisenstein (1957). For an extended analysis of Eisenstein's theories of montage, see Aumont (1987). See also Xavier (1983, pp. 175–7).
2   See Michelson (1972, p. 66). See also Michelson's introduction to Vertov (1984).

Russian Formalism and the Bakhtin School

1   Roman Jakobson, "The Dominant," in Ladislav Matejka and Krystyna Pomorska (eds), *Readings in Russian Poetics: Formalist and Structuralist Views* (Cambridge, MA, and London: MIT Press, 1971), pp. 105–10.

The Historical Avant-Gardes

1   Michael Newman, "Postmodernism," in Lisa Spiganesi (ed.), *Postmodernism: ICA Documents* (London: Free Association Books, 1989).
2   Linda Williams has argued that the 1920s writings of the Surrealists bifurcate into two lines of thinking, a "naive" line represented by writers like Desnos, for whom film could literally transcribe the content of dreams, and a more sophisticated line, for example that of Artaud, for whom film could constructively approximate the *forms* of unconscious desire. See Williams (1984).
3   Robert Desnos, "Le Reve t le cinéma," *Paris-Journal* (April 27, 1923), in Abel (1988, p. 283).
4   Antonin Artaud, "Sorcellerie et cinéma," quoted in Virmaux and Virmaux (1976, p. 28).

The Debate after Sound

1   See Dulac's "The Expressive Techniques of the Cinema," in Abel (1988, Vol. I, p. 305).
2   René Clair, "Talkie versus Talkie," in Abel (1988, Vol. II, p. 39).
3   Gertrud Koch, "Rudolf Arnheim: the Materialist of Aesthetic Illusion," in *New German Critique*, No. 51 (Fall 1990).
4   See Gertrud Koch, "Bela Bálázs: The Physiognomy of Things," *New German Critique*, No. 40, Winter 1987.

The Frankfurt School

1   Quoted in Anton Kaes, "The Debate about Cinema: Charting a Controversy (1909–1929)," *New German Critique*.

Notes

2　Noël Carroll points out that Benjamin's emphases on "distraction" on the one hand, and "shock" on the other, "appear to pull in opposite directions" (lazy focus and concentration) but also admits that Benjamin might be thinking of these mental postures as occurring "sequentially." See Carroll (1998). Like Adorno, but in analytical language, Carroll argues that Benjamin's radical claims for the cinema are overly optimistic and technologically deterministic.

The Phenomenology of Realism

1　See Thomas Elsaesser, "Cinema: The Irresponsible Signifier or 'The Gamble with History': Film Theory or Cinema Theory," *New German Critique.*
2　Peter Wollen, "Introduction to *Citizen Kane," Film Reader,* No. 1 (1975).
3　See Hansen's introduction to Kracauer (1997), p. xxv.
4　Ibid., p. 304.
5　Maurice Merleau-Ponty, "The Film and the New Psychology," pp. 58–9.

The Cult of the Auteur

1　Astruc's essay was first published in *Ecran Français,* No. 144, 1948, and is included in Peter Graham (ed.), *The New Wave* (London: Secker and Warburg, 1969), pp. 17–23.

Third World Film and Theory

1　See Fernando Solanas and Octavio Getino, "Towards a Third Cinema," in Nichols (1985).

The Advent of Structuralism

1　Much of the material in this section draws and slightly elaborates on materials from *New Vocabularies in Film Semiotics: Structuralism, Poststructuralism, and Beyond* (London: Routledge, 1992).

The Question of Film Language

1　See "Francesco Casetti and Italian Film Semiotics," *Cinema Journal,* 30, No. 2 (Winter 1991).

Notes

Cinematic Specificity Revisited

1   See Metz (1974a). An egregiously inept translation turned Metz's somewhat arid text into an unreadable monstrosity. Two of Metz's key terms – *langue* and *langage* – were more or less systematically mistranslated into their opposites, thus transforming much of the book into nonsense.

2   See David Bordwell, "Textual Analysis, etc," *Enclitic* (Fall 1981/ Spring 1982).

Interrogating Authorship and Genre

1   Godard, to take a more upscale example, was notoriously fond of oxymoronic genre collages: *Breathless* as an "existentialist gangster film," *A Woman is a Woman* as a "cinema verité musical," and *Numéro Deux* as "feminist pornography." Most films participate in various genres.

2   Preston Sturges's *Sullivan's Travels* forms a kind of generic palimpsest which includes (1) social consciousness film like *Grapes of Wrath*; (2) picaresque; (3) satire; (4) the Hollywood film about Hollywood; (5) Sennett-style slapstick; (6) the screwball comedy; (7) the depression documentary *à la* Pare Lorentz; (8) chain-gang films like *I Am a Fugitive from a Chain Gang*; (9) the all-black musical like *Hallelujah!*; and (9) the animated cartoon (see Stam, 1992).

3   Woody Allen's films, especially those in which he appears, are often mistaken for self-indicting autobiography, the critical equivalent of equating Shakespeare with Iago.

1968 and the Leftist Turn

1   Quoted in Thomas Levin, "The Cinema of Guy Debord," in Elizabeth Sussman (ed.), *On the Passage of a Few People through a Rather Brief Moment in Time: The Situationist International* (Cambridge, MA: MIT Press, 1989), p. 95.

2   Daniel Dayan, "The Tutor Code of Classical Cinema," *Film Quarterly*, Vol. 28, No. 1 (Fall 1974); reprinted in Gerald Mast et al. (eds), *Film Theory and Criticism* (New York: Oxford University Press, 1992).

3   William Rothman, "Against the System of Suture," *Film Quarterly*, Vol. 29, No. 1 (Fall 1975); reprinted in Mast et al. (eds), *Film Theory and Criticism* (New York: Oxford University Press, 1992).

The Presence of Brecht

1   See Baudry (1967).

2   See "Entretien avec Christian Metz," *Ça* 7/8 (May 1975), p. 23.

Notes

The Politics of Reflexivity

1   This reflexivity need not be literal. According to Annette Michelson (in Sitney, 1970) the films of Michael Snow and Hollis Frampton promote an epistemological reflexivity, simultaneously modeling the processes of cinema and those of cognition itself.

The Search for Alternative Aesthetics

1   Antonin Artaud, *Le Theatre et son double* (Paris: Gallimard, 1964), pp. 211–12.
2   Patricia Mellenkamp, "Jokes and their Relationships to the Marx Brothers," in Heath and Mellenkamp (1983).

The Feminist Intervention

1   Claire Johnston, "Women's Cinema as Counter Cinema," in Nichols (1985).
2   Teresa de Lauretis, "Rethinking Women's Cinema: Aesthetic and Feminist Theory," in Erens (1990).
3   See Shohat (1991).
4   Tania Modleski, "Femininity and Mas(s)querade, a Feminist Approach to Mass-Culture," in MacCabe (1986).

The Poststructuralist Mutation

1   See, for example, Julia Kristeva, "Word, Dialogue, and Novel," in Kristeva (1980). For more on the relation between Bakhtin and poststructuralism, see Robert Young, "Back to Bakhtin," *Cultural Critique*, No. 2 (Winter 1985–6); and Allon White, "The Struggle over Bakhtin: Fraternal Reply to Robert Young," *Cultural Critique*, No. 8 (Winter 1987–8).

Textual Analysis

1   Quoted in Pechey (1986), pp. 113–14. Shklovsky made the comparison both in *Rozanov* (1921) and in *Theory of Prose* (1925).
2   See "Discourse in the Novel," in Bakhtin (1981), p. 292.
3   For a provocative and informative analysis of these institutional factors in the rise of cinema studies, see Bordwell (1989).

Notes

Interpretation and its Discontents

1   One wonders if other acronymic coalitions, for example VBGH (Volosinov/ Bakhtin/Gramsci/Hall) or MBJZ (Mulvey/Jessica Benjamin/Jameson/ Žižek), might have been more acceptable.

2   For a critique of *Making Meaning* from a different perspective, see Berys Gaut, "Making Sense of Films: Neoformalism and its Limits," in *Forum for Modern Language Studies*, XXXI: I (1995). See also Malcolm Turvey, "Seeing Theory," in Allen and Smith (1997).

From Text to Intertext

1   See Arlindo Castro, *Films About Television*, Ph.D. dissertation, Cinema Studies, New York University (1992).

2   Genette's highly suggestive categories tempt one to coin additional terms within the same paradigm. One might speak of "celebrity intertextuality," i.e. filmic situations where the presence of a film or television star or celebrity intellectual evokes a genre or cultural milieu (Marshall McLuhan in *Annie Hall*, or the gallery of high-profile names in Altman's *The Player* or Allen's *Celebrity*). "Genetic intertextuality" would evoke the process by which the appearance of the sons and daughters of well-known actors and actresses – Jamie Lee Curtis, Liza Minnelli, Melanie Griffith – evokes the memory of their famous parents. "Intratextuality" would refer to the process by which films refer to themselves through mirroring, microcosmic, and mise-en-abyme structures, while "auto-citation" would refer to an author's self-quotation, as when Vincent Minnelli cites his own *The Bad and the Beautiful* within *Two Weeks in Another Town*. "Mendacious intertextuality" would evoke those texts, e.g. the pseudo-newsreels of *Zelig* or the ersatz Nazi films in *Kiss of the Spider Woman*, which invent a pseudo-intertextual reference.

The Amplification of Sound

1   For a critique of these claims, see Noël Carroll, "Cracks in the Acoustic Mirror," in Carroll (1996).

The Coming Out of Queer Theory

1   See Julia Erhart, "She Must Be Theorizing Things: Fifteen Years of Lesbian Criticism, 1981–1996," in Gabrielle Griffin and Sonya Andermahr (eds), *Straight Studies Modified: Lesbian Interventions in the Academy* (London: Cassell, 1997).

Notes

Multiculturalism, Race, and Representation

1   For Roger Kimball multiculturalism implies "an attack on the … idea that, despite our many differences, we hold in common an intellectual, artistic, and moral legacy, descending largely from the Greeks and the Bible [which] preserves us from chaos and barbarism. And it is precisely this legacy that the multiculturalist wishes to dispense with." See Roger Kimball, *Tenured Radicals: How Politics has Corrupted Higher Education* (New York: HarperCollins, 1990), postscript.

2   The phrase "the West and the Rest," to the best of our knowledge, goes back to Chinweizu's *The West and the Rest of Us: White Predators, Black Slaves and the African Elite* (New York: Random House, 1975). It is also used in Stuart Hall and Bram Gieben (eds), *Formations of Modernity* (Cambridge: Polity Press, 1992).

3   Many of these ideas are developed in greater depth in Shohat and Stam (1994).

4   See Y. N. Bly, *The Anti-Social Contract* (Atlanta: Clarity Press, 1989).

5   Samir Amin speaks of economic polycentrism in similar terms in his book *Delinking: Towards a Polycentric World* (London: Zed Books, 1985).

6   For a similar view, see Joan Scott, "Multiculturalism and the Politics of Identity," *October* 61 (Summer 1992), and Stuart Hall, "Minimal Selves," in *Identity: The Real Me* (London: ICA, 1987).

7   Steve Neale (1979–80) points out that stereotypes are judged simultaneously in relation to an empirical "real" (accuracy) and an ideological "ideal" (positive image).

8   Shohat and Stam (1994) develops these ideas at much greater length.

9   Mercer and Julien (1988), in a similar spirit, distinguish between "representation as a practice of depicting" and "representation as a practice of delegation."

Third Cinema Revisited

1   For more on "post-third-worldism" see Shohat and Stam (1994) and Ella Shohat, "Post-Third Worldist Culture: Gender, Nation and the Cinema," in Jacquie Alexander and Chandra Mohanty (eds), *Feminist Genealogies, Colonial Legacies, Democratic Futures* (London: Routledge, 1996).

2   From Anthony Guneratne's proposal for a book entitled *Rethinking Third World Cinema* (given me by the author).

3   See, for example, David McDougall, "Beyond Observational Cinema," in Paul Hockings (ed.), *Principles of Visual Anthropology* (The Hague, 1975).

4   Faye Ginsburg, "Aboriginal Media and the Australian Imaginary," *Public Culture*, Vol. 5, No. 3 (Spring 1993).

Notes

5 Indigenous media have remained largely invisible to the First World public except for occasional festivals (for example, the Native American Film and Video Festivals held regularly in San Francisco and New York City, or the Latin American Film Festival of Indigenous Peoples held in Mexico City and Rio de Janeiro).

6 Faye Ginsburg, "Indigenous Media: Faustian Contract or Global Village?," *Cultural Anthropology*, Vol. 6, No. 1 (1991), p. 94.

7 Ibid.

8 For a critical view of the Kayapo project, see Rachel Moore, "Marketing Alterity," *Visual Anthropology Review*, Vol. 8, No. 2 (Fall 1992); and James C. Faris, "Anthropological Transparency: Film, Representation and Politics," in Peter Ian Crawford and David Turton (eds), *Film as Ethnography* (Manchester: Manchester University Press, 1992). For an answer by Turner to Faris, see "Defiant Images: The Kayapo Appropriation of Video," Forman Lecture, RAI Festival of Film and Video in Manchester 1992, forthcoming in *Anthropology Today*.

9 Appadurai (1990).

10 Jameson (1986). For an excellent critique of the Jameson essay, see Ahmad (1987).

11 Behroze Gandhy and Rosie Thomas make this point in their essay "Three Indian Film Stars," in Gledhill (1991).

The Social Valence of Mass-Culture

1 Kluge develops these ideas in *Die Patriotin* (Frankfurt: Zweitausendeins, 1979). Hansen (1991) expands on the implications of Kluge's ideas. See also the special issues of *October* (No. 46, Fall 1988) and *New German Critique* (No. 49, Winter 1990).

2 Horace M. Newcombe deploys a Bakhtinian framework to speak of the "heteroglot environment" and "dialogic nature of the [televisual] medium," arguing that television is in many ways more "novelistic" than the novel. "From the collaborative writing process common in film and television, to the negotiation between writer and producer, producer and network, network and internal censor, dialogue is the defining element in the creation of television content." See Horace M. Newcombe, "On the Dialogic Aspects of Mass Communication" (1984), and Horace M. Newcombe and Paul M. Hirsch, "Television as a Cultural Forum: Implications for Research," *Quarterly Review of Film Studies* (Summer 1983).

3 I develop these ideas in more detail in Stam (1989).

Notes

Post-Cinema: Digital Theory and the New Media

1   In a recent essay in *Cinema Journal* Robert Baird explains the success of films like *Jurassic Park* by its "thoughtful anticipation of human cognition and emotion, and the cognitive universality of its threat-scene narrative." While Baird acknowledges the role of "big money," he emphasizes the films' appeal to hard-wired universal cognitive schemata. While suggestive, this approach has the downside of naturalizing the Hollywood domination of world cinema. While it admittedly takes in-finitely more talent to produce a *Jurassic Park* than to make a hamburger, talk of universal schemata is on another level like saying that the "Big Mac corresponds to hard-wired culinary schemata." It doesn't explain why middle-class Middle Easterns will come to pay more for Big Macs when they have subtly seasoned kebab at home. The notion of "contingent universals," on this level, replays the old notion of Europe (in the broad sense) as "universal" and the "rest of the world" as "local."

2   G. L. Ulmer, "Grammatology (in the Stacks) of Hypermedia," in Truman (ed.), *Literary Online*, pp. 139–64.

3   For an excellent critique of the ethnocentrism of cyberdiscourse, see Gerald Lombardi's Ph.D. dissertation, *Computer Networks, Social Networks and the Future of Brazil*, Dept. of Anthropology, NYU (May 1999).

Select Bibliography

Listed here are works either cited or recommended. For a more comprehensive bibliography, see Toby Miller and Robert Stam (eds), *Film and Theory* (Oxford: Blackwell Publishers, 1999).

Abel, Richard 1988. *French Film: Theory and Criticism 1907–1939*, 2 vols. Princeton: Princeton University Press.
— (ed.) 1996. *Silent Film*. New Brunswick, NJ: Rutgers University Press.
Adams, Parveen 1996. *The Emptiness of the Image: Psychoanalysis and Sexual Differences*. London: Routledge.
Adams, Parveen and Elizabeth Cowie (eds) 1990. *The Woman in Question*. Cambridge, MA: MIT Press.
Adorno, T. W. 1978. *Minima Moralia: Reflections From a Damaged Life*. Trans. E. F. Jeph. London: Verso.
Adorno, T. W. and Hanns Eisler 1969. *Composing for the Films*. New York: Oxford University Press.
Adorno, T. W. and Max Horkheimer 1997. *The Dialectic of Enlightenment*. Trans. John Cummings. New York: Verso.
Affron, Charles 1982. *Cinema and Sentiment*. Chicago: University of Chicago Press.
Ahmad, Aijaz 1987. "Jameson's Rhetoric of Otherness and the National Allegory," *Social Text* 17 (Fall).
Alea, Tomás Gutiérrez 1982. *Dialectica Del Espectador*. Havana: Ediciones Union.
Allen, Richard 1989. *Representation, Meaning, and Experience in the Cinema: A Critical Study of Contemporary Film Theory*. Ph.D. Dissertation, University of California, Los Angeles.
— 1993. "Representation, Illusion, and the Cinema," *Cinema Journal* No. 32, Vol. 2 (Winter).
— 1995. *Projecting Illusion: Film Spectatorship and the Impression of Reality*. New York: Cambridge University Press.

Select Bibliography

Allen, Richard and Murray Smith (eds) 1997. *Film Theory and Philosophy*. Oxford: Clarendon Press.

Allen, Robert C. and Douglas Gomery 1985. *Film History: Theory and Practice*. New York: Alfred A. Knopf.

Alternative Museum of New York 1989. *Prisoners of Image: Ethnic and Gender Stereotypes*. New York: The Museum.

Althusser, Louis 1969. *For Marx*. Trans. Ben Brewster. New York: Pantheon Books.

Althusser, Louis and Balibar 1979. *Reading Capital*. Trans. Ben Brewster. London: Verso.

Altman, Rick (ed.) 1981. *Genre: The Musical*. London: Routledge and Kegan Paul.

— 1984, "A Semantic/Syntactic Approach to Film Genre," *Cinema Journal*. Vol. 23, No. 3.

— 1987. *The American Film Musical*. Bloomington: Indiana University Press.

— (ed.) 1992. *Sound Theory, Sound Practice*. New York: Routledge.

Anderson, Benedict 1991. *Imagined Communities: Reflexions on the Origins and Spread of Nationalism*. 2nd edition. London: Verso.

Anderson, Perry 1998. *The Origins of Postmodernity*. New York: Verso.

Andrew, Dudley 1976. *The Major Film Theories*. New York: Oxford University Press.

— 1978a. "The Neglected Tradition of Phenomenology in Film," *Wide Angle* Vol. 2, No. 2.

— 1978b. *André Bazin*. New York: Oxford University Press.

— 1984. *Concepts in Film Theory*. New York: Oxford University Press.

Ang, Ien 1985. *Watching "Dallas": Soap Opera and the Melodramatic Imagination*. Trans. Della Couling. London: Methuen.

— 1996. *Living Room Wars: Rethinking Media Audiences for a Postmodern World*. London: Routledge.

Appadurai, Arjun 1990. "Disjunction and Difference in the Global Cultural Economy," *Public Culture* Vol. 2, No. 2 (Spring).

Aristarco, Guido 1951. *Storia delle Theoriche del Film*. Turin: Eimaudi.

Armes, Roy 1974. *Film and Reality: An Historical Survey*. Harmondsworth: Penguin.

— 1987. *Third World Filmmaking and the West*. Berkeley: University of California Press.

Armstrong, Dan 1989. "Wiseman's Realm of Transgression: *Titicut Follies*, the Symbolic Father and the Spectacle of Confinement," *Cinema Journal* Vol. 29, No. 1 (Fall).

Arnheim, Rudolf 1933 [1958]. *Film*. Reprinted as *Film as Art*. London: Faber.

— 1997. *Film Essays and Criticism*. Trans. Brenda Benthien. Madison: University of Wisconsin Press.

Astruc, Alexandre 1948. "Naissance d'une novelle avant-garde: la camera-stylo,"

Ecran Français, No. 144.

Auerbach, Erich 1953. *Mimesis: The Representation of Reality in Western Literature*. Trans. Willard R. Trask. Princeton: Princeton University Press.

Aumont, Jacques 1987. *Montage Eisenstein*. Trans. Lee Hildreth, Constance Penley, and Andrew Ross. Bloomington: Indiana University Press.

— 1997. *The Image*. Trans. Claire Pajackowska. London: British Film Institute.

Aumont, Jacques and J. L. Leutrat 1980. *Théorie du film*. Paris: Albatross.

Aumont, Jacques and Michel Marie 1989a. *L'Analyse des films*. Paris: Nathan-Université.

— 1989. *L'Oeil interminable*. Paris: Seguier.

Aumont, Jacques, Andre Gaudreault, and Michel Marie 1989. *Histoire du cinéma: nouvelles approaches*. Paris: Publications de la Sorbonne.

Aumont, Jacques, Alain Bergala, Michel Marie, and Marc Vernet 1983. *Esthetique du film*. Paris: Fernand Nathan.

Austin, Bruce A. 1989. *Immediate Seating: A Look at Movie Audiences*. Belmont: Wadsworth.

Bad Object-Choices 1991. *How Do I Look? Queer Film and Video*. Seattle: Bay Press.

Bahri, Deepika and Marya Vasudeva 1996. *Between the Lines: South Asians and Postcoloniality*. Philadelphia: Temple University Press.

Bailble, Claude, Michel Marie, and Marie-Claire Ropars 1974. *Muriel, histoire d'une recherche*. Paris: Galilee.

Bailey, R. W., L. Matejka, and P. Steiner (eds) 1978. *The Sign: Semiotics Around the World*. Ann Arbor: Michigan Slavic Publications.

Bakari, Imruh and Mbye Cham (eds) 1996. *Black Frames: African Experiences of Cinema*. London: British Film Institute.

Baker Jr., Houston, Manthia Diawara, and Ruth H. Lindeborg (eds) 1996. *Black British Cultural Studies: A Reader*. Chicago: University of Chicago Press.

Bakhtin, Mikhail 1981. *The Dialogical Imagination*. Trans. Michael Holquist, ed. Caryl Emerson and Michael Holquist. Austin: University of Texas Press.

— 1984. *Rabelais and His World*. Trans. Helense Iswolsky. Bloomington: Indiana.

— 1986. *Speech Genres and other Late Essays*. Trans. Vern W. McGee, ed. Caryl Emerson and Michael Holquist. Austin: University of Texas Press.

Bakhtin, Mikhail and P. M. Medvedev 1985. *The Formal Method in Literary Scholarship*. Trans. Albert J. Wehrle. Cambridge, MA: Harvard University Press.

Bal, Mieke 1985. *Narratology: Introduction to the Theory of Narrative*. Toronto: University of Toronto Press.

Bálász, Bela 1930. *Der Geist des Films*. Frankfurt: Makol.

— 1972. *Theory of the Film: Character and Growth of a New Art*. Trans. Edith Bone. New York: Arno Press.

Barnouw, Erik and S. Krishnaswamy 1980. *Indian Film*. New York: Oxford University Press.

Barsam, Richard Meran (ed.) 1976. *Nonfiction Film Theory and Criticism*. New York: E. P. Dutton.
— 1992. *Nonfiction Film: A Critical History*. Revd. edn. Bloomington: Indiana University Press.
Barthes, Roland 1967. *Elements of Semiology*. Trans. Annette Lavers and Colin Smith. New York: Hill & Wang.
— 1972. *Mythologies*. Trans. Annette Lavers. New York: Hill & Wang.
— 1974. *S/Z*. New York: Hill & Wang.
— 1975. *The Pleasure of the Text*. Trans. Richard Miller. New York: Hill & Wang.
— 1977. *Image/Music/Text*. Trans. Stephen Heath. New York: Hill & Wang.
— 1980. *Camera Lucida*. Hill & Wang.
Bataille, Gretchen M. and Charles L. P. Silet (eds) 1980. *The Pretend Indians: Image of Native Americans in the Movies*. Ames: Iowa State University Press.
Baudrillard, Jean 1975. *The Mirror of Production*. St Louis: Telos Press.
— 1983. *Simulations*. Trans. Paul Foss, Paul Patton, and Phillip Beitchman. New York: Semiotext(e).
— 1988. *The Ecstasy of Communication*. Trans. Bernard Schutze and Caroline Schutze. New York: Semiotext(e).
— 1991a. "The Reality Gulf," *Guardian* January 11.
— 1991b. "La Guerre du Golfe n'a pas eu lieu," *Libération* March 29.
Baudry, Jean-Louis 1967. "Écriture/Fiction/Ideologie," *Tel Quel* 31 (Autumn). Trans. Diana Matias, *Afterimage* 5 (Spring 1974).
— 1978. *L'Effet cinéma*. Paris: Albatros.
Bazin, André 1967. *What is Cinema?* 2 vols. Trans. and ed. Hugh Gray. Berkeley: University of California Press.
Beauvoir, Simone de 1952. *The Second Sex*. Trans. H. M. Parshley. New York: Knopf.
Beckmann, Peter 1974. *Formale und Funktionale Film- und Fernsehanalyse*. Dissertation, Stuttgart.
Bellour, Raymond 1979. *L'Analyse du film*. Paris: Albatross.
— (ed.) 1980. *Le Cinéma américain: analyses de films*. 2 vols. Paris: Flammarion.
Belton, John (ed.) 1995. *Movies and Mass Culture*. New Brunswick, NJ: Rutgers University Press.
Benjamin, Walter 1968. *Illuminations*. Trans. Harry Zohn. New York: Harcourt, Brace & World.
— 1973. *Understanding Brecht*. Trans. A. Bostock. London: New Left Books.
Bennett, Tony, Susan Boyd-Bowman, Colin Mercer, and Janet Woolcot (eds) 1981. *Popular Television and Film*. London: British Film Publishing and Open University Press.
Berenstein, Rhona Joella 1995. *Attack of the Leading Ladies: Gender, Sexuality, and Spectatorship in Classic Horror Cinema*. New York: Columbia University Press.
Bernardet, Jean-Claude 1994. *O Autor No Cinema*. São Paulo: Editora Brasiliense.

344

Select Bibliography

Bernardi, Daniel (ed.) 1996a. *The Birth of Whiteness: Race and the Emergence of US Cinema*. New Brunswick, NJ: Rutgers University Press.

— (ed.) 1996b. *Looking at Film History in "Black and White"*. New Brunswick, NJ: Rutgers University Press.

Bernstein, Matthew and Gaylyn Studlar (eds) 1996. *Visions of the East: Orientalism in Film*. New Brunswick, NJ: Rutgers University Press.

Best, Steven and Douglas Kellner 1991. *Postmodern Theory: Critical Interrogations*. New York: Guilford Press.

Bettetini, Gianfranco 1968 [1973]. *The Language and Technique of the Film*. The Hague: Mouton.

— 1971. *L'indice del realismo*. Milan: Bompiani.

— 1975. *Produzione del senso e messa in scena*. Milan: Bompiani.

— 1984. *La Conversazione Audiovisiva*. Milan: Bompiani.

Betton, Gerard 1987. *Esthetique du cinéma*. Paris: Presses Universitaires du France.

Bobo, Jacqueline 1995. *Black Women as Cultural Readers*. New York: Columbia University Press.

Bogle, Donald 1989. *Toms, Coons, Mulattos, Mammies, and Bucks: An Interpretive History of Blacks in American Films*. New York: Continuum.

Bordwell, David 1985. *Narration in the Fiction Film*. Madison: University of Wisconsin Press.

— 1989. *Making Meaning: Inference and Rhetoric in the Interpretation of Cinema*. Cambridge, MA: Harvard University Press.

— 1993. *The Cinema of Eisenstein*. Cambridge, MA: Harvard University Press.

— 1997. *On the History of Film Style*. Cambridge, MA: Harvard University Press.

Bordwell, David and Noël Carroll (eds) 1996. *Post-Theory: Reconstructing Film Studies*. Madison: University of Wisconsin Press.

Bordwell, David and Kristin Thompson 1996. *Film Art: An Introduction*. 5th edition. New York: McGraw-Hill.

Bordwell, David, Janet Staiger, and Kristin Thompson 1985. *The Classical Hollywood Cinema: Film Style and Mode of Production to 1960*. New York: Columbia University Press.

Bourdieu, Pierre 1998. *On Television*. New York: New Press.

Brakhage, Stan 1963. *Metaphors on Vision*. New York: Film Culture.

Branigan, Edward 1984. *Point of View in the Cinema: A Theory of Narration and Subjectivity in Classical Film*. The Hague: Mouton.

— 1992. *Narrative Comprehension and Film*. New York: Routledge.

Bratton, Jacky, Jim Cook, and Christine Gledhill (eds) 1994. *Melodrama: Stage, Picture, Screen*. London: British Film Institute.

Braudy, Leo 1976. *The World in a Frame*. New York: Anchor Press.

Braudy, Leo and Gerald Mast (eds) 1999. *Film Theory and Criticism*. 5th edition. New York: Oxford University Press.

Brecht, Bertolt 1964. *Brecht on Theatre*. New York: Hill & Wang.

345

Select Bibliography

Brennan, Teresa and Martin Jay (eds) 1996. *Vision in Context: Historical and Contemporary Perspectives on Sight.* New York: Routledge.

Brooker, Peter and Will Brooker (eds) 1997. *Postmodern After-Images: A Reader in Film, Television and Video.* London: Arnold.

Brooks, Virginia 1984. "Film, Perception, and Cognitive Psychology." *Millennium Film Journal* 14.

Brown, Royal S. 1994. *Overtones and Undertones: Reading Film Music.* Berkeley: University of California Press.

Browne, Nick 1982. *The Rhetoric of Film Narration.* Ann Arbor: UMI.

— (ed.) 1990. *Cahiers du Cinéma 1969–1972: The Politics of Representation.* Cambridge, MA: Harvard University Press.

— (ed.) 1997. *Refiguring American Film Genres: History and Theory.* Berkeley: University of California Press.

Brunette, Peter and David Wills 1989. *Screen/Play: Derrida and Film Theory.* Princeton: Princeton University Press.

Brunsdon, Charlotte and David Morley 1978. *Everyday Television: "Nationwide".* London: British Film Institute.

Bryson, Norman, Michael Ann Holly, and Keith Moxey 1994. *Visual Culture: Images and Interpretations.* Hanover: Wesleyan University Press.

Buckland, Warren (ed.) 1995. *The Film Spectator: From Sign to Mind.* Amsterdam: Amsterdam University Press.

Bukatman, Scott 1993. *Terminal Identity: The Virtual Subject in Postmodern Science Fiction.* Durham, NC: Duke University Press.

Burch, Noël 1973. *Theory of Film Practice.* Trans. Helen R. Lane. New York: Praeger.

— 1990. *Life to those Shadows.* Trans. and ed. Ben Brewster. Berkeley: University of California Press.

Burch, Noël and Jorge Dana 1974. "Propositions," *Afterimage* No. 5.

Burger, Peter 1984. *Theory of the Avant-Garde.* Trans. Michael Shaw. Minneapolis: University of Minnesota Press.

Burgoyne, Robert A. 1990. *Bertolucci's 1900: A Narrative and Historical Analysis.* Detroit: Wayne State University Press.

Burgoyne, Robert A., Sandy Flitterman-Lewis, and Robert Stam 1992. *New Vocabularies in Film Semiotics: Structuralism, Post-Structuralism and Beyond.* London: Routledge.

Burton, Julianne 1985. "Marginal Cinemas." *Screen* Vol. 26, Nos. 3–4 (May–August).

— (ed.) 1990. *The Social Documentary in Latin America.* Pittsburgh: University of Pittsburgh Press.

Butler, Jeremy G. (ed.) 1995. *Star Texts: Image and Performance in Film and Television.* Detroit: Wayne State University Press.

Butler, Judith P. 1990. *Gender Trouble: Feminism and the Subversion of Identity.* New York: Routledge.

Select Bibliography

Caldwell, John Thornton 1994. *Televisuality: Style, Crisis and Authority in American Television*. New Brunswick, NJ: Rutgers University Press.

Carroll, John M. 1980. *Toward a Structural Psychology of Cinema*. The Hague: Mouton.

Carroll, Noël 1982. "The Future of an Allusion: Hollywood in the Seventies and (Beyond)." *October* Vol. XX (Spring).

— 1988a. *Mystifying Movies: Fads and Fallacies in Contemporary Film Theory*. New York: Columbia University Press.

— 1988b. *Philosophical Problems of Film Theory*. Princeton: Princeton University Press.

— 1996. *Theorizing the Moving Image*. Cambridge: Cambridge University Press.

— 1998. *A Philosophy of Mass Art*. Oxford: Clarendon Press.

Carson, Diane, Linda Dittmar, and Janice R. Welsh (eds) 1994. *Multiple Voices in Feminist Film Criticism*. Minneapolis: University of Minnesota Press.

Carter, Angela 1978. *The Sadeian Woman and the Ideology of Pornography*. New York: Harper & Row.

Casebier, Allan 1991. *Film and Phenomenology: Toward a Realist Theory of Cinematic Representation*. Cambridge: Cambridge University Press.

Casetti, Francesco 1977. *Semiotica*. Milan: Edizione Academia.

— 1986. *Dentro lo Sguardo, il Filme e il suo Spettatore*. Rome: Bompiani.

— 1990. *D'un regard l'autre*. Lyon: Presses Universitaires de Lyon.

— 1993. *Teorie del cinema: (1945–1990)*. Milan: Bompiani. Published in French as *Les Théories du Cinema depius 1945* (Paris: Nathan, 1999).

Caughie, John (ed.) 1981. *Theories of Authorship: A Reader*. London: Routledge and Kegan Paul.

Cavell, Stanley 1971. *The World Viewed*. Cambridge, MA: Harvard University Press.

— 1981. *Pursuits of Happiness*. Cambridge, MA: Harvard University Press.

Cesaire, Aimé 1972. *Discourse on Colonialism*. Trans. Joan Pinkham. New York: MR.

Cham, Mbye B. and Claire Andrade-Watkins (eds) 1988. *Critical Perspectives on Black Independent Cinema*. Cambridge, MA: MIT Press.

Chanan, Michael (ed.) 1983. *Twenty-Five Years of the New Latin American Cinema*. London: British Film Institute.

Chateau, Dominique 1986. *Le Cinema comme langage*. Paris. AISS IASPA.

Chateau, Dominique and François Jost 1979. *Nouveau cinéma, nouvelle sémiologie*. Paris: Union Generale d'Editions.

Chateau, Dominique, André Gardies, and François Jost 1981. *Cinémas de la modernité: films, théories*. Paris: Klincksieck.

Chatman, Seymour 1978. *Story and Discourse: Narrative Structure in Fiction and Film*. Ithaca, NY: Cornell University Press.

Chion, Michel 1982. *La Voix au cinéma*. Paris: Cahiers du Cinéma/Editions de l'Etoile.

— 1985. *Le Son au cinéma*. Paris: Cahiers du Cinéma/Editions de l'Etoile.

— 1988. *La Toile trouée*. Paris: Cahiers du Cinéma/Editions de l'Etoile.

— 1994. *Audio-Vision: Sound on Screen*. Trans. and ed. Claudia Gorbman. New York: Columbia University Press.

Chow, Rey 1995. *Primitive Passions: Visuality, Sexuality, Ethnography, and Contemporary Chinese Cinema*. New York: Columbia University Press.

Church, Gibson, Pamela Gibson, and Roma Gibson (eds) 1993. *Dirty Looks: Women, Pornography, Power*. London: British Film Institute.

Churchill, Ward 1992. *Fantasies of the Master Race: Literature, Cinema and the Colonization of American Indians*. Ed. M. Annette Jaimes. Monroe: Common Courage Press.

Clerc, Jeanne-Marie 1993. *Littérature et cinéma*. Paris: Editions Nathan.

Clover, Carol J. 1992. *Men, Women, and Chain Saws: Gender in the Modern Horror Film*. Princeton: Princeton University Press.

Cohan, Steve and Ina Rae Hark (eds) 1992. *Screening the Male: Exploring Masculinities in the Hollywood Cinema*. New York: Routledge.

Cohen-Seat, Gilbert 1946. *Essai sur les principes d'une philosophie du cinéma*. Paris: PUF.

Colin, Michel 1985. *Language, Film, Discourse: prolégomènes à une sémiologie générative du film*. Paris: Klincksieck.

Collet, Jean, Michel Marie, Daniel Percheron, Jean-Paul Simon, and Marc Vernet 1975. *Lectures du film*. Paris: Albatross.

Collins, Jim 1989. *Uncommon Cultures: Popular Culture and Post-Modernism*. London: Routledge.

Collins, Jim, Hillary Radner, and Ava Preacher Collins (eds) 1993. *Film Theory Goes to the Movies*. New York: Routledge.

Comolli, Jean-Louis and Narboni, Jean 1969. "Cinema/Ideology/Criticism." *Cahiers du cinéma*.

Cook, Pamela 1985. *The Cinema Book*. London: British Film Institute.

— 1996. *Fashioning the Nation: Costume and Identity in British Cinema*. London: British Film Institute.

Cook, Pamela and Philip Dodd (eds) 1993. *Women and Film: A Sight and Sound Reader*. Philadelphia: Temple University Press.

Copjec, Joan 1989. "The Orthopsychic Subject: Film Theory and the Reception of Lacan." *October* 49.

— (ed.) 1993. *Shades of Noir*. New York: Verso.

Cowie, Elizabeth 1997. *Representing the Woman: Cinema and Psychoanalysis*. Minneapolis: University of Minnesota Press.

Crary, Jonathan 1995. *Techniques of the Observer*. Cambridge, MA: MIT Press.

Creed, Barbara 1993. *The Monstrous-Feminine: Film, Feminism, Psychoanalysis*. New York: Routledge.

Creekmur, Corey K. and Alexander Doty (eds) 1995. *Out in Culture: Gay, Lesbian and Queer Essays on Popular Culture*. Durham, NC: Duke University Press.

Select Bibliography

Cripps, Thomas 1979. *Black Film as Genre.* Bloomington: Indiana University Press.

Culler, Jonathan 1975. *Structuralist Poetics: Structuralism, Linguistics and the Study of Literature.* Ithaca, NY: Cornell University Press.

— 1981. *The Pursuit of Signs: Semiotics, Literature, Deconstruction.* Ithaca, NY: Cornell University Press.

Currie, Gregory 1995. *Image and Mind.*

David, Joel 1995. *Fields of Vision: Critical Applications in Recent Philippine Cinema.* Quezon City: Ateneo de Manila University Press.

Debord, Guy 1967. *Society of the Spectacle.* Paris: Éditions Champ Libre.

de Certeau, Michel 1984. *The Practice of Everyday Life.* Trans. Steven Rendall. Berkeley: University of California Press.

de Lauretis, Teresa 1985. *Alice Doesn't: Feminism, Semiotics, Cinema.* Bloomington: Indiana University Press.

— 1989. *Technologies of Gender: Essays on Theory, Film and Fiction.* Bloomington: Indiana University Press.

— 1994. *The Practice of Love: Lesbian Sexuality and Perverse Desire.* Bloomington: Indiana University Press.

de Saussure, Ferdinand 1966. *Course in General Linguistics.* Trans. Wade Baskin. New York: McGraw Hill.

Deleuze, Gilles 1977. *Anti-Oedipus: Capitalism and Schizophrenia.* Trans. Robert Hurley, Mark Seem, and Helen R. Lane. New York: Viking Press.

— 1986. *Cinema I: The Movement-Image.* Trans. Hugh Tomlinson and Barbara Habberjam. London: Athlone Press.

— 1989. *Cinema II: The Time-Image.* Trans. Hugh Tomlinson and Robert Galeta. Minneapolis: University of Minnesota Press.

Dent, Gina (ed.) 1992. *Black Popular Culture.* Seattle: Bay Press.

Denzin, Norman K. 1991. *Images of Postmodern Society: Social Theory and Contemporary Cinema.* London: Sage Publications.

— 1995. *The Cinematic Society: The Voyeur's Gaze.* London: Sage Publications.

Derrida, Jacques 1976. *Of Grammatology.* Trans. Gayatri Chakravorty Spivak. Baltimore: Johns Hopkins University Press.

— 1978. *Writing and Difference.* Trans. Alan Bass. Chicago: University of Chicago Press.

Desnos, Robert 1923. "Le Rêve et le cinéma." *Paris Journal* April 27.

Diawara, Manthia 1992. *African Cinema: Politics and Culture.* Bloomington: Indiana University Press.

— (ed.) 1993. *Black American Cinema.* New York: Routledge.

Dienst, Richard 1994. *Still Life in Real Time: Theory after Television.* Durham, NC: Duke University Press.

Dissanayake, Wimal (ed.) 1988. *Cinema and Cultural Identity: Reflections on Films from Japan, India, and China.* Lanham: University Publications of America.

— (ed.) 1994. *Colonialism and Nationalism in Asian Cinema*. Bloomington: Indiana University Press.

Doane, Mary Ann 1987. *The Desire to Desire: The Woman's Film of the 1940s*. Bloomington: Indiana University Press.

Doane, Mary Ann, Patricia Mellencamp, and Linda Williams (eds) 1984. *Revision: Essays in Feminist Film Criticism*. Frederick, MD: University Publications of America.

Donald, James, Anne Friedberg, and Laura Marcus 1998. *Close-Up 1927–1933: Cinema and Modernism*. Princeton: Princeton University Press.

Dorfman, Ariel 1983. *The Empire's Old Clothes: What the Lone Ranger, Babar, and other Innocent Heroes do to our Minds*. New York: Pantheon.

Dorfman, Ariel and Armand Mattelart 1975. *How to Read Donald Duck: Imperialist Ideology in the Disney Comic*. London: International General.

Doty, Alexander 1993. *Making Things Perfectly Queer: Interpreting Mass Culture*. Minneapolis: University of Minnesota Press.

Downing, John D. H. (ed.) 1987. *Film and Politics in the Third World*. New York: Praeger.

Drummond, Phillip, et al. (eds) 1979. *Film as Film: Formal Experiment in Film 1910–1975*. London: Arts Council of Great Britain.

Duhamel, Georges 1931. *America, the Menace: Scenes from the Life of the Future*. Trans. Charles M. Thompson. Boston: Houghton Mifflin.

Dyer, Richard 1986. *Heavenly Bodies: Film Stars and Society*. New York: St Martin's Press.

— 1990. *Now You See It: Studies on Lesbian and Gay Film*. New York: Routledge.

— 1993. *The Matter of Images: Essays on Representations*. London: Routledge.

— 1997a. *Stars*. 2nd revd. edition. London: British Film Institute.

— 1997b. *White*. London: Routledge.

Eagle, Herbert (ed.) 1981. *Russian Formalist Film Theory*. Ann Arbor: Michigan Slavic Publications.

Eco, Umberto 1975. *A Theory of Semiotics*. Bloomington: Indiana University Press.

— 1979. *The Role of the Reader: Explorations in the Semiotics of Texts*. Bloomington: Indiana University Press.

— 1984. *Semiotics and the Philosophy of Language*. Bloomington: Indiana University Press.

Ehrlich, Victor 1981. *Russian Formalism: History–Doctrine*. London: Yale University Press.

Eikhenbaum, Boris (ed.) 1982. *The Poetics of Cinema*. In *Russian Poetics in Translation*, Vol. 9. Trans. Richard Taylor. Oxford: RPT Publications.

Eisenstein, Sergei 1957. *Film Form and Film Sense*. Cleveland: Merieian.

— 1988. *Selected Works, Vol. 1: Writings 1922–1934*. Trans. and ed. Richard Taylor. Bloomington: Indiana University Press.

— 1992. *Selected Works, Vol. 2: Towards a Theory of Montage*. Trans. Michael Glenny, ed. Richard Taylor and Michael Glenny. Bloomington: Indiana University Press.

Ellis, John 1992. *Visible Fictions: Cinema, Television, Video.* 2nd edition. London: Routledge & Kegan Paul.

Elsaesser, Thomas 1973. "Tales of Sound and Fury: Observation on the Family Melodrama," *Monogram* No. 4.

— 1989. *New German Cinema: A History.* New Brunswick, NJ: Rutgers University Press.

— (ed.) 1990. *Early Cinema Space, Frame, Narrative.* London: British Film Institute.

Enzensberger, Hans Magnus 1974. *The Consciousness Industry: On Literature, Politics and the Media.* New York: Seabury Press.

Epko, Denis 1995. "Towards a Post-Africanism," *Textual Practice* No. 9 (Spring).

Epstein, Jean 1974–5. *Écrits sur le cinéma, 1921–1953: édition chronologique en deux volumes.* Paris: Seghers.

— 1977. "Magnification and Other Writings." *October* No. 3 (Spring).

Erens, Patricia 1979. *Sexual Stratagems: The World of Women in Film.* New York: Horizon.

— 1984. *The Jew in American Cinema.* Bloomington: Indiana University Press.

— (ed.) 1990. *Issues in Feminist Film Criticism.* Bloomington: Indiana University Press.

Fanon, Frantz 1963. *The Wretched of the Earth.* Trans. Constance Farrington. New York: New Grove Press.

Ferro, Marc 1985. *Cinema and History.* Berkeley: University of California Press.

Feuer, Jane 1993. *The Hollywood Musical.* 2nd edition. Bloomington: Indiana University Press.

Fischer, Lucy 1989. *Shot/Countershot: Film Tradition and Women's Cinema.* Princeton: Princeton University Press.

Fiske, John 1987. *Television Culture.* London: Methuen.

— 1989a. *Understanding Popular Culture.* Boston: Unwin Hyman.

— 1989b. *Reading the Popular.* Boston: Unwin Hyman.

Fiske, John and John Hartley 1978. *Reading Television.* London: Methuen.

Flinn, Caryl 1992. *Strains of Utopia: Gender, Nostalgia, and Hollywood Film Music.* Princeton: Princeton University Press.

Flitterman-Lewis, Sandy 1990. *To Desire Differently: Feminism and the French Cinema.* Urbana: University of Illinois Press.

Forgacs, David and Robert Lumley (eds) 1996. *Italian Cultural Studies: An Introduction.* New York: Oxford University Press.

Foster, Hal 1983. *The Anti-Aesthetic: Essays on Postmodern Culture.* Port Townsend: Bay Press.

Foucault, Michel 1971. *The Order of Things: An Archeology of the Human Sciences.* New York: Pantheon.

— 1978. *The History of Sexuality.* New York: Pantheon.

— 1979. *Discipline and Punishment: Birth of the Prison.* New York: Vintage.

351

Freeland, Cynthia A. and Thomas E. Wartenberg (eds) 1995. *Philosophy and Film*. New York: Routledge.

Fregoso, Rosa Linda 1993. *The Bronze Screen: Chicana and Chicano Film Culture*. Minneapolis: University of Minnesota Press.

Friar, Ralph E. and Natasha A. Friar 1972. *The Only Good Indian: The Hollywood Gospel*. New York: Drama Book Specialist.

Friedan, Betty 1963. *The Feminine Mystique*. New York: Norton.

Friedberg, Anne 1993. *Window Shopping: Cinema and the Postmodern*. Berkeley: University of California Press.

Friedman, Lester 1982. *Hollywood's Image of the Jew*. New York: Ungar.

— (ed.) 1991. *Unspeakable Images: Ethnicity and the American Cinema*. Chicago: University of Illinois Press.

Frodon, Jean-Michel 1998. *La Projection nationale: cinéma et nation*. Paris: Odile Jacob.

Fuss, Diana 1989. *Essentially Speaking: Feminism, Nature and Difference*. New York: Routledge.

— 1991. *Inside/Out: Lesbian Theories, Gay Theories*. New York: Routledge.

Gabbard, Krin and Glen O. Gabbard 1989. *Psychiatry and the Cinema*. Chicago: University of Chicago Press.

Gabriel, Teshome H. 1982. *Third Cinema in the Third World: The Aesthetics of Liberation*. Ann Arbor, MI: UMI Research Press.

Gaines, Jane 1991. *Contested Culture: The Image, the Voice, and the Law*. Chapel Hill: University of North Carolina Press.

— (ed.) 1992. *Classical Hollywood Narrative: The Paradigm Wars*. Durham, NC: Duke University Press.

Gaines, Jane and Charlotte Herzog (eds) 1990. *Fabrications: Costume and the Female Body*. London: Routledge.

Gamman, Lorraine and Margaret Marshment (eds) 1988. *The Female Gaze: Women as Viewers of Popular Culture*. London: Women's Press.

Garcia, Berumen and Frank Javier 1995. *The Chicano/Hispanic Image in American Film*. New York: Vantage Press.

Gardies, Andre 1980. *Approche du récit filmique*. Paris: Albatros.

Garroni, Emilio 1972. *Progetto di Semiotica*. Bari: Laterza.

Gates, Jr., Henry Louis 1988. *The Signifying Monkey*. New York: Oxford University Press.

Gaudreault, André 1996. *Du littéraire au filmique: système du récit*.

Gaudreault, André and François Jost 1990. *Le Récit cinématographique*. Paris: Nathan.

Genette, Gérard 1976. *Mimologiques: voyages en cratylie*. Paris: Seuil.

— 1980. *Narrative Discourse: An Essay in Method*. Ithaca, NY: Cornell University Press.

— 1982a. *Figures of Literary Discourse*. New York: Columbia University Press.

— 1982b. *Palimpsestes: la littérature au second degré*. Paris: Seuil.

Gersch, Wolfgang 1976. *Film bei Brecht: Bertolt Brechts praktische und theoretische Auseinandersetzung mit dem Film*. Munich: Hanser.

Getino, Octavio and Fernando Solanas 1973. *Cine, Cultura y Decolonizacion*. Buenos Aires: Siglo XXI.

Gever, Martha, John Greyson, and Pratibha Parmar (eds) 1993. *Queer Looks: Perspectives on Lesbian and Gay Film – Videos*. New York: Routledge.

Gidal, Peter 1975. "Theory and Definition of Structural/Materialist Film," *Studio International* Vol. 190, No. 978.

— (ed.) 1978. *Structural Film Anthology*. London: British Film Institute.

— 1989. *Materialist Film*. London: Routledge.

Gledhill, Christine 1987. *Home is Where the Heart Is: Studies in Melodrama and the Woman's Film*. London: British Film Institute.

— (ed.) 1991. *Stardom: Industry of Desire*. London: Routledge.

Godard, Jean-Luc 1958. "Bergmanorama." *Cahiers du cinéma* No. 85 (July).

Gorbman, Claudia 1987. *Unheard Melodies: Narrative Film Music*. Bloomington: Indiana University Press; London: British Film Institute.

Gramsci, Antonio 1992. *Prison Notebooks*. New York: Columbia University Press.

Grant, Barry Keith (ed.) 1986. *The Film Genre Reader*. Austin: University of Texas Press.

— 1995. *Film Genre Reader II*. Austin: University of Texas Press.

Grant, Barry Keith and Jeannette Sloniowski 1998. *Documenting the Documentary: Close Readings of Documentary Film and Video*. Detroit: Wayne State University Press.

Greenaway, Peter 1998. "Virtual Irreality." *Cinemais* No. 13 (September–October).

Greenberg, Harvey Roy 1993. *Screen Memoires: Hollywood Cinema on the Psychoanalytic Couch*. New York: Columbia University Press.

Guerrero, Ed 1993. *Framing Blackness: The African American Image in Film*. Philadelphia: Temple University Press.

Gunning, Tom 1990. *D. W. Griffith and the Origins of American Narrative Film*. Champaign: University of Illinois Press.

Guzzetti, Alfred 1981. *Two or Three Things I Know About Her: Analysis of a Film by Godard*. Cambridge, MA: Harvard University Press.

Hall, Stuart and Paul du Gay (eds) 1996. *Questions of Cultural Identity*. London: Sage Publications.

Hall, Stuart, Dorothy Hobson, Andrew Lowe, and Paul Willis (eds) 1980. *Culture, Media, Language*. London: Hutchinson.

Hammond, Paul (ed.) 1978. *The Shadow and its Shadow: Surrealist Writings on the Cinema*. London: British Film Institute.

Hansen, Miriam 1991. *Babel and Babylon: Spectatorship in American Silent Fim*. Cambridge, MA: Harvard University Press.

Harvey, Sylvia 1978. *May '68 and Film Culture*. London: British Film Institute.

Haskell, Molly 1987. *From Reverence To Rape: The Treatment of Women in the Movies*. 2nd edition. New York: Holt, Rinehart and Winston.

Hayward, Phillip and Tana Wollen (eds) 1993. *Future Visions: New Technologies of the Screen*. London: British Film Institute.

Hayward, Susan 1996. *Key Concepts in Cinema Studies*. London: Routledge.

Heath, Stephen 1981. *Questions of Cinema*. Bloomington: Indiana University Press.

Heath, Stephen and Teresa de Lauretis (eds) 1980. *The Cinematic Apparatus*. London: Macmillan.

Heath, Stephen and Patricia Mellencamp (eds) 1983. *Cinema and Language*. Frederick, MD: University Publications of America.

Hebdige, Dick 1979. *Subculture: The Meaning of Style*. London: Methuen.

— 1988. *Hiding in the Light: On Images and Things*. London: Routledge.

Hedges, Inez 1991. *Breaking the Frame: Film Language and the Experience of Limits*. Bloomington: Indiana University Press.

Henderson, Brian 1980. *A Critique of Film Theory*. New York: E. P. Dutton.

Hilger, Michael 1986. *The American Indian in Film*. Metuchen, NJ: Scarecrow Press.

— 1995. *From Savage to Nobleman: Images of Native Americans in Film*. Lanham: Scarecrow Press.

Hill, John and Pamela Church Gibson (eds) 1998. *The Oxford Guide to Film Studies*. Oxford: Oxford University Press.

Hillier, Jim (ed.) 1985. *Cahiers du Cinéma: The 1950s: Neo-Realism, Hollywood, New Wave*. Cambridge, MA: Harvard University Press.

Hodge, Robert and Gunther Kress 1988. *Social Semiotics*. Ithaca, NY: Cornell University Press.

hooks, bell 1992. *Black Looks: Race and Representation*. Boston, MA: South End Press.

— 1996. *Reel to Real: Race, Sex and Class at the Movies*. New York: Routledge.

Horton, Andrew and McDougal, Stuart Y. 1998. *Play It Again, Sam: Retakes on Remakes*. Berkeley: University of California Press.

Humm, Maggie 1997. *Feminism and Film*. Bloomington: Indiana University Press.

Hutcheon, Linda 1988. *A Poetics of Postmodernism: History, Theory, Fiction*. New York: Routledge.

Irigaray, Luce 1985a. *Speculum of the Other Woman*. Trans. Gillian C. Gill. Ithaca, NY: Cornell University Press.

— 1985b. *This Sex Which is Not One*. Trans. Catherine Porter with Carolyn Burke. Ithaca, NY: Cornell University Press.

Jacobs, Lewis 1960. *An Introduction to the Art of the Movies*. New York: Noonday.

James, David E. 1989. *Allegories of Cinema: American Film in the Sixties*. Princeton: Princeton University Press.

James, David E. and Rick Berg (eds) 1996. *The Hidden Foundation: Cinema and the Question of Class*. Minneapolis: University of Minnesota Press.

Jameson, Fredric 1972. *The Prison-House of Language: A Critical Account of Structuralism and Russian Formalism*. Princeton: Princeton University Press.

— 1981. *The Political Unconscious: Narrative as a Socially Symbolic Act*. Ithaca, NY: Cornell University Press.

— 1986. "Third World Literature in the Era of Multinational Capitalism." *Social Text* No. 15 (Fall).

— 1991. *Postmodernism, or, The Cultural Logic of Late Capitalism*. Durham, NC: Duke University Press.

— 1992. *The Geopolitical Aesthetic: Cinema and Space in the World System*. Bloomington: Indiana University Press.

— 1998. *The Cultural Turn: Selected Writings on the Postmodern 1983–1998*. London: Verso.

Jay, Martin 1994. *Downcast Eyes: The Denigration of Vision in Twentieth Century French Thought*. Berkeley: University of California Press.

Jeancolas, Jean-Pierre 1995. *Histoire du cinéma français*. Paris: Nathan.

Jenkins, Henry 1992. *What Made Pistachio Nuts? Early Sound Comedy and the Vaudeville Aesthetic*. New York: Columbia University Press.

Jenkins, Henry and Kristine Brunovska Karnick (eds) 1994. *Classical Hollywood Comedy*. New York: Routledge.

Jenks, Chris (ed.) 1995. *Visual Culture*. London: Routledge.

Johnston, Claire 1973. *Notes on Women's Cinema*. London: Society for Education in Film and Television.

— (ed.) 1975. *The Work of Dorothy Arzner: Toward a Feminist Cinema*. London: British Film Institute.

Jost, François 1987. *L'Oeil – camera: entre film et roman*. Lyon: Presses Universitaires de Lyon.

Jullier, Laurent 1997. *L'Ecran post-moderne: un cinéma de l'allusion et du feu d'artifice*. Paris: Hartmattan.

Kabir, Shameem 1997. *Daughters of Desire: Lesbian Representations in Film*. London: Cassell Academic.

Kaes, Anton 1989. *From Hitler to Heimat: The Return of History as Film*. Cambridge, MA: Harvard University Press.

Kalinak, Kathryn 1992. *Settling the Score: Music and the Classical Hollywood Film*. Madison: University of Wisconsin Press.

Kaplan, E. Ann (ed.) 1988. *Postmodernism and its Discontents: Theories and Practices*. London: Verso.

— 1990. *Psychoanalysis and the Cinema*. London: Routledge.

— 1997. *Looking for the Other*. London: Routledge.

— (ed.) 1998. *Women in Film Noir*. London: British Film Institute.

Karnick, Kristine Brunovska and Henry Jenkins (eds) 1995. *Classical Hollywood*

Comedy. New York: Routledge.

Kay, Karyn and Gerald Pear (eds) 1977. *Women and the Cinema*. New York: E. P. Dutton.

Kellner, Douglas 1995. *Media Culture*. London: Routledge.

King, John, Ana M. Lopez, and Manuel Alvarado (eds) 1993. *Mediating Two Worlds: Cinematic Encounters in the Americas*. London: British Film Institute.

Kitses, Jim 1969. *Horizons West*. London: Secker and Warburg/British Film Institute.

Klinger, Barbara 1994. *Melodrama and Meaning: History, Culture and the Films of Douglas Sirk*. Bloomington: Indiana University Press.

Kozloff, Sarah 1988. *Invisible Storytellers*. Berkeley: University of California Press.

Kracauer, Siegfried 1947. *From Caligari to Hitler: A Psychological History of the German Film*. Princeton: Princeton University Press.

— 1995. *The Mass Ornament: Weimar Essays*. Trans. and ed. Thomas Y. Levin. Cambridge, MA: Harvard University Press.

— 1997. *Theory of Film: The Redemption of Physical Reality*. Princeton: Princeton University Press.

Kristeva, Julia 1969. *Semeiotike: récherches pour une sémanalyse*. Paris: Seuil.

— 1980. *Desire in Language: A Semiotic Approach to Literature and Art*. Trans. Thomas Gora, Alice Jardine, and Leon S. Roudiez. New York: Columbia University Press.

— 1984. *Revolution in Poetic Language*. Trans. Margaret Waller. New York: Columbia University Press.

Kuhn, Annette 1982. *Women's Pictures: Feminism and Cinema*. London: Routledge.

— 1985. *The Power of the Image: Essays on Representation and Sexuality*. London: Routledge and Kegan Paul.

Kuleshov, Lev 1974. *Kuleshov on Film: Writings of Lev Kuleshov*. Trans. and ed. Ronald Levaco. Berkeley: University of California Press.

Lacan, Jacques 1977. *Écrits: A Selection*. Trans. Alan Sheridan. New York: W. W. Norton.

— 1978. *The Four Fundamentals of Psycho-Analysis*. Trans. Alan Sheridan. New York: W. W. Norton.

Laffay, Alfred 1964. *Logique du cinéma*. Paris: Masson.

Lagny, Michele 1976. *La Révolution figurée: film, histoire, politique*. Paris: Albatross.

— 1992. *De l'histoire du cinéma: méthode historique et histoire du cinéma*. Paris: Armand Colin.

Lagny, Michele, Marie-Claire Ropars, and Pierre Sorlin 1976. *Octobre: écriture et idéologie*. Paris: Albatross.

Landow, George P. (ed.) 1994. *Hyper/Text/Theory*. Baltimore: Johns Hopkins University Press.

Landy, Marcia (ed.) 1991. *Imitations of Life: A Reader on Film and Television*

Melodrama. Detroit: Wayne State University Press.
— 1994. *Film, Politics and Gramsci*. Minneapolis: University of Minnesota Press.
— 1996. *Cinematic Uses of the Past*. Minneapolis: University of Minnesota Press.
Lang, Robert 1989. *American Film Melodrama*. Princeton: Princeton University Press.
Langer, Suzanne 1953. *Feeling and Form*. New York: Scribner.
Lapierre, Marcel 1946. *Anthologie du cinéma*. Paris: Nouvelle Edition.
Laplanche, J. and J. B. Pontalis 1978. *The Language of Psycho-Analysis*. Trans. Donald Nicholson-Smith. New York: Norton.
Lapsley, Robert and Michael Westlake 1988. *Film Theory: An Introduction*. Manchester: Manchester University Press.
Lawrence, Amy 1991. *Echo and Narcissus: Women's Voices in Classical Hollywood*. Berkeley: University of California Press.
Lebeau, Vicky 1994. *Lost Angels: Psychoanalysis and Cinema*. London: Routledge.
Lebel, J. P. 1971. *Cinéma et idéologie*. Paris: Editions Sociales.
Lehman, Peter 1993. *Running Scared: Masculinity and the Representation of the Male Body*. Philadelphia: Temple University Press.
— (ed.) 1997. *Defining Cinema*. New Brunswick, NJ: Rutgers University Press.
— 1998. "Reply to Stuart Minnis." *Cinema Journal* Vol. 37, No. 2 (Winter).
Lemon, Lee T. and Marion J. Reis (eds) 1965. *Russian Formalist Criticism: Four Essays*. Lincoln: Nebraska University Press.
Leutrat, Jean-Louis 1987. *Le Western archéologie d'un genre*. Lyon: PUL.
Lévi-Strauss, Claude 1967. *Structural Anthropology*. Trans. Claire Jacobson and Brooke Grundfest Schoepf. Garden City, NY: Doubleday.
— 1990. *The Raw and the Cooked*. Trans. John and Doreen Weightman. Chicago: University of Chicago Press.
Leyda, Jay 1972. *Kino: A History of the Russian and Soviet Film*. London: Allen and Unwin.
L'Herbier, Marcel 1946. *Intelligence du cinématographe*. Paris: Correa.
L'Herminier, Pierre 1960. *L'Art du cinéma*. Paris: Seghers.
Liebman 1980. *Jean Epstein's Early Film Theory, 1920–1922*. Ann Arbor, MI: University Microfilms.
Lindermann, Bernhard 1977. *Experimentalfilm als Metafilm*. Hildesheim: Olms.
Lindsay, Vachel 1915. *The Art of the Moving Image*. Revd. 1922. New York: Macmillan.
Lipsitz, George 1998. *The Possessive Investment in Whiteness: How White People Profit From Identity Politics*. Philadelphia: Temple University Press.
Lister, Martin (ed.) 1995. *The Photographic Image in Digital Culture*. London: Routledge.
Loomba, Ania 1998. *Colonialism/Postcolonialism*. London: Routledge.
Lotman, Juri 1976. *Semiotics of Cinema*. Trans. Mark E. Suino. Ann Arbor: Michigan Slavic Contributions.

Lovell, Terry 1980. *Pictures of Reality: Aesthetics, Politics and Pleasure*. London: British Film Institute.

Lowry, Edward 1985. *The Filmology Movement and Film Study in France*. Ann Arbor: UMI.

Lyotard, Jean-François 1984. *The Postmodern Condition*. Trans. Geoff Bennington and Brian Massumi. Minneapolis: University of Minnesota Press.

MacCabe, Colin 1985. *Tracking the Signifier: Theoretical Essays: Film, Linguistics, Literature*. Minneapolis: University of Minnesota Press.

— (ed.) 1986. *High Theory/Low Culture: Analyzing Popular Television and Film*. New York: St Martin's Press.

Machado, Arlindo 1997. *Pre-Cinema e Pos-Cinemas*. São Paulo: Papirus.

Macheray, Pierre 1978. *Theory of Literary Production*. Trans. Geoffrey Wall. London: Routledge.

Marchetti, Gina 1994. *Romance and the "Yellow Peril": Race, Sex, and Discursive Strategies in Hollywood Fiction*. Berkeley: University of California Press.

Marie, Michel and Marc Vernet 1990. *Christian Metz et la théorie du cinéma*. Paris: Meridiens Klincksieck.

Martea, Marcel 1955. *Le Langoge cinématographique*. Paris: Le Cerf.

Martin, Michael T. 1993. *Cinemas of the Black Diaspora: Diversity, Dependence and Oppositionality*. Detroit: Wayne State University Press.

— (ed.) 1997. *New Latin American Cinema*. 2 vols. Detroit: Wayne State University Press.

Masson, Alain 1994. *Le Récit au cinéma*. Paris: Editions de l'Etoile.

Matejka, Ladislav and Irwin R. Titunik (eds) 1976. *Semiotics of Art: Prague School Contributions*. Cambridge, MA: MIT Press.

Mattelart, Armand and Michele Mattelart 1992. *Rethinking Media Theory: Signposts and New Directions*. Trans. James A. Cohen and Marina Urquidi. Minneapolis: University of Minnesota Press.

— 1994. *Mapping World Communication: War, Progress, Culture*. Trans. Susan Emanuel and James A. Cohen. Minneapolis: University of Minnesota Press.

Mayne, Judith 1989. *Kino and the Woman Question: Feminism and Soviet Silent Film*. Columbus: Ohio State University Press.

— 1990. *The Woman at the Keyhole: Feminism and Women's Cinema*. Bloomington: Indiana University Press.

— 1993. *Cinema and Spectatorship*. London: Routledge.

— 1995. *Directed by Dorthy Arzner*. Bloomington: Indiana University Press.

Mellen, Joan 1974. *Women and their Sexuality in the New Film*. New York: Dell.

Mellencamp, Patricia 1990. *Indiscretions: Avant-Garde Film, Video and Feminism*. Bloomington: Indiana University Press.

— 1995. *A Fine Romance: Five Ages of Film Feminism*. Philadelphia: Temple University Press

Mellencamp, Patricia and Philip Rosen (eds) 1984. *Cinema Histories/Cinema Prac-*

tices. Frederick, MD: University Publications of America.

Mercer, Kobena and Isaac Julien 1988. "Introduction: De Margin and De Center." *Screen* Vol. 29, No. 4.

Messaris, Paul 1994. *Visual Literacies: Image, Mind, and Reality*. Boulder, CO: Westview Press.

Metz, Christian 1972. *Essais sur la signification au cinéma*, Vol. II. Paris: Klincksieck.

— 1974a. *Language and Cinema*. Trans. Donna Jean. The Hague: Mouton.

— 1974b. *Film Language: A Semiotics of the Cinema*. Trans. Michael Taylor. New York: Oxford University Press.

— 1977. *Essais sémiotiques*. Paris: Klincksieck.

— 1982. *The Imaginary Signifier: Psychoanalysis and the Cinema*. Trans. Celia Britton, Annwyl Williams, Ben Brewster, and Alfred Guzzetti. Bloomington: Indiana University Press.

— 1991. *La Narration or impersonelle, ou le site du film*. Paris: Klincksieck.

Michelson, Annette 1972. "*The Man With the Movie Camera*: From Magician to epistemologist." *Artforum* (March).

— 1984. Introduction to *Kino-Eye: The Writing of Dziga Vertov*. Berkeley: University of California Press.

— 1990. "The Kinetic Icon in the Work of Mourning: Prolegomena to the Analysis of a Textual System." *October* 52 (Spring).

Miller, Toby 1993. *The Well-Tempered Self: Citizenship, Culture, and the Postmodern Subject*. Baltimore: Johns Hopkins University Press.

— 1998. *Technologies of Truth: Cultural Citizenship and the Popular Media*. Minneapolis: University of Minnesota Press.

Miller, Toby and Robert Stam (eds) 1999. *A Companion to Film Theory*. Blackwell Publishers.

Mirzoeff, Nicholas (ed.) 1998. *The Visual Culture Reader*. London: Routledge.

Mitchell, Juliet 1974. *Psychoanalysis and Feminism*. New York: Vintage.

Mitchell, Juliet and Jacqueline Rose (eds) 1982. *Feminine Sexuality: Jacques Lacan and the école freudienne*. New York: W. W. Norton.

Mitchell, William J. 1992. *The Reconfigured Eye: Visual Truth in the Post-Photographic Era*. Cambridge, MA: MIT Press.

Mitry, Jean 1963. *Esthétique et psychologie du cinéma: les structures*. Paris: Editions Universitaires.

— 1965. *Esthétique et psychologie du cinéma: les formes*. Paris: Editions Universitaires.

— 1987. *La Sémiologie en question: language et cinéma*. Paris: Editions du Cerf.

— 1997. *The Aesthetics and Psychology of the Cinema*. Trans. Christopher King. Bloomington: Indiana University Press.

Modleski, Tania 1988. *The Women Who Knew Too Much*. New York: Methuen.

— 1991. *Feminism Without Women: Culture and Criticism in a "Postfeminist" Age*. New York: Routledge.

Mora, Carl J. 1988. *Mexican Cinema: Reflections of a Society 1896–1988*. Los Angeles: University of California Press.

Morin, Edgar 1958. *Le Cinéma ou l'homme imaginaire: essai d'anthropologie*. Paris: Editions de Minuit.

— 1960. *The Stars: An Account of the Star-System in Motion Pictures*. Trans. Richard Howard. New York: Grove Press.

Morley, David 1980. *The Nationwide Audience: Structure and Decoding*. London: British Film Institute.

— 1992. *Television Audiences and Cultural Studies*. London: Routledge.

Morley, David and Kuan-Hsing Chen (eds) 1996. *Stuart Hall: Critical Dialogues in Cultural Studies*. London: Routledge.

Morrison, James 1998. *Passport to Hollywood: Hollywood Films, European Directors*. Albany, NY: SUNY Press.

Morse, Margaret 1998. *Virtualities: Television, Media Art and Cyber-Cultures*. Bloomington: Indiana University Press.

Mukarovsky, Jan 1936 [1970]. *Aesthetic Function, Norm and Value as Social Facts*. Ann Arbor: University of Michigan Press.

Mulvey, Laura 1989. *Visual and Other Pleasures*. Bloomington: Indiana University Press.

— 1996. *Fetishism and Curiosity*. Bloomington: Indiana University Press.

Munsterberg, Hugo 1970. *Film: A Psychological Study*. New York: Dover.

Murray, Janet H. 1997. *Hamlet on the Holodeck: The Future of Narrative in Cyberspace*. Cambridge, MA: MIT Press.

Musser, Charles 1991. *Before the Nickelodeon: Edwin S. Porter and the Edison Manufacturing Company*. Berkley: University of California Press.

Naficy, Hamid 1993. *The Making of Exile Cultures: Iranian Television in Los Angeles*. Minneapolis: University of Minnesota Press.

Naremore, James 1998a. *Acting in the Cinema*. Berkeley: University of California Press.

— 1998b. *More than Night: Film Noir in its Contexts*. Berkeley: University of California Press.

Naremore, James and Patrick Brantlinger (eds) 1991. *Modernity and Mass Culture*. Bloomington: Indiana University Press.

Nattiez, J. J. 1975. *Fondéments d'une sémiologie de la musique*. Paris: Union Generale d'Editions.

Neale, Steve 1979–80. "The Same Old Story: Stereotypes and Difference." *Screen Education* Nos. 32–3 (Autumn/Winter).

— 1980. *Genre*. London: British Film Institute.

— 1985. *Cinema and Technology: Image, Sound, Color*. Bloomington: Indiana University Press.

Nichols, Bill 1981. *Ideology and the Image*. Bloomington: Indiana University Press.

— (ed.) 1985. *Movies and Methods*. 2 vols. Berkeley: University of California Press.

— 1991. *Representing Reality*. Bloomington: Indiana University Press.

Noguez, Dominique 1973. *Cinéma: théorie, lectures*. Paris: Klincksieck.

Noriega, Chon A. (ed.) 1992. *Chicanos and Film: Essays on Chicano Representation and Resistance*. Minneapolis: University of Minnesota Press.

Noriega, Chon A. and Ana M. Lopez (eds) 1996. *The Ethnic Eye: Latino Media Arts*. Minneapolis: University of Minnesota Press.

Norris, Christopher 1982. *Deconstruction: Theory and Practice*. London and New York: Methuen.

— 1990. *What's Wrong With Postmodernism: Critical Theory and the Ends of Philosophy*. Baltimore: Johns Hopkins University Press.

— 1992. *Uncritical Theory: Postmodernism, Intellectuals, and the Gulf War*. Amherst: University of Massachussetts Press.

Noth, Winfried 1995. *Handbook of Semiotics*. Bloomington: Indiana University Press.

Odin, Roger 1990. *Cinéma et production de sens*. Paris: Armand Colin.

Ory, Pascal and Sirinelli, Jean-François 1986. *Les Intellectuels en france, de l'affaire dreyfus à nos jours*. Paris: Armand Colin.

Pagnol, Marcel 1933. "Dramaturgie de Paris." *Cahiers du film* No. 1 (December 15).

Palmer, R. Barton 1989. *The Cinematic Text: Methods and Approaches*. New York: AMS Press.

Panofsky, Erwin 1939. *Studies in Iconology*. Oxford: Oxford University Press.

Pechey, Graham (ed.) 1986. *Literature, Politics and Theory: Papers from the Essex Conference 1976–84*. London: Methuen.

Peirce, Charles Sanders 1931. *Collected Papers*. Ed. Charles Hartshorne and Paul Weiss. Cambridge, MA: Harvard University Press.

Penley, Constance (ed.) 1988. *Feminism and Film Theory*. London: Routledge.

— 1989. *The Future of an Illusion: Film, Feminism and Psychoanalysis*. Minneapolis: University of Minnesota Press.

Penley, Constance and Sharon Wills (eds) 1993. *Male Trouble*. Minneapolis: University of Minnesota Press.

Perkins, V. F. 1972. *Film as Film: Understanding and Judging Movies*. Harmondsworth: Penguin.

Petro, Patrice 1989. *Joyless Streets, Women and Melodramatic Representation in Weimar Germany*. Princeton: Princeton University Press.

— (ed.) 1995. *Fugitive Images: From Photography to Video*. Bloomington: Indiana University Press.

Pettit, Arthur G. 1980. *Images of the Mexican American in Fiction and Film*. College Station: Texas A & M University Press.

Piaget, Jean 1970. *Structuralism*. Trans. and ed. Chaninah Maschler. New York: Harper/Colophon.

Pietropaolo, Laura and Ada Testaferri (eds) 1995. *Feminisms in the Cinema*.

361

Bloomington: Indiana University Press.

Pines, Jim and Paul Willemen (eds) 1989. *Questions of Third Cinema*. London: British Film Institute.

Polan, Dana 1985. *The Political Language of Film and the Avant-Garde*. Ann Arbor, MI: UMI Research Press.

— 1986. *Power and Paranoia: History, Narrative and the American Cinema, 1940–1950*. New York: Columbia University Press.

Powdermaker, Hortense 1950. *Hollywood: The Dream Factory*. Boston: Little Brown.

Pribram, Deidre (ed.) 1988. *Female Spectators: Looking at Film and Television*. London: Verso.

Propp, Vladimir 1968. *Morphology of the Folktale*. Trans. Laurence Scott. Austin: University of Texas Press.

Pudovkin, V. I. 1960. *Film Technique*. New York: Grove.

Ray, Robert B. 1988. "The Bordwell Regime and the Stake of Knowledge." *Strategies* Vol. I (Fall).

Reeves, Geoffrey 1993. *Communications and the "Third World"*. London: Routledge.

Reid, Mark A. 1993. *Redefining Black Film*. Berkeley: University of California Press.

Renov, Michael (ed.) 1993. *Theorizing Documentary*. New York: Routledge.

Renov, Michael and Erika Suderburg (eds) 1995. *Resolutions: Contemporary Video Practices*. Minneapolis: University of Minnesota Press.

Rich, Adrienne 1979. *On Lies, Secrets, and Silence*. New York: Norton.

Rich, Ruby 1992. "New Queer Cinema." *Sight and Sound* (September).

— 1998. *Chick Flicks: Theories and Memories of the Finest Film Movement*. Durham, NC: Duke University Press.

Ritchin, Fred 1990. *In Our Own Image: The Coming Revolution in Photography*. New York: Aperature Foundation.

Rocha, Glauber 1963. *Revisao Critica do Cinema Brasilaiso*. Rio de Janerio: Editora Civilizacao Brasileira.

— 1981. *Revolucao do Cinema Novo*. Rio de Janeiro: Embrafilme.

— 1985. *O Seculo do Cinema*. Rio de Janeiro: Alhambra.

Rodowick, D. N. 1988. *The Crisis of Political Modernism: Criticism and Ideology in Contemporary Film Theory*. Urbana: University of Illinois Press.

— 1991. *The Difficulty of Difference: Psychoanalysis, Sexual Difference and Film Theory*. New York: Routledge.

— 1997. *Deleuze's Time Machine*. Raleigh, NC: Duke University Press.

Rogin, Michael 1996. *Blackface, White Noise: Jewish Immigrants in the Hollywood Melting Pot*. Berkeley: University of California Press.

Ropars-Wuilleumier, Marie-Claire 1981. *Le Texte divisé*. Paris: Presses Universitaires de France.

— 1990. *Écramiques: le film du texte*. Lille: PUL.

Rose, Jacqueline 1980. "The Cinematic Apparatus: Problems in Current Theory."

In Teresa de Lauretis and Stephen Heath (eds), *Feminist Studies/Critical Studies*. New York: St Martin's Press.

— 1986. *Sexuality in the Field of Vision*. London: Verso.

Rosen, Marjorie 1973. *Popcorn Venus: Women, Movies and the American Dream*. New York: Coward McCann & Geoghegan.

Rosen, Philip (ed.) 1986. *Narrative, Apparatus, Ideology: A Film Theory Reader*. New York: Columbia University Press.

— 1984. "Securing the Historical: historiography and the classical cinema, in Patricia B. Mellencamp and Philip Rosen (eds), *Cinema Histories, Cinema Practices*. Fredericksburg: AFI.

Rowe, Kathleen 1995. *The Unruly Woman: Gender and the Genres of Laughter*. Austin: University of Texas Press.

Rumble, Patrick and Bart Testa, 1994. *Pier Paolo Pasolini: Contemporary Perspectives*. Toronto: University of Toronto Press.

Rushdie, Salman 1992. *The Wizard of Oz*. London: British Film Institute.

Russo, Vito 1998. *The Celluloid Closet: Homosexuality in the Closet*. New York: Harper & Row.

Ryan, Michael and Douglas Kellner 1988. *Camera Politica: The Politics and Ideology of Contemporary Hollywood Film*. Bloomington: Indiana University Press.

Salt, Barry 1993. *Film Style and Technology: History and Analysis*. Revd. edition. London: Starword.

Sarris, Andrew 1968. *The American Cinema: Directors and Directions 1929–1968*. New York: Dutton.

— 1973. *The Primal Screen: Essays in Film-Related Subjects*. New York: Simon and Schuster.

Schatz, Thomas 1981. *Hollywood Genres: Formulas, Filmmaking, and the Studio System*. Philadelphia: Temple University Press.

— 1998. *The Genius of the System: Hollywood Filmmaking in the Studio Era*. 2nd edition. New York: Pantheon Books

Schefer, Jean-Louis 1981. *L'Homme ordinaire du cinéma*. Paris: Gallimard.

Schneider, Cynthia and Brian Wallis (eds) 1988. *Global Television*. New York: Wedge Press.

Schwarz, Roberto 1987. *Que Horas Sao?: Ensaios*. São Paulo: Compania das Letras.

Screen Reader I: Cinema/Ideology/Politics. 1977. London: SEFT.

Screen Reader II: Cinema & Semiotics. 1981. London: SEFT.

Sebeok, Thomas A. 1979. *The Sign and Its Masters*. Austin: University of Texas Press.

— 1986. *The Semiotic Sphere*. New York: Plenum.

Sedgewick, Eve Kosofsky 1985. *Between Men: English Literature and Male Homosocial Desire*. New York: Columbia University Press.

— 1991. *Epistemology of the Closet*. London: Harvester Wheatsheaf.

Seiter, Ellen, Hans Borchers, Gabriele Kreutzner, and Eva-Marie Warth (eds) 1991.

Remote Control: Television, Audiences and Cultural Power. London: Routledge.

Seldes, Gilbert 1924. *The Seven Lively Arts*. New York and London: Harper & Brothers.

— 1928. "The Movie Commits Suicide," *Harpers* (November).

Shaviro, Steven 1993. *The Cinematic Body*. Minneapolis: University of Minnesota Press.

Shohat, Ella 1989. *Israeli Cinema: East/West and the Politics of Representation*. Austin: University of Texas Press.

— 1991. "Imaging Terra Incognita." *Public Culture* Vol. 3m, No. 2 (Spring).

— 1992. "Notes on the Postcolonial." *Social Text* Nos. 31–2 .

— (ed.) 1999. *Talking Visions: Multicultural Feminism in the Transnational Age*. Cambridge, MA: MIT Press.

Shohat, Ella and Robert Stam 1994. *Unthinking Eurocentrism*. London: Routledge.

Silverman, Kaja 1983. *The Subject of Semiotics*. New York: Oxford University Press.

— 1988. *The Acoustic Mirror: The Female Voice in Psychoanalysis and Cinema*. Bloomington: Indiana University Press.

— 1992. *Male Subjectivity at the Margins*. New York: Routledge.

— 1995. *The Threshold of the Visible World*. New York: Routledge.

Sinclair, John, Elizabeth Jacka, and Stuart Cunningham (eds) 1996. *New Patterns in Global Television Peripheral Vision*. Oxford: Oxford University Press.

Sitney, Adams (ed.) 1970. *The Film Culture Reader*. New York: Praeger.

— (ed.) 1978. *The Avant-Garde Film: A Reader of Theory and Criticism*. New York: New York University Press.

Smith, Jeff 1998. *The Sounds of Commerce: Marketing Popular Film Music*. New York: Columbia University Press.

Smith, Murray 1995. *Engaging Characters: Fiction, Emotion, and the Cinema*. Oxford: Clarendon Press.

Smith, Valerie 1996. *Black Issues in Film*. New Brunswick, NJ: Rutgers University Press.

— (ed.) 1997. *Representing Blackness Issues In Film and Video*. New Brunswick, NJ: Rutgers University Press.

Snead, James 1992. *White Screens/Black Images: Hollywood from the Dark Side*. New York: Routledge.

Snyder, Ilana 1997. *Hypertext: The Electronic Labyrinth*. Washington Square: New York University Press.

Sobchack, Vivian 1992. *The Address of the Eye: A Phenomenology of Film Experience*. Princeton: Princeton University Press.

Sorlin, Pierre 1977. *Sociologie du cinéma: ouverture pour l'histoire de demain*. Paris: Editions Aubier Mongaigne.

— 1980. *The Film in History: Restaging the Past*. New Jersey: Barnes & Noble Books.

Select Bibliography

Spigel, Lynn 1992. *Make Room for TV: Television and the Family Ideology in Postwar America*. Chicago: University of Chicago Press.

Spivak, Gayatri Chakravorty 1987. *In Other Worlds: Essays in Cultural Politics*. New York: Routledge.

Stacey, Jackie 1994. *Star Gazing: Hollywood Cinema and Female Spectatorship*. London: Routledge.

Staiger, Janet 1992. *Interpreting Films: Studies in the Historical Reception of American Cinema*. Princeton: Princeton University Press.

— (ed.) 1995a. *The Studio System*. New Brunswick, NJ: Rutgers University Press.

— 1995b. *Bad Women: Regulating Sexuality in Early American Cinema*. Minneapolis: University of Minnesota Press.

Stallabrass, Julian 1996. *Gargantua: Manufactured Mass Culture*. New York: Verso.

Stam, Robert 1985. *Reflexivity in Film and Literature*. Ann Arbor: University of Michigan Press. Reprinted 1992 by Columbia University Press, New York.

— 1989. *Subversive Pleasures: Bakhtin, Cultural Criticism and Film*. Baltimore: Johns Hopkins University Press.

— 1992. "Mobilizing Fictions: The Gulf War, the Media, and the Recruitment of the Spectator." *Public Culture* Vol. 4, No. 2 (Spring).

Stam, Robert and Ella Shohat 1987. "*Zelig* and Contemporary Theory: Meditation on the Chameleon Text." *Enclitic* Vol. IX, Nos. 1–2, Issues 17/18 (Fall).

Stam, Robert, Robert Burgoyne, and Sandy Flitterman-Lewis 1992. *New Vocabularies in Film Semiotics: Structuralism, Post-Structuralism and Beyond*. London: Routledge.

Stone, Allucquere Rosanne 1996. *The War of Desire and Technology at the Close of the Mechanical Age*. Cambridge, MA: MIT Press.

Straayer, Chris 1996. *Deviant Eyes, Deviant Bodies: Sexual Re-Orientations in Film and Video*. New York: Columbia University Press.

Studlar, Gaylyn 1988. *In the Realm of Pleasure*. Urbana: University of Illinois Press.

— 1996. *This Mad Masquerade: Stardom and Masculinity in the Jazz Age*. New York: Columbia University Press.

Tan, Ed S. H. 1996. *Emotion and the Structure of Narrative Film: Film as an Emotion Machine*. Mahwah: Lawrence Erlbaum.

Tasker, Yvonne 1993. *Spectacular Bodies: Gender, Genre and the Action Cinema*. New York: Routledge.

Taylor, Clyde 1998. *The Mask of Art: Breaking the Aesthetic Contract in Film and Literature*. Bloomington: Indiana University Press.

Taylor, Lucien (ed.) 1994. *Visualizing Theory: Selected Essays From V.A.R. 1990–1994*. New York: Routledge.

Taylor, Richard (ed.) 1927 [1982]. *The Poetics of Cinema: Russian Poetics in Translation, Vol. IX*. Oxford: RPT Publications.

Thomas, Rosie 1985. "Indian Cinema: Pleasure and Popularity." *Screen* Vol. 26,

Nos. 3–4 (May–August).

Thompson, Kristin 1981. *Ivan the Terrible: A Neo-Formalist Analysis*. Princeton: Princeton University Press.

— 1988. *Breaking the Glass Armor: Neo-Formalist Film Analysis*. Princeton: Princeton University Press.

Tomlinson, John 1991. *Cultural Imperialism: A Critical Introduction*. London: Pinter.

Trinh, T. Min-Ha 1991. *When the Moon Waxes Red: Representation, Gender and Cultural Politics*. New York: Routledge.

Tudor, Andrew 1974. *Theories of Film*. London: Secker and Warburg.

Turim, Maureen 1989. *Flashbacks in Film: Memory and History*. New York: Routledge.

Turovskaya, Maya 1989. *Cinema as Poetry*. London: Faber.

Tyler, Parker 1972. *Screening the Sexes: Homosexuality in the Movies*. New York: Holt, Rinehart and Winston.

Ukadike, Nwachukwu Frank 1994. *Black African Cinema*. Berkeley: University of California Press.

Ulmer, Gregory 1985a. *Applied Grammatology*. Baltimore: Johns Hopkins University Press.

— 1985b. *Teletheory: Grammatology in the Age of Video*. London: Routledge.

Vanoye, Francis 1989. *Récit écrit/récit filmique*. Paris: Nathan.

Vernet, Marc 1988. *Figures de l'absence*. Paris: Cahiers du Cinéma.

Veron, Eliseo 1980. *A Producao De Sentido*. São Paulo: Editora Cultrix.

Vertov, Dziga 1984. *Kino-Eye: The Writings of Dziga Vertov*. Trans. Kevin O'Brien, ed. Annette Michelson. Berkeley: University of California Press.

Viano, Maurizio 1993. *A Certain Realism: Making Use of Pasolini's Film Theory and Practice*. Berkeley: University of California Press.

Virilio, Paul 1989. *War and Cinema: The Logistics of Perception*. Trans. Patrick Camiller. London: Verso.

— 1991. "L'acquisition d'objectif," *Liberation* (January 30).

— 1994. *The Vision Machine*. Bloomington: Indiana University Press.

Virmaux, Alain and Odette Virmaux 1976. *Les Surréalistes et le cinéma*. Paris: Seghers.

Volosinov, V. N. 1976. *Marxism and the Philosophy of Language*. Trans. Ladislav Matejka and I. R. Titunik. Cambridge, MA: Harvard University Press.

Walker, Janet 1993. *Couching Resistance: Women, Film, and Psychoanalytic Psychiatry*. Minneapolis: University of Minnesota Press.

Walsh, Martin 1981. *The Brechtian Aspect of Radical Cinema*. London: British Film Institute.

Wasko, Janet 1982. *Movies and Money: Financing the American Film Industry*. Norwood: Ablex.

Waugh, Thomas (ed.) 1984. *"Show Us Life!": Toward a History and Aesthetics of the Committed Documentary*. Metuchen, NJ: Scarecrow Press.

— 1996. *Hard to Imagine: Gay Male Eroticism in Photography and Film from their Beginnings to Stonewall*. New York: Columbia University Press.

Wees, William C. 1991. *Light Moving in Time: Studies in the Visual Aesthetics of Avant-Garde Film*. Berkeley: University of California Press.

Weis, Elizabeth and John Belton 1985. *Theory and Practice of Film Sound*. New York: Columbia University Press.

Weiss, Andrea 1992. *Vampires and Violets: Lesbians in the Cinema*. London: Jonathan Cape.

Wexman, Virginia Wright 1993. *Creating the Couple: Love, Marriage, and Hollywood Performance*. Princeton: Princeton University Press.

Wiegman, Robyn 1995. *American Anatomies: Theorizing Race and Gender*. Durham, NC: Duke University Press.

Willemen, Paul 1994. *Looks and Frictions: Essays in Cultural Studies and Film Theory*. Bloomington: Indiana University Press.

Williams, Christopher (ed.) 1980. *Realism and the Cinema: A Reader*. London: Routledge and Kegan Paul.

— (ed.) 1996. *Cinema: The Beginnings and the Future*. London: University of Westminster Press.

Williams, Linda 1984. *Figures of Desire*. Urbana: University of Illinois Press.

— 1989. *Hard Core: Power, Pleasure and the Frenzy of the Visible*. Berkeley: California University Press.

— (ed.) 1994. *Viewing Positions: Ways of Seeing Film*. New Brunswick, NJ: Rutgers University Press.

Williams, Raymond 1985. *Keywords: A Vocabulary of Culture and Society*. New York: Oxford University Press.

Wilson, George M. 1986. *Narration in Light: Studies in Cinematic Point of View*. Baltimore: Johns Hopkins University Press.

Wilton, Tamsin (ed.) 1995. *Immortal Invisible: Lesbians and the Moving Image*. London: Routledge.

Winston, Brian 1995. *Claiming the Real*. London: British Film Institute.

— 1996. *Technologies of Seeing: Photography, Cinematography and Television*. London: British Film Institute.

Wolfenstein, Martha and Nathan Leites 1950. *Movies: A Psychological Study*. Glencoe, IL: Free Press.

Woll, Allen L. 1980. *The Latin Image in American Film*. Los Angeles: UCLA Latin American Center Publications.

Wollen, Peter 1982. *Readings and Writings: Semiotic Counter-Strategies*. London: Verso.

— 1993. *Raiding the Icebox: Reflections on Twentieth-Century Culture*. Bloomington: Indiana University Press.

— 1998. *Signs and Meaning in the Cinema*. 4th edition. London: British Film Institute.

Wollen, Tana and Phillip Hayward (eds) 1993. *Future Visions: New Technologies of the Screen*. Bloomington: Indiana University Press.

Wong, Eugene Franklin 1978. *On Visual Media Racism: Asians in American Motion Pictures*. New York: Arno Press.

Wright, Will 1975. *Sixguns and Society*. Berkeley: University of California Press.

Wyatt, Justin 1994. *High Concept: Movies and Marketing in Hollywood*. Austin: University of Texas Press.

Xavier, Ismail 1977. *O Discurso Cinematografico*. Rio de Janeiro: Paz e Terra.

— 1983. *A Experiencia do Cinema*. Rio de Janeiro: Graal.

— 1996. *O Cinema No Seculo*. Ed. Arthur Nestrovski. Rio de Janeiro: Imago.

— 1998. *Allegories of Underdevelopment*. Minneapolis: University of Minnesota Press.

Young, Lola 1996. *Fear of the Dark: "Race," Gender and Sexuality in the Cinema*. London: Routledge.

Young-Bruehl, Elisabeth 1996. *The Anatomy of Prejudices*. Cambridge, MA: Harvard University Press.

Zizek, Slavoj 1989. *The Sublime Object of Ideology*. New York: Verso.

— 1991. *Looking Awry: An Introduction to Jacques Lacan Through Popular Culture*. Cambridge, MA: MIT Press.

— (ed.) 1992. *Everything You Always Wanted to Know About Lacan But Were Afraid To Ask Hitchcock*. London: Verso.

— 1993. *Enjoy Your Symptom! Jacques Lacan in Hollywood and Out*. New York: Routledge.

— 1996. *For They Know Not What They Do: Enjoyment as a Political Factor*. New York: Verso.

Index

369

Index